CULTURE, PLACE, AND NATURE

STUDIES IN ANTHROPOLOGY AND ENVIRONMENT

Devon Peña and K. Sivaramakrishnan,

Series Editors

CULTURE, PLACE, AND NATURE

Centered in anthropology, the Culture, Place, and Nature series encompasses new interdisciplinary social science research on environmental issues, focusing on the intersection of culture, ecology, and politics in global, national, and local contexts. Contributors to the series view environmental knowledge and issues from the multiple and often conflicting perspectives of various cultural systems.

*The Kuhls of Kangra:
Community-Managed Irrigation
in the Western* Himalaya
by J. Mark Baker

*The Earth's Blanket:
Traditional Teachings for Sustainable Living*
by Nancy Turner

*Property and Politics in Sabah, Malaysia:
Native Struggles over Land Rights*
by Amity A. Doolittle

*Border Landscapes:
The Politics of Akha Land Use
in China and Thailand*
by Janet C. Sturgeon

*From Enslavement to Environmentalism:
Politics on a Southern African Frontier*
by David McDermott Hughes

*Ecological Nationalisms: Nature, Livelihoods,
and Identities in South Asia*, edited by
Gunnel Cederlöf and K. Sivaramakrishnan

*The Tropics and the Traveling Gaze:
India, Landscape, and Science, 1800–1856*
by David Arnold

The Tropics
AND THE
Traveling Gaze

INDIA, LANDSCAPE, AND SCIENCE, 1800–1856

David Arnold

UNIVERSITY OF WASHINGTON PRESS

Seattle and London

THIS PUBLICATION WAS SUPPORTED IN PART
BY THE DONALD R. ELLEGOOD INTERNATIONAL
PUBLICATIONS ENDOWMENT

© 2006 by the University of Washington Press
First paperback edition © 2014 by the University of Washington Press
Printed and bound in the United States of America
18 17 16 15 14   5 4 3 2 1

Published in the United States of America
by University of Washington Press
www.washington.edu/uwpress

Published in South Asia by Permanent Black
D-28 Oxford Apts., 11 I.P. Extension, Delhi 110092

All rights reserved. No part of this publication may be reproduced or transmitted in any form or by any means, electronic or mechanical, including photocopy, recording, or any information storage or retrieval system, without permission in writing from the publisher.

Library of Congress Cataloging-in-Publication Data
Arnold, David, 1946– .
The tropics and the traveling gaze :
India, landscape, and science, 1800–1856 / David Arnold.
p. cm. — (Culture, place, and nature)
Includes bibliographical references and index.
ISBN 978-0-295-99383-6 (pbk : alk. paper)
1. Human ecology—India—History—19th century.
2. India—Colonization—History—19th century.
3. Europeans—Travel—India—History —19th century.
4. Travelers' writings, European—History and criticism.
5. India—Description and travel. I. Title. II. Series.
GF661.A76 2006   304.2'0954'09034—dc22   2005023751

The paper used in this publication is acid-free and meets the minimum requirements of American National Standard for Information Sciences—Permanence of Paper for Printed Library Materials, ANSI Z39.48–1984

*For Juliet
and all our traveling days*

CONTENTS

Acknowledgments xiii

Introduction 3

ONE Itinerant Empire 11

TWO In a Land of Death 42

THREE Romanticism and Improvement 74

FOUR From the Orient to the Tropics 110

FIVE Networks and Knowledges 147

SIX Botany and the Bounds of Empire 185

Conclusion 225

Notes 233

Bibliography 267

Index 289

ILLUSTRATIONS

Fig. 1: The Bhutanese Himalaya, Assam and the Brahmaputra Valley, from J.D. Hooker, *Himalayan Journals*, vol. 2 (1854).   23

Fig. 2: *Larix griffithii*, from J.D. Hooker, *Illustrations of Himalayan Plants* (1855), drawn by W.H. Fitch from a sketch by Hooker.   66

Fig. 3: Pilgrims at Hardwar, from R. Montgomery Martin, *The Indian Empire Illustrated* (1861), engraved by J.M.W. Turner.   70

Fig. 4: The Ruins of Old Delhi, from R. Montgomery Martin, *The Indian Empire Illustrated* (1861).   78

Fig. 5: The Jama Masjid at Mandu, from R. Montgomery Martin, *The Indian Empire Illustrated* (1861).   79

Fig. 6: The River Yamuna in the Himalaya, from R. Montgomery Martin, *The Indian Empire Illustrated* (1861).   101

Fig. 7: The Ruins at Etawa, Rajasthan, from T. Bacon (ed.), *Oriental Annual* (1839).   120

Fig. 8: Surf at Fort St George, Madras, from R. Montgomery Martin, *The Indian Empire Illustrated* (1861).   138

Fig. 9: Sir William Hooker, photograph, late 1850s. National Portrait Gallery, London.   150

Fig. 10: *Amherstia nobilis*, from Nathaniel Wallich, *Plantae Asiaticae Rariores*, vol. 1 (1830), by Vishnu Prasad. 153

Fig. 11: *Phytocrene gigantea*, from Nathaniel Wallich, *Plantae Asiaticae Rariores*, vol. 3 (1832), drawn by Vishnu Prasad, with anatomical sections by William Griffith. 173

Fig. 12: Joseph Hooker, daguerreotype, c. 1852. National Portrait Gallery, London. 187

Fig. 13: Punkabaree Bungalow at the Foot of the Himalaya, from J.D. Hooker, *Himalayan Journals*, vol. 1 (1854), from a sketch by Hooker. 195

Fig. 14: The Tambur Valley, Nepal, from J.D. Hooker, *Himalayan Journals*, vol. 1 (1854), from a sketch by Hooker. 197

Fig. 15: *Rhododendron dalhousiae*, from J.D. Hooker, *Rhododendrons of Sikkim-Himalaya* (1849), by W.H. Fitch, from a sketch by Hooker. 219

Figures 2, 10, 11, and 15 are reproduced by kind permission of the Royal Botanic Gardens, Kew; figures 9 and 12 appear by kind permission of the National Portrait Gallery, London, and figures 1, 3 to 8, 13, and 14, by kind permission of the School of Oriental and African Studies, London.

MAPS

1: India in 1856   14

2: The North Indian Travels of Reginald Heber, Victor Jacquemont and Joseph Hooker. 128

ACKNOWLEDGMENTS

In the course of researching and writing this book, I have accumulated a great many debts of gratitude, which it is my pleasure to acknowledge here. I am extremely grateful to the Leverhulme Trust for a research fellowship in 2002–4, which freed me from teaching and administrative responsibilities for two years and enabled me to research and write most of this book. My research has made particular use of two invaluable repositories. I wish particularly to thank Kate Pickard, the archivist at the Royal Botanic Gardens, Kew, for her help in locating material on William and Joseph Hooker and their Indian correspondents, and Craig Brough and his obliging colleagues in the Library at Kew. Particular thanks to John Flanagan and James Kay for generously permitting me to reproduce illustrations from works at Kew and making copies available for this book.

I am indebted, too, to Rosemary Seton as the former archivist at SOAS and the staff of the School's Special Collections Reading Room for their ready assistance in locating much of the travel literature used in this book, and to Lance Martin and Glenn Ratcliffe for help with illustrations. I have further benefited from use of the archives of the Zoological Society of London, and the library and archives of the Natural History Museum (with particular thanks to Ann Datta for directing me to the NHM's Hodgson Papers). The archives and library of the Royal Asiatic Society were a further major source for this work, and I am most grateful to David Waterhouse for suggesting I use the RAS collection of Hodgson material. My thanks, too, to James Kilvington at the National Portrait Gallery in London for help with the Hooker photographs used in this work. I am further indebted to Deepak Erasmus for permission to see the original proceedings of the

Agricultural and Horticultural Society in Calcutta, and most appreciative of the locational and logistical help I received from Anna Balickci-Denjongpa, Tharchen Sherpa, and A. Shakeel in Sikkim, Darjeeling, and Varanasi.

A preliminary exploration of the arguments developed here first appeared as "India's Place in the Tropical World, 1770–1930," in the *Journal of Imperial and Commonwealth History* 26 (1998). An earlier variant of Chapter 2 has been published as "India's Deathscapes" in *Nineteenth Century Contexts* (2005), and preliminary versions of Chapter 6 in Felix Driver and Luciana Martins (eds), *Tropical Views and Visions* (2005) and David M. Waterhouse (ed.) *The Origins of Himalayan Studies: Brian Houghton Hodgson in Nepal and Darjeeling, 1820–1858* (2004). Early drafts were also presented at conferences and seminars in Delhi, London, Oxford, Cambridge, St Andrews, Milwaukee, and Princeton between 1995 and 2004, and I am grateful to all those who kindly and critically commented on work presented on those occasions.

I have greatly benefited from discussions with many scholars working in related fields and on similar subjects, including Alan Bewell, Dan Clayton, Richard Drayton, Felix Driver, Jim Endersby, Richard Grove, Mark Harrison, Michael Hutt, Shruti Kapila, David Livingstone, Luciana Martins, Nancy Leys Stepan, Giles Tillotson, and Tom Trautmann. Particular thanks to Henry Noltie for his critical reading of an earlier version of Chapter 5 and for introducing me to the Royal Botanic Garden Edinburgh. Also to Ranajit Guha for his prescient study *A Rule of Property for Bengal*, first published forty years ago. Special thanks to Catherine Lawrence for the maps and to the SOAS Arts and Humanities research fund for supporting the cost of illustrations in this book. For their encouragement and assistance in seeing this work into print, I am particularly beholden to Rukun Advani and Anuradha Roy in Delhi and Lorri Hagman in Seattle, to K. Sivaramakrishnan and Mahesh Rangarajan as editors of the respective Permanent Black and University of Washington Press series on environmental history, and to the anonymous reviewers for both presses. I am especially grateful to Mahesh for his detailed and wide-ranging comments on an earlier version of this book. As ever, my greatest and abiding debt is to Juliet Miller, without whose love and companionship this and many other journeys might never have been undertaken—or been even half so much fun.

Chiswick
September 2005

The Tropics
AND THE
Traveling Gaze

INTRODUCTION

THIS IS A BOOK ABOUT LAND. IT IS ABOUT A LAND—ABOUT INDIA AND how that vast and diverse region came to be known to, and conceptualized by, British and other European travelers and observers in the first half of the nineteenth century. But it is also a book about *the* land, about the ways in which India's material environment became increasingly subject to the colonial understanding of landscape and nature, and to the scientific scrutiny of itinerant naturalists. Although there have previously been scholarly works that have individually discussed various aspects of travel, landscape, and science in colonial India, none has attempted, as this does, to see them as part of an interrelated process of observation and appropriation. Like Paul Carter's fine study *The Road to Botany Bay*,[1] *The Tropics and the Traveling Gaze* is an essay in "spatial history." It is concerned with European responses to an unfamiliar landscape, about the land as an object of colonial fear and desire, utility and aesthetics. It seeks to show how India, in passing under British control, was evaluated in ways that combined scenic delight and practical opportunity with a harsher appraisal of India as a land of death and disease, of desolation and deficiency. It is an attempt to understand how India, while recognized as having its own distinctive physical and cultural identity, was nevertheless annexed to ideas of landscape and nature that were external and alien to itself, and which aligned it, in science as in sentiment, with distant places and other times.

This book is, therefore, primarily concerned with colonialism as "a cultural process," "imagined and energized through signs, metaphors and narratives."[2] Since it is about "the colonization of space," and how landscapes acquire a "moral and even redemptive significance,"[3] it does not purport to be an environmental history in the widely practiced sense of trying to describe the "real" world of nature, captured objectively at a given moment in time. That is a possible, even necessary, task, but it is one that requires caution and discernment. Indeed, one of the underlying impulses behind the writing of this book has been precisely a concern that historians and others who have looked back at the early nineteenth century in South Asia are in danger of being greatly misled if they read the sources of the time as if they were transparently objective, scientifically dependable, statements of "reality." Rather, these are cultural texts deeply imbued, in their concepts and phraseology, in their expectations and judgments, with the aesthetic and utilitarian values of their age and, more often than not, whether they emanate from the state or from independent investigators, with the colonizing ethos of the era. Instead of ignoring the sentiment—individual and collective—that informs so much of the scenic description and natural history writing of the early nineteenth century, it makes more sense to confront it and try to unravel its significance.

This book seeks, then, to examine how, at a time when the now pervasive term "environment" was never employed,[4] nature and the place of humans within the natural world were conceptualized and contextualized. What we in the late twentieth and early twenty-first centuries have come to identify and integrate as "the environment" coalesced for early nineteenth-century writers in India (and elsewhere) around rather different visual, experiential and conceptual nodes—around "climate" (in a broader and generally more determinist sense than we would recognize today) and its neo-Hippocratic linkages with health and disease; around ideas of natural history and "nature;" around agriculture and "improvement;" and, not least, around ideas of landscape and scenery. This study does not attempt to engage with all of these domains of socially constructed nature in equal measure, in part because some, such as climate and disease, have already been the subject of extended discussion elsewhere.[5] It does seek, though, especially in the opening chapters, to suggest some of the connections and correspondences that existed between them. The book makes extensive use of what Bernard Cohn described as the "observational/travel modality" in the formation and articulation of colonial knowledge in India.[6] It further seeks to use what is referred to here as "the traveling gaze" as a means to prise open for closer examination the European understanding of India (largely as generated within India rather than more distantly from Europe) through representations of its landscape and through botany as a science specifically concerned with what we now in part understand as "the environment."

There has, of course, been a large and impressive body of scholarly work that has interpreted the environment (including climate, disease, and vegetation) deterministically, as primary forces in the making of human history—not least in determining which lands became suited to European settlement ("neo-Europes" in Alfred W. Crosby's challenging phrase),[7] or which, situated largely within the tropics, remained largely beyond the pale of the white races. Certainly, many Europeans in the late eighteenth and early nineteenth centuries worked with a roughly similar model, finding something ineluctably alien and uncomfortable about a land like India that was clearly so different from Britain, France, or Germany, though they were often reluctant in practice to accept such a stark dichotomy and to be entirely governed by the apparent prohibitions of nature.[8] While duly recognizing the part that disease and other environmental factors have played in history, this book is part of a wider, more recent trend to reverse the environmentalist paradigm and to see environments in a more subjective, socially constructed way and to question whether there was anything "natural" about some parts of the globe becoming "neo-Europes" and others tropical no-go areas for whites. In other words, this book examines the possibility (with respect to India) that "the tropics" were invented quite as much as they were encountered.

Central, then, to the argument and the approach adopted here is the conviction that ideas of landscape, far from being peripheral to the exercise of power or merely reflective of a material reality, formed a central and integrating element in the wider constitution of colonial knowledge and a critical ingredient in the larger colonizing process. In understanding landscape in this way, I follow Denis Cosgrove and Stephen Daniels in believing that a landscape "is a cultural image, a pictorial way of representing, structuring or symbolizing surroundings," though, like them, I would hasten to add that this is not to say that landscapes are therefore "immaterial."[9] In taking this route into the understanding of early colonial India and the "environmental" consciousness of the time, I have been influenced by the example of recent work, notably on Africa, Australia, and North America that has similarly demonstrated the importance of externally derived perceptions and practices imposed by Europeans (or peoples of European origin) upon very different landscapes and the part that imported images and ideals had upon local land-use policies, agricultural practices, scientific and technological intervention and state management of the land.[10]

In the Indian case, I would argue, this was an appropriation, begun (or extended) through words and images, "associations" and expectations, through scientific terminologies and texts, travel narratives and literary representations, that was, in its way, quite as fundamental to the colonial enterprise as the more familiar story of conquering armies, revenue systems and imperial bureaucracies. In early nineteenth-century India, as much as in contemporary Britain or France, "nature," especially as represented through ideas and images of landscape, was "an historically specific construct," articulated through and informed by a bourgeois "vision" or "gaze."[11] And, lest it be thought that terms like "vision" and "gaze" imply appraisal but inaction, aesthetic taste rather than material transformation, it should be recognized that "seeing," or (hardly less literally) "reading," a landscape in a certain way was commonly the prelude to, or necessary precondition for, the physical transformation of the Indian countryside. Of primary importance in this, whether as landscape aesthetic, the embodiment of Christian virtue and capitalist morality, or as a far-reaching program of rural reformation, was the pervasive belief in "improvement." This has been extensively written about, both in the context of imperial agendas and of revenue policies in late eighteenth- and early nineteenth-century India;[12] yet the extent to which the ethos of "improvement" was embedded in—and had an enduring impact upon—the British understanding of the Indian landscape and the outlook and activities of naturalists and other scientists has yet to be fully recognized. Like the Romanticism with which it was so intimately associated, "improvement" was one of the foundational influences of the period and one of the principal links between such seemingly diverse (but broadly "environmental") fields as botany, agriculture, and even (given its historical and symbolic location within idealized topographies) religion. Nature was an element conspicuously if not always consciously invoked in its various manifestations, especially as landscape, in attempts to legitimize colonial rule and to establish through nature a corresponding authority over human subjects.

In seeking to understand the landscape and environment of India in this culturally attentive way, the present study also aims to raise other questions of interpretive significance. One of these relates to the issue of how the history of India itself is to be understood and situated in this early colonial period. Although it is less the case now than it was twenty or thirty years ago, the overwhelming tendency remains to see India either strictly in relation to its own past and indigenous traditions and legacies, or as increasingly locked into a relationship (whether reciprocal or asymmetrical) with Britain as the colonial power (or, perhaps, in some subtle combination of these two). The importance of these two elements, separately or entwined, cannot be denied, but they must often appear insufficient in themselves. It was, thus, not only Britain, but Europe as a whole (its travelers, artists, and naturalists) that shaped perceptions of early nineteenth-century India and fashioned its scientific activities and "improving" agendas.[13] Equally, while Britain (and, even more strikingly, its constituent regions) provided one set of ideals and images against which the landscape of India was adjudged, the colonial imagination also drew upon a rich and varied repertoire of examples and idioms from other parts of the globe, from Africa to Arabia, from Australia and New Zealand to Antarctica and the Alps, and, most significantly of all, from the "tropical" archetypes of the West Indies and Brazil. Some of these scenic tropes were summoned up from personal, often childhood, experiences, but many originated from works of science and travel, while others existed nowhere except in fiction and fantasy.

Although, as the seminal work of Edward Said would lead us to expect,[14] "the Orient" figured prominently in much of this, it was the idea of the tropics—warm, fecund, luxuriant, paradisiacal and pestilential—that was in many respects the most influential source of inspiration and innovation and had the most prodigious effect upon scenic appraisal and scientific practice.[15] Certainly, colonial India drew upon the diverse landscape images and ideals present in Britain's own varied landscape, just as these were imported into other areas of British settlement overseas,[16] though the projected Anglicization of the Indian landscape, even to the extent of creating European homesteads in the hills, was a prospective vision that never actually materialized. But ideas of landscape and land-use were drawn no less powerfully from outside Britain, and especially from the American tropics. Part of the significance of this "tropicalization" of India lay in the extent to which it marginalized or denied indigenous precedent. Far more than Orientalism, to which, despite Said, the East did not fail to make its contribution, this was an overwhelmingly European epistemological maneuver, founded in "nature" but pregnant with economic, political, and cultural significance.

In thus highlighting the transforming role of "improvement" and "tropicalization," this work departs from many recent studies of colonial science, knowledge, and power in South Asia. There has been a tendency of late to argue that colonialism here had a "soft landing," whether because its impact was slow to be felt, or because of the practical limitations of colonial power and knowledge, which spread like an impossibly thin layer of treacle over a vast, subcontinental mass and an ancient, complex, and resilient society. There is a view that the process of knowing, and hence ultimately of ruling, India (not least in the period before the mid-century Mutiny and Rebellion) was "dialogic," involving interaction and exchange, and a fair measure of mutual respect and reciprocal borrowing, between Europeans and Indians.[17] Such a reassuring view of the intellectual openness of the colonial encounter stands in stark contrast with the idea that the colonial interest in knowledge was almost entirely self-serving, and that colonialism represented not just physical coercion and enforced social, economic, and political change but also profound cultural disjuncture and a high degree of "epistemological violence" directed against indigenous forms and systems of knowledge.[18]

It is certainly not the intention here to suggest that indigenous ideas of landscape or the agency of Indians (as plant collectors, say, or illustrators) played no significant part, whether in the scenic representation of India or the botanical pursuits of the period. India was, in Mary Louise Pratt's terms, a series of important "contact zones," places where disparate cultures met: but in these "zones", the relationship of power (and of power over knowledge) was often highly asymmetrical.[19] It would be a mistake, on the basis of the kind of evidence presented here, to presume that indigenous ideas and agency had an equal role or that some kind of open, mutually respectful, discourse existed between Indian science and its European counterpart. As far as botany was concerned, indigenous knowledge and agency was, even by the 1830s, assigned a secondary, subaltern status, and though both were undoubtedly taken up and utilized by European travelers and India-based naturalists, this was more often akin to exploitation than a recognition of epistemological equality. What Indians knew and did was seldom given credence as "science," nor (with rare exceptions) were they allowed to share in the authorial role that Europeans reserved for themselves, as opposed to the humbler task of collecting plants or providing raw data about vernacular uses. Our ideas of what constituted Western science, especially as it functioned in the colonies, also need critical investigation and discipline-specific disaggregation. Accordingly, one of the concerns especially of the later chapters of this book is with the tensions that divided colonial from metropolitan science as well as the networks and patterns of mutual reliance that linked the two. For this purpose, too, the physical experience of travel, the observational and authorial practices to which it gave rise, and the metaphorical applications of travel to science in South Asia or between India and Europe, are seen here as having great utility and significance, especially for the still unsettled world of early nineteenth-century colonialism.[20]

Much of the scholarly consideration of colonial science and the Indian environment has hitherto focused on the latter part of the century, a period for which scientific and bureaucratic source material is more readily available and in which the role of the state and colonial scientific and technical services is more clearly evident. But the colonial engagement with India was a long one and looking at the early nineteenth century, a period when the East India Company ruled rather than the Crown, and looking at different kinds of sources (especially non-governmental sources such as travel narratives and journal literature) often suggests a rather different picture from the increasingly familiar one for late nineteenth-century India. It is not the purpose of this book to trace the many changes that overtook the Indian environment in the second half of the nineteenth century, and the further appropriation and reinterpretation of that landscape—by science, technology, and the state—that occurred, especially from the 1870s onwards. But it is hoped that by looking afresh at the first half of the century and taking a wide view of how ideas of landscape were constituted and how sciences like botany functioned, it is possible to arrive at a more accurate and nuanced understanding of the interrelations between landscape, science, and empire in this earlier period.

The Tropics forms, in part, a sequel to my *Colonizing the Body: State Medicine and Epidemic Disease in Nineteenth-Century India* (1993) and to my earlier monograph *Police Power and Colonial Rule: Madras, 1859–1947* (1986). All three form part of a cumulative attempt to try to determine the nature and evolution of colonialism in India, and to investigate the phenomenon of colonialism historically, as a distinct form of power and knowledge. Taken together, these three studies function (to my mind at least) as a kind of triangulation—taking body, land, and state as three fixed points from which to survey the complex and varied terrain of nineteenth- and early twentieth-century colonialism. If the presence of the state is less immediately obvious in this book than in the previous two, its facilitating role and governing intentions (or inhibitions) should nonetheless be discernible from the scenic and scientific literature of the period. At this foundational moment the colonial regime of power was often made manifest more through experiment and exploration than through formal pronouncements, policies, and institutions, and it is partly in order to capture this as yet unfixed quality in early colonialism in India that so much emphasis has been placed here upon travel and its effect upon an emerging system of colonial knowledge. While science in this period was certainly not reducible simply to politics by another means and naturalists, as some scholars have been anxious to remind us,[21] might individually adhere to ideas and objectives that kept them at a seemly distance from the crude materiality and commanding ambitions of their imperial masters, science and empire seldom failed to communicate with each other and, indeed, often found patronage and agency in one and the same person.

Equally, if the corporality of colonial discourse and practice was more central to *Colonizing the Body*, it is by no means absent here. The role of medical topography and the experiential element in the elaboration of India's incipient "tropicality" are further indications of the importance of the body (taken as instrument as well as subject) within the emergent colonial project. And while my study of the police twenty years ago sought to direct attention to the coercive role of the mature and late colonial state in India, this book looks back to an earlier phase in the evolution of colonialism in which a seemingly more tenuous (but still tenacious) hegemony of "affect" and "association" held an ideological prominence and a practical significance that was already in retreat even before the mid-century climacteric of the Mutiny and Rebellion.

1
ITINERANT EMPIRE

Empire on the Move

THROUGHOUT ITS LONG HISTORY INDIA HAS, IN NO SMALL PART, BEEN defined through travel. This might be said of the restless movement of its kings, courts, and armies, the peregrinations of warriors, merchants, and scribes, the wanderings of pilgrims, *sanyasis*, and saints, or the periodic or enforced migrations of pastoralists, laborers, religious refugees, and the famine poor. But it is surely also true of the way in which India has repeatedly been described and characterized by a long series of foreign travelers—from the Greek Megasthenes in the fourth century BC to the Chinese Buddhist monk Fa Hsien in the fifth century AD, from the Moroccan Ibn Battuta in the fourteenth to the Frenchman François Bernier in the mid-seventeenth century—whose work colored contemporary perceptions or has weighed heavily in the historical appraisals of the present.

But while the accounts of travelers have so richly—at times so perversely—informed the understanding of India and helped to create and sustain some of its most abiding images, it is equally important to recognize how much the manner as well as the content of that external representation changed, and has continued to change, over time. Travelers to India necessarily brought with them the expectations and sensibilities of their age as well as the styles of observation and recording with which they were familiar. Even within the wide canon of European travel writing about India, and despite the frequent, almost mesmeric, reiteration of familiar tropes and images, the variations were enormous. Thus, although Europeans had been visiting India and writing accounts of their travels from the time of the Portuguese navigator Vasco da Gama in the late fifteenth century (or even earlier), the early nineteenth century—the period with which this book is principally concerned—saw a dramatic increase in the number of Western travelers and the volume of travel narratives produced, as well as a qualitative change in the nature of their writing.

The reasons for this double shift are many and various. One cause lay in growing British domination over South Asia. Acting through the English East India Company, the power of the British expanded rapidly in the late eighteenth and early nineteenth centuries, and in consequence many hitherto inaccessible areas of India[1] were opened up to European observation and travel. Despite earlier misgivings about the morality of British rule and concern about the rapacity of Company officials, by the early nineteenth century, the British began to exhibit a new sense of ownership toward India. It became common for travel writers to justify their accounts in terms of a need for the British public to know more about "our Eastern empire,"[2] or they stressed the value of first-hand experience of India, still in the 1830s represented as a little-known—and "much-neglected"—country.[3]

Emma Roberts, one of the leading travel writers of the period, once remarked that the "native inhabitants of India appear to be addicted to locomotion,"[4] an observation that might have applied with equal force to the British themselves. Well into the middle decades of the nineteenth century, the empire in India appeared to be constantly on the move. The pattern of British expansionism was itself a factor in creating this restlessness. Founded in 1600, for a century and a half, the activities of the English East India Company had been largely confined to trade, its territorial hold upon India restricted to a small number of coastal enclaves, principally Surat, Calcutta (now Kolkata), Madras (Chennai), and Bombay (Mumbai). However, in the mid-eighteenth century this localized presence and limited engagement with India changed dramatically. Between the late 1740s and mid-1760s a combination of military force and diplomatic stealth provided the British a substantial foothold in India, principally in Bengal and Bihar and in the Northern Circars of the southeast.

Over the next fifty years the Company embarked on a long series of wars and political maneuvers that steadily swelled its dominions. Between

1772 and 1818 the British fought three wars against the Marathas, by the end of which much of western and central India had passed into their hands. They also engaged in three wars against the South Indian state of Mysore, ending with the death of its ruler Tipu Sultan at the siege of Seringapatam in 1799 and the appropriation of large areas of the Deccan. They conducted a fiercely fought campaign against the Gurkhas of Nepal from 1815 to 1816, which threw open to British control the southern Himalaya. There followed two wars against Burma (1824–5 and 1852), the annexation of Sind in 1843 and the Anglo-Sikh Wars from 1846 to 1849, which culminated in the British takeover of the Punjab. Not all of the Company's military ventures ended favorably or added either to its territory or to its reputation: success in the first Burma war proved costly of both British and Indian soldiers' lives, and armed intervention in Afghanistan (1838–42) was widely regarded as a military and diplomatic debacle. But the setbacks appeared no more than temporary. As well as the second Burma war, during the governor-generalship of Lord Dalhousie (1848–54) the British made further annexations, with Awadh in the North and Nagpur in Central India the largest gains. By the eve of the Mutiny in 1857, Company rule had encompassed two-thirds of India.

This sustained pattern of military activity and territorial aggrandizement provided the context, and to a degree the incentive, for the travel and itinerant science of the early nineteenth century. Fueled by the global struggle against Revolutionary and Napoleonic France, as well as by regional conflict against Mysore and the Marathas, the spirit of military expansionism reached its apogee during the governor-generalship of Lord Wellesley (1798–1805); but a cautious recognition of the military underpinning of British power informed many of the more reflective assessments of the period as a whole. "Our empire in India has arisen from the superiority of our military prowess," wrote Sir Charles Metcalfe in 1814. "Its stability rests entirely on the same foundation."[5] Reckless expansionism and aggressive militarism were officially frowned upon by the British government and the Company's Court of Directors in London, but for much of the early nineteenth century, despite the rise of a professional civil service, the army played a leading part in the governance of India. The large British military presence, amounting to some 30,000 white troops by the 1830s, along with a third of a million Indian sepoys and their European officers, helped set the administrative tone (and class agenda) for British rule in India.[6] But while white soldiers in the Royal

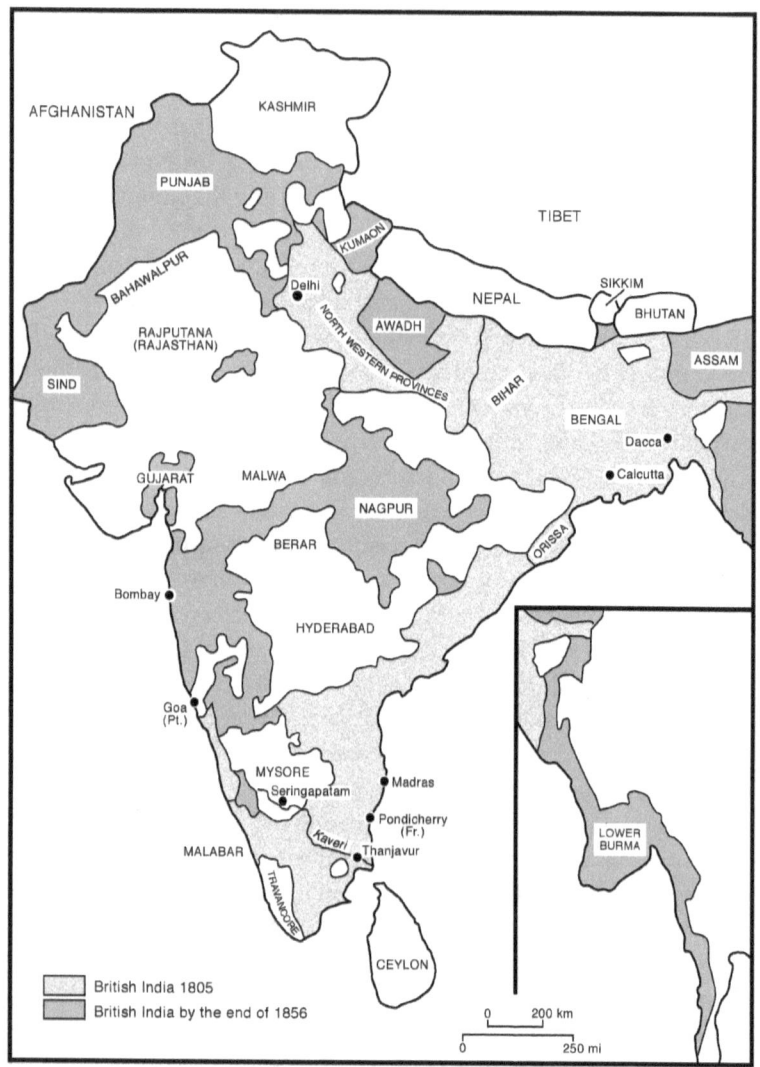

MAP 1. India in 1856

and Company armies were—except when campaigning or marching between military stations—confined to their crowded and suffocating barracks, the officer class enjoyed much greater mobility.

It was not just the boundaries of British India that were almost constantly on the move: so, too, were its military and administrative personnel. Accounts of European travel in India have tended to focus on outsiders new to India, but much of the travel writing of the period, including much of that written in a scientific vein, was produced by Europeans resident in the country and so reflected their more informed perspectives. The rapid growth of the Company's dominions facilitated and encouraged European travel, and it removed the prohibitions that many Indian rulers, wary of British intentions, had previously placed upon foreigners. With the close of the Maratha wars it became possible for Europeans to pass, relatively unhindered, from the straits of Ceylon to the Himalaya mountains, from the island of Bombay in the west to the Brahmaputra in the east.[7] In the more confident and overtly imperial environment of the early nineteenth century, the days were past when a European traveler felt it necessary to disguise himself as a Turkish merchant (as George Forster had done in order to cross North India safely in 1782) or to cloak his scientific and commercial mission with the pretense of being an indigent physician (like the naturalist Anton Hove in the Maratha domains).[8] By the 1830s even travelers in the Indus valley, still outside British control, might disdain to travel in disguise and decline to feel that their security depended on it.[9] Although the exercise of an imperial "right to roam" remained a contentious issue (as it proved to be for the naturalist Joseph Hooker in Sikkim in 1849), by mid-century, middle-class Europeans, women as well as men, continental Europeans as well as Britons, generally found few political obstacles to journeying from one part of India to another.

Officers and administrators, whether military or civilian, rarely stayed in one posting very long before they were moved elsewhere or were obliged by promotion or illness to transfer to another station. The constant need for surveys and reports—on matters as diverse as geology, topography, forest resources, and revenue settlements—further fueled this restless movement. The expansion of the Company's domains itself provided the incentive for much of the travel of the period, as military officers, or doctors, engineers, and surveyors attached to the army,[10] journeyed to the far reaches of the subcontinent, whether in the course of their duties, in traveling to or from official postings, on botanical excursions or hunting expeditions, or during periods of leave and recuperation. Many of the travel accounts of the period, like a large number of scientific works, were written by individuals who belonged to, or were in various ways attached to, the armed services in India—if not as serving officers, then as the relatives (including wives, sisters, and daughters) of military personnel.[11]

Traveling India

The history of colonial India has often been understood, reasonably enough, through the establishment and functioning of its principal administrative institutions, such as the army, the civil service, the police or the revenue administration, much as its science has been most closely identified with such prominent organizations and agencies as the Asiatic Society of Bengal (founded in 1784), the Indian Medical Service (present in embryonic form in each of the three "presidencies" or provinces of British India by the late eighteenth century), and the trigonometrical survey (established during the early nineteenth century). But focusing on such institutions tends to detract from the raw kinetics of early colonialism and the restlessness of an empire materially as well as ideologically still in the making; it overlooks the importance this mobility had for the European understanding and representation of India.

The point can briefly be made with respect to three individuals whose careers are discussed more fully later on in this book. In the course of his short India career (1832–45) and in connection with various military duties or scientific assignments, the surgeon-botanist William Griffith hurtled from one end of the expanding Indian empire to another. First appointed to the medical service in Madras, he was subsequently sent to Malacca in Sumatra (then still part of the Company's territories), before being dispatched on expeditions to Assam (in search of tea trees), Bhutan (as physician to a diplomatic embassy), Afghanistan (with the invading British forces), and Burma (to report on teak forests). In thirteen years of botanizing, Griffith amassed a collection of 9,000 plant species, a record even by the gargantuan standards of the time. As well as the mobility required by his dual profession of army physician and state botanist, Griffith's constant movement is indicative of an unsatisfied thirst for practical knowledge and the perceived need to build a more systematic understanding of Indian flora on the opportunities for personal observation and acquisition available only through travel. When he died, aged only 34, it was as much from exhaustion as from the effects of debilitating disease.[12] Griffith's careering around India (and beyond) was extreme but not entirely exceptional. There were naturalists like Edward Blyth, curator of the Asiatic Society's museum, whose duties confined them to Calcutta or the other presidency towns; but most spent a large part of their time traveling and, quite apart from what the Company required of them officially, regarded it as essential to the furtherance of science that they did so.[13]

This restless, itinerant lifestyle was not true only of the Company's servants. In his short term as Bishop of Calcutta (1823–6), Reginald Heber made, from curiosity as much as from responsibility for his far-flung flock, two extensive tours of the subcontinent, during the first visiting Bengal, North India and the Himalaya, western India, Madras, and Ceylon, before dying at Tiruchirapalli in South India during his second, exhausting perambulation. Heber's account of his travels became almost immediately after his death a model of Romantic writing about India, a template against which other travelers judged their own wanderings and impressions.[14] There had been a time, too, when the governor-general of India (an office first held by Warren Hastings in 1774) barely stirred from his official seat in Calcutta, or ventured far beyond the encircling ditch excavated in the 1740s to defend the city from Maratha invasion. But by the latter part of this period several governors-general had become far more mobile. In his first four years in office (from January 1848 to February 1852), Lord Dalhousie spent less than twelve months in Calcutta: he lived for long periods in North India, overseeing operations against the Sikhs and residing at Simla, the fledgling summer capital of British India, where he and his wife recovered from the heat and illnesses of the plains. He also visited Sind, Bombay, the Madras Presidency, Ceylon, Penang, and Singapore before returning to Calcutta.[15] It is not surprising that Dalhousie recognized, if only from personal experience, the imperative need to facilitate travel and communication through railroads, telegraphs, and an efficient postal service. He was criticized for spending so much time away from Calcutta, but the extent and engrossing complexity of the Indian empire seem to require that he, like so many of his contemporaries, spend much of his time on the road.

The extent to which British India itself partook more of the character of a temporary camp than a settled colony was much debated at the time.

As early as 1782, George Forster, writing from Benares, declared, somewhat wishfully, that "the English should no longer account themselves sojourners in this country."[16] But, since few middle-class Britons regarded India as their permanent home, rather as a place where they might well die but were unlikely to retire, and from which they painfully dispatched their young children to grow up and be educated in Britain, the idea of being "settled" in India made little sense. Seventy years after Forster, one leading member of the Bengal Medical Service still referred to the British, and British women in particular, as "sojourners in the sun."[17] It was not uncommon for Britons in their more melancholy moments to think of themselves not merely as exiles, but as convicts, "transported," as Dalhousie put it, "to this penal settlement."[18] Although by the 1850s advances in land and sea transport, and attempts to emulate the successes of Canada, Australia, and New Zealand through projected schemes of white colonization, led some writers to suggest that India was at last moving from the transient status of "an encampment" to the settled fixity of a colony,[19] it was generally accepted that India remained, in imperial terms, a great anomaly, and was likely to remain so. Before the mid-century Mutiny, the want of a permanent white population, like the reliance upon the military underpinning of British rule, emphasized the rootless, restless nature of the Indian empire. This want of fixity could only reflect, in turn, upon the nature of the science that empire produced.

As British rule in India became more established and institutionally grounded, the potential for personal mobility increased. By the 1850s, India and its interior provinces had become far more accessible to European travelers than they had been at the close of the previous century. Improvements in maritime technology, especially the advent of steamships in the Indian Ocean, and the adoption of the overland route across Egypt from Alexandria to the Red Sea in place of the longer, more perilous, passage via the Cape of Good Hope, substantially reduced journey times between British and Indian ports and lowered the cost of travel. By 1840 a ship might depart for India and return home to Britain within eight months, instead of the year or more required in the previous century.[20] One writer reckoned in 1851 that India was now—in terms of travel time—only one-sixth the distance from Britain it had been in the days of Robert Clive and Warren Hastings ninety years earlier, adding that in "that simple fact a revolution of the most momentous kind is expressed."[21] It became possible for well-heeled travelers to visit India and Ceylon on a seven-month winter ramble, and even, to the indignation of "old India hands," to publish a serviceable account of their experiences on their return.[22] Especially once the Suez Canal opened in 1869, the age of organized international tourism was not far off.[23]

Communications, too, benefited from advances in transportation and improved postal services. By the 1840s letters moved with a speed and dependability unimaginable decades earlier. Instead of eighteen months' delay, letters might now receive a reply within six months or less. In the late 1840s Joseph Hooker, based at Darjeeling in the eastern Himalaya, three hundred miles from Calcutta, was able to maintain a regular correspondence with his father, William Hooker, at Kew: some letters went missing, but most reached their destination within two months. When Joseph Hooker returned to Darjeeling from one of his Himalayan expeditions in January 1849, he found 47 "English letters" waiting for him.[24] The volume of this correspondence and the speed with which it moved between Darjeeling and Kew is indicative of the extent to which individuals could maintain a strong sense of connectedness with Britain, with family, friends, and professional circles. By the mid-1840s 30,000 letters were dispatched by steamers each month from Bombay alone. Remarking on this, one observer suggested that whereas formerly correspondence "even between intimate friends and dear relatives" had "soon flagged" and eventually "ceased altogether," now regular steamship services "made every Englishman and Englishwoman, in the three presidencies, a periodical letter-writer."[25]

The emotional as well as intellectual gulf between Britain and British India might not thereby have vanished, but the possibilities for travel and communication—for articulating difference as well as promoting interconnectedness—were greatly enhanced.

Within India an expanding network of travelers' bungalows (an Anglicized term that spread almost as rapidly as the improvement in communications), a relatively reliable palki or palanquin service (with relays of bearers booked through local postmasters), the building of new roads and bridges (especially along the Grand Trunk Road that linked Calcutta with Benares and the northwest), and the advent of steamboats on the Ganges and Indus, ensured that even before the much-heralded arrival of the railroads in the mid-1850s, the interior of the country could be traversed more easily and speedily than had been possible before 1800.[26]

Even so, no small part of the writing of the period was devoted to the frustrations and discomforts of Indian travel, especially by palanquin, which many authors likened to traveling in a half-closed coffin or a portable oven.[27] It is remarkable, nonetheless, how far and how fast Europeans could travel even by this primitive means of transport. In 1807 Sir James Mackintosh, Recorder at the Bombay High Court, claimed to have traveled a thousand miles across South India, from Goa to Madras and back via Mysore, by palanquin in a month (at the rate of more than thirty miles a day); two decades later John Lawrence, then a young civil servant, was said to have covered the 900 miles from Calcutta to Delhi in only eighteen days (fifty miles a day).[28] Most pre-Mutiny travel was more leisurely, averaging ten to fifteen miles a day, thus allowing for close observation of the passing countryside, coupled with frequent stops along the way, at scenic temples or in the obliging shade of mango trees. But travelers varied widely in their expectations and habits. Some, like Mackintosh, used their palanquin time less as an opportunity to see India than to catch up on their reading of European novels and essays. As a naturalist, Joseph Hooker, who had his first taste of palanquin travel in 1848, was rapidly convinced of the physical discomfort of traveling in a conveyance "horsed by men." "Then, too," his complaint continued,

> you pass plants and cannot stop to gather them; trees and don't know what they are; houses, temples, and objects strange to the traveller's eye, and have no one to teach where and what they may be; no fellow-traveller with whom to change one curious remark.[29]

Others, by contrast, like Emma Roberts, regarded palanquin travel as providing—at least to a woman—unique opportunities to see India first-hand, to stop at and savor its remoter, more romantic, places. The best time to travel, she explained to her readers, was just after the rains, when the doors of the palanquin could be kept wide open:

> various beauties of the jungles display themselves to view; every spot is covered with the richest verdure, and creepers of luxuriant growth, studied with myriads of stars, fling their bright festoons from tree to tree. Those beautiful little mosques and pagodas, which in every part of India embellish the landscape, look like gems as they rise from the soft green turf which surrounds them . . .[30]

In some respects, while removing the evident discomforts and inconveniences of palanquin travel, the coming of the railroads, by making rapid (and in its own way even more secluded) travel much easier, rendered the countryside far less visible to European travelers, less subject to both the critical and the admiring gaze.

Writing India

The physical expansion of the Company's domains and concurrent advances in transport and communications were not the only factors that helped usher in a new age of travel and travel writing. The greatly augmented British military and administrative engagement with India in the early nineteenth century brought with it a new generation of educated men (and, in far smaller numbers, women), with minds attuned to the literary, artistic, and scientific interests of their day. These were individuals who were better able to absorb and articulate impressions of India than had earlier travelers, whose accounts of India, especially of its landscape, appear, by contrast, sparse and superficial. A sixteenth- or seventeenth-century traveler might dwell at length on intrigues at the Mughal court, describe the principal items of trade to be found in a "spacious and fruitfull kingdome" like Bengal, or comment on the "false gods" of the Hindus and their strange manners and customs; he might even remark on the unfamiliar fruits and exotic animals.[31] India might emerge from such accounts as a place of marvels and wonders,[32] but, with few exceptions (like François Bernier amidst the delights and enchantments of Mughal Kashmir), the traveler was unlikely to say much about the landscape or pass judgment on forests, hills, and plains beyond briefly noting that they were pleasing to the eye or, according to local opinion, unhealthy.[33]

By the late eighteenth and early nineteenth centuries, however, European descriptions of India had become far more elaborate and expressive, as the just-quoted passage from Emma Roberts indicates. Scarcely later than in Europe, British India became subject to a new sensitivity to nature.[34] The travel writing of the period (along with the personal correspondence and other forms of more intimate literary expression) exhibited a new, romantically charged awareness of the richness and diversity of the physical environment. It is enthused with a new vocabulary of place and taste and an unprecedented medical and scientific interest in topography, climate, vegetation, and landscape. This change might be dated to the 1780s or even slightly earlier. One early manifestation is to be found in the narrative of the painter William Hodges, who worked and traveled in India between 1780 and 1783. With his experience of the South Pacific, where he had been an artist on Captain Cook's second expedition (1772–5), and his taste for the "picturesque" properties of waterfalls, woods and other "beauties of nature," Hodges was a significant pioneer in India of this newfound sensibility to nature.[35]

Some of this novel feeling gained expression in pictorial representations of India and in the publication of "views" portraying India's main historical, architectural, and scenic sites. After about 1800, however, when Hodges and the uncle and nephew partnership of Thomas and William Daniell (active in India from 1785 to 1794) had left the country,[36] India was poorly supplied, by comparison with Europe or North America, with professional landscape artists. Even so, the kinds of "Oriental" images produced in this early period, especially by the Daniells, lingered on (as will be further seen in Chapter 4) in the minds of travelers and were reproduced and emulated—in mood, subject, and style—in other illustrative and literary work well into the 1830s and 1840s.[37]

Some of this new expressiveness found its way, too, into the novels and poetry produced in this period in India. *Hartly House*, a novel published anonymously in 1789, is constructed through the letters of Sophia Goldsborne, newly arrived in Calcutta; writing to her friend Arabella in England, she makes frequent reference to the physical experience of being in India, but despite her apparent curiosity about India, Sophia barely ventures beyond the immediate environs of Calcutta. And although her opinion of the country oscillates between praise for "this Arcadian climate" and delight that "Nature is here lavish of her most beautiful productions" and laments about "this all subduing climate" and its "fervid heat," she (or the author) lacks the vocabulary through which to express what is idiosyncratic about India or distinct from England's "soft" and "temperate" climate.[38] Indeed, her most common reference point is to the poem "Summer" from James Thomson's *Seasons*, a quintessential piece of English pastoralism written sixty years earlier.[39] In so far as this novel can serve as a guide, the peculiar properties of India's climate and physical environment remain elusive and non-specific.

By contrast, by the early nineteenth century, and certainly by the 1830s, there had emerged a far more complex, expressive and distinctive discourse of Indian landscape, topography, and travel. This literature pointedly and repeatedly invoked the authority and authenticity of "knowing" India first-hand, not least by drawing attention to its physical features as much as to its cultural characteristics, while yet maintaining a host of literary and geographical references (or "associations" as they were commonly called) that situated India within a much wider mental field of comparisons and contrasts. While pictorial representations were frequently employed as familiar—and, in the more didactic of these works, instructive— reference points, and were used to supplement textual accounts, or provide the model for scenic descriptions that were self-consciously "picturesque," the written word served as the primary vehicle for the articulation of landscape ideas and sentiments. The representation of India through a series of "scenes" and "views," often through a combination of written text and accompanying engravings, so common by the 1820s and 1830s, created a cumulative impression of the diversity and interest of India as presented to the traveler's discerning eye. But the frequent

FIG. 1. The Bhutanese Himalaya, Assam, and the Brahmaputra Valley, from J.D. Hooker, *Himalayan Journals*, vol. 2 (1854).
Reproduced by kind permission of the School of Oriental and African Studies, London.

invocation of "prospects," "spectacles," and "*coups d'oeil*"—standard expressions in the travel literature and itinerant science of this period—also suggests a kind of panopticism exercised through the critical gaze of the European observer.[40] The naturalist Joseph Hooker was as likely as any of his contemporaries to use the expression "*coup d'oeil*" to describe nothing more momentous than the imposing appearance of European houses along Calcutta's stylish Chowringhee Road. But he also used it in a more significant manner, to describe—and so expose for scientific scrutiny—the commanding view to be obtained from a hill near Shillong in Assam, with its distant views of the Brahmaputra and Himalaya (see Fig. 1), or the flooded forests of the Sundarbans as seen from the mast of a Calcutta-bound steamer.[41] The quest for visual vantage points, the better to understand and represent the configuration of the land, the appearance of sky and vegetation, or the human impact on nature, was a recurring motif in the literature of the period. It was also a demonstration of the importance attached in the late eighteenth and early nineteenth centuries to the ocular authority of the traveler, who (it was assumed) brought a discerning eye, a sharp intelligence, and the benefits of education, sensibility, and experience to the spectacle exposed to his or her view.

Reliance upon the written word did not simply arise from the lamented absence of skilled landscape artists. Prose descriptions communicated even more powerfully and comprehensively than could most landscape art, the sense of India being scrutinized and appraised by outsiders. There was, besides, much about India (and its elusive, contradictory nature) that did not lend itself to pictorial representation: the "air of squalor," for instance, about many Indian towns and pilgrimage places which, Roberts wrote, "disgusts the eye,"[42] or the abrupt and dramatic transformation (unparalleled in Britain) that took place in the appearance of the Indian landscape between the parched vegetation of the dry season and the luxuriant greenery that followed the monsoon. Although seeing remained the most privileged of the senses, smelling, hearing, tasting, and touching were also prominent in the writings of the time, not least in the accounts of naturalists like Joseph Hooker and Victor Jacquemont, as they strove to relate the reality of India to the glories of the long anticipated tropics. There was a sensual quality about India, its plant-life and landscape, the smell of its flowers or the taste of exotic fruit, that could only be communicated through words. Scientifically as well as scenically, the investigation and representation of India called for elaborate word-pictures and narrative structures that could record not merely significant detail but also convey the totality and the experiential qualities of an entire landscape. And there was much about the European understanding of India—not least its many "horrors"—that was not satisfied with the deceptive pleasures of the "picturesque" and seemed to call for a more judgmental (and hence textual) strategy of representation.

Although a number of recent scholars have adopted the idea of the "picturesque" as a key to understanding Western representations of India in this period,[43] the term (though certainly frequently used) often had a very trite meaning, suggesting something that was pretty rather than profound, appealing to the eye rather than troubling the soul, worthy of being made into a picture but otherwise of little arresting importance. Representations of India, at least in prose and particularly in the more earnest travel and scientific literature, strove to express something about India that reached beyond the framing confines and shallow conventions of the picturesque. As subsequent chapters will show, writers sought to narrativize the Indian landscape and not merely depict it caught in a single moment in time, to represent it as a series of interconnected moral as well as scenic tropes that cumulatively signified progression (or regression) from the familiar into the exotic and from the civilized to the heathen, or, conversely, from the torrid and oppressive to the temperate and uplifting. The scenic complexity of India and the great diversity of its landscapes made it possible to build such narratives of contrast and contradiction within India and not merely in terms of a journey from Europe to India. Simultaneously, without ever entirely sacrificing their own privileged externality, writers invoked the language and sentiments of Romanticism to situate themselves and their readers within the landscape, seeking to evoke its distinctive moods, characteristics, and associations, to make interconnections between sentiment and science. The picturesque, as understood at the time, was a woefully inadequate vehicle for such grand representational ambitions.

In the opening decades of the nineteenth century, India appeared to command unprecedented interest in Britain, which was sustained by reports of military successes and fiascos, debates about the future of the Company (as its charter came up for periodic review before Parliament), and by the growing number of British families with India connections. As Thomas De Quincey remarked in 1839, "everybody has an India uncle,"[44] and many middle-class children were brought up in households where "Indo-mania" ruled and India was talked of almost incessantly.[45] As controversy raged over the Company, and as British economic ambitions and religious policies came under critical scrutiny, so educated British public interest in India also increased—or was presumed to have. If at the turn of the century there appeared to be few non-specialist books about India,[46] by the 1830s there was seen to be a lively market for Indiana, one which book publishers and review editors in London and Edinburgh were eager to exploit. The early nineteenth century saw the publication in Britain of hundreds, if not thousands, of books about India: histories, biographies, political commentaries, economic analyses, evangelical tracts, chronicles of military campaigns, and tales of sport and hunting, and, above all, travel narratives. At its height between the 1820s and 1840s, this vogue for travel writing about India constituted one of the principal means by which India was known to the West and through which ideas about the subcontinent were processed and disseminated.[47]

It is important to recognize, though, how rapidly, despite (arguably, because of) this prodigious tide of publication, the subject of India began to bore the British public,[48] and how often works, whether written by travelers or "old Indians," as they liked to honor themselves, aroused only expressions of exasperation, tedium, and regret. As early as 1825 one writer (himself only briefly resident in India) remarked that books about the country were "notorious for being devoid of general interest, and are usually regarded as almost unreadable by the British public, who give much more attention to works upon even the most obscure and useless of our colonial dominions." "Indeed," he added, "the indifference which the majority of people at home manifest towards India seems rather difficult to account for, when one considers that there is scarcely a family in the middle classes that has not some connexion, friend, or relation residing in the country."[49] Others complained that to the outsider works on India were often "long treatises," full of "hard names" and "perplexing allusions" that British readers could barely understand, or were written in a "sapless, inanimate style" that was "repulsive to the general reader."[50] "Heaviness" was "the besetting sin of most works on India."[51]

Despite this unfavorable response, most travel writers believed they had something new to contribute to Europe's still insufficient stock of knowledge about India and the East. The late eighteenth- and early nineteenth-century European "discovery" of India advanced on many different fronts—through the investigation of Hinduism and Oriental texts, for instance, by Sir William Jones and other scholarly minded judges, doctors, and civil servants, grouped around the Asiatic Society of Bengal; or through the physical measuring and surveying of India, which by 1857 had made possible the accurate mapping of virtually the whole of India from Kanyakumari in the south to the Himalaya in the north.[52] Although ideas of "discovery" in a geographical sense are more commonly associated with the European voyages of the fifteenth and sixteenth centuries, or with the interior of Africa in the eighteenth and nineteenth, the period from the 1780s through to the 1850s was as close as the British in India came to a comparable "age of discovery." The sense of excitement was particularly intense between the 1820s and the 1840s as the Himalaya, the desert regions of western India and the Indus valley, and the densely forested regions of Assam and Burma in the east, came under increasing scrutiny. Being an explorer, visiting places previously untrodden by Europeans, let alone surveyed for science, was one of the compulsions that drove Joseph Hooker to reach the bleak Himalayan frontier between Sikkim and Tibet in the late 1840s.

Such travel was significantly more than a geographical exploration and mapping of India. It will be argued here that the travel literature, especially in the hands of those who, if not "ardent" naturalists, were at least knowledgeable travelers, was of crucial importance for the perceptual reconnaissance of India and the complex relationship thereby established between India's material existence—its terrain, climate, vegetation, wildlife, and so on—and the identity created for India from out of this physical base. Although much has (rightly) been written in recent years about the importance of the mechanical and technological means of extending this control—by surveys and censuses, by railroads, steamships, and telegraphs,[53] the importance of these "tools of empire" to the wider annexation of India by the British, especially before the 1850s, can easily be exaggerated. In the early nineteenth century much of the work of subordinating and appropriating India was conducted at a discursive level and through such means as travel writing and the scientific and literary appropriation of the Indian landscape.

Romanticism is frequently discussed in representations of the East in Europe, where Indian literature and philosophy were among the movement's many sources of inspiration; but this in particular is a subject that has been remarkably neglected in the context of colonial India itself. "Romantic India" has often been taken to mean the "cultural imaginary" that poets, novelists, and painters imposed upon the East and summoned up out of their own fertile imaginations.[54] This was the distant view of India presented by Robert Southey, Samuel Taylor Coleridge, and Thomas Moore (author of that seductive poetic narrative *Lalla Rookh*), writers who, while certainly well informed about India, had never actually been there.[55] Even among historians of British India there has been a singular reluctance to see Romanticism as more than a fleeting and relatively superficial phenomenon—of lesser moment than the contemporaneous doctrines of the utilitarians and evangelicals or the revenue-hungry policies of the East India Company.[56] However, recent discussion of Romanticism as a historical phenomenon as much as a literary movement has shown (not least through a critical reappraisal of travel writing and its "complicity" in, or "anxiety" over, empire) how Romanticism was closely bound up with colonialism and the contradictory ideas and sentiments generated by early nineteenth-century nationalism and imperialism.[57] In looking at the travel writing of the Romantic era in India and at the scientific, medical, and topographical literature with which it was enmeshed, it is possible to see more clearly the contribution Romanticism made to the colonial appropriation of India and its function as a bridge between an earlier phase of Orientalism (in the pre-Saidian sense of that term) and a later move (especially marked after the suppression of the Mutiny) toward a colonial version of Foucauldian governmentality.[58]

Science and the Traveling Gaze

Since reference is made at various points in this book to "the traveling gaze," it is worth commenting on the intended use of that expression from the outset. Like the allusion already made to panopticism and governmentality, the idea of a traveling gaze is necessarily indebted to the seminal writings of Michel Foucault, especially *The Birth of the Clinic* and *Discipline and Punish* and also his investigation of the human sciences in *The Order of Things*.[59] In this Foucauldian sense "the gaze" ranges from the disciplining power of constant monitoring and surveillance (as over prisoners or hospital inmates) to the investigative, ordering, and interpretative intelligence that pervades the practice of a modern science like botany or zoology. Both usages imply an asymmetrical relationship of power in which the viewer occupies a position of authority and control over the subject of his or her penetrating gaze. The viewer might be an individual but his or her vision articulates, as if in microcosm, a far wider regime of power, and though physical force might underpin the exercise of power (by, for instance, placing the prisoner in the penitentiary in the first place) it is through superior knowledge, by the precision and pervasiveness of the gaze, or even by the commanding physical presence of the gaze over its subject (as in seeing a landscape from an elevated and hence uniquely revealing viewpoint) that this power is principally exercised.

In recent, post-Foucauldian scholarship, "the gaze," or its equivalents, have come to be used in a wide variety of contexts (often with scant reference to Foucault's own work). Part of the value of the idea to the present work is that it usefully spans discussion of the development of the natural sciences (in this instance botany) and, though this was not Foucault's own usage, the conceptualization of nature in terms of landscape.[60] Indeed, the idea of "the gaze"—especially as exercised by the white male explorer, missionary, administrator, or itinerant naturalist— has rapidly come to be seen as one of the principal expressions of the wider colonizing process. The concept advanced by Mary Louise Pratt of the "seeing-man . . . whose imperial eyes passively look out and possess," embodied for her in imperial travelers like Richard Burton in Africa in the 1860s, and the representative "monarch of all I survey" style of travel writing, has effectively combined the Foucaldian paradigm of power/ knowledge with imperial themes of travel and landscape, nature, art, and literature. The exercise of "the gaze" is the prelude to possession in more material and institutional forms, just as travel is more about imposing upon, than learning from, the landscape subject to the itinerant gaze.[61]

These applications and elaborations of Foucault are not effected without hazard, but they can open up new interpretive possibilities. Moving "the gaze" from the prison and the natural sciences and into the landscape raises questions as to how far an inanimate, or at least non-human, object like the landscape can be subjected to or "reformed" by a disciplining gaze in the same way as criminals in prison. One answer is to substitute "improvement" for "reform," or to recognize the challenging noncompliance between external expectations of a landscape and its material reality or pre-existing understandings and usages. This contestation over landscapes and nature understood not simply as objective fact but also as social construction, makes it possible to think analytically of "terrains of resistance."[62] Again, while Foucault's panopticon was a structure built of stone and iron, intimidating in its very physicality and immobility, "the gaze," it is increasingly realized, can also be highly mobile and yet still exercise a powerful and enduring disciplinary effect. The point here must be, as Paul Carter has indicated, that travel in a colonial or colonizing situation like that of Australia from the time of Cook's exploration onwards, was more than a merely physical activity. It was also "an epistemological strategy, a mode of knowing."[63] What Carter calls "the travelling mode of knowledge," and the ability of early explorers and cartographers to transform space into "an object of knowledge,"[64] finds a direct parallel in early British India and enables us to take the authority of the Foucauldian gaze well beyond the physical confines of the prison.

For the purposes of this discussion, then, the idea of a traveling gaze relates, firstly, to the process by which much of the observation, and hence the understanding, of India was conducted through travel. Although part of the scientific investigation of India during the early colonial period was conducted by and through such institutional sites as the army, hospitals, prisons, and lunatic asylums, or botanic gardens, museums, and observatories, a large portion of this process of observation and representation (and often a prior element in both a temporal and structural sense) was performed by European travelers, situated outside, or moving between, the main centers of colonial administration and science, whether through official expeditions or in the course of other occupations and pursuits. Many an up-country official in this period was engaged in survey and settlement work that not only required him personally to travel extensively but also placed him at the core of an "ambulatory court,"[65] to which information of various kinds was constantly being relayed and within which it was assembled and collated for onward transmission or subsequent use. In moving frequently from place to place, the "observant officer" had, as one writer put it, "not only an opportunity of investigating the geological formation, natural history, and productions of the country;" he also enjoyed "great facilities for studying the history, religion, and civilization of the people, from the various monuments and inscriptions, both ancient and modern, which lie on his route."[66] In other words, travel (and the subsequent production of scientific texts, travel narratives, or works combining elements of both genres) was one of the principal ways in which India was captured not just for empire, but also for science.

References to "the scientific traveller" abound in the literature of this period,[67] well before the term "scientist" was in common use. The term needs to be understood not only in terms of the contemporary Western passion for scientific inquiry (which spread well beyond the scientific community as such) but also as part of an evolving strategy within colonial epistemology, as an attempt to use direct European observation to supplement or even displace the written texts (mainly in Sanskrit and Persian) and the high-caste intermediaries (particularly Brahmin pandits) that had informed and characterized the early Orientalist project. The converse of this epistemological reorientation was, however, that colonial science itself, in becoming so heavily tied to travel, often assumed a sketchy, *ad hoc* character, suggestive of incomplete or interrupted conversations. An extreme, but not unrepresentative, example of this was an anonymous article published in 1839 in the *Journal of the Asiatic Society of Bengal*, describing places and sights observed during a march through Central India the previous year. It began with the frank declaration that:

> Many of the places visited in this journey, were unavoidably visited ... at a gallop; the descriptions are not therefore offered as minute and faultless details, but rather as sketches claiming every indulgence; whose aim is to stimulate the curiosity of future travellers over the same ground, who may have more leisure to pursue the inquiry.[68]

It is not intended to suggest that "the traveling gaze" was either passive or impartial. External to the cultural and physical landscape through which the European traveled, this scientific and scenic gaze was itself an ordering, even disciplining, mechanism that edited as well as elicited information and actively meddled in the construction of the knowledge it sought to shepherd and cajole into meaningful shapes and approved scientific forms. In some fields—such as ethnography—this disciplinary gaze and the discourse it engendered had hardly moved by the 1850s beyond a preliminary reconnaissance,[69] while in others—such as medical topography (discussed in Chapter 2 in connection with India's "deathscapes")—it had already begun to define the lines along which colonial policy and ideology were later to advance.

Aided by increased European mobility and observational opportunity, the seemingly contradictory role of the traveling gaze was to render the novel and exotic more familiar by attaching it to the cultural norms and epistemological systems of Western Europe while simultaneously emphasizing what was alien about India's Oriental or tropical landscape and all the varied forms of human, animal, and vegetable life that it contained. And while part of the function of the gaze was to disaggregate—to break down larger entities (patterns of vegetation, disease environments, racial categories) and so enable them to become objects of more precise and exacting scientific scrutiny—it was also deemed necessary to view and to interpret such entities as a whole, as "tableaux," as "spectacles," or "scenes," whose collective significance amounted to more than their constituent parts, or which communicated to the observant traveler as much as, if not more than, what intricate dissection and microscopic analysis might reveal. In this holistic approach there was much to indicate the influence of Romanticism on scientific as well as scenic ideas and representations. While Foucault ignored Romanticism and privileged Enlightenment (much as he neglected land for the body) the investigation of early nineteenth-century India makes it essential to recognize the importance of the Romantic gaze as an integral part of the colonial scientific enterprise of the period and as a critical means by which India was appropriated to European imagination, experience, and exploitation.

This leads to a second set of meanings of the traveling gaze. Travel, it is argued here, was central to the way in which science was constructed in and around early colonial India. Without travel much of the science of the period would not have been practically or technically possible. Even if it was in danger of producing no more than the most preliminary or superficial results, as in the case of the traveler quoted above, cumulatively such observation provided the bedrock upon which later, more systematic, surveys and analyses were constructed. Before the 1860s, it was commonly the case in India, as elsewhere, that scientific accounts were presented in the forms of journeys, in which narratives of personal experience and the unfolding of nature intersected or were mutually reinforcing.[70] But it is possible to go further and argue that, as far as ideas of science and landscape were concerned, travel was constitutive and not merely contextual.[71] India's immense size, great physical diversity and often baffling cultural complexity at times led to its being considered a "continent" rather than the "subcontinent" it subsequently more modestly became,[72] and with the experience of travel it accordingly came to be understood in narrative terms, as a series of stages, advancing from one region (as defined by climate, topography, vegetation, diet, and latterly race) to another, or, as in the case of Joseph Hooker in the Himalaya, constantly crossing from one zone to another. These marked internal differences, played out across the varied landscape of India, acquired a strong emotional and moral identification from which neither scientific observation nor literary representation was entirely immune.

By the 1850s, travel, and the scientific reconnaissance that accompanied it, had helped reveal the diversity of India and the difficulty of characterizing it through a single scenic trope. In their report on the "tropical forests" of India in 1851, a group of colonial scientists, led by Hugh Cleghorn of the Madras Medical Service, aptly observed:

> British India is so extensive an empire, so diversified in soil and climate, as well as in natural and agricultural products, that it is impossible to predicate anything respecting it generally; that which is descriptive of one part is not necessarily applicable to another. Thus some parts are covered with primaeval forests ... while others are not only bare of trees, but of vegetation of any kind.[73]

The point must be made, however, that, despite the recognition of India's diversity, this did not in fact preclude attempts to characterize India as a whole or to look for environmental tropes and models of nature and culture that would make it possible to locate India, or its constituent regions, within a large schema.

Further, although Europeans often sought to impose their own understanding of landscape upon India, an understanding derived from Europe itself or from other tropical regions, India did not always match up to these expectations. It might be more difficult to speak of a "resistance against the gaze" in speaking of landscapes than of bodies, but a similar principle of non-compliance applies. Indeed, the observer's disappointment with the India of his or her expectations was a recurrent motif, and was one point of departure for those seeking to "improve" the country. Thus, the sciences of India—especially the natural sciences discussed here—led by botany, evolved symbiotically with travel in ways that were mutually constitutive. While science as authored and authorized in Europe never failed to exercise its gravitational pull on India, the archeology of colonial knowledge, as far as the natural sciences were concerned, can only be adequately understood by reference to the landscape through which it was constructed.

Thirdly, the traveling gaze of the early nineteenth century needs to be situated within a specific historical context. It possessed a pronounced significance only at a particular moment in the long-term evolution of science and colonialism in India. As already indicated, before the 1770s or even 1800s there was little opportunity (or requirement) for science to "travel" in India. With a few notable exceptions (such as Samuel Turner's mission to Bhutan and Tibet in 1783, the account of which became one of the foundational texts of colonial travel writing in India),[74] political and military circumstances made such mobility extremely difficult. Scientific investigations were as a consequence largely confined to those parts of the coastline that had already passed under Company rule (Bengal and the Northern Circars) or to the presidency towns of Calcutta, Madras, and Bombay.

Conversely, after the 1850s, as rail travel expanded and tourism became more routine, and as the requirements of science grew more exacting, travel lost much of its utility for science and, as laboratories and research institutes grew in importance, the landscape became a less significant site of colonial appraisal and scientific enquiry. Before the middle decades of the century the "spectacle" of India was largely only available to the European gaze through arduous travel. Subsequently, as the trend set by the Great Exhibition in London in 1851 gathered pace, that "spectacle" itself became mobile and accessible to the West in the West, or it was replicated in urban India through exhibitions, museum displays and such ceremonial occasions as the imperial durbars.[75] Both British public anxiety and British interest grew because of the Mutiny of 1857–8, yet the genre of travel writing about India was itself in decline by mid-century.[76] In the age of the railroad, such writing had become clichéd and stale, as passé as a palanquin, and was only effectively revived by the genius of Rudyard Kipling (as much through his imaginative fiction as his early journalism) toward the century's close.

Moreover, in the second half of the century, as it sought to distance itself from Romanticism's subjectivity and emotionalism, science became more comprehensively professionalized and institutionalized—in the work of the colonial medical and scientific services, in hospitals, agricultural colleges and research institutes—just as India itself became more systematically embodied in the censuses, gazetteers, and administrative manuals, in the sanitary reports and ethnographic surveys of the late nineteenth century.[77] By the 1860s and 1870s, as colonial governmentality took firm hold, the age of itinerant science and the traveling gaze was almost over.

Under the Tropics

Travel forms one of the organizing ideas of this book; the other is concerned with India's increasingly assured but never unproblematic place within "the tropics." Even a superficial glance at the travel, and more especially the scientific, literature of the latter part of this period will show a frequent evocation of India as part of a wider tropical world: its climate and vegetation, its forests and diseases, even (more tentatively) its inhabitants have come to be designated "tropical" in ways that suggest that this was deliberate and not an absent-minded aside. At it most basic the term "tropics" signified to contemporaries those lands (presumably between the tropics, but not invariably so) that were characterized by "heat, moisture, and a luxuriant vegetation."[78] But the use of the term, and in so many different contexts, clearly extended well beyond this specific meaning.

There is now an extensive academic literature about the nature and evolution of the idea of the tropics, especially as it developed in the course of the eighteenth and nineteenth centuries and influenced European medical, scientific, and artistic ideas. It has accordingly become possible to understand the tropics "as a conceptual, and not just physical, space." Designating a portion of the globe the tropics became a "Western way of defining something culturally and politically alien, as well as environmentally distinctive, from Europe and other parts of the temperate zone."[79] By invoking the tropics, early nineteenth-century writers brought to India a host of scientific and scenic ideas that ranged from the paradisiacal to the pestilential, from the impressionistic and Romantic to the narrowly technical characterization of plant and animal species. India's incorporation into the tropics was thus one way (among others) of defining its "otherness" from Europe as well as stressing its interconnectedness with what was increasingly thought of, in contradistinction to the northern and southern "temperate" zones, as the "tropical world." Tropicality might thus complement or supplant the alterity of "Orientalism" in fashioning the imaginative geography of the non-European world.[80]

And yet, for all the power of the tropical idea, India was always something of a misfit, a troublesome site for tropicality. Much (but by no means all) of the subcontinent lay within the tropics, though paradoxically, some of its most "tropical" locations lay north of the Tropic of Cancer in the foothills of the Himalaya, and yet it failed in many scenic and scientific respects to conform to the idealized notion of the tropics derived from European encounters with the Pacific, Central America, and the Caribbean, or even neighboring Ceylon, Burma, and Sumatra. If the term "luxuriant" so habitually applied to tropical vegetation were elided, as it often appeared to be, with a more general notion of "luxury" and "luxurious" then India, once famed for its riches but now apparently so prone to famine and deficient in basic staples, only partly satisfied European ambitions and desires. Indeed, India appeared to many disappointed contemporaries to be *in* the tropics yet not truly *of* the tropics. Even so, whereas the term "tropical" was seldom applied to India before 1800, after that date, and especially by the 1840s, the term was extensively used in a wide variety of scientific and scenic contexts. Why, how, and to what extent, India became "tropical" is one of the central concerns of this book.

In an age preoccupied with "associations," with establishing connections and correspondences, India was not allowed to simply be itself. The tropicalization of India points to Europe's political and cultural dilemma as to where India should be located in the geographical schema of the expanding imperial world—whether to see it as an extension of the more familiar Orient of the Middle East and Persia (or even the Holy Land of the Bible), as a transitional zone between the deserts of Arabia and the exuberant landscapes of Southeast Asia, or, even, looking north, as an appendage to the frozen wastes and windswept steppes of Tibet and Central Asia. Each of these hypothetical orientations had its scientific as well as scenic advocates, but it was India as tropical that had most widely come to prevail by the mid-nineteenth century. By becoming tropical, India's disease environment, its climate, plant life, and human inhabitants took on a new meaning in European eyes. India's tropicalization was also a sweeping act of erasure, as well as of identity formation: it countered the appreciative evaluation of India's ancient achievements by Orientalist scholars with an insistence upon the subordination of the country (and, implicitly, its civilization) to the dominant power of nature, a nature that Europeans prided themselves on having increasingly understood and overcome.

Tropicality was thus critical to the "discovery" and representation of India in several ways. It helped capture the European experience of India as an alien and exotic land—of its sights, but also the smell and taste of the land and its products, the physical sensations involved in living in a territory in many respects singularly different from northwest Europe. Tropicality, in departing from and in part contrasting with, ideas of "the Orient," was an important means of situating India in a wider geographical and cultural context, relative not only to its own neighbors, but also to its past and prospective future. The emerging literature on India's tropicality might serve to glorify aspects of nature, but it also highlighted what were understood to be its inherent deficiencies—why it was not and never could be Europe. This was to be of long-term importance both in contesting the positive impressions of India created by Orientalist scholarship and in giving weight to ideas that were eventually to characterize India as a "backward," at best an "undeveloped," society. If India did, indeed, belong to the tropics then it was more as the representative of the "bad tropics" than as an exemplar of the "good tropics" of so much European imagining.

Exploring the emergence of India's tropicality also opens up for consideration another central theme of this work—the emergence of the natural sciences as a prominent form and fashioner of "colonial knowledge." Although there has been some fruitful discussion of "colonialism and its forms of knowledge,"[81] much more remains to be said about how such forms of knowledge were constituted in nineteenth-century India, especially in the realms of science, what distinguished the production of knowledge in a colonial context from that in a metropolitan setting, and how colonial epistemology incorporated or rejected indigenous knowledge. As the last two chapters of this book suggest, botany provides an important case study of how these processes of knowledge formation occurred and what their consequences were. The tropics, botany helps demonstrate, were a scientific project as well as a scenic ideal.

Joseph Hooker

This book is far from being the biography, or even the part-biography, of a single scientific figure. Indeed, part of its underlying argument is that the ideas and practices surrounding Indian tropicality and botany were the result of a long process of investigation and collaboration. Nonetheless, the British botanist Joseph Dalton Hooker (1817–1911) appears frequently in these pages, particularly in connection with his three-year visit to eastern India and the Himalaya, 1848–51. There are several reasons for invoking Hooker in this way. By the time he returned from India in the early 1850s Hooker was one of the most highly regarded and widely traveled naturalists of his time, able through his own observation and extensive network of contacts to oversee and coordinate the vast botanical knowledge of the expanding British empire.[82] His four-year voyage (1839–43) as a naturalist on board HMS *Erebus* in Sir James Ross's expedition to the Antarctic took him to Tasmania, New Zealand, the Cape of Good Hope, and the Falkland Islands, as well as to the edge of Antarctica itself.

Having seen the southern temperate and south polar region, Hooker was keen to see a tropical region and for this purpose resolved to visit India. His wide experience of scientific travel and his expectations of a tropical India make him a key figure in any discussion of the natural sciences of the period and the characterization of India's landscapes and vegetation. In one of its several guises, this book can be understood as an extended commentary on, and an attempt to provide a regional and colonial context for, Hooker's *Himalayan Journals*, published in 1854, along with the "Introductory Essay" he and his collaborator Thomas Thomson wrote for their combined *Flora Indica* of 1855 and Hooker's *Illustrations of Himalayan Plants*, which also appeared in 1855 (and which in turn built on the earlier success of his *Rhododendrons of Sikkim-Himalaya*). Not only does this trinity of interlocking texts collectively embody Hooker's own very diverse understanding of India and the various ways in which it needed to be represented (through travel narrative, scientific discourse, and botanical illustration); it also demonstrates the importance of several forms of collaboration (as between the scientific traveler and the stay-at-home savant or between Western epistemology and indigenous knowledge) in the making of nineteenth-century science.

Hooker certainly did not invent India's tropicality: that was the outcome of a far longer and more complex discursive maneuver. But, along with Alexander von Humboldt, Charles Darwin, and Alfred Russel Wallace, he did become one of its most influential and authoritative scientific exponents. Moreover, as a close friend of Darwin and with a keen interest of his own in the geographical distribution of plants and the variability of species, Hooker was by the early 1850s emerging as one of the leading "philosophical" naturalists of his day. And yet, although it was not his greatest personal concern in India, he was also conscious of the importance of economic botany in the service of empire—a preoccupation that became more evident in his later career, especially after he became director of Kew Gardens, in succession to his father, Sir William Hooker, in 1865.[83] Just as he (and his father) exercised considerable influence over the development of botany in India, so Joseph Hooker's experience of India, and, reciprocally, its profound influence upon him, had a great impact on his wider scientific thinking and on the evolution of the natural sciences in nineteenth-century Europe.[84]

By 1848, especially following his return from the Antarctic expedition five years earlier, Hooker had a growing reputation as a botanist in Europe; however, he was still an outsider to the colonial establishment in India, a "griffin," to use a term favored by the British in India. He was not a member of the East India Company's medical, military, or civil services, from the ranks of which so many of the naturalists, and so large a proportion of the India travelers, of the period were drawn. Hooker had the compensating advantage of seeing British India with fresh eyes, as a newcomer to its peculiar customs and strange obsessions. And yet, like many other members of the British middle classes and the scientific community in Britain, he had many personal as well as professional contacts with India. These included an uncle, Gurney Turner, in the Bengal Medical Service (thus fulfilling De Quincey's remark about everyone having an "India uncle"). In another Company surgeon, Thomas Thomson, also on the Bengal establishment, he had a friend whom he had known since childhood and who became his collaborator in producing the only volume of the *Flora Indica* of 1855, yet a work that in turn paved the way for Hooker's definitive seven-volume *Flora of British India* (1872–97). Hooker never returned to India after 1851, yet with his commanding position at the heart of botany's empire, as director at Kew, and with the wide network of scientific and administrative contacts he had acquired for himself or inherited from his father, he was a remarkably authoritative and enduring figure in Indian botany, a position he retained virtually until his death in 1911.[85]

In many respects, Hooker enjoyed an exceptionally privileged position in India. Few outsiders, even the eminent German naturalist Alexander von Humboldt, were allowed by the Company to visit its Indian domains and to conduct scientific research there. The French botanist Victor Jacquemont in the 1830s was one of the few exceptions to this general prohibition, and his personal and scientific experience of India (discussed in Chapter 4) form an illuminating contrast with Hooker's a little more than a decade later. In the late 1840s and early 1850s Hooker enjoyed influential local support in India, notably from the governor-general, Lord Dalhousie. But while this patronage aided his scientific enterprise, it also brought him into closer (and, with respect to Sikkim, controversial) association with the politics of Company rule and the management of India's imperial frontiers. As an outsider, Hooker was able to view British India with a certain (at times skeptical) detachment; but, as the later chapters of this book will show, he was also heavily reliant in his scientific work and botanical excursions on local assistance and information. Part of this came both from resident Britons, notably the self-taught naturalist and Buddhist scholar Brian Houghton Hodgson in Darjeeling, but also, in rather different ways, from Indian assistants and informants. In Hooker, then, we can see at work an itinerant, metropolitan-based naturalist, actively engaging with (or aspiring to rise above) the various forms of "colonial science" and "indigenous knowledge." In that respect, Hooker helps us to understand one of the underlying issues of this book—how far science itself was able to "travel"—not just between different places around the globe but between one culture, one episteme, and another.

Long before Joseph Hooker arrived in India in January 1848, his father, William Jackson Hooker (1785–1865), had established an extensive network of correspondents in the country. As a professor of botany in Glasgow and then, from 1841, as director of the Royal Botanic Gardens at Kew, the elder Hooker had gained the acquaintance of a large number of individuals drawn to the pursuit of botany. In visiting India, where his father had never been, Joseph Hooker was the beneficiary of these invaluable contacts. Even more significantly for the present purpose, the published work of both Hookers, father and son, along with their vast private and botanical correspondence, and the journals Joseph Hooker kept while in India, provide an exceptional rich body of material for examining the inner workings of tropical botany in a formative stage of its development and as a complex scientific enterprise in nineteenth-century India. They further afford the means by which to relate the formal world of botanical science to its more personal meanings and experiences as well as to its wider social and political context.

Joseph Hooker's account of his journey, his *Himalayan Journals*, was not only a scientific narrative after the much admired model of Humboldt's *Personal Narrative* and Darwin's *The Voyage of the "Beagle"* but also one of the last major travel works about India produced during the Company period. That it enjoyed considerably less popular and scientific success than either Humboldt's or Darwin's narratives is perhaps a telling comment upon its relative failure to combine travelogue and scientific research in a single piece of writing. But stylistic shortcomings do not detract from the *Himalayan Journals*' historical value, read alongside Hooker's extensive private correspondence, and his other published works of the period, as an illuminating example of scientific travel and of the Romantic representation and increasingly tropicalized framing of Indian nature. The *Himalayan Journals* thus represent more than one naturalist's views and experiences: they also stand as a kind of apogee and a closing testimony for itinerant science and the traveling gaze in British India before the upheaval of 1857–8 and the imperial transformation it helped to bring about.

2
IN A LAND OF DEATH

IN THE EARLY NINETEENTH CENTURY INDIA COMMONLY APPEARED IN the European perception as a land of encircling death. This was not just from the high levels of white mortality, which were, after all, matched (if not exceeded) at other intra-tropical locations, notably the West Indies and West Africa.[1] Nor was it solely because the experience of European sickness and mortality gave form and urgency to the medical topography of the period and so helped to substantiate ideas of India as a disease-laden and deadly landscape and to fashion ameliorative sanitary and scientific measures. It was also that the Indian countryside—with its highly visible deathscapes—seemed, to Europeans, to epitomize the negatively tropical attributes of the Indian environment and, further, to reflect many of the religious abominations and moral deficiencies of Indian society. The experience of journeying to India—hailed, even from afar, as "the grave of thousands"[2]—and the first-hand impression formed by travel within India, strongly reinforced this spatial sense of a mortality inscribed on the landscape itself. From the outset, the prevalence and visibility of death framed many a European traveler's understanding of India, and conditioned his or her scenic sensibilities, just as untimely death, or the effort to evade it, helped shape the careers and inform the attitudes of many of its scientific observers.

White Death

Visiting Australia in 1836, the young naturalist Charles Darwin remarked in a now much-quoted observation: "Wherever the European has trod, death seems to pursue the aboriginal. We may look to the wide extent of the Americas, Polynesia, the Cape of Good Hope, and Australia, and we shall find the same result."[3] But in early nineteenth-century India, it was Europeans who saw themselves as being hounded by death, and, while not seeing themselves as threatened, like Australia's Aborigines, with racial extinction, still subject to an almost unremitting tide of mortality.

The severity of this mortality, especially from cholera, malaria, and dysentery, the "three grand divisions of tropical disease,"[4] was greatest among European rank-and-file soldiers in India, and it was this constant hemorrhaging of white manpower—expensive to recruit, costly to replace—that impelled the colonial administration toward such measures of sanitary reform as were attempted, prior to the Mutiny of 1857, in barracks and cantonments.[5] In a colonial epidemiology constructed as much around class as around race, debate raged: were these high levels of sickness and mortality the direct consequence of "tropical diseases" and the undermining of "unseasoned" European constitutions through unaccustomed heat and humidity? Or did they owe more to social factors—the drunken and dissolute habits of the European soldiery?

James Ranald Martin, one of the leading authorities on European health in India at the time, noted in 1851 that while unmarried European army officers died at the rate of 3.8 per cent a year (and married officers at 2.7 per cent), the figure among European soldiers was a staggering 7.4 per cent. "This wide difference in sickness and mortality," he concluded, "is referable almost solely to the difference of habits of life." And if drink were the principal cause of disease and indiscipline, its effects were hardly mollified by barrack life in general, which he described as "a world of wretchedness and misery, moral and physical."[6] Although few figures were available as testimony, it was also believed that levels of mortality among the soldiers' barrack-bred children were "frightful" as well and that even those who survived into adolescence were "languid" and "feeble."[7] Some disapproving soldiers themselves shared the view that excessive drinking was the principal cause of so much misery and mortality. One disillusioned Irish infantryman, stationed in Sind in the 1840s, attributed half the deaths among his comrades to the effects of drink.[8] But other commentators took a different view. Writing in the immediate aftermath of the Mutiny, Joseph Ewart of the Bengal Medical Service also noted the enormous disparity between the mortality rates of European soldiers and their officers, and accepted that drink and the "dreadful ennui" of barrack life contributed to this startling differential and the "remarkable immunity" of the officer class to death and disease.⁹ But he was more inclined than some of his contemporaries to argue that class differences in health occurred everywhere, not just in India, and that the diseases prevalent among the army in India, especially malaria, hepatitis, and cholera, resulted more from the effects of climate and defective sanitation than from drink and its attendant evils.¹⁰

Despite the sense of radical class difference that the growing volume of medical statistics helped engender, high levels of mortality certainly did not leave the white middle classes untouched, especially in the early years of the century and particularly in Bengal, the deadliest province of British India, and home to the largest number of its European inhabitants. Among this group comparisons with rank-and-file soldiers (many of them, especially in the Company's infantry regiments, Irish Catholics) were deemed in many respects less pertinent than with those who came from similar class backgrounds or followed comparable professions in Britain. Thus it was calculated by Henry Prinsep of the Bengal Civil Service that in the first three decades of the century civil servants in India suffered a death-rate three times that of similarly employed individuals in Britain and that in Bengal this amounted to just over twenty-five per thousand each year.¹¹

While the authority of statistics was undoubtedly growing, they often carried less immediate weight than anecdotal evidence and personal observation. Even without the statistics, there was much individual testimony to the effect that death and near-death debility were much on the minds of Europeans at the time and that India was often seen through the depressing prism of their own mortality. It was not that the British did not die in their own country in this period (they did, and in formidable numbers), but that death in India seemed exceptionally violent, swift, and wasteful of human life, and dying abroad (far from family and friends) was even more distressing than at home.

The mood was set as early as the 1760s. Writing of Calcutta, Mrs Kindersley observed:

> Life and death so rapidly succeed, that medicines very frequently have not time to operate before the great event has taken place. People live, as if in a camp, talk of death familiarly, and as if it was an event more probable to take place tomorrow than the next day.¹²

To judge by contemporary accounts, not only was mortality perceived to be alarmingly high, the visible effects of disease were also everywhere apparent. According to the Reverend William Tennant of Calcutta in 1796 "a sallow and livid complexion" was "almost universal" among European residents in Bengal. He continued:

> The climate of India proves a severe trial to every European constitution; many fall sacrifice to its first attacks; many more linger on in a state of increasing debility, and painful disease, which reduces them to a state more resembling ghosts than men; the remainder, who for years continue to combat its influence, finding that they also are at last to be worsted in the conflict, are glad to retreat to Europe, there to eke out, or to husband, the remains of life.[13]

The ghostly, not merely sickly, appearance of European residents was much remarked upon, especially by newcomers. John Howison in the 1820s was struck by the "spectral" appearance of the European "constitutionalists" who took their daily exercise on the beach at Bombay. Mounted on equally "melancholy and dispirited" horses, they silently appeared and vanished in the morning mist as if "on a journey to the other world."[14] A decade later, Emily Eden, sister to the governor-general, Lord Auckland (1836–42), remarked that in India "those that are well look about as fresh as an English *corpse*." She did add, though, that, despite the "very violent illnesses," mortality among the more affluent Europeans was now no greater there than in any other country and that "the old-fashioned days of imprudence about health are quite as much gone by as the times of great extravagance."[15]

While malaria and dysentery remained significant causes of white mortality, as they had for decades past, the eruption of epidemic cholera in 1817, initially in Bengal and then across a large part of India, seemed to give further deadly confirmation of the peculiarly pestilential nature of the country and its climate.[16] While the poorer classes of both Europeans and Indians were acknowledged to be the principal victims, no one seemed immune. Colonel James Tod, the British Political Agent to the Western Rajput States, was traveling in Rajasthan (or Rajputana as it was then more commonly known) between 1820 and 1821 when the disease first struck. He remarked that "although for some time we flattered ourselves that it was only the intemperate, the ill-fed, or ill-clothed that fell victim to it," the disease soon proved to be "no respecter of persons." Among its first victims in Rajasthan was the Raja of Boondi, whose dying agony Tod witnessed with compassionate anguish. In his experience, "the prince and the peasant, the European and the native, the robust and the weak, the well-fed and the abstinent," might all fall to this foul and often fatal disease.[17] The death from cholera in 1827 of Sir Thomas Munro, Governor of Madras, seemed to endorse this sentiment: even British India's administrative elite was not immune.[18] Contemporary descriptions of cholera emphasized the sudden onset and rapid conclusion of the disease—Munro died within twelve hours of the first signs of an attack—but they also portrayed the excruciating agony endured by its sufferers. The patient, by one doctor's account, "tosses about continually, and evinces the utmost distress." His skin turned cold and corpse-like, the pulse grew sluggish and breathing labored; his voice became "feeble, sepulchral, and unnatural." For the hardened physician, no less than the novice, this was an experience not endured without "sentiments of the most anxious and painful nature."[19]

Even without cholera, there was much to mourn. Almost every writer had tales to tell of individuals who had been "carried off very suddenly," as were many of the acquaintances of William Hickey in late eighteenth-century Calcutta, by the "burning climate of Asia" or "one of those violent fevers so prevalent in the East Indies."[20] The newly wed Ulsterwoman Honoria Lawrence, recalling her first impressions of India in 1837 said, "During my short residence in this country I have been struck by the depth of colouring with which the scenes of existence are here painted. Life is so uncertain, disease so rapid . . ."[21] She recounted, among other "startling occurrences," the story of two women, not unlike herself, who had landed in India to find their fiancé or husband had died only hours earlier from cholera or similar causes. She was left with the gloomy and foreboding impression of the "frightful rapidity of death, and all belonging to it, in this climate."[22]

Nor had matters seemingly much improved even by the 1850s. During his term as governor-general, Lord Dalhousie's thoughts repeatedly strayed toward death and dying. In August 1851 he recorded the story of a "poor young fellow" at Simla (founded, ironically, as a European health resort), who "was dancing here in my house last Wednesday; he was buried today, Monday!" "If nothing else goes fast in this country," added the man credited with introducing railways, telegraphs, and a modern postal service into India, "disease and death speed."[23]

Although Dalhousie temporarily diverts us away from the British middle classes to the family of a Scottish Tory aristocrat, his experience of the deadliness of India had a wider resonance. His father, the ninth earl, was appointed commander-in-chief of the Indian Army in 1829 and took Ramsay, his eldest son and heir, with him to Calcutta as an aide-de-camp. Both men were quickly wrecked by dysentery and fever. The invalided earl, who returned home in 1832 a ghost of his former self, was hardly recognizable to his family, and both he and Ramsay died soon after. In the circumstances, it is not surprising that the younger and only surviving son, elevated to the Dalhousie title in 1838, saw India as having been "the death of my father, and of my brother before me."[24] And yet when in 1847 he was approached by the government of the day he readily agreed to accept the office of governor-general, despite all that the country had already cost his family, despite his wife's poor health and the need to leave their two daughters behind in Britain. He believed it was his patrician duty to accept high office when asked to do so and hoped, more pragmatically, that his Indian salary would help restore the family estate and recoup his depleted finances. Despite his youth—he was only 35 when he accepted the governor-generalship—Dalhousie's life in India soon became "a continual struggle against pain, weakness, and disease."[25] His wife found India almost unbearable and her health deteriorated to such a degree that in 1853 she had to return to Britain alone, plunging the Dalhousies into the miseries of separation (husband from wife, parents from children) that so many British families in India faced with the deepest dread. Lady Dalhousie died on the voyage home, almost within sight of England, leaving her widowed husband bereft and broken in spirit.[26] He himself died, aged only 49, a few years after leaving India.

Against this familiar background of death and debility, in the wake of epidemic cholera and in response to soaring military mortality, especially during the costly campaigns of the first Burma war, there began to emerge from the mid-1820s a voluminous body of work on India's medical topography. Written by East India Company surgeons, this literature effectively mapped mortality onto the landscape of India, detailing the apparent effects of climate and disease on European "constitutions" and proposing means by which fatal or incapacitating conditions might be evaded or actively countered.[27] James Ranald Martin's *Notes on the Medical*

Topography of Calcutta, published in 1837, was one of the earliest and most influential studies of this kind. Martin and his contemporaries recognized the influence that social practices (among caste-ridden Hindus as among drink-sodden European soldiers) might have on the incidence of disease; but mostly in this morbid, neo-Hippocratic geography, it was the land itself that appeared most deadly—malignant miasmas emanated from every swamp, graveyard, paddy field and jungle, summoned up by tropical humidity and a powerful sun, wafted along on insalubrious winds, or rising up in invisible clouds from rotting vegetation, human detritus, and putrid mud. The perceived deadliness of the Indian climate and landscape served as an authorizing commission for medical science. While the inherent malevolence of India's physical environment was repeatedly emphasized in these works, their authors were not necessarily environmental fatalists. Sometimes, in the spirit of "improvement" we will consider in the next chapter, they argued for the ameliorating effects that human intervention—through such activities as draining marshes, clearing wasteland and jungle, and the relocation of cantonments or realignment of barracks—might have upon the incidence of disease.[28]

Medical topography was certainly not unique to India;[29] but in an alien setting it served to highlight what was seen to be particularly perilous, from a European perspective, about such an unfamiliar landscape and its associated seasons and climatic peculiarities, its distinctive vegetation and even its abundant insect and animal life. It authoritatively directed attention to the exceptional hazards not only of India but also of the tropics within which India was increasingly incorporated, and it mapped out a complex terrain of tracts and localities, each of which seemed to harbor some different combination of malign (more rarely, benign) characteristics. While it could be—and often was—represented as an almost undifferentiated whole, as being both tropical and deadly, this was also a landscape that needed, for practical purposes, to be read with close attention to climatic, topographical, and socio-economic detail. So ingrained and instinctive had this medico-topographical way of thinking about the Indian landscape become that when Joseph Hooker traversed northeast India, from Darjeeling to Chittagong in 1850, every place he visited was instantly identified in terms of its reputed unhealthiness (or, more occasionally, its salubriousness), whether for Europeans or for Indians, even though in many cases no convincing explanation could be offered as to why one place was intensely malarial while another, though lying dangerously close to lakes and marshes, was not.[30]

Although the representation of this disease-laden landscape was primarily conducted by Europeans and articulated through European experience, reference was sometimes made to Indian perceptions of a given landscape and its relationship with disease. The Tarai, the narrow belt of forest and swamp that ran across the northern rim of India between the plains and the Himalaya, was commonly invoked as a region almost defined by death. This tract was considered so deadly as to be impassable for Indians and Europeans alike through a large part of the year. Early in the nineteenth century, the surgeon-naturalist Francis Buchanan noted that local testimony ascribed the local "*awl*" or fever to the foul breath of the huge serpents that inhabited the region. For Buchanan this expression of indigenous opinion served little purpose other than to show the superstition of the "natives" and to exhibit his own superiority. "Rational men," he averred, knew better than to assign malaria to such a spurious cause: it was undoubtedly due to the bad air arising from rotting leaves and the resulting miasmas, triggered by the onset of the seasonal rains.[31] More often, though, at least early in the century, Indian and European experience seemed to converge and proffer mutual confirmation. In his travels through drought- and famine-prone Marwar (Jodhpur) in southwest Rajasthan, James Tod repeatedly spoke of "this region of death." In so doing he echoed local terminology (using the expression "*Maroost'hali*," a place of aridity and death); but, as he and his companions sickened and some of them died, he also used this indigenous understanding of the region to color his own melancholy reflections on mortality and loss.[32]

Dying Abroad

Medical topography was far from being the only means by which ideas of landscape and mortality became textually entwined. While the white community remained small relative to the Indian population around it, far larger numbers of Britons (women as well as men) went to India in the early nineteenth century than before. Members of this new colonial elite were generally well educated and widely read; they were also sufficiently familiar with the tastes of the time to be able to write articulately about their emotions and experiences as earlier generations of India travelers had seldom done, and to see scenery and death as fit subjects for their cultured sensibilities. It is particularly in the writings of women, through their letters and journals as well as their published works, and drawing upon their own harrowing experiences of separation and loss, that one gains the most powerful impression of India as a land of encircling death. Certainly, women like Emma Roberts and Honoria Lawrence contributed much to the language and literature of British Indian sensibility. But men were by no means impervious to such sentiments, and highly placed government servants and army officers, like Sir Thomas Munro, Governor of Madras, and Sir James Mackintosh, Recorder at the Bombay High Court, also wrote with great feeling and eloquence about their experience of exile, separation and death.

Evidence of a newfound sensibility about the subject of European mortality in India can be found early in the century in the writing of one woman visitor, Maria Graham.[33] She captured the melancholy mood of the time in visiting the Park Street cemetery, the main British burial ground in Calcutta, in 1810. Although barely forty years had passed since it had opened, Graham found that:

> There are many acres covered so thick with columns, urns, and obelisks, that there scarcely seems to be room for another; it is like a city of the dead; it extends on both sides of the road, and you see nothing beyond it; and the greater number of those buried here are under five-and-twenty years of age! It is a painful reflection . . . to consider the number of young men cut off in the first two or three years' residence in this climate.[34]

Another observer was Emily Eden, who found much about "this horrid country" to dislike—sickness and mortality not least among them. In 1836 she described the military cemetery at Barrackpore, near Calcutta:

> It was a melancholy sight . . . We could not find one instance of a death later than twenty-five. Then the monuments are always erected by "brother officers," or a "circle of friends," and never by relations: "By stranger's hands his dying eyes were closed," I could not help thinking.[35]

While the physical evidence of their mortality was, for many Europeans, a significant and visible presence in the Indian landscape, the "melancholy" it occasioned (melancholy and sensibility being "close sisters")[36] seemed to call for sober reflection rather than constituting a rationale for a hasty British retreat from India. Rather than avoid any mention of cemeteries, crowded with their dead countrymen, writers found them "deeply affecting,"[37] and seemed to regard it as part of their responsibility to report on them (much as they did on the state of jails and European orphanages), and thus to reflect on what they implied about British rule and residence in so foreign a place.

This was notably the case with Emma Roberts, whose widely read *Scenes and Characteristics of Hindostan* revealed her as something of a connoisseur of graveyards (an entire chapter of her book was devoted to "cemeteries and funeral obsequies"). Despite her desire to encourage tourists to quit the spas of Europe to visit the sights of India, the deathscapes she surveyed seemed superficially to convey a less inviting message. "Strangers," she remarked, "visiting our Eastern territories, cannot fail to be impressed with painful feelings, as they survey the gloomy receptacles appropriated to those Christians who are destined to breathe their last in exile."[38] At Berhampore, a sickly station in central Bengal abandoned after years of heavy troop mortality, cholera had decimated several British regiments: "doleful records upon the tombstones chronicle its gloomy triumphs," Roberts noted: "neither age nor sex are spared." Indeed, "no cemetery in India ... contains the mortal remains of so many juvenile mothers and young brides as that at Berhampore."[39] The neglect and decay of funeral monuments added to somber reflections about the transience of human existence. Roberts deplored the state of many of these dilapidated tombs, and the "disgusting images which sicken the spirit in cemeteries, owing their dreariness and desolation to the indifference of the living." They should, she urged, be made more pleasing to the eye and less objects of horror to "those who have little hope of living to return to their native land."[40]

Perhaps these burial-ground descriptions disclose something of Roberts' personal sense of loss (the sister she had accompanied to India having recently died) or even foreboding about her own death (which came barely five years later, in 1840). But it might be a mistake to overpersonalize such sentiments. Some of this writing about death and cemeteries clearly reflected the conventions of the time or was done for literary effect. Thus, warming to the Gothic possibilities of her subject, Roberts observed that all the cemeteries in India were overcrowded,

> and many exhibit the most frightful features of a charnel-house, dilapidated tombs, rank vegetation, and unburied bones whitening in the wind. The trees are infested with vultures and other hideous carrion-birds; huge vampire-bats nestle in the walls, which too often present

apertures for the admission of wolves and jackalls crowding to their nightly resort, and tearing up the bodies interred without the expensive precautions necessary to secure them from some frightful desecration.[41]

Even so, the tragedy of dying abroad seemed genuinely to haunt Roberts and her contemporaries. There seemed something uniquely "melancholy" about the fate of Europeans who perished abroad, especially alone, a feeling that troubled men and women alike. These, in Pat Jalland's terms, were decidedly "bad" deaths.[42] Roberts dwelt at length on "the exceedingly melancholy" fate of European travelers who, falling sick, were abandoned by their palanquin bearers, and left to expire by the roadside or be devoured by wild animals.[43] Even when Europeans died among friends and attended by doctors, the rapidity with which corpses decayed and had to be interred in the tropics added "a cruel aggravation" to the proceedings. So profoundly shocking were these sudden deaths and hasty internments that Roberts claimed (skirting the possibility of contagion) that attending a funeral became a "death-warrant to the living," with those present liable to fall ill and die from sheer distress. That women attended funerals in India, unlike in Britain at the time, was thought to add to the emotional trauma.[44] At times, perhaps for want of any weightier explanation, disappointment and the "depressing passions," as much as actual evidence of disease, were held responsible for the death of Europeans. Even common soldiers and sailors, not normally credited with much sensibility, were said to become depressed and hence more susceptible to the destructive effects of climate, especially when they witnessed the death of a comrade or allowed homesickness to engulf them.[45] A constant state of melancholy was itself sufficient to "prepare the body for the seeds of fever."[46]

Even if life—for the white middle classes in India—grew more secure as the nineteenth century advanced, death still seemed to haunt their imaginings. In 1851, Richard Burton, still a lieutenant in the Bombay Army, before he turned his ambitious eyes to Arabia and the African lakes, told the story of a Company officer who, having left England in his youth and retaining few links with the country, married a nautch (dancing) girl and adopted an Indian lifestyle. When the officer died, his body was cremated like the Hindu he had very much become. For Burton this was a desperately sad end. Visiting the place where the man's ashes had been scattered, he reflected:

It is always a melancholy spectacle, the last resting-place of a fellow-countryman in some remote nook of a foreign land, far from the dust of his forefathers—a grave prepared by strangers, around which no mourners ever stood, and over which no friendly hand raised a tribute to the memory of the lamented dead. The wanderer's heart yearns at the sight. How soon may not such fate be his own?[47]

While Burton was clearly pondering his own possible fate (he was at the time *en route* to the Nilgiri hills in South India to recuperate his health), his comments reflected wider European anxieties about dying in India, about having a "good" death and a "proper" burial. As was so often the case, Europe saw itself reflected in the mirror of Indian mortality. In the 1850s, with cremation still exceptional in the West, most Europeans in India identified it unfavorably with the practice of sati.[48] Widow-burning, formally outlawed in 1829 by the government of Lord Bentinck (1828–34), was still in Burton's day one of the most repugnant (and mesmerizing) images the West had of India. Accounts of European travel up the Ganges valley from the anglicized environs of Calcutta into the far less familiar territory of northern India (like Bishop Reginald Heber's in 1824–5),[49] commonly became journeys into Hinduism's "heart of darkness," narratives of a succession of unfolding "horrors"—as tales of sati were quickly followed by reports of female infanticide, human sacrifices, and murderous Thugs. Hindus were castigated for the way in which, it was alleged, they cruelly ejected their sick and dying, abandoning them to die at the side of the Ganges, even stuffing their mouths and noses with mud to hasten their demise, or indifferently leaving the half-burned limbs of their deceased relatives floating in the river, to be fought over by snarling pariah dogs and squabbling vultures.[50] These scenes of "superstition, cruelty, and horror" surrounding death in India,[51] seemed to display a "want of normal feeling" among Hindus and to show that among them there existed "none of the tender feeling cherished in burying the dead among Christians."[52] Repugnance at Hindu death practices intensified Europeans' concern that their dead be afforded proper dignity and respect.

By invoking an acceptable mood of melancholy and making the contrast with Hindus' apparent want of humanity toward the dead and dying, writing about their own deaths, about dispiriting funerals and dismal cemeteries, may, paradoxically, have made it easier for Britons to reconcile themselves to the high personal cost of empire. Even in such a land as this, the scene of such squalor and misery, the death of Europeans and the monuments to their mortality were the deserving occasion for the exercise of noble sentiments. It was possible to see European deaths, even on such a scale, as constituting a kind of melancholy title to India. Mortality formed part of the "sentimental conquest" of India.[53] If the country had already cost so many worthy and innocent lives, how could it now be abandoned or the responsibilities of imperial ownership abjured?

Already by the 1830s the Indian landscape was thickly populated, if not by actual monuments, at least by the memories of those who had died in establishing British rule and in bringing "peace" and "civilization" to India. Few travelers passed through the Rajmahal hills on the western margins of Bengal without noting and reflecting on the monument to Augustus Cleveland, the pioneer administrator who, in subduing the "tribal" inhabitants, had first effectively implanted British rule in the area.[54] James Tod concluded the narrative of his Rajasthan travels by recalling officer friends who had fallen victim to cholera and fever, their memories inseparable from the places where they had lived and died.[55] Surgeon John M'Cosh similarly interrupted his medical topography of Assam to recall the "brave officers" who had died in the course of "our taking possession of Assam." In this litany of lives lost, the hostility of nature appeared as fraught with danger as the uncowed Assamese: Dr Leslie died of fever brought on by two days' exposure in the "pestilential jungle;" Lieutenants Beddingfield and Burlton were massacred by Khasi tribesmen; Dr Beadon in seeking their revenge was killed by an arrow; Lieutenant Brodie fell victim to fever "caught scouring the jungles at a season of the year when no European ought to be exposed, and without European aid of any kind;" and Captain Cathcart perished from jungle fever, "induced by being exposed to a whole day's rain, and being obliged to spend the night without any of the comforts of life." Even if now "unhonoured," M'Cosh concluded, their graves remained as "melancholy proof" of their sacrifices and achievements.[56]

India and the Empire of Affect

One can understand the preoccupation of the British in early nineteenth-century India with death and "death-like separation"[57] as constituting a major strand within a wider empire of affect. Employing this phrase is not meant to imply a stark opposition between an Empire of Emotion and an Empire of Reason—indeed, emotion and reason seemed to many at the time to complement, not to contradict, each other and to be equally important in representing personal feelings and responses. I do, however, want to suggest that empire, in this period especially, was about far more than formal structures and public rhetoric. For many of its participants, for their families and friends, it had a much stronger personal signification.

Among the middle classes (and to a degree among the aristocracy as well) empire was largely known about and understood through personal contacts and associations. It was made meaningful either through the experience of travel itself or through the letters, journals, and family conversations that communicated an intimate and impressionistic notion of what life in countries like India actually entailed. As we have already seen in the case of the aristocratic Dalhousies, this more immediate sense of empire was strongly imbued with anxious feelings of danger, separation, and loss, only partly redeemed by recognition of empire as the means for pursuing personal opportunities or fulfilling a sense of public duty. I want further to suggest that ideas of landscape and nature formed an important part of this discourse of imperial affect—whether in terms of the sensibilities considered appropriate to middle-class observation and experience (not least in communication between men and women),[58] as the vehicle for nostalgia for "home" and an abiding sense of alienation abroad, or even as a surrogate for rawer emotions—of loss and longing— that were hard to articulate more openly.

The widely shared experience of serving the empire, especially in the early nineteenth century when the twin "tropical" territories of the West Indies and India commanded almost equal importance in British minds, created a common awareness of the career opportunities available overseas and of the personal adventures (from military campaigning to hunting and natural history excursions) life abroad might allow. But this awareness was also tinged with profound anxiety, born of bitter experience, over the prospect of long-term separation from family, friends, and society at home and the possibility, even likelihood, of severe debility and an early grave. Whether manifested through nostalgia and melancholy, metaphor or surrogacy, the intertwining of ideas of death and separation with images of landscape and nature was an important part of the way in which this more intimate understanding of empire and its personal opportunities and costs was expressed.

As with the discussion of white morality and mortality, this empire of affect had strong class connotations. There was little sense that lower-class Europeans could—or ever should—be party to this world of cultured sensibility and mutual affect. At best, they might be the deserving objects of middle-class philanthropy as were the army children recruited into Henry Lawrence's military orphan asylums at Sanawar, Ootacamund, and other hill-stations from the early 1850s onwards, "rescued from the heat and danger (both physical and moral) of barrack-life in the plains."[59] At worst, they were condemned for their drunkenness, their lewd and dissolute behavior, for their want of self-discipline and general "intemperance" (a term that had particular resonance in "tropical" India where a "temperate" lifestyle was considered essential for preserving European health and prestige).

That working-class whites should be tolerated in India at all was felt by many to be no better than a necessary (military) evil, for they otherwise appeared physically and socially out of place, or were appropriately confined to (and largely concealed within) a few isolated localities. The contrast between the spatial mobility of the itinerant middle class and the institutional fixity of the lower classes was striking.[60] In a telling passage, Honoria Lawrence described how India in the hot weather was only made tolerable for European women of the officer class by their being able to flee to the cool of the hills; when necessary, they could take a sea voyage to recover their health. But for the poorer white women, confined to crowded and ill-ventilated barracks with their soldier husbands and sickly offspring, there was no such mobility, no escape from "the full misery of a tropical climate."[61]

In the course of their own journeys, middle-class travelers commonly visited the white inmates of orphanages and jails or called in on the veteran and invalid stations created by the Company for its European soldiery. On his north Indian tour of 1824–5, Bishop Heber stopped at one of these at Chunar, near Benares, and gave communion to a group of European veterans. In a passage revealing of his own mixed emotions, Heber observed:

> The majority ... are men still hardly advanced beyond youth, early victims of a devouring climate, assisted, perhaps, by carelessness and intemperance; and it was a pitiable spectacle to see the white emaciated hands thrust out under a soldier's sleeve to receive the Sacrament, and the pale cheeks, and tall languid figures of men, who if they had remained in Europe,

would have been still overflowing with youthful vigour and vivacity, the best ploughman, the strongest wrestlers, and the merriest dancers of the village . . .[62]

As nostalgia for rural England contended with a sense of how out of place these poor Europeans were in India, Heber returned from his reverie with the harsher thought that the invalids of Chunar "have borne a very bad character for their profligacy and want of discipline."[63]

Conversely, if deemed largely unfit for poor whites, India by the early nineteenth century appeared a much worthier middle-class destination than it had twenty or thirty years earlier. Following the devastating Bengal famine of 1770 and the protracted impeachment of Warren Hastings in London (1786–95) criticism of the Company's greed and rapacity was rife and the decadence of the "nabobs" attracted notoriety and disgust.[64] As India passed more firmly under parliamentary control, as the presence of army officers, civil servants, and doctors increased, and the new middle-class mores affecting Britain began to infiltrate the subcontinent, so perceptions of white morality (and, to a degree, the attendant mortality) in India began to change. It was sometimes suggested that the greatest "improvement" India had seen in recent decades was not in the country itself but in the lifestyle of its European elite.[65] The British middle classes saw themselves as sloughing off the excesses of the past and assuming even in India the standards of respectability and responsibility that prevailed at home.[66] In its administrative personnel as in its moral aspirations, this was essentially a middle-class empire, though it certainly strayed, through its governors-general and their families, into the ranks of the aristocracy—from the ancient Dalhousies to the recently ennobled Edens.

The novelist Maria Edgeworth captured this shift in opinion about India in a letter to her stepmother in 1822. She was concerned about the prospects of her young half-brother Thomas Pakenham Edgeworth (who later joined the Company's medical service and became an accomplished botanist before ill-health forced him to retire from India). On a visit to Hertfordshire, she engaged in conversation with a relative of the Prinseps, one of the most celebrated families to serve in British Bengal in the early nineteenth century, before making a visit to Haileybury, the college at which from 1806 entrants to the Company's civil service were trained prior to being sent to India. "In consequence of the improved education and regulations for the Company's servants in India," Edgeworth reported, "the whole system[,] manners and morals have changed." Her informant assured her that there were "no young men better informed[,] better principled or better conducted than those who go out as Writers to India. With the danger to their morals much of the danger for their health has [also] decreased." As evidence of this, the Prinsep sons were all said to be "in good health and speak without any horror of the climate."[67]

As indicated in the previous chapter, improvements in transport and the increasing volume of mail and passenger traffic meant that India was in many respects becoming less remote from Britain than it had appeared in the previous century. Even so, a strong sense of physical distance remained, and given the long periods of separation between family members, and the way in which service in India commonly divided family members, much of the affective nature of this empire of sentiment was articulated through letters and journals. Many of these in turn (such as those of Munro, Mackintosh and Heber) rapidly found their way into print after the author's death, thus becoming further points of reference for other essays in affect.

In this epistolary empire, women—mothers, sisters, wives—were not only articulate correspondents (like Honoria Lawrence), writing to family and friends from the outposts of empire, but also the subjects to whom lonely males expressed their pent-up emotions and their often contradictory feelings about India. Until he married, relatively late in life, Thomas Munro wrote his most personal and passionate letters to his sister Erskine in Glasgow; so did Henry Lawrence (until he married Honoria Marshall) to his sister Letitia in northern Ireland. Sensibility, about nature and landscape as about personal feelings of longing and despair, was often, it seemed, most openly directed toward the opposite sex.[68] The intensity of these communications was sometimes almost unbearable—or increasingly inappropriate. Brian Hodgson, isolated for almost twenty years in the British Residency in Kathmandu, frankly declared himself in his letters to his younger sister "a very solitary man," desperate for "feminine affection." It was eventually necessary for Fanny, the sister to whom such soulful confidences were addressed, to remind Hodgson that she was no longer the child she had been when last they had met and now had a husband and family of her own to whom she owed affection.[69]

At a time when Company servants might remain in India for decades before returning to Britain on leave, the sense of communicating across time as well as space could be almost overwhelming. In 1805 Munro, who at 44 had not seen his sister Erskine since he was 18, wrote to her:

> This correspondence between India and Scotland, between persons who have not seen each other for near thirty years, and who may never meet again, is something like letters from the dead to the living. We are both so changed from what we were, that when I think of home, and take up one of your letters, I almost fancy myself listening to a being from another world.[70]

In these familial letters, as well as many direct expressions of emotion, feeling was often routed through and around sentiments linked to the landscape and scenery of India. The physical presence of India, which kept family and friends apart, became a powerful symbol of separation, of nostalgia and longing and, often enough, fear of threatening or encroaching death.

The letters of Thomas Munro provide an interesting example of this, not least because they cover a period in which British sensitivity to nature, including the aesthetic qualities of the Indian landscape, was clearly increasing. Further, Munro is one of the most written about figures in the history of early colonial South India, cast (in an earlier historiography at least) as an exemplary man of action, a heroic soldier, a wise administrator and an individual with a rare degree of empathetic understanding of India, its past, and its people.[71]

Born in 1761, the son of a Glasgow merchant, Munro received only a grammar school education before he left for India in 1779 at the age of eighteen. Embroiled with administrative and revenue matters, caught up in the ongoing military struggle with Mysore, there was little in Munro's early letters to suggest any marked interest in nature or in the natural sciences. Indeed, when his younger brother, James, took up botany in the early 1790s he ridiculed the sexual obsessions of Linnaean taxonomy and sensibly advised him: "Burn your books rather than hurt your health by study."[72] But Thomas Munro mellowed with age and grew more Romantic with his times. In a letter to Erskine in 1790 he described sitting on a hilltop near Ambur, in North Arcot, surveying the scene:

> This spot has for me a certain charm, which I always strongly feel, but cannot easily describe. It is a kind of enjoyment derived from the wide views of the diversified country below me,—from the thoughts that its rivers, woods, and villages, give rise to; but above all, from the temporary return that I make to my native country, while memory contrasts the far distant with the surrounding objects. While seated on the rock, I am, or fancy I am, more thoughtful than when below. The extent and grandeur of the scene raises my mind, and the solitude and silence make me think that "I am conversing with Nature here."[73]

After twenty years' service in the Baramahal districts of the Madras Presidency, where he helped devise the new ryotwari (peasant-based) land revenue system, Munro seemed to feel deeply engaged with India, not least through its landscape. He declared to Erskine in 1799 that this was a "romantic country," where "every tree and mountain has some charm which attaches me to them." He had begun to make a garden for himself near Dharmapuri in Salem district, where he grew mangoes, oranges, and grapes: the thought of now having to leave it, he once wrote, "goes as much to my heart as forsaking my old friends."[74] Munro was not alone in his horticultural habits. Gardens formed an important focus for early nineteenth-century European sentiment about India—combining elements of nostalgia for gardens known in childhood at home with an adult appetite for nature in its more cultivated and productive forms. They represented a pleasing hybridity, expressed through a diversity of fruit trees and flowers, combining Eastern exoticism with European familiarity. In North India, too, there was some sense of continuity with the Islamic gardens of the Orient, as places of contemplation as well as pleasure, of quiet, order, and seclusion in contrast with the rootlessness of an itinerant existence and the heat and dust of the weary road.[75]

Conscious of how many of his former friends and colleagues had died and how his own health had been undermined by long years in India, in 1807 Munro returned to Britain for the first time in 27 years. Seven years later, aged 52, he married a fellow Scot, Jane Campbell, and returned with her to Madras. Becoming governor of the province in 1819, Munro made a new garden for his wife (herself a keen gardener) at Guindy, his official country residence. This, with their two children and the house they shared together, became a place of solace, away from the hardships and responsibilities of office that weighed heavily on a man who now regarded himself as being more at home in India than in Britain. This private world of cultivated nature helped sustain Munro through advancing old age and the enervating ordeal of a "tropical climate." When he was away on tour, Munro's letters to his wife made frequent reference to the pleasures and solaces of the Indian landscape. In a letter in May 1821 from Nanguneri in the southern district of Tirunelveli, he described a landscape that was cool and verdant after the rains, "a beautiful wild scene of mingled rocks and jungle, and aged trees and water." Despite missing his wife, and remembering that she had once visited the spot with him, the vista evoked nostalgia for past times "and beings which have long since passed away. I wish I could indulge in these dreams," he wrote, "and wander about in this romantic country, instead of returning to the dull and endless task of public business."[76]

When in 1826, for health reasons, his wife and children departed for Britain, Munro's descriptions of the garden and the rural scenes they had enjoyed together, but which he now visited alone, became the poignant expression of his deep sense of separation and loss. In one letter to Jane he wrote of visiting the garden where formerly he had always been sure of finding her and their son Campbell, nicknamed "Kamen." Now he found nobody "except a boy guarding the mangoes and figs from the squirrels." It was "a great change from the time when I was always sure of finding you and Kamen there. It is melancholy to think that you are never again to be in a place in which you took so much pleasure."[77]

Munro died a year later from cholera, without seeing his wife and children again. But his correspondence was published within four years of his death, in part because, as his biographer put it, these "beautiful" last letters showed "how deeply this rendering asunder of the tenderest ties of nature" was felt by Munro.[78] And they were read by, among others, Maria Edgeworth (who found them "delightful" and an aid to her own distant understanding of India),[79] as evidence of the sentiments and sensibilities worthy of an imperial proconsul.

Death and Botany

Since death, its fear and remembrance, infiltrated so many other aspects of European life in early nineteenth-century India, it is not surprising that it crept into the pursuit of science as well. The apparent threat to European health posed by India's climate and terrain was, as we have seen, an important stimulus to the development of colonial medical topography. But a pervasive awareness of death also informed the way in which naturalists thought about their personal prospects, about the fate of friends and professional colleagues, and about the fitting objects of their own scientific enquiries.

This interconnectedness was most striking in the case of botany. In India as in Europe, flowers and plants were ready vehicles for emotion and affect, and lent themselves to a stream of willed and unconscious associations, not least with childhood and death. The professionalization of botany did little to remove or impair this burden of sentiment. When William Hooker's daughter Mary Hariette lay dying of tuberculosis in Jersey in June 1841, he brought with him to her bedside a vasculum of roses from Kew Gardens.[80] For his son, Joseph Hooker, traveling in Sikkim eight years later, the very sight of certain Himalayan plants, redolent of European flora or bearing the names of fellow botanists, was enough to "excite lively and pleasing emotions." It was, he added, "the ignorant and unfeeling alone who can ridicule the association of the names of travelers and naturalists with those of animals and plants."[81] Flowers familiar from a British childhood evoked intense nostalgia and fond recollection, just as the sight of palm-fronds or bamboos swaying in the wind made observers think instinctively of the dark plumes nodding on the heads of horses in a funeral procession.[82] An interest in botany and horticulture was widespread among Europeans in India and across a wide social spectrum. Gardening was an approved alternative to drunkenness among the white soldiery and cantonments boasted some of the finest flower and vegetable gardens in India.[83] More than any other science of the period, botany was practiced by women as well as men and so entered middle-class epistolary conversations and affective discourse to an extent unmatched by chemistry or geology.[84]

But the active pursuit of botany in a country like India was also fraught with its particular perils and added the death of many of its young practitioners to its emotional freight and professional hazards. We will return to some of these issues in later chapters, but the nature of botanists' often fatal engagement with India's deathscapes and its empire of affect deserves some preliminary consideration here. As a field science, botany in early nineteenth-century India could be a high-risk business. In the course of official missions or in search of plant "novelties," zealous botanists plunged into jungles or subjected themselves to privations that ended in debility or death from dysentery or malaria. A number of promising botanists perished in this way. In 1817, after four years' service with the Bengal Army, which included time spent in Nepal, the young Scottish surgeon and naturalist William Jack was recruited by Sir Stamford Raffles to botanize in Sumatra. After a series of fruitful botanical forays, which helped reveal the riches of Malayan flora to Western botanical science, Jack died in Singapore in 1822, aged only 27. The French naturalist Victor Jacquemont, to whom we will turn in more detail in Chapter 4, died in Bombay in 1832, after three years' arduous traveling and plant collecting in India: he was 32. Likewise, in his brief career as a surgeon-botanist, William Griffith, first appointed to Madras in 1832, but soon journeying from one end of the Indian empire to the other, died in 1845, shortly before his thirty-fifth birthday. Another, less renowned, East India Company surgeon, John Ellerton Stocks of the Bombay Medical Service, conducted a series of single-handed botanical expeditions into Sind and Baluchistan, where he contracted malaria. He returned to England in 1854 but died shortly after, also aged 34.

These almost Keatsian deaths shocked the scientific community in Britain as well as in India and cast a pall over future scientific endeavor. In November 1842, musing on his own future and the possibility of visiting either the Andes or India, Joseph Hooker remarked only half in jest to the taxonomist George Bentham (who had suggested that he "see a little of Tropical Vegetation" after his "Antarctic herborizations"), "Have not you Botanists killed collectors a-plenty in the Tropics?"[85] There was much justification, not only with respect to India, for such a gloomy association between botany, death and the tropics. In 1840 Joseph Hooker's father had been responsible for nominating a naturalist for the ill-fated Niger expedition: his choice fell on the young German botanist J.R.T. Vogel. Within weeks of their arrival in West Africa, Vogel and most of the expedition were dead from malaria. It then fell to William Hooker, with the assistance of his son Joseph (who, had he not been heading for the Antarctic in 1839, might well have been selected for the Niger expedition instead), to edit Vogel's diary and botanical notes for publication.[86]

Hooker's own visit to India, barely a year later, was overshadowed by frequent deaths just as his itinerary was partly dictated by a personal determination to avoid sickness and death. During the first year of his Indian journey no less than four of the surgeons and naturalists Hooker had known or befriended died. Among them was the geologist

D.H. Williams, who had recently been appointed by the East India Company to investigate the coal seams of eastern India and with whom Hooker camped and traveled for two pleasant months on the first stage of his journey into the interior. The geologist Charles Lyell, who had a brother of his own in the army in India and so had additional reason for anxiety, noted Williams's death from fever, contracted while geologizing in the jungles of Bengal, with alarm and indignation. Already, he wrote to his father, one out of every five geologists sent to India "had been cut off in the prime of life," and he had protested against sending the able Williams on such a "forlorn hope." Now, having "done his business, poor fellow," and helped the Company locate coal, he was "left like his predecessors to die in a ditch." Lyell's thoughts then turned to Hooker. "Heaven grant that poor Joseph Hooker may be spared, but I dread Assam and Borneo [where Hooker was meant to continue his botanical investigations], and would rather have the work on the Antarctic regions and still unpublished notes than all the magnolias in the Himalaya."[87]

Hooker, too, was shocked by Williams's sudden death and made a substantial contribution to a bereavement fund set up for his widow and children.[88] Moreover, the geologist's demise was soon followed by that of Joseph's uncle, Gurney Turner (his mother's younger brother), a member of the Bengal Medical Service. Hooker, by now safely ensconced in Darjeeling, struggled to cope with so much "melancholy news." "I do feel his death very deeply," he wrote to his father of Turner. But Hooker was quick to reassure him of his own safety, urging his father to trust his "prudence" and announcing his decision to remain in the Himalaya "where there is a perfect immunity from disease."[89] Staying in Darjeeling with Brian Hodgson confirmed him in this intention; Hodgson had been ill almost from the time of his arrival in India thirty years earlier and had accordingly sought appointments in the Himalaya, at first in Kumaon and subsequently in Kathmandu, where he could hope to nurse his fragile health.[90] Neither of the postings in fact absolved him from illness. Hodgson's interest in hunting and shooting might never have matured into the study of zoology and ornithology had ill-health not forced him into Himalayan seclusion. And, as if to confirm his own dismal experience, Hodgson further witnessed the death of his two brothers in India, one of whom died within hours of contracting fever while out snipe shooting in the plains.[91]

Hooker might himself have felt safe ensconced in the hills, but reports and rumors of death continued to haunt and harass him. He soon learned of another death, that of George Gardner, a fellow botanist who, having previously studied Brazilian flora, had made the pan-tropical leap to become superintendent of the botanic garden at Peradeniya in Ceylon in 1844. When Hooker visited the island in December 1847, *en route* to Calcutta, Gardner had been his enthusiastic host. Another naturalist had fallen victim to the tropics, "cut off," as William Hooker put it, "in the midst of his useful labours."[92]

Such untimely deaths as those of Vogel, Williams, Turner, and Gardner not only evoked a sense of promising lives cruelly—perhaps needlessly—cut short; they often left a mournful legacy in their wake as well. The botanists' vast collections of plants (gathered at such cost to their own lives) had to be sorted and disposed of, their scattered notes and unpublished writings either left to rot (which they rapidly did in India's heat and humidity or in the obscure basement of India House in London) or edited for posthumous publication. Much of the personal knowledge of where and how plants grew, painstakingly acquired by itinerant botanists, died with them, thereby making their collections of limited use to other naturalists.[93] One of the most striking cases was that of William Griffith, around whom a coterie of appreciative naturalists rapidly formed, praising him as "a man of genius" and "undying fame," "India's brightest botanical ornament . . . taken away even before the prime of life."[94] Nearing death, Griffith requested his friend and fellow surgeon, John M'Clelland, to publish his scientific essays and travel notes. Despite not being a botanist, M'Clelland regarded his promise to a dying man as a "sacred duty." He secured financial support from the East India Company, and, accompanied by warm tributes to Griffith's achievements (and, still more, to his great potential) as a botanist, his papers appeared in several volumes from 1848 onwards.[95] Botanical texts, with their attendant eulogies and dedications, thus became scientific memorials to the dead, though there were those, including Joseph Hooker, who felt that in this instance the labor was misguided and that Griffith's reputation was ill-served by the publication of a mass of "crude" and disorganized material.[96]

In 1855 Joseph Hooker published his *Illustrations of Himalayan Plants*, a stunning book with thirty glowing, imperial-sized color plates. The book was based on drawings commissioned locally by J.F. Cathcart, a civil servant and keen amateur botanist, who had died while returning from India four years earlier. Hooker had met Cathcart in Darjeeling and visited his remarkable hillside garden. The *Illustrations* were thus both a

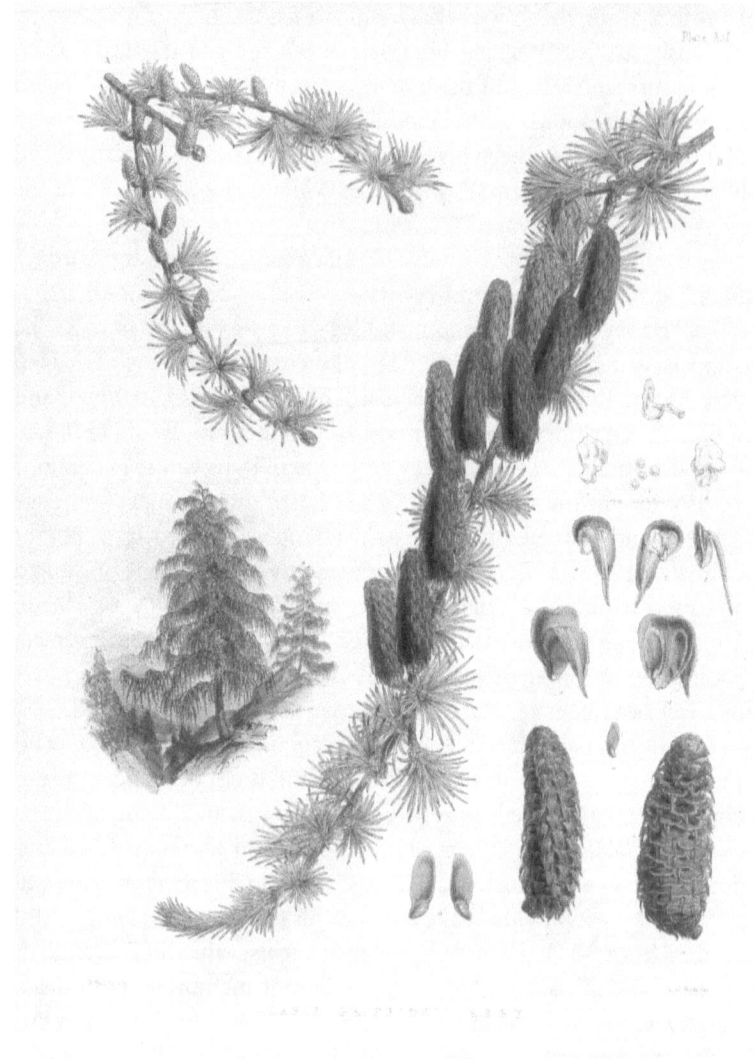

FIG. 2. *Larix griffithii*, from J.D. Hooker, *Illustrations of Himalayan Plants* (1855), drawn by W.H. Fitch from a sketch by Hooker. Reproduced by kind permission of the Royal Botanic Gardens, Kew.

celebration of the Himalaya's spectacular flora, through a volume designed to appeal to "the lovers of art and horticulture," and a memorial to a friend and patron of Indian botany. In addition to Hooker's personal memoir of Cathcart, in which his life was commemorated and his contribution to botany praised,[97] the book described and depicted many new species, several of them named after Cathcart and other European residents or botanists. Thus one Himalayan larch (*Larix griffithii*, see Fig. 2) was named after Griffith, whom Hooker (despite his personal dislike of the man) honored as "one of the most active and promising of the many naturalists who have devoted their energies and sacrificed their lives to the pursuit of botany in India."[98] Flora could be a melancholy muse.

Gothic Christianity

The contemplation of India's deathscapes was, however, more than just an occasion for European anxiety and introspection. Ideas of death and dying went well beyond a sense of fear and foreboding among middle-class exiles: they also profoundly affected the ways in which Britons thought about India and the society that inhabited it. The Indian landscape, far from being an uncultured void, was everywhere replete with the signs and symbols of its established religions: this was especially so of Hinduism, with its holy rivers and hilltop temples, its sati stones and sacred groves. Nature itself—from the mountains to the seas, from the tiger to the peacock,[99] from the sacred pipal or bo tree (which even Western science, in deference to Hindu and Buddhist belief, acknowledged as *Ficus religiosa*) to the resplendent lotus (the throne of goddess Lakshmi)—had already been conspicuously appropriated by local myth and religious practice. Only the most impervious of European travelers failed to recognize that India's landscape had already been colonized by others.

The consequences of this prior appropriation were many and various. Its recognition facilitated a representation of India that located the "horrors" attached to Hindu "superstition" within an equally deadly and desolate "heathen" landscape, thus using one negative attribute to reinforce another. Or it provoked a determined effort to wrest the Indian countryside away from its vernacular associations, seeking to make a contrast between the splendor of nature and the squalor of man (as by making a distinction between the quiet beauty of the Ganges and the ghastly practices Hindus reputedly perpetrated along its banks).[100] But, in general, landscape and nature were reinterpreted in terms that were essentially Western in character, and scenic vistas, like colorful plants and curious animals, became annexed to an aesthetic and a morality that were alien to India but more accessible to European observers.

Religion provided one route by which this was done, overlaying the pre-colonial acculturation of the Indian landscape with an imported religiosity. For many Christian newcomers to the East, India served as a kind of biblical exegesis. Botany—in part because it was seen by many of its amateur practitioners as a celebration of God's handiwork ("every flower is a sermon of divine power, wisdom and goodness," William Jones averred)[101]—was particularly complicit in this exercise in re-appropriation. Flowers and trees, spices, aromatic gums and other plant substances hitherto known only through reading the Bible were here witnessed for the first time. In the 1830s, Edward Madden, an Irish-born artillery officer and respected botanist, compiled for his personal use a list of "biblical plants" he had observed on his travels, complete with scriptural references and supporting texts.[102] Travelers similarly saw animals and birds that recalled Bible scenes and parables; they observed with the Scriptures "a land whose stones are iron" or whose villagers built thorn fences to "hedge about kine;" they glimpsed, as if in the Holy Land two thousand years earlier, men dressed in flowing white robes, women with veils and shy glances, drawing water from wells and bearing home pots on their heads. Along with flat-roofed houses baking in the sun, there was even the humble charpoy to make sense of Christ's injunction to Lazarus to take up his bed and walk.[103] But, even more intensely, India's landscape served to summon up images of evil, of a pagan land crying out for moral reform and spiritual redemption. The newly arrived Honoria Lawrence commented that those parts of the Bible "that treat of idolatry have a force, when read here, such as in our land they cannot have."[104]

One of the factors which led to the fashioning of a new and more intense language around the Indian landscape in the early nineteenth century was undoubtedly the evangelical movement. Until the revision of its charter in 1813 the East India Company, concerned not to alienate its subjects, had prohibited Christian missionaries from operating in India. But even before that date, Baptist missionaries based at the Danish settlement of Serampore, near Calcutta, and even the Company's own chaplains, had begun to unleash a barrage of righteous condemnation against Hinduism. Despite the Company's attempt to maintain a politically expedient distance between itself and missionary discourse, by the 1820s and 1830s evangelical ideas had become widespread and permeated much of the private thinking and unguarded expression even of its own officials, as well as the letters, diaries, and travelogues of those who toured the country. The effect of the rise of evangelical Christianity among Europeans resident in India may in part have been to reconcile them to personal ordeals of sickness and death. Individuals like Reginald Heber and Honoria Lawrence brought with them to India a conviction that the God who gave them life could also as easily take it away.[105] Heber remarked in 1824, on hearing that cholera was again rife in Bengal, that this was a timely reminder of how near "even in the midst of life we are to death." "Surely," he added, "there is no country in the world where this recollection ought to be more perpetually present with us than India."[106]

Within weeks of arriving in India Honoria Lawrence believed "my days may be numbered,"[107] and she anticipated that she might not survive the birth of her first child. When the eight-month-old Letitia died in November 1840 she could only make the tragedy bearable by thinking that it came "directly from a Father's hand." In her search for "composure" in the face of adversity, Honoria found a consoling "holy calm" in the belief that her daughter had gone to join Christ in heaven and that her tragic death had brought Honoria closer to her Savior. This was "one of the blessed fruits of that sorrow" and made it possible for her to face her own eventual death in India (in 1854), after years of illness, with "resignation," even "joy."[108]

Projected outwards, however, onto the landscape of India, the impact of evangelical Christianity was rather different. From early in the century evangelicals remorselessly attacked Hinduism as a religion of gross superstition and extreme physical cruelty, pillorying the East India Company for allowing such "barbaric" practices as sati, infanticide, and pilgrims crushing themselves to death under the massive wheels of the temple car of the god Jagannath at Puri. "Impurity and cruelty," wrote the Serampore missionary William Ward in 1822, "have been, in all ages, the prominent features of every form of pagan superstition. But nowhere have all these features presented a more disgusting and horrible appearance than among the Hindoos."[109] The evangelicals flailed Hinduism with an impassioned prose that seemed at times to draw as much inspiration from the Gothic novel as from Christian scripture. The tone was set early on by Claudius Buchanan, a Calcutta chaplain, who gave a vivid and widely read account of his visit in 1806 to Puri, the town on the coast of Orissa that housed the temple of Jagannath. Earlier descriptions of Puri and its pilgrims had assumed a far more neutral tone, but for Buchanan the town, situated in a veritable "valley of death," was a place where deluded Hindus worshiped "obscene" idols, which he likened to the Moloch of Old Testament Canaan.[110] While "appalled at the magnitude and horror of the spectacle" of the temple, Buchanan was no less disgusted by all that surrounded it. Puri was filled with "famished pilgrims, many of whom die in the streets from want or of disease." Outside the town, and scattered across the plains for fifty miles around this Indian "Golgotha," lay the rotting and dismembered corpses of dead pilgrims, with dogs and vultures picking at their bones.[111]

Missionaries or merely Christian travelers, many subsequent writers echoed Buchanan's stark descriptions, recycling his expressions of "horror" and "disgust," reiterating his characterization of Jagannath as "the Moloch of Hindustan" and his gruesome depiction of Puri and its environs as India's "Golgotha."[112] Such fierce hostility was not, it should be noted, directed at all Hindu pilgrimage sites. Hardwar, the place where the Ganges

FIG. 3. Pilgrims at Hardwar, from R. Montgomery Martin, *The Indian Empire Illustrated* (1861), engraved by J.M.W. Turner.
Reproduced by kind permission of the School of Oriental and African Studies, London.

issued from the Himalaya into the Indian plains, was regarded with particular favor and picturesque appreciation. But the pleasure to be derived from Hardwar—"one of the places best worthy of a traveller's attention in India," according to Roberts[113]—contrasted with the cold shiver Puri sent down European spines. In a passage that seemed to combine Mary Shelley's *Frankenstein* with Buchanan's evangelical repulsion, Roberts's impressions of Puri were of a "dark and frowning pagoda," rising abruptly from the seashore, "its huge and shapeless mass not unlike some ill-proportioned giant." Seeing this "mighty Moloch," with bright sunshine overhead and attractive green foliage all around, seemed to her only to "deepen its horrors." It was a "foul blot upon the fair face of nature," a "frightful monument" to the human perversion of God's designs.[114]

Puri was not the only stage on which such monstrous dramas were enacted. Travelers arriving by ship had often remarked on the depressing sight of the mud-banks, flooded forests and tangled vegetation of the Sundarbans that they passed through before arriving at Calcutta. But from early in the nineteenth century, as the censorious discourses of topography, medicine, and religion matured and coalesced, this region acquired a new signification. It was seen as a hostile and pestilential region, a place of deadly fever, of marauding tigers and man-eating crocodiles. But, more than that, it became identified with the infanticide practiced by Hindu devotees on the shores of Sagar island, close to the entrance to the river Hugli. Shortly before he died in Java in 1811, John Leyden, surgeon and linguist, poet and former collaborator of Sir Walter Scott, composed a grim set of verses about Sagar's "dreary isle." Here, Leyden wrote, "where crimson'd Ganga shines in blood, and man-devouring monsters swarm," "strange deeds of blood" were performed in honor of the "Dark Goddess" Kali. The uncompromising second stanza ran:

To glut the shark and crocodile
A mother brought her infant here:
She saw its tender playful smile,
She shed not one maternal tear:-
She threw it on a watery bier:-
With grinding teeth sea monsters tore
The smiling infant which she bore:-
She shrunk not once its cries to hear![115]

Leyden did not openly espouse the missionary cause,[116] but the connection he made between barbaric Hinduism on the one hand and the savagery of flesh-eating "monsters" and pestiferous jungle on the other, helped set the tone for writers who were unapologetically evangelical. By the 1820s and 1830s European descriptions of the Sundarbans were regularly filled with images in which savage creatures and jungle miasmas combined to evoke a "heathen" landscape redolent of all the excesses and abominations attributed to Hinduism. In 1823 Bishop Heber penned one of the most powerful descriptions of this kind, portraying Sagar island as a dreary and dreadful place full of "tygers, serpents and fevers" at the sight of which any true Christian would recoil.[117] His account was taken up and elaborated upon by Alexander Duff of the Church of Scotland Mission in Calcutta. Writing in 1839 of the "superstitions and idolatries" of eastern India, Duff scoffed at William Jones's "inexpressible pleasure" at first arriving in India in 1783 and his Orientalist enthusiasm for investigating "the vast regions of Asia," "fertile in the productions of human genius" and its "abounding natural wonders." The "dismal mud banks," "dingy forests," and "impenetrable thickets" of the Sundarbans, Duff wrote instead, were "the receptacle for ages of all manner of destructive creatures, and still more destructive exhalations which load the atmosphere with pestilence and death." Amidst these awesome solitudes, silence reigned "deep, awful, and unbroken as that of the sepulchre."[118]

Beyond these "dreary regions," though, the banks of the Hugli became "enlivened by the presence of man." Flowering plants and fruit trees lined the river, and the "rich variegated foliage" and "groves of towering cocoa-palms" waving their "feathery plumes in the breeze" all spoke of "the exuberant bounties of a gracious God." The richly scented air and hothouse atmosphere were "calculated to regale the senses, exhilarate the spirits, and diffuse through the whole soul a strange delirium of buoyant hope and joy."[119] And yet, Duff was quick to add, such "pleasurable sensations" were "doomed to be transient and short-lived":

> You have escaped from the region of jungle and of pestilence. But you have not escaped, you cannot escape, from the emblems and memorials of a loathsome superstition. These seem ever present, and everywhere present. It is truly a land of bright and glorious sunshine; yet a land of moral darkness that may be felt at every step.[120]

Nature in India thus seemed complicit in the "horrors" of Hinduism. For Duff, as for many other Europeans, evangelicals or not, one of the earliest and most enduring impressions of India as a land of death came from seeing corpses floating in the Hugli, with vultures and alligators tearing at the bloated, rotting flesh. Close by, and clearly visible from the passing ship, was a further "degrading spectacle"—that of the sick and aged left to die on the riverbanks.[121] So disturbing, so alien, were these first enframing images of India that they remained vivid in the minds of many Europeans when they came to write up their memoirs, even twenty or thirty years later.[122] But for devout Christians like Heber, Duff, and Honoria Lawrence such scenes were not simply shocking in themselves. They reinforced the deeply held conviction that India was more than a "darkened land." Morally and physically, it was "this very land of death."[123]

3

ROMANTICISM AND IMPROVEMENT

DESPITE INDIA'S RECURRING—IF DISTANT—PRESENCE IN THE ROMANTIC writing of early nineteenth-century Britain, Romanticism has been curiously ignored in discussion of India itself. Perhaps this is because Romanticism appears a fanciful and delusory way to comprehend a regime as addicted to warfare and the remorseless extraction of revenue as the East India Company appeared to be,[1] or to represent a period when the subcontinent was repeatedly ravaged by famine and epidemic disease. One might further explain this neglect of Romanticism in India as a consequence of the way in which Orientalism (in both its classical scholarly sense and, following Edward Said, its critical discursive meaning) has dominated consideration of India under Company rule, almost to the exclusion of any other mode of analysis. At best, Romanticism appears a sickly child, failing to thrive in India, or elbowed aside by the sturdier forces of Benthamite utilitarianism and Christian evangelism.[2]

Recent attempts to rethink Romanticism see it less as a literary movement confined to Europe and more as an aspect of Europe's understanding of, and engagement with, the rest of the world, as through the ambivalences of travel literature, or alarm at the intrusion of "colonial" diseases into Britain, or perceptions of Africa and the slave trade;[3] such rethinking suggests that in ignoring or undervaluing Romanticism, scholars of early nineteenth-century India have overlooked one of the most significant influences on the imperial mentalities of the time and missed out on a valuable tool of analysis. Romanticism has, of course, been recognized as a complex, elusive, even "inchoate," phenomenon, calling for close contextual reading.[4] This chapter does not aspire to a new theorization of Romanticism, but it does seek to explore the multiple connections between Romantic literature, imagery and landscape sensibility in European writing about travel and topography in early nineteenth-century India. It thereby tries to show how externally derived ideas were assembled and applied, extensively and influentially, to the Indian environment, in ways which any scholarly reading of these sources should critically encompass. Although some recent writing about the travel literature of the period is skeptical about its ties to Romanticism,[5] the example of colonial India indicates that the two were closely interconnected and that travel writing was one of the principal literary genres through which colonial Romanticism was expressed.[6] Equally, scholarship on the relationship between Romanticism and early nineteenth-century science[7] suggests important but hitherto largely unexplored linkages between travel, science, and Romanticism in the colonial literature of the period and the need to be cautious about presuming that the imperial order in early nineteenth-century India was essentially the embodiment of "Enlightenment rationality."

As one might expect, within this extensive body of colonial literature there were wide differences of style and interpretation, arising as much from individual taste and experience as from professional orientation and training. Even so, the Romantic vein of writing was remarkably successful in establishing itself in India after 1800, and flourished between the early 1820s and late 1840s. Despite the diversity of observer perspectives, Romanticism in India was only in part about the idealization of the past and of untamed nature, still so often identified as primary tropes of Romantic writing, or about escape from an increasingly industrialized society. In India, as in Britain, Romanticism articulated a visceral discontent with what actually existed and a hankering after a very different existence. But through association with the doctrines and imagery of capitalism and Christianity, it also helped forge a program for change, emphasizing the need to transform the ruined and debased Indian landscape to create a peaceful and prosperous civilization modeled after an "improved" and industrious Britain.

The Ambiguity of Ruins

As indicated in the previous chapter, the European envisioning of India as a land of death went far beyond melancholy reflections on white mortality. The recurrent representation of India as a series of morally framed deathscapes was a projection of what many Europeans felt was wrong, not so much with themselves, as with India and Indians. A further expression of this was the common trope of India as a land in ruins. There were two aspects to this. As in Europe, ruined buildings could be seen as picturesque objects, worthy subjects of Romantic contemplation. In this regard they were morally inspiring and aesthetically pleasing landscape features. Indeed, the conspicuous presence of such "objects of antiquity" was one of the factors that distinguished India from the seemingly uncivilized wilds of North America and, to a significant degree, spared it from being similarly designated a domain of pure nature.[8] And yet the idea of India in ruins, especially when it extended beyond "picturesque" views of crumbling palaces and decaying tombs to become a metaphor for the country at large, communicated a far more censorious meaning.

Before the landscape of India became visibly transformed by canals, railroads, and land reclamation—a process well under way by the mid-1850s—the remains of forts and tombs, of abandoned palaces and cities, were among the most visible features of the landscape, especially once travelers moved from the coastal cities of Calcutta, Bombay, and Madras into the interior provinces. Many Indian cities appeared, in European eyes, to be little more than extended ruins. As late as the 1840s, one army engineer observed:

> All the towns in India, with a very few exceptions, are in ruins. Delhi is surrounded by ruins. Agra, Booranpore [Berhampore], Aurungabad, have immense suburbs in ruins. The Deckan is a heap of ruins. Many towns in central India that had their hundreds of thousands of inhabitants, are now literally without one, and are swarming with leopards, tigers, elks, and buffaloes. In deep forests you stumble upon Hindoo gateways, stone tanks eight hundred yards square, brick walls of large dimensions; scores of acres of burying-grounds, and all the other concomitants and proofs of [former] wealth, power and population.[9]

Writing in 1840, Lieutenant Tickell of the Bengal Army recounted how, "engulphed in the labyrinths of untenanted forests," he had found the half-hidden remains of many ancient buildings. In one locality, these occurred in great numbers,

> and the road leading to them is replete with debris of the most melancholy and dreary nature, rank grass waving over tanks [reservoirs], some of great magnitude, which lie on every side. Thickets and briars matting over richly carved ghauts and temples; old avenues and plantations, whose symmetry can now scarcely be detected amidst overwhelming jungle, offer a vivid picture of what these deserted tracts once were; and the mind instinctively pictures to itself a once opulent and prosperous people, whose forgotten dust rests perhaps within the funereal shades of these ancient forests, as their fates and fortunes, alike unknown, lie buried in the elapsed vastness of time![10]

Similar accounts of India's desolation could be gleaned almost indefinitely from the literature of the time. Bishop Heber in the 1820s was just one among dozens of travelers to be struck by the "decayed, but most striking and romantic, magnificence" of Delhi, the old Mughal capital.[11] "From the gate of Agra," he wrote, "to Humaiöon's tomb is a very aweful scene of desolation, ruins after ruins, tombs after tombs, fragments of brick-work, freestone, granite and marble, scattered everywhere over a soil naturally rocky and barren."[12] He noted the remains of an old Pathan palace, which had once been part of a "large and solid fortress." It was built in a "plain and unornamented style of architecture," and it would have been "picturesque had it been in a country where trees grow, and ivy was green." But here, in India, it was "only ugly and melancholy."[13]

Musing on the remains of lost civilizations, as if on India's Ozymandias,[14] was a common pastime, and often accompanied the Orientalist investigation of Indian antiquity. In the 1790s William Tennant found the ruined palace of Rajmahal, with its "empty halls, marble parlour, and half decayed vaults," still expressive of its "former magnificence": "the despotism of the East," he concluded, "is great even in its ruins."[15] Such sites were not merely evocative of the past; they could also serve as a salutary reminder to the British of their own imperial transience. Touring the half-deserted towns and crumbling Mughal palaces of North India in the late 1820s, Major Archer was moved to reflect on the decline of the house of Timur, "whose inheritance we have acquired," from its

FIG. 4. The Ruins of Old Delhi, from R. Montgomery Martin,
The Indian Empire Illustrated (1861).
Reproduced by kind permission of the School of Oriental and
African Studies, London.

former "magnitude and grandeur." Anyone who was aware of their "greatness of power" must, he believed, feel regret at their passing and "acknowledge the instability of their own name and fame."[16] But appreciation was not the traveler's only response. Visiting the Buddhist monuments of Aurangabad and Ellora in 1810, James Mackintosh declined, despite his own Orientalist interests, to be impressed. Their function was, he observed, to "display power": they had nothing about them that was "reasonable, useful or beautiful; all is fatalistic, massy, and monstrous." The object of such art was "to overwhelm the mind, rather than delight it, and to excite wonder, not admiration."[17] He speculated that more useful labor had been employed in Britain over the previous fifty years on "docks, canals, and other useful works" than on "all the boasted works of Asia, from the wall of China to the Pyramids." "To pierce a country in all directions with canals" was, to his "improving" mind, "a greater work than any of them."[18]

Emma Roberts was another author who frequently portrayed India through half-pleasing, half-horrifying vignettes of desolation and decay. Visiting Delhi shortly after Heber, she too found a great plain "strewed with fragments of ruined tombs, temples, serais, and palaces." Pools of

FIG. 5. The Jama Masjid at Mandu, from R. Montgomery Martin, *The Indian Empire Illustrated* (1861). Reproduced by kind permission of the School of Oriental and African Studies, London.

stagnant water had "formed themselves in the hollowed foundations of the prostrate edifices, adding to the wildness and dreariness of the scene."[19] Ruins could, however fleetingly, be enchanting. Roberts described with more feeling than many of her male contemporaries the eerie beauty of a ruined edifice on the nearby banks of the Yamuna, the "full-orbed moon shining in virgin majesty over plain, and grove, and gently gliding river." But, as so often with Roberts, a chillier tone quickly crept in: far from human habitation, the river teemed with alligators, wild birds ("untamed tenants of the waste") cried overhead, and the atmosphere of "profound solitude" was oppressive. So strongly did she recoil from the scene that she thought with anticipatory pleasure of the day when steamships would ply the river and bring a reassuring animation to the scene, and then the "lonely site of these crumbling ruins can be divested of its savage grandeur."[20] Earlier in the same work, Roberts described the long-deserted Water Palace at Mandu. In a passage that echoed her uneasy account of the European cemetery at Berhampore (and which edgily anticipated Kipling's "Cold Lairs" by half a century), she described how "desolate creatures, the jackall, the vulture, the serpent, and the wolf" had gained "undisputed possession of the halls and gardens" that "so mournfully" attested to the "former magnificence of a city overspread with jungle, and abandoned to the beasts of the field." As on the banks of the moonlit Yamuna, she concluded that even "the most exuberant and buoyant spirit becomes depressed by the solemn stillness and utter devastation of this unbroken solitude."[21]

Evocative though the "magnificent yet sad memorials of fallen grandeur" might be,[22] there was an intense and (as British rule grew more secure) increasing feeling that the morose monuments of the past needed to be left behind and that India had more inspiring sights to offer. Having seen the Taj Mahal and Akbar's mausoleum, Major Lloyd seemed greatly relieved in March 1822 to be heading for the Himalaya, thus quitting "the perishing records of man, for the imperishable records of nature."[23] Three months later, having delighted in "scenes of eternal beauty," he returned with reluctance to the "heated plains, where the crimson tide of barbarian conquests had rushed, and left behind the dregs of desolation." After the solace of the mountains, returning to heat and history was, at best, a "melancholy pleasure."[24]

Jungle

The evidence of India's ruination lay not only in deserted palaces and crumbling mausoleums; it was also inscribed in nature. Of all the many terms used by travelers and topographers to describe the Indian terrain—jheels, ghats, nullahs, and the like—none was more expressive than the word "jungle." It was, however, a term used in a bewildering variety of ways. There were "wet" jungles as well as "dry" ones, jungles of grass, thorn-scrub, and bamboo, "low jungles" as well as "tree jungles." For some travelers the word was simply synonymous with "wood" or "forest,"[25] and by mid-century it generally appeared without any explanation at all.

Following the original Sanskrit and vernacular meaning of the term,[26] some early writers, like Benjamin Heyne in the 1790s and 1800s, equated "jangal" with "desert," to describe dry, stony landscapes, thinly vegetated with thorn-bush and scrub.[27] Something of this usage and the accompanying spelling persisted (at least among botanists) into the late 1830s.[28] More commonly by that date, though, "jungle" had come to signify dense, tangled vegetation, so thick as to be virtually impenetrable.[29] For the hunter "jungle" might, for all its hazards, signify the likely hiding place of wild boar, deer, and other game, but for most other Europeans it suggested danger, disorder, and vegetative excess. One argument for clearing jungles was that they harbored dacoits (bandits) and dangerous, predatory beasts.[30] In a number of early military campaigns, such as the Poligar War in South India in 1801, the British had to clear a broad swathe through dense jungle in order to allow their troops and artillery to advance against their well-protected opponents.[31] Jungles acquired further negative connotations through their association with disease, especially the malarial fevers that killed or incapacitated so many Europeans and their Indian subordinates. This identification with disease went back at least to British military expeditions in the 1770s into areas like the sub-Himalayan Tarai and Bengal's "Jungle Mahals."[32] By the 1820s it was not uncommon for military men and medical officers to speak in a single phrase of "jungle, pestilence, and fever."[33] As we saw in the last chapter, this kind of multiple association between physical harm and moral evil leant itself to Christian representations of a landscape that was perceived to be both heathen and deadly, as entangled with rank, miasmatic, over-fecund plant life as Hinduism appeared to teem with primitive beliefs and convoluted superstitions.[34] By extension, even Europeans who spent too long up-country, isolated from their own kind, were likely to turn "jungly" or, in Emily Eden's expressive phrase, to have their civilized manners "jungled out of them."[35]

Occasionally, jungles might be "picturesque" or contain "spots of romantic beauty." Roberts, for one, wrote appreciatively of "the rich tapestry" of trees and flowers in north Indian jungles, and the army botanist Edward Madden described hills "clothed from base to summit with impenetrable jungle, the deep verdure of which adds much to the beauty of the scene."[36] But as the negative connotations of "jungle" hardened this perception became less common. In travel narratives and topographies a contrast was frequently made between tangled, disease-laden, and dangerous "jungles" on the one hand and on the other pleasing "topes" of mango trees (sometimes tamarinds) that had been planted to provide travelers with shade and villagers with fruit. Unlike the jungles, hurried through as quickly as possible, these were designated "groves," or even "orchards," and welcomed as pleasant spots at which to breakfast or camp. The lustrous foliage and noble stature of the mango trees reminded British travelers patriotically of oaks, and topes held comforting associations with English woods and parks.[37] It was perhaps only among the growing ranks of professional botanists and foresters that a more discriminating view of jungle began to emerge. In their 1851 report on India's "tropical forests" to the British Association for the Advancement of Science, Hugh Cleghorn and his colleagues wrote of topes of mango and tamarind "embowering every village," but also, somewhat defensively, of tracts of jungle consisting of grass and shrub (including dhak, jujube, and acacia trees) "which by some are accounted so much waste" but which, rather than "disfiguring the rich appearance of a cultivated country," were a valuable source of fodder and timber.[38]

Underlying all these differences was the double meaning jungle had. It was frequently used, as the Indian equivalent of the American "wilderness," as primordial nature, untouched and untenanted by humankind. One writer in 1848 thus referred to "real natural jungle" as the "opponent of agricultural wealth" and "the mainstay of primeval barbarism," but, he observed, this was now fast disappearing from Bengal through the spread of cultivation and "under the stability of our rule."[39] Jungle, however, also signified land which had once been tilled but had since fallen out of cultivation. Given the common connection at the time between "culture," "cultivation," and "civilization" (as when William Lloyd wrote of "jungle of all shades broken by shreds of culture"),[40] jungle used in this sense was a ready emblem of India's more general decline, just as jungles symbolically as well as physically enshrouded the remains of many once thriving cities and prosperous empires. In the early 1820s, Sir John Malcolm described one central Indian district as a "fertile undulating plain, once perfectly open, flourishing, and highly cultivated, but of late years overgrown in many parts with low jungle, or brushwood." With the suppression of banditry, the return of wasteland to cultivation, and the spread of a new "spirit of improvement," he anticipated the rapid revival of "peaceful occupations" and a renewed flow of revenue from the land.[41]

The idea of jungle as signifying the neglect of cultivation and lapse of civilization was further reinforced by its faunal associations. Just as abandoned fields and villages were said to have "gone to jungle," so the proliferation of tigers, bears, and wild elephants was seen, as in the aftermath of the Bengal famine of 1770, as a sorry index of human decline and depopulation.[42] Conversely, in seeking to restore and "improve" Central India following the Maratha wars, Malcolm was anxious to reclaim tracts of land that had been "usurped by wild beasts" and where tigers "literally fought with the returning inhabitants for their fields." These enemies of improvement had killed 84 villagers in one tract alone in 1818; but with the advent of British rule the number of deaths fell dramatically, and in 1820 there was "hardly one."[43] But tigers and bears "infested" many parts of Central India a decade or more later, and indeed "infest"—with its implication of unwanted vermin—long remained the word habitually used to describe these and other wild animals.[44]

Buchanan in South India

In early 1800 the Bengal-based surgeon-naturalist Francis Buchanan was sent to Madras by the governor-general, Lord Wellesley, to report on territory recently seized from Tipu Sultan, the ruler of Mysore.[45] Although many of the European travel accounts of the period began from Calcutta rather than from Madras (or Bombay), Buchanan's journey followed a broadly characteristic pattern, in moving from the anglicized environs of a colonial port city into the cultural and topographical unfamiliarity of the Indian interior.[46] Traveling into the hinterland might signify novelty, excitement and a welcome escape from the constraints and conventions of European society in the cities (as it did for the naturalists Victor Jacquemont and Joseph Hooker); but contemporary travel narratives instead often took the form of a journey into India's "heart of darkness," in which a censorious view of landscape and nature elided with, and reinforced, a moral critique of the human inhabitants. But equally, and more in keeping with the Romantic's quest, beyond the sterile plains and the pervasive despotism of custom and caste, might lie the delightful prospect of unbridled nature—in the uplifting sight of snow-capped mountains or the colorful and exhilarating vision of tropical vegetation.

As he left Madras in late April and headed inland Buchanan found what he saw as abundant evidence not only of the destruction caused by recent warfare and Mysorean depredations but also the ruined or defective state of Indian agriculture. Like so many early nineteenth-century European travelers, Buchanan found it hard to comprehend a landscape in which dry and wet seasons were so strongly marked and not subject, like his native Scotland, to mist and rain throughout much of the year. Despite the fact that he was traveling at the driest time of the year, when much of the vegetation was dormant and parched, and cultivation was at a virtual standstill, Buchanan repeatedly disparaged the territory he traversed as being devoid of "verdure" and having a "desert appearance," as if this were its permanent state. Like many of his contemporaries, Buchanan found the dry plains "barren," and "bare,"[47] the "nakedness" of the countryside unappealing. To be pleasing to the European eye, India needed to be "clothed," whether with flowery meadows and well-kempt woodlands, or with the kind of dense and exuberant forest vegetation that was said to "clothe the tropical plains of South America."[48] Instead, relieved by only occasional patches of cultivation, the Carnatic landscape reminded Buchanan of the Scottish moors, except that it was "still more barren."[49]

Apart from the unimproved wastes of his own country, Buchanan had in mind two very different models of landscape against which to assess South India. One was the luxuriant vegetation (he did not call it "tropical") of southeast Bengal and Chittagong on the eastern shore of the Bay of Bengal, where he had traveled and botanized between 1796 and 1798. He had found little about the dense and exotic vegetation of this region, with its palms, bamboos, and creepers, to remind him of his native scenery, but he still declared it "highly pleasing," both for its novelty and for its "beauty and grandeur."[50] But the second, in many ways more dominant, image in Buchanan's mind was that of rural Britain, as transformed by the agrarian revolution, with its enclosed fields, stone walls and tidy hedges, with fattened livestock grazing on improved pastures or snug in stables and barns.[51] South Indian cultivators appeared by contrast to be indolent and "slovenly," though it seemed to Buchanan that the land itself, far from being naturally deficient, was "perfectly fitted for the English manner of cultivation" if only it were "enclosed . . . and planted with hedge-rows."[52] To Buchanan, as to many other travelers, the absence of enclosed fields reinforced the impression of "nakedness" and compared unfavorably with England and "with all that is rural and secure in its crowded and neatly dressed inclosures."[53] Such was the apparent backwardness of Indian agriculture that, according to Buchanan, a "meliorating succession of crops" was "utterly unknown," and "scarcely any attention" was paid to "the improvement of the breed of labouring cattle, and still less providing them with sufficient nourishment."[54]

That Buchanan, like so many of his contemporaries, thought in terms of "improvement" and judged India's agriculture and landscapes accordingly, is hardly surprising. This, after all, was Britain's "age of improvement," in which ideas of progressive change—in agriculture, manufacturing, and society at large—were rife, and were seen to combine moral worth and scientific rationality with the benefits of capitalist enterprise and private property.[55] Nor was it surprising that ideas of improvement and "improving landlords" should readily establish themselves overseas and become a basis for colonial agrarian policy and the "rule of property." In India, particularly in Bengal, Buchanan's home province, they had become firmly embodied in the principles behind the Permanent Settlement of 1793.[56] It was little more than a decade before Buchanan's south Indian journey that Major James Browne had advanced a plan for "improving" the Jungle Mahals,[57] and Philip Francis had spoken of Bengal as an "estate"—"the greatest, the most improvable, and the most secure, that ever belonged to any state."[58] By the early 1800s ideals of improvement were present in the mind of almost every British traveler in India and framed almost every account of its landscape.

As he neared Seringapatam, at the heart of Tipu's former domains, Buchanan saw "waste" and "desolation" almost everywhere, partly caused, he believed, by recent warfare but also by the "wanton caprice of Tippoo" and his "bad system of government." Reading the evil effects of tyranny into the dilapidated state of the countryside, Buchanan remarked: "The temples, villages, and dams have been broken down, the canals choked, and every plantation of trees totally ruined, while a great extent has been laid waste for hunting ground."[59] However, he sought to emphasize the benefits that had already resulted from British rule and the contrast, inscribed on the landscape, between present tranquility and former rapacity. Since Tipu's defeat, he claimed, everything had begun to wear a look of "restoration." "The villages are rebuilding, the canals are clearing; and in place of antelopes and forest guards, we have the peaceful bullock returning to his useful labour."[60]

This last comment reflected the fact that bullocks, as well as their agricultural uses, had been essential to the conduct of war in this region, the means by which heavy ordnance was hauled from place to place and food supplied to armies criss-crossing the ravaged countryside. But it was suggestive, too, of the dual symbolism of animals in the writing of the period. Domesticated animals, like the "peaceful bullock" evoked an idyll of rural stability, order, and productivity. At the same time, animals outside this domesticated sphere, like the countryside they inhabited, symbolized the threatening hostility of untamed nature and the decline of the good government needed to keep them at bay. In his travels, Buchanan repeatedly remarked upon the presence of tigers, leopards, and others of the "tiger kind," seeing them as a persistent danger to village livestock (even to his own camp).[61] In the interior of Mysore, as in other parts of South India, there were also wild elephants to threaten villagers and their crops, and cause further rural depopulation.[62]

But not all of Buchanan's narrative was darkened by a pessimistic view of Indian agriculture and the human and animal tyrants that preyed upon it. Indeed, Buchanan was one of the first European travelers (especially scientific travelers) to write in what we can begin to recognize as a Romantic vein. To some extent Buchanan's Romantic inclinations were most evident in his constant disappointment at the "barrenness" and apparent lack of beauty in the arid and desolate landscape of South India. But, as Peter Womack has cogently argued for the Scottish Highlands in the period following the suppression of the Jacobite rebellion in 1746—an example the many Scots in East India Company employ knew well—ideas of capitalist improvement were far from incompatible with Romanticism. "Officially," he notes, "Romance and Improvement were opposites: naïve and imported, past and present, tradition and innovation. But in reality they were twins."[63] In North Britain the process of reconciling the two was effected in various ways—through the literary output of authors like Sir Walter Scott, through the application to Highland landscapes of the pictorial conventions of the picturesque, and through narratives of travel, like those of James Bosworth and Thomas Pennant. In Buchanan's time, or later, each of these had its counterpart in British India: indeed, in several instances precisely the same figures were involved and had a comparable influence on perception and taste.[64]

As he quit the plains of the Carnatic and entered the hills of Mysore, Buchanan began to see, and appreciate, "a wild but romantic country," consisting of "low hills, intermixed with little cultivated vallies," and occasional "very stately" forests.[65] In October 1800 he reached one of the scenic high points of his journey—the falls on the River Kaveri at Gangana. As in Britain, waterfalls in India were prominent objects of Romantic observation and reflection (though there was some resentment that they were often prior sites of Hindu worship, their beauty disfigured by "superstitious" practices).[66] The "grandeur" of the 200-foot-high Kaveri falls drew from Buchanan one of the few passages of unreserved enthusiasm in his entire journey: significantly it was for a sight of pure nature rather than one of human toil and husbandry. "I have never seen any cataract that for grandeur could be compared with this," he began, quickly adding:

> but I shall not attempt to describe its broken woody banks, its cloud of vapour, its rainbow, its thundering noise, nor the immense slippery rocks from whence the dizzy traveller views the awful whirlings of its tumultuous abyss. All these, except in magnitude and sublimity, exactly resemble those of the other waterfalls I have seen. The pencil of an artist might well be employed in imitating its magnificent scenery, and would convey a better idea of its grandeur than my power of description can venture to attempt.[67]

Nor was it only the waterfall that delighted him and tested his "power of description." In late November 1800, as he crossed the Ghats into Malabar, Buchanan was impressed by the changes he saw in the vegetation and scenery. On the road to Palghat he noted: "The country through which I passed is the most beautiful that I have ever seen. It resembles the finest parts of Bengal; but its trees are loftier, and its palms more numerous."[68] A few days later, still thinking of Bengal and Chittagong, Buchanan found himself in a "very beautiful country," its luxuriant vegetation fed by the southwest monsoon and cascading streams. Here there were rural scenes unmatched on the eastern side of the Ghats, with "fine verdant fields of corn" and "groves of fruit-trees," with mangoes, plantains, and jackfruit in abundance.[69]

For scientific travelers like Buchanan the zealous pursuit of botany and the aesthetic enjoyment of scenery were seldom far apart. For him, as for several of the naturalists who sought to follow after him (such as Jacquemont and Hooker, neither of whom actually reached the region), Malabar possessed the alluring quality of an enchanted garden. As a botanical province, it was already known from the large number of plants that had been described by, and illustrated for, the Dutch naturalist Hendrick van Rheede in his *Hortus Malabaricus* in the seventeenth century.[70] Although the word "tropical" never seems to have entered Buchanan's vocabulary, the *Hortus* had made Malabar a tropical Eden in the botanists' collective imagination, its rich and varied vegetation the epitome of what "tropical" vegetation ought to be, the reverse, in fact, of what so much of India actually appeared to be.[71]

Tod's Rajasthan

In Francis Buchanan, armed with an official mission and an "improving" brief, the Romantic evocation of nature remained a subdued motif. But even before Buchanan left India in 1815, a Romantic sensibility had widely imbued British residents and travelers. James Tod, writing two decades after Buchanan, showed a far more empathetic engagement with the landscape of Rajasthan than did Buchanan with the Carnatic and Mysore, and brought to his account of the region a style of writing and a wealth of historical and literary allusions that heralded Romanticism's growing ascendancy in India.

Tod's *Annals and Antiquities of Rajasthan*, first published in 1829, rapidly established itself as one of the most influential accounts of India as a "feudal" society.[72] In detailing the lives, deeds, and legends of the Rajput princes and princesses of a region that remained only indirectly under British control, the *Annals* were partly an attempt to give Hindus the kind of "national" history that earlier Orientalists had believed to be lacking.[73] It was Tod's hope that, "however slight the analogy between the chronicles of the Hindus and those of Europe, as historical works"— that is, despite the mythology and "fictions" that marred so many Indian sources—they would "serve to banish the reproach which India has so long laboured under of possessing no record of past events."[74] Given Tod's historical task, and his evidently affectionate feeling for the land and people of Rajasthan, his work has often been represented as a classic example of Orientalist scholarship; but it might with equal justice be deemed an essay in high Romanticism. Giving India a history, and endowing that "pre-bourgeois past" with lively characters and stirring events, was itself characteristic of much Romantic writing about India, as it was in Europe.[75]

The *Annals* were enthused with a Romantic delight in the Rajput princely order, by Tod's day much decayed and unthreatening to British power, and set against the scenery of Rajasthan whose distinct and dramatic landscape had already attracted the attention of earlier writers.[76] Medievalism was one of the central tropes of Romanticism in India as it was in Europe, but, like the appreciation of ruins, to which it was closely allied, it bore a highly ambivalent character. On the one hand, it leant itself to a pleasurable and nostalgic indulgence in the epic deeds and picturesque legacies of a distant time, where things seemed simpler and more stable than the inexorable change and encroaching mechanization of the present-day.[77] Tod approvingly quoted Byron:

... there is a power
And magic in the ruin'd battlement,
For which the palace of the present hour
Must yield its pomp, and wait till ages are its dower.[78]

Emma Roberts was likewise one of several authors who, in praising Tod's "admirable work," saw in North India and Rajasthan fond echoes of Europe's Middle Ages (the subject of her own earlier writing), and objects of "feudal grandeur" which transported "the European stranger back to the ages of chivalry."[79] But at the same time India's still extant medievalism often appeared barbaric and cruel, or, at best, as an anachronism in a bustling and enlightened age of industry and empire. In this underlying ambiguity India's medievalism was expressive of the constant dualism that shaped colonial Romanticism, combining a desire to luxuriate in India's past, to enjoy the "picturesque" ruin or revel in the colorful and animated sight of a cavalcade of Sikh or Maratha horsemen, with a superior imperative to censure, moralize, and "improve."

Interweaving his personal experiences with Rajput history and legend, Tod recounted his own journeys through Rajasthan between 1819 and 1822, and it is in these sections of the *Annals* that his Romantic sensibilities become most evident. Unlike Buchanan and many other travel writers of the period, Tod's narrative begins *in medias res*, with the author already ensconced in Rajasthan and Romantically involved with the land, its people and culture, rather than as an outsider, peering in from outside, venturing into a new and alien land. Even so, Tod's travelogue begins with a characteristically external allusion to European literature (albeit refracted through an imagined Africa). He and his fellow officers had been camped in the Udaipur valley in Mewar, "the most diversified and most romantic spot on the continent of India," but after two years in this enchanted place, ennui had set in. "Never," Tod wrote, invoking Samuel Johnson's Ethiopian prince, "did Rasselas sigh more for escape" from such "blissful captivity."[80] In October 1819 Tod and his party quit this tranquil spot and set out for the "sterile plains of the sandy desert of Marwar" (Jodhpur).[81]

In the course of his travels, Tod observed large tracts of cultivable land that should have supported flourishing crops, but which, like the Carnatic plains traversed by Buchanan, exhibited instead "the effects of warfare and rapine." Here the territory had been subject not to the rulers of Mysore, but to the "predatory hordes" of the Marathas and freebooting Pindaris, or even earlier to the Mughals and Pathans, the "Goths and Vandals" of Rajasthan. The countryside had not been freed from its oppressors until 1817, when, according to Tod, it was at last able to enjoy the "blessings of peace" and the protection of the British.[82] Nature's bounty, and the human ability to enhance natural beauty and productivity through diligent toil, was a common theme of Tod's. Combining the ethos of Romanticism with the doctrine of improvement, it also served to heighten an underlying contrast between the abundance of nature and the bitter consequence of human misrule. "Nature," he remarked of one well-favored valley, adorned with the "useful mangoe" and the "picturesque tamarind," "has been lavish of her beauties to this romantic region."[83] Experiencing a similar scene of abundance and contentment on a later journey, Tod remarked that "the peasantry were smiling at the sight of the luxuriant young crops of wheat, barley, and gram, aware that no ruthless hand could now step between them and the bounties of Heaven."[84]

In the wilder parts of Rajasthan Tod and his companions passed through scenery that was rugged and mountainous, presenting a very different kind of Romantic landscape from the cultivated plains and fecund valleys. Without extensive jungles to mar the view and menace the traveler, here was a landscape that leant itself to the commanding eye and the roving imagination. This was a landscape of craggy outcrops, dotted with picturesque temples and ruined forts, steeped in history and myth. In the Aravalli mountains that divided Mewar from Marwar there was scarcely a rock or stream that had not "some legend attached to it."[85] Mountains and solitude were the cue for a Romantic soliloquy: crossing one pass, Tod remarked,

> Who, that has a spark of imagination, but has felt the indescribable emotion which the gloom and silence of a Gothic cathedral excites? The very extent provokes a comparison humiliating to the pygmy spectator, and this is immeasurably increased when the site is the mountain pinnacle, where man and his works fade into nothing in contemplating the magnificent expanse of nature.[86]

"What a sight for the antiquary!" Tod exclaimed as he attempted to describe this wild locality and the "solitary" temple that sat in its midst, even while modestly disclaiming that: "It would present no distinct picture to the eye, were I to describe each individual edifice within the scope of vision." Nearby, on the opposite side of the valley, stood a "simple monumental shrine":

> It was most happily situated, being quite isolated, overlooking the road leading to Marwar, and consisted of a simple dome of very moderate dimensions, supported by columns, without any intervening object to obstruct the view of the little monumental altar arising out of the centre of the platform. It was the Sybilline temple of Tivoli in miniature. To it, over rock and ruin, I descended. Here repose the ashes of the Troubadour of Mewar, the gallant Prithwiraj, and his heroine wife, Tarra Bahe whose lives and exploits fill many a page of the legendary romances of Mewar.[87]

In this passage the reader is presented with the narrator's personal musing upon (and physical engagement with) the landscape, but also a scene that has both Indian historical and legendary associations and (via "Sybilline" temples and troubadours) connections with European history, architecture, literature, and scenery. The whole, moreover, forms in the traveler's all-seeing eye a scenic ensemble in which the diverse elements—nature, God, history, legend, architecture, topography—merge to create a single visual and emotional impression. The attempt to depict "scenes," to make vivid word-pictures out of landscapes, to fuse elements of a remembered Europe with an imagined India, was common not only to Tod but many other Romantic writers in India.[88]

From this vantage point, Tod and his party began their descent into the plains of Marwar, already identified as "the region of death." Mountains rose up every side,

> their summits, as they caught a ray of the departing sun, reflecting on our sombre path a momentary gleam from the masses of rose-coloured quartz which crested them. Noble fortresses covered every face of the hills and the bottom of the glen, through which, along the margin of the serpentine torrent which we repeatedly crossed, lay our path ... [P]artly from the novelty and grandeur of the scene, and partly from the invigorating

coolness of the air, our mirth became wild and clamorous: a week before, I was oppressed with a thousand ills; and now I trudged the rugged path, leaping the masses of granite which had rolled into the torrent.[89]

The highland scene, and an encounter with wild-looking Meras, the "mountaineers" (mountain-dwellers) of Rajasthan, made Tod wish, by a common conceit, that, rather than his deficient prose, he had "the pencil of a master to paint the scene." Inevitably, his thoughts turned to the artist almost invariably cited on these occasions: "It was a subject for Salvator Rosa."[90] But even in the depths of his romanticizing, Tod did not lose sight of a more utilitarian agenda. No scientist himself, he nevertheless interspersed his narrative with remarks on geology, ethnography, climate, and vegetation, remarking that he knew "no portion of the globe which would yield to the scientific traveller more abundant materials for observation than the alpine Aravulli."[91] He called for a "scientific party" to be appointed to "anatomise" this "important portion of India" and report on its "antiquaries" and natural history. But Tod's zeal in calling for the production of a work on "*Aravali delineated* by the hand of science," was tempered by the chastening thought that John Tod, his cousin, chosen for precisely this task had died, aged 22, only six months after his arrival in India.[92] As so often, death haunted Tod's Romantic sensibilities.

Tod commenced a second journey through southern Rajasthan in late January 1820, but this time the pleasures of travel were blighted by illness and the death of several of his companions. Cholera, having erupted in Bengal three years earlier, was now rife in central and western India. But even though sickness and death cast a lengthening shadow over this narrative, Tod still found time to rhapsodize over the landscape and revel in its historical associations. In this second journey, the dual perspective of Tod's improving Romanticism was even more evident. Having immersed himself in the history and culture of the Rajputs, he was able to identify and empathize with the warrior elite of Rajasthan while at the same time standing apart from them, from their barbarism and medievalism, and so be a modern man, the representative of a more scientific civilization. Romanticism could thus be both retrospective and prospective, immersing itself one moment in "feudal" antiquity while almost simultaneously championing the seemingly contrary cause of capitalist modernity.

In February 1820, Tod looked down from a high escarpment onto the plains of Mewar stretched out below. The ridge afforded him a stunning *coup d'oeil* and "one of the most diversified scenes, whether in a moral, political, or picturesque point of view," he had ever beheld. From this commanding height his eye traversed "all the grand theatres of the history of Mewar"—from Chittoor, "the palladium of Hinduism," through the mountainous Aravalli, "the shelter of her heroes," to the lands seized by the "barbarian Toork" (the Muslims) and Marathas. "What associations, what aspirations," Tod exulted, "does this scene conjure up for one who feels as a Rajpoot for this fair land." The flat plain through which he and his party had passed appeared

> as a deep basin, fertilised by numerous streams, fed by huge reservoirs in the mountains, and studded with towns which once were populous, but are for the most part now in ruins, though the germ of incipient prosperity is just appearing. From this height I condensed all my speculative ideas on a very favourite subject—the formation of a canal to unite the ancient and modern capitals of Mewar, by which her soil might be made to return a tenfold harvest, and famine be shut out for ever from her gates. My eye embraced the whole line of the Bairis, from its outlet at the Oodisagar, to its passage within a mile of Cheetore, and the benefit likely to accrue from such a work appeared incalculable. What new ideas would be opened to the Rajpoot, on seeing the trains of oxen, which now creep slowly along with merchandise for the capital, exchanged for boats gliding along the canal; and his fields, for miles on each side, irrigated by bilateral cuts, instead of the creaking Egyptian wheel.[93]

Heber: Romanticism and the "Egregious Griffin"

One of the most influential—but also one of the most contentious—figures in Romantic travel writing in India was Reginald Heber, the Anglican Bishop of Calcutta from 1823 until his death in 1826. Already a mature man and an established literary figure when he arrived in India, Heber brought with him to India a language suffused with literary Romanticism and a plethora of imported images and associations which he freely transferred to the subcontinent during his travels, especially in North India in 1824–5. That Heber, unlike Buchanan and Tod, was a relative newcomer to India when he wrote his *Narrative* made him more dependent on the ideas he brought with him than if he had lived and worked in India for twenty years.

There was surely some justice in the view of those who saw Heber as an "egregious griffin,"[94] whose Romanticism obscured rather than illuminated his understanding of India and whose travel writing was marred by inaccuracy, superficiality and a failure to appreciate the essential differences between India and Europe.[95] Few travel writers in India were more criticized than Heber and yet his literary style and pious reputation (aided by the widely felt tragedy of his death) made him a figure of exceptional authority. As late as the 1850s his *Narrative of a Journey through the Upper Provinces of India* was reputed to be "pre-eminently the *magnum opus* as the guide to the traveller in India."[96] His work was, besides, widely emulated and cited by other travelers, including Emma Roberts, who observed that Heber "possessed a true relish for the sublime and beautiful" and "delighted with all a poet's enthusiasm in the picturesque."[97] In fact, Heber's *Narrative* and the response to it epitomizes the ambivalent triumph of colonial Romanticism and the difficulty of reconciling a moral and poetic representation of India with the more strictly scientific observation of India aspired to (despite their own Romantic inclinations) by Jacquemont, Hooker, and other later writers.

Heber was born in Cheshire in 1783. After traveling in eastern Europe and Scandinavia in 1805–6, he married Amelia, the daughter of Dr William Shipley, Dean of St Asaph in North Wales, and settled down to the life of a country vicar in Shropshire. In 1822, at the age of 39, he was unexpectedly offered the post of Bishop of Calcutta. Heber believed there was much he could do to serve Christianity in India, but wondered whether it was in his family's best interest to live in the tropics. He and his wife had recently lost their first child, Amelia's own health was poor, and a brother of hers had died of fever in the West Indies a decade earlier. Both were concerned whether their second child—Amelia was pregnant again—would survive in India. Heber consulted several doctors (including Charles Darwin's father, their family physician) about the likely effects of India on their health; but they offered contradictory advice. One said that going to Calcutta was to invite certain death; another that for Europeans who guarded their health the risk was no greater than in staying at home.[98] Heber decided that his evangelical calling outweighed the uncertain risks to his family's health, and in June 1823 they sailed for India, "that land of disappointment, and sorrow, and death."[99]

Reginald Heber had long been interested in the spread of Christianity in the East, but, in addition, "these regions had a romantic charm in his mind."[100] Certainly, Heber was well versed in Romantic literature before he arrived in India. As a poet and writer of hymns (including the one of 1819 which began brightly with "Greenland's icy mountains" and concluded darkly with "heathens" bowing down to "wood and stone"), he was well known in British literary circles and had reviewed the work of several leading Romantics, including Southey and Byron.[101] The combination of Romanticism and Christianity gave Heber a ready-made language and a rich array of sensibilities, images, and associations through which to render exotic India intelligible to himself and his correspondents. As even his harshest critics noted, though, the narrative of his north Indian travels was taken, after his death and without the revisions he might otherwise have made, from the journal he had written for his wife. It was thus, like the letters and journals of Thomas Munro and others discussed in Chapter 2, initially intended for an intimate, female audience. As such its evocation of the Indian landscape belonged more to the empire of affect than to any more rigorous or scientific attempt to describe India. But with its publication Heber's journal crossed the slender dividing line between private sentiment and shared sensibility, between how one individual saw India and how it came to be collectively represented in print.

On the voyage out, when not studying Persian and Hindustani, Heber read *Quentin Durward* and commended the works of Sir Walter Scott to his somewhat bemused fellow passengers. The "hot and coppery sky" lowering over Sagar island at the mouth of the Hugli, and the corpses drifting past the ship, reminded him of Coleridge's *Rime of the Ancient Mariner*, with its "extremely vivid, and scarcely exaggerated ... descriptions of natural objects in tropical countries;" while lightning flashing across the night sky as they neared Calcutta recalled the "echoing vaults" of Padalon, the hellish underworld in Southey's *Curse of Kehama*.[102] In thus viewing India through the lens of Romantic literature, Heber was an extreme (but not exceptional) case. References to such self-consciously "Oriental" works as Southey's *Kehama* (1810) and Moore's *Lalla Rookh* (1817) infuse the travel literature of the period and, though their authors had never visited India, their works were repeatedly taken as authoritative guides to the country, its society and scenery.[103]

The circularity involved in such textual appropriation and recycling was extraordinary. Even as Southey reworked and embellished others' first-hand accounts of sati, Jagannath, and the famine of 1770,[104] his (and Milton's) poetic depictions of elephants and banyan trees were considered sufficiently accurate to be quoted in scientific texts and guidebooks to India.[105] But more than Southey and Moore and apart from Shakespeare, Milton, and Defoe, if there was one writer who, more than any other, was invoked by Europeans in India at this time it was Scott. Significantly, this was not for his only Indian novel, *The Surgeon's Daughter*, but for his early collections of Scottish ballads and for his historical novels, particularly *Rob Roy, Ivanhoe* and *Quentin Durward*.[106] India too seemed an antique land, barely touched by the age of improvement, still populated by warring tribes and feudal chiefs, and if much of India, like Scotland or pre-modern Europe appeared "rude and wild," so too did other parts resemble a "Highland Arcadia," with picturesque views and grand, romantic vistas.[107] To believe travel writers of the time, there was hardly a Maratha camp or troop of Sikh cavalry, a rugged pass or a misty glen that was not worthy of Scott's pen—or a painting by Salvator Rosa. Heber made repeated use of Scott and Rosa, occasionally working them both into a single scenic description.[108]

In their personal evaluation of India, Europeans employed many different literary tropes and topographical templates. At times, as we saw in Chapter 2, India served as a kind of biblical exegesis. At others, it echoed the *Arabian Nights*, recalled *Paradise Lost* or replayed scenes from *Hamlet* and *Macbeth*. Many of the most favored works—*Pilgrim's Progress, Don Quixote, Robinson Crusoe*—were themselves, however allegorically, tales of travel. Such familiar texts were the mental companions of almost every middle-class, early nineteenth-century traveler, and they helped give India, despite its evident exoticism, much of its "already-known," "pre-scribed" quality. Romanticism played upon and enlarged this pre-existing trove of literary texts, but it also showered upon India a wealth of new images and allusions from writers such as Moore, Coleridge, Southey, Wordsworth, the Shelleys, Byron, and Scott. These literary references were the common property of the British bourgeoisie, but (until the Indian middle classes adopted them as their own) they were clearly external and alien to India itself. By the 1820s and 1830s, as the Orientalist interest in India's literature and history (still evident in Tod) waned, so the need to attach India to Europe's more familiar literary, historical, and geographical associations increased in proportion.

Heber's sin was to carry these un-Indian associations to ludicrous lengths. Thus, Calcutta immediately reminded him of St Petersburg, that other "city of palaces;" Dhaka, still more implausibly, looked like Moscow. Every Indian river, if it did not resemble the Dee or Mersey, recalled the Don. The sight of Bengali cows contentedly grazing put him instantly in mind of the Dutch painter Cuyp; the "gothic architecture" of old mosques and palaces resembled Bolton Abbey. Fatehpur Sikri looked like Oxford while Delhi had him reaching for *Lalla Rookh*. The tribal chiefs of the Rajmahal hills had strayed out of the pages of *Rob Roy*; and the history of the Rajputs (as recounted Tod) came straight from *Ivanhoe*.[109] Seeing Bengal (or Ceylon, it seemed not to matter which) recalled the illustrations in Captain Cook's voyage to an equally tropical Tahiti.[110] When someone in Heber's camp cried out "the camels are coming," he misheard and, thinking they had said "The Campbells are coming," his mind spun off on a long train of childhood reverie.[111]

Even when not straining for geographical comparisons and literary companionship, Heber's sentimental Romanticism was seldom suppressed. In "An Evening Walk in Bengal," written for Amelia in July 1824, Heber began:

> Come walk with me the jungle through;
> If yonder hunter told us true,
> Far off, in desert dark and rude,
> The tyger holds his solitude . . .

And he continued:

> So rich a shade, so green a sod,
> Our English fairies never trod!
> Yet who in Indian bow'r has not stood,
> But thought on England's "good green wood?"
> And bless'd, beneath the palmy shade,
> Her hazel and her hawthorn glade,
> And breath'd a prayer (how oft in vain!)
> To gaze upon her oaks again?[112]

The extreme (and often absurd) subjectivity of these colonizing images and associations might seem to suggest that the European travelers of the period were seriously homesick men and women, with nothing but nostalgia on their minds and devoid of any intellectual capacity to see what actually passed before their eyes. That may indeed have been the case, especially with Heber; but there could be more to this almost constant invocation of other, more familiar, landscapes. In associationist thought, invoking comparisons and seeing resemblances was thought to aid critical observation and facilitate subsequent reflection and recall.[113] The need to make connections underpinned not merely the Romantic travel writing of the period but also much of its itinerant science. The medical topographer J.R. Martin was fond of quoting the Scottish Enlightenment philosopher Adam Ferguson to the effect that "all observation is suggested by comparison."[114]

Similarly, Joseph Hooker once remarked that part of the value of making mental associations was to focus more clearly on the "violation of the details," thus revealing how one apparently similar scene (of mountains, say, or vegetation) departed significantly from another that it otherwise closely resembled.[115] In 1854, shortly after the publication of the *Himalayan Journals,* Darwin asked his friend whether the "tropical vegetation" of Brazil was "as beautiful or nearly as beautiful" as that of the Himalaya. Hooker replied that that of Sikkim was "uncommonly fine," but did not match that of Brazil, the Khasi hills, or Chittagong. He added, though, as a cautionary aside, that the more he read and traveled, the more convinced he became "that our impressions are more the effects of association than ever."[116] As Hooker was aware, associations could mislead (as they often did through an excess of nostalgia or from a purely instinctive response), but, in the perceptive traveler, they could also stimulate detailed observation and render the local and exotic accessible to a universalizing discourse of travel, sentiment, and place. In Heber's *Narrative* such a discerning use of associationism seemed to be singularly lacking. But to his admirers this apparent superficiality in fact made India's strangeness and complexity more, not less, intelligible to the traveler's gaze, more open to the musings of the Romantic spirit.[117] To his detractors, however, the result was neither conducive to scientific observation nor faithful to the many, far-reaching differences that divided East from West.

Romancing the Himalaya

Since mountains were among the principal objects toward which the Romantic imagination and Europe's newfound feeling for nature were directed,[118] the Himalaya promised some of the most Romantic scenery on earth. Certainly, to many jaded Europeans, tired of being forever confined indoors by the heat or boxed up in a palanquin, the Himalaya offered a rare opportunity to roam with relative freedom and, through the physical enjoyment of walking and riding, stimulate their previously stifled Romantic inclinations. If the rest of India resembled "a vast prison," the mountains offered instead "emancipation" through the "power of wandering at will in the open air."[119] This pleasure was enhanced by the dramatic change in climate, vegetation, and scenery that accompanied the traveler who ascended into the Himalayan foothills. For visitors who felt "as if transported by some good genii from India to Europe,"[120] the change was as much corporeal as scenic: they felt as if they had gained a "new lease of life" after the "apathetic indolence" of hot, humid Calcutta.[121] Moreover, by entering the hills they found themselves traveling through time as well as space, returning to a distant home and a fondly recalled childhood. If the Himalayan landscape served to evoke "memory," it was a memory of a far distant land, not of India.[122]

Little known to the West before the 1800s,[123] the Himalaya became accessible to the British as a result of the Anglo-Gurkha war of 1815–16. The Scot James Baillie Fraser, who traveled in Kumaon in the western Himalaya during the later stages of the war, was one of the many Europeans who felt relief at leaving behind the "low Dhak jungle" of the plains, with their "desolate and barren aspect," and finding views instead that, "to one accustomed to the sober, though rich monotony of the level plains of Hindostan," were "quite bewitching and almost confounding."[124] He began to notice by the wayside "many old friends": brambles, wild strawberries and raspberries, pine trees and oaks. Ascending further into the mountains he saw "wild and rugged peaks": "Imagination," he declared, "cannot paint a wilder, more beautiful, or in some places more horrid glen." Reveling in associations that emotionally annexed the Himalaya to his own homeland, he continued:

> Asia was almost lost in our imagination: a native of any part of the British isles might here have believed himself wandering among the lovely and romantic scenes of his own country. The delight of such association of feeling can only be understood by those, who have lingered out a long term of expatriation, and who anxiously desire the moment of reunion with their native land.[125]

As another appreciative traveler, Major William Lloyd, similarly put it a few years later, this was "Europe not Asia"; in his case it was his boyhood in the Welsh hills that the vegetation and scenery of the Himalaya nostalgically conjured up.[126] Not only did Fraser find trees, flowers and rural scenes familiar from childhood: the vista so reminded him of home that he half wondered what Indians were doing there:

> The large extent of corn under the eye was nearly ripe; the reapers were at work; the wild brown hill with swelling round peaks rose above us, and but for the colour of the attendants, the whole scene had so highland an air, that it was difficult to believe it to be Indian.[127]

A few days' march took Fraser into a "noble forest" of oak, holly, rhododendron, and larch, interspersed with meadows filled with "European" flowers, a sight he "hailed with great satisfaction." Fraser confessed to being no botanist, but the "beautiful" ferns and "humble" buttercups gave rise to a "pleasing recollection," for in such "wild and remote regions, the remembrance of early days and youthful pleasures recurs, even when excited by trifles, with redoubled interest."[128] Higher still, there were birches and alders ("exactly similar to that which grows so commonly on the sides of the rivulets in Scotland") to stimulate his Proustian powers of recall.[129]

In time, through the researches of J. Forbes Royle, Joseph Hooker, and others, the botany of the Himalaya came to be extensively investigated and scientifically described, though seldom, even in the most technical of texts, without similar observations on the emotions and associations aroused by the sight so far from home of "European" trees and flowers.[130] In this respect, botanists, for all their professionalism, shared with their countrymen a common aesthetic sensibility. But nostalgia was only one of the many powerful responses the Himalaya provoked. The vast forests Fraser observed did more than appeal to his Romantic imagination; they also excited his "improving" indignation. "What a seeming waste of noble timber!" he exclaimed, "and how uselessly do these grand trees appear to flourish and decay!" The villagers could never "make use of them;" their consumption of timber was small, and even if it were greater they had "not tools with which to avail themselves of the abundance which these endless forests afford."[131] Mentally converting "noble" trees into "valuable" timber, he mused that, if it were only possible to transport

FIG. 6. The River Yamuna in the Himalaya, from R. Montgomery Martin, *The Indian Empire Illustrated* (1861). Reproduced by kind permission of the School of Oriental and African Studies, London.

this wealth of wood to the plains below, "it would be a most important acquisition."[132] For Fraser the Himalayan forests seemed inexhaustible, timeless, and under-exploited. Only a few decades later, as the commercial extraction of timber gathered pace, many European observers began to doubt whether the Himalayan forests were as anything like as inexhaustible as Fraser had imagined.[133]

Few Europeans were unmoved by the Himalaya. Honoria Lawrence, who in 1843 accompanied her husband Henry to the Residency in Kathmandu, described the mountains' extraordinary, almost unearthly, beauty, which put her in mind of Wordsworth's "Ode to Immortality."[134] Others, elated by their own emotional and aesthetic responses, were correspondingly dismayed at the "total insensibility" of the local population, or that of their guides and coolies, to such spectacular sights. So intense was this reaction against what was believed to be the local population's total lack of aesthetic appreciation that some British travelers felt an inherent right to appropriate such remarkable scenes of natural grandeur for themselves.[135] Such a privileging of European emotions could, however, give rise to its own bathos. When in May 1828 Major Archer gazed in admiration at one magnificent Himalayan panorama he turned to his Muslim servant and asked whether "the sight was not grander than any he had ever seen?" He was taken aback when the servant replied that he had been more impressed by the Vauxhall pleasure gardens in London, which "beat it hollow," as did the illuminations "when the English took Buonaparte." Archer admitted that this remark made him "come down a peg from the height to which my enthusiasm had elevated me;"[136] but even this unexpectedly deflating response served to reinforce the idea that Indians did not have the capacity to appreciate such magnificent scenery, that the aesthetics of landscape were simply beyond them.

There was, however, recognition that the Himalaya were "the peculiar abodes of the gods of the Hindoos," as Archer put it,[137] and that even the remotest parts of the mountains were far from being culturally uncolonized. Most European travelers, especially in the western Himalaya where pilgrims and shrines were most in evidence, had some awareness of the reverence in which the Hindus held the mountains and the sources of the sacred Ganges and Yamuna. Some even felt an affinity between the profundity of their own response to the Himalayan scenery and the religious sentiments of the "poor Hindoo" who paused "on his painful pilgrimage" at some "lovely spot" to rest and pray.[138] And yet, for many this did not significantly alter their sense of ownership of a landscape which seemed by its appearance and associations to belong more to Europe than to India. In late 1824 Heber characteristically drew both Christian inspiration and Romantic pleasure from "the Indian Caucasus." Not only did the mountains of Kumaon remind him of Snowdonia and arouse feelings of "intense delight and awe," but, as he ascended through "glens, forests, and views of the most sublime and beautiful description," he felt "as if climbing the steps of the altar of God's great temple."[139] Embarked on a pilgrimage of his own, and having crossed the heathen plains, approaching the mountains seemed to bring Heber measurably close to the Christian god. Spiritually as much as scenically, the Himalaya seemed to be the high point of his journey.

Inevitably, the Himalaya invited comparison with the mountains of Europe and especially with the Alps, which many European travelers had visited, read about, or knew from illustrations. Although the superior height of the Himalaya was duly acknowledged, there was often a feeling that they could not compete with the greater beauty and more appealing scale of the Alps. Extolling the mountain panorama to be seen from the house of his host Brian Hodgson at Darjeeling, Joseph Hooker confessed to his readers that the Swiss Alps, "though barely possessing half the sublimity, extent, or height of the Himalaya, are yet more beautiful." Even individual peaks, like the "stupendous mass" of Junnoo in east Nepal, he considered to be "far less picturesque" than the Matterhorn.[140] There was, indeed, a bleakness about the high Himalaya that appalled the Romantic imagination. The icy wastes of peaks and passes strayed well beyond the picturesque, beyond "delightful melancholy," into something far more sinister. The unbroken stillness of the peaks was "death-like" (an expression frequently used of the Himalaya), and the rugged scenes among the intervening passes were judged "awesome" and "very distressing."[141]

When, in the early 1840s, J.D. Cunningham reached upper Kanawar, he found the scenery "grand" but its "vastness and barrenness" "fatiguing." There were scenes of "naked grandeur," but he could not recall any as being "pleasing from their variety, or such as we would term picturesque from their contrasts." He warned "the admirer of nature unadorned" not to venture too far into the Himalaya, or even to go beyond Chini, where he or she could still "revel amidst scenes of surpassing luxuriance and beauty."[142] Cunningham was, however, one of the few early travelers to visit the high mountains in wintertime. He found the experience daunting:

Hills of snow are heaped high upon hills of snow, range retires beyond range, and naught relieves the drear and hoary waste or interferes with the awful stillness of the scene, save perhaps a dark and frowning precipice, or the voice of the blue river below, struggling with its fetters of rocks and ice. In contemplating these vast solitudes, illuminated by the setting sun, the mind of man is for a moment raised, and he feels and admires their sublimity. He stands majestic, the sole living being on the circumference of a world, but of a world half-formed or in ruin, or not fitted for him. The broad expanse of desolation wearies and appalls; the fatal cold and the waning day recall other thoughts, and he turns silent and subdued to seek relief and sympathy among his fellow mortals, and in the ordinary occupations of life.[143]

For all his excitement at reaching his long-sought-after goal, Joseph Hooker experienced similar sentiments when he looked out across the Tibetan plateau from the Donkia Pass in northeast Sikkim in September 1849: "There is no loftier country on the globe than that embraced by this view, and no more howling wilderness," he recorded. "Never, in the course of all my wanderings, had my eye rested on a scene so dreary and inhospitable."[144] Such dismal prospects drove some travelers to think of Mary Shelley—if not of the icy wastes of *Frankenstein*, then of the scenes of desolation in *The Last Man*.[145] For others, the "death-like" solitudes of the Himalaya, the "deadly paleness" of the eternal snows and the mist-enshrouded peaks, and the "sterility" and "nakedness" of the high passes,[146] seemed not to resemble anything remembered from Britain or continental Europe, but only eerily to echo the arid plains below.

Improving India

Romanticism in India, as in the West, assumed many different, often contradictory, forms. The glorification of wild nature was certainly one of these, though in India as we have seen this was frequently done obliquely through approving (or disappointed) comparisons with European scenery or by reference to its literary and pictorial representations. But more often than not a Romantic appreciation of nature was coupled with a simultaneous desire to "improve" India, both in the capitalistic sense of generating enhanced income and profit from the land and in terms of the aesthetic sense of transforming landscape that presently seemed either "naked" or obscurely overgrown with unsightly jungle.

The preference for a humanized, cultivated and orderly landscape over a wild and unkempt one was widely shared. Reporting on Dehra Dun in the western Himalaya in 1827, F.J. Shore, the Assistant Commissioner, wrote a long and lyrical description of the valley, extolling the remarkable beauty of its scenery. His eye descended from the "grand and sublime" mountains in the far distance to the changing seasonal hues of the sal (*Shorea robusta*) and sissoo (*Dalbergia latifolia*) forests of the lower slopes. But what at first appeared to be unstinting praise for the glories of untouched nature concluded with the abrupt observation: "Were there but cultivation and the habitations of man on the level between the river and hills, the scenery would be perfect."[147] The idea of an "improved" landscape often dovetailed with the perceived need for European enterprise to replace Indian ignorance and sloth. Reporting a few years before Shore on the geology of the western Himalaya, Captain J.D. Herbert was similarly struck by the physical beauty and productive potential of the Kumaon hills. He believed that if the "visionary" experiment of European settlement were to be tried anywhere in India, it stood the greatest chance of success in Dehra Dun, amid a landscape of "picturesque scenery," with green fields, hedges, and streams "that might almost remind one of the scenery of England." It was here, in this already seemingly idyllic spot, that Herbert believed there was the greatest need and opportunity for "European improvements."[148]

The doctrine of improvement, well established in India by the 1820s and 1830s, thus meant considerably more than ridding India of its ruins and restoring it to what it had been at an earlier, more peaceful and prosperous time. It also signified a desire to transform the country into something that looked and functioned like the rural landscape and agrarian economy of contemporary Britain. Certainly, this view was not without influential critics. Reacting against the zamindari system created by the Permanent Settlement of 1793, which sought to stimulate agrarian productivity by installing "improving" landlords, Thomas Munro in Madras argued against needless meddling by a government anxious "to make everything as English as possible in a country which resembles England in nothing." It was time, he urged in 1824, "that we should learn, that neither the face of the country, its property nor its society, are things that can be suddenly improved by any contrivance of ours, though they may be greatly injured by what we mean for their good... we should take every country as we find it."[149] But in general the aesthetics of landscape and the widely held perception that Indian agriculture was anachronistic and defective served to reinforce and lend legitimacy to the revenue-hungry ambitions of the Company and its servants. Buchanan's desire for enclosures in the Carnatic, Tod's plea for canals in Rajasthan, Herbert's penchant for European homesteads in Dehra Dun—these were but three manifestations of a widely held "improving" mindset.

Nor was the ideology of improvement confined to officials. Indeed, it was particularly marked among Christian clergymen and missionaries, like William Tennant, Reginald Heber, and Alexander Duff, in whose writings (covering, between them, the period from the 1790s to the 1840s) improvement took on a strong moral as well as economic purpose.[150] Especially revealing in this regard was the formation of the Agricultural and Horticultural Society of India, set up in Calcutta in 1820, largely through the efforts of the Baptist missionary, William Carey. Carey was a keen amateur botanist and close friend of William Roxburgh, superintendent of the Calcutta botanic garden. He undertook the posthumous publication of Roxburgh's *Flora Indica*, a tribute, like so many other botanical works, to a deceased friend but also a floral hymn to nature as God's handiwork.[151] That the initiative for the Agricultural and Horticultural Society came from a missionary in part demonstrated the government's own reluctance to act in such matters, but it also showed how an improving agenda might simultaneously be an evangelizing one, replacing "heathen" jungles and "indolent" agriculturalists with the more morally acceptable prospect of tidy villages and industrious laborers toiling in their orderly fields.[152]

In his manifesto calling for the creation of the Society, Carey declared that it would "tend to enlarge the ideas of the peasantry, to dissipate their prejudices, to call forth their latent energies, to encourage their industry, and promote their respectability and usefulness in society."[153] He continued:

> The draining of marshes, the cultivation of large tracts of country now not only useless, but the resort of savage beasts and the source of severe diseases—the improvement of stock—the creation of a larger quantity

of the necessaries and conveniences of life, and of raw materials for manufactures—the gradual conquest of the indolence which in Asiatics is almost become a second nature,—and the interdiction of habits of cleanliness, and a neat arrangement of domestic conveniences, in the place of squalid wretchedness, neglect and confusion; in a word, of industry and virtue in the room of idleness and vice, might all, by an association of this nature in time become obviously important even to the natives themselves.[154]

Once established, the Agricultural and Horticultural Society enjoyed a fair degree of success: after the Asiatic Society, it was the most influential and best-known society in India and it similarly spawned a number of up-country imitators and affiliates. It claimed successive governors-general as its patrons (some of whom, like Lord Bentinck, showed a keen personal interest in its operations) and by the late 1830s it boasted a membership of around 460, including military and medical officers, lawyers, clergymen, merchants, British indigo planters, and Bengali zamindars. It had outposts in towns and military stations across northern India, including, thanks to the enterprising Major Napleton, a particularly active branch at Bhagalpur in the planter country of east Bihar.[155] The Society further enjoyed the support of successive superintendents of the Calcutta botanic garden, who saw its activities as complementing the more strictly scientific work of their own under-funded establishment.[156]

The commitment to "improvement" outlasted Carey's death in 1834 and officially the Society's mission remained, as one of its presidents put it, to rescue Indian agriculture from a state "more rude ... than that of England two centuries ago."[157] But such "improving" ambitions proved difficult to sustain. Although members of the Society amassed a vast repository of knowledge about Indian agricultural practices and energetically encouraged the introduction of new food crops, like potatoes or improved varieties of sugarcane,[158] for many among its predominantly European membership the Society had a more self-regarding role. It was the principal agency for the distribution of seeds and fruit trees which it imported, principally from Britain. Branch societies held regular flower, fruit, and vegetable shows at which prizes were awarded to European residents, Indian zamindars or their malis (gardeners) for the finest displays of larkspur and lupins or—even more outlandishly—for the best celery, kale and mangel-wurzels.[159] It was not difficult for skeptical travelers to ridicule such expatriate obsessions, as their hosts insisted they admire their beds of "stunted, shrivelled, and worm-eaten exotics" or fed them coarse and inedible "British vegetables" for their supper.[160] The partial shift in the Society's focus from agriculture to floriculture in the 1840s further suggested that "improvement" could easily degenerate into little more than the recreational pursuit of European pastimes.

There was, nonetheless, a growing sense by the 1840s and 1850s that India was changing and that the face of the country was very different from what it had been half a century earlier. In some areas, such as the lower slopes of the Kumaon hills or in the Ganges–Yamuna doab (interfluvial tract), there was mounting concern at the rapid rate of deforestation and the effect this might have in reducing rainfall and thereby causing drought and famine.[161] But it would be a mistake to overemphasize the impact of desiccationist ideas on European perceptions of the Indian landscape before the 1850s. In the eyes of many travelers and observers the British deserved the credit for positively transforming the landscape, liberating it from its former barrenness and "desolation." In their estimation, through the construction of roads and irrigation canals, and the planting of many thousands of trees (mainly from the botanic garden at Saharanpur) along roadsides and canal banks, the Indian countryside was beginning to exhibit clear signs of "improvement."[162] The transformation was most marked in the semi-arid Punjab, where cultivated fields were rapidly replacing desert, "bushy jungle," and "pastoral waste."[163]

More than anything else in the pre-railroad age, irrigation canals were transforming the landscape. The excavation of the West Yamuna Canal (1823–43) and the opening of the Ganges Canal in 1854 were hailed as a boon to agriculture and a check to famine that as recently as 1838 had devastated large parts of northern India. Canal construction symbolized an age in which British engineering had begun to outstrip the achievements of the Mughals and to imprint itself no less visibly upon the surrounding landscape than had Mughal tombs and palaces. One clergyman rhapsodized that the Ganges Canal was a work which "in grandeur of design and wisdom of purpose, throws into the shade all, even the greatest, works of the Mahomedan emperors."[164] There were some for whom this marked the advance of Christian civilization across a heathen landscape. One former army officer remarked in his account of the Anglo-Sikh War:

When the Punjaub, paralysed and withered under the military authority of Runjeet Singh, first became ours, it never entered into the imagination of the most sanguine, to conceive the change which a few short years of wise and enlightened rule would produce in the outward face of the country. Whole tracts of forest and jungle have been cleared and brought under cultivation; canals, hundreds of miles in extent ... are in course of construction; commerce and agriculture are encouraged, and every possible facility is afforded to the native mind to develop the resources which nature has placed within the reach of its inhabitants. We cannot but feel that it is only a Christian power, which could have exercised this happy influence; for Christianity has been in all ages, and under all circumstances, the pioneer of enlightenment and civilisation.[165]

Captain Baird Smith, writing in 1849, appeared no less convinced of the immense improvements that canals would bring to northern India and the stimulus they would provide to "tropical agriculture." "This great tract," he wrote of the Ganges–Yamuna doab, "will become the garden of the North-Western Provinces; and we shall hear no more of the devastating famines, which have hitherto swept across it, bringing physical wretchedness and moral degradation in their train."[166] The landscape of India, depicted not long before as desolate and ruined, had from the perspective of many a European, now begun to bear the imprint of an "improving" regime, colonizing a once barren countryside. Across a landscape where Romanticism and improvement had helped pioneer an ideology of aesthetic distaste and moral dismay, science and technology had—it seemed—begun to work their transforming effect.

4
FROM THE ORIENT TO THE TROPICS

THAT INDIA WAS, IN CERTAIN FUNDAMENTAL RESPECTS, DIFFERENT from Britain and from Europe was not seriously in question in the early nineteenth century. Although writers on travel, nature, and topography (especially those of a Romantic persuasion) repeatedly made comparisons with Europe, India's alterity remained profound and often perplexing: it was multifaceted, inconclusive, enigmatic.[1] India was more than the merely strange, a Europe lost in another place and time. The testing question was how India's differences most cogently manifested themselves, how far India stood alone, a "continent" in its own right, or was best understood and represented by being aligned with such other geo-cultural domains as "the Orient" and "the Tropics." Like Romanticism, with which it had many affinities, but in a manner more amenable to science than Orientalism, the idea of India's "tropicality" was one externally imposed but increasingly resonant means of trying to define, compare, and contextualize India, to render it more accessible to the European imagination and ultimately to its colonizing processes.

The Emergence of Tropicality

The term "tropicality" has recently come to signify the conceptualization and representation of the tropics in European imagination and experience. The tropics are commonly treated as a geographical fact, technically defined by the lines of latitude 23°–28' north and south of the Equator that correspond to the seasonal oscillations of the earth relative to the sun; but the idea of such a region, and the varied associations it has given rise to, have a long and complex history in European thought. If Orientalism, in Edward Said's influential formulation, appears to have a timeless quality, transcending conventional historical periodization, tropicality can be seen as having (as well as a continuing essentialization of tropical otherness) a close and evolving relationship with the history of European expansionism. Although one can trace the origins of such a mental construct further back, into classical and medieval European thought, the idea of the tropics developed primarily as a result of the European "voyages of discovery" in the fifteenth and sixteenth centuries, the subsequent opening up of maritime routes, and the establishment of the Iberian empires in, or on the margins of, Africa, America, and Asia. In this way, the perceived contrast between Europe and the tropics (registered through scenery, climate, vegetation, disease, animal life, and human diversity) began to emerge. So did a perception of the common characteristics of the tropical regions themselves, aided by intra-tropical linkages and the transfers of plants, animals, peoples, and diseases.[2]

The gathering pace of exploitation, as well as exploration, fostered perceptions of the tropics as places of Edenic plenitude and fecundity, enlivened and elevated to heights of wonder and enchantment by the brilliant colors and curious appearance of the animals, birds, fish, and other creatures that inhabited these regions, as well as by strange fruits and exotic spices, by the apparent abundance of minerals, precious stones, and natural resources. There was about the tropics an exhilarating and alluring air of novelty, of untouched nature and of "innocent" and "primitive" peoples inhabiting a primordial, almost dreamlike world.[3] But the tropics were also the "torrid zone" and came to signify abundance and excess in more troubling ways—diseases of a kind or intensity unknown in Europe, seasons of intolerable heat and enervating humidity (unrelieved by the moderating seasons of more temperate lands), plagues of insect pests, violent storms and crashing surf, and a predation and savagery in nature that ranged from the sharks circling menacingly at sea and tigers prowling in dark jungles to the superstition and savagery of the "tropical races" themselves.[4] Seemingly so inimical to white health and settlement, the American tropics also came to signify the home (whether considered a necessity dictated by climate or a cruel and abhorrent aberration) of black slavery.[5]

Onto this original stock of early European impressions was grafted a more systematic and scientific understanding of the tropics. The opening phase of what might be termed scientific tropicality (rather than the more casual and piecemeal observations made over the previous three hundred years) can be dated from roughly the 1750s to the 1820s. This phase was particularly associated with the apogee of British and French plantation societies in the West Indies (and the accompanying investigations into the islands' diseases, climate, and natural history), the Anglo-French exploration of the South Pacific (through such celebrated figures as George Anson, Louis Antoine de Bougainville, and James Cook),[6] and the scientific labors of such itinerant naturalists as Joseph Banks, Johan Reinhold Forster and his son Georg, and Alexander von Humboldt.[7] It was at this time that the "great world of the tropics" began to "exert its influence on conceptions of nature."[8] However, in this first phase of scientific tropicality, and certainly in terms of medicine and arrival history, much of the scientific investigation was coastal and insular (a point which Richard Grove's work on "tropical island Edens" has helped emphasize),[9] based in the West Indies, West Africa, Mauritius, Ceylon, Java, and Sumatra.[10]

But science did not stand alone and the scientific discovery of the tropics was accompanied, and in part informed, by its literary counterpart. Much as the British adopted Daniel Defoe's seventeenth-century classic *Robinson Crusoe* as their principal depiction of the island tropics, so the French found in Henri Bernardin de Saint-Pierre's Rousseau-esque novel *Paul et Virginie* (set in Mauritius and first published in 1788), one of their most influential works of tropical Romanticism.[11] By the 1840s these and other literary, scientific, and travel accounts of the tropics had cross-pollinated and coalesced to form a single impression of color, light, exuberance, and adventure. As one India-bound traveler enthused (not without the irony born of experience):

> With what feelings of delight does the youth first enter upon the fairy region of the tropics, a region which Cook and Anson, and the immortal fictions of St. Pierre and De Foe, have invested in his estimation with a sweet and imperishable charm! The very air to him is redolent of a spicy aroma, of a balmy and tranquillizing influence, whilst delicious but indefinable visions of the scenes he is about to visit—of palmy groves, and painted birds, and coral isles, "in the deep sea set," float before him in all these roseate hues

with which the young and excited fancy loves to paint them. Paul and Virginia—Robinson—Friday—goats—savages and monkeys—ye are all for ever bound to my heart by the golden links of early association and acquaintanceship.[12]

This chapter is principally concerned, however, with a second phase of tropicality, roughly dating from the end of the Napoleonic wars in 1815, and extending through to the late 1850s, during which time the work of earlier tropical travelers was greatly extended in geographical range and, as the natural sciences themselves progressed, elaborated and refined through interlinked processes of observation, mapping, and classification. By the 1830s, as Warwick Anderson has remarked, the existence of the tropics was scientifically assured. Whether a tropical region was "defined most accurately by vegetation, parallels of latitude, isotherms, humidity, or a relative discomfort index" might remain open to dispute, "but that such a place did exist, and was peculiar in some definable way, was no longer in doubt."[13]

In this second phase, while islands and coasts, and the floating laboratories of shipboard naturalists, remained significant scientific sites, large areas of the interior landmasses came under closer scrutiny— Amazonian Brazil, Central America, West Africa, South and Southeast Asia, northern Australia—and their tropical characteristics were minutely examined and incorporated into Western scientific knowledge.[14] In this second phase of scientific tropicality Humboldt was much the most influential figure, revered almost as a god among the naturalists of his day. Through his powerful descriptions of "equinoctial" America, which he visited with Aimé Bonpland between 1799 and 1804, Humboldt gave a new scenic vision as well as scientific authority to the idea of a tropical world filled with vibrant nature—most characteristically through its abundant and luxuriant vegetation—and driven by a dynamic interdependence between diverse biogeographical elements. He brought a commanding intelligence and (through the use of scientific instruments) new standards of scientific precision to the study of the climate, topography, geology, and natural history of the tropics. In particular, his pioneering work on plant geography vividly demonstrated the influence of altitude and aspect on the zoning of vegetation, from tropical, through temperate, to alpine forms.[15]

But, more even than this proto-ecological accomplishment, Humboldt's understanding of the tropics was enriched by his personal impressions of its "organic richness," "luxuriant fullness" and "abundant fertility." He found in equatorial America, with its snow-capped peaks, dense forests, and vast plains, a "grand and imposing spectacle" that left him with "feelings of astonishment and awe."[16] After Humboldt, whose impassioned prose inspired artists as well as naturalists, it was widely accepted that the "dazzling tropics" required sentiment as well as science if their intrinsic vibrancy and visual impact were to be properly understood and their dreamlike quality captured and communicated.[17] His *Personal Narrative*, first published in French in 1814–25 and translated into English soon after, profoundly influenced later naturalists, among them Charles Darwin, Joseph Hooker, and Alfred Russel Wallace, who in turn did much to extend and popularize scenic appreciation and scientific understanding of the tropics.[18]

But where did this spectacular flowering of tropicality leave India— a land which Humboldt, Darwin, and Wallace never visited? In the late eighteenth century and opening years of the nineteenth, India did not appear to belong to the tropics in as self-evident a way as the Pacific, the West Indies, or West Africa did. India was *in* the tropics, but not necessarily *of* the tropics. In the 1780s outsiders like Joseph Banks, another leading naturalist who never visited the subcontinent, certainly thought of India, as much by analogy with the West Indies as by virtue of its geographical location, as having (or being capable of yielding) "tropical productions" that would eventually contribute handsomely to Britain's expanding system of trade and manufacturing.[19] But writers in India at the same period appeared less sure, considering themselves, like William Jones, as being "between the tropics" or "under the Tropick," but not otherwise regarding the country in which they resided as being closely aligned by nature, let alone by history and culture, with other parts of the tropical world.[20] Indeed, in seeking to demonstrate India's ancient philological and religious connections with Europe, Jones seemed intent upon using India to complete and complement Europe's classical and Christian past.[21]

Until about the 1830s India's "tropical" status remained remarkably ill-defined. In the opening years of the century, as noted in Chapter 3, Francis Buchanan did not employ the term, even when in Chittagong or Malabar he encountered and described exactly the kind of vegetation that later writers would eagerly call "tropical." On the other hand, James Forbes, whose *Oriental Memoirs* (based on his years in India, 1765–84) was an important landmark in the emerging topographical and ethnographic representation of India, referred more substantially to the "tropical sun" and the contrast between "tropical climates" like India's and the "temperate climes of Europe." He even suggestively described Hindus as "natives of the torrid zone."[22] In order to establish more clearly the emergence of India's tropicality, it is necessary to turn first to the late eighteenth century and to one of the most significant scientific figures of the period—the surveyor and cartographer James Rennell.

Rennell's *Memoir*

Rennell was born in Devon in 1742. Following service in the navy, he was appointed in 1764 to conduct surveying operations in eastern India. In 1767 he became Surveyor-General of Bengal and in 1779, after his return to Britain, he produced his *Bengal Atlas*, a work remarkable for "the large scale of its maps and the unprecedented accuracy of its details."[23] In 1782 Rennell published his *Map of Hindostan* with an accompanying *Memoir*: the latter appeared in enlarged form in 1788 and in a revised edition in 1792. Although much of his published work appeared after he left India in 1777, Rennell has long been seen as an innovative surveyor and cartographer. He was hailed by his Victorian biographer as Britain's "greatest geographer" and praised for the combination of logical principles and detailed data on which his *Memoir* was based. Recent scholarship has tended to be similarly appreciative of Rennell's achievements and to see him as a representative Enlightenment figure.[24]

Despite the praise heaped upon the *Memoir* and the map it accompanied, one cannot but be struck by its historical limitations. Like his contemporaries, Rennell was heavily reliant upon the use of route or traverse surveys, some of which he had personally carried out in eastern India, while others had resulted from the observations of army officers engaged in military operations and route marches in India over the previous thirty years. In route surveys the observer's gaze was directed toward such prominent landmarks as the course of rivers and roads or the location of lakes and mountains. The resulting maps thus functioned as the cartographic equivalent of descriptive travel narratives, guiding future travelers through the landscape or giving the map's readers a sense of the sights and hazards of the country to be traversed.[25] This method of map-making and the journey-like quality it conveyed were, however, soon to be superseded by the more comprehensive trigonometric surveys carried out by William Lambton, George Everest, and the Survey of India, though it might be noted that the route survey method remained a basic tool of scientific reconnaissance in several other fields, including botany.

Apart from traverse surveys and campaign memoirs, Rennell used information from earlier European travelers and map-makers.[26] He did, however, look further afield for information, particularly for his *Memoir*. Typically enough for the time, he turned to ancient writers like Arrian, whose account of the invasion of India by Alexander of Macedonia in 326 BC not only provided geographical data about the northwest but also, in a more ethnographic vein, indicated "how nearly the ancient inhabitants resembled the present." Through the use of such works, India's history and geography remained appended to Europe and its classical antiquity.[27] Rennell also used more recent European travelers like the Frenchman François Bernier (who visited India in the 1660s), as well as recently translated sources from the Mughal period, notably Abu'l Fazl's *Ain-i Akbari* and the Persian chronicles of his sixteenth-century contemporary Firishta. Since for Rennell "Hindoostan" remained largely coterminous with the former Mughal Empire, its boundaries and provinces were a still relevant guide to the country and its constituent regions. As presented in Rennell's *Memoir*, India's geography was thus less the consequence of a new imperial vision (or cartographic technology) than an eclectic amalgam, with recent route surveys supplementing gazetteers and histories that stretched back to Mughal times and beyond to the ancient Greeks.

The *Memoir* was, moreover, a geography represented largely through the recitation of place names, through a digest of distances between principal towns, and a record of historic boundaries and divisions. Apart from Bengal and Kashmir (for which Bernier provided a vivid account based on both his own experience and Mughal delight in this "paradise of the Indies"),[28] there was little attempt to typify or evoke the varied landscape of India or to represent more than superficially its different zones of climate and vegetation. This lacuna is not perhaps surprising, given the constraints on European knowledge at the time, though such sensibilities were fast developing in Britain at the time that Rennell compiled his *Memoir*. In commenting on India's cities (many of which he considered greatly decayed since Mughal times) Rennell blandly remarked that, "generally speaking," the "description of one Indian city, is a description of all; they being all built on one plan, with exceeding narrow, confined and crooked streets; with an incredible number of reservoirs and ponds, and a great many gardens, interspersed."[29] Elsewhere, in these pre-evangelical days, he summarily described the Jagannath temple at Puri as "a shapeless mass" and not "otherwise remarkable" except as "one of the first objects of Hindoo veneration" and as an "excellent seamark" on an otherwise flat and featureless coast.[30] Similarly, when Rennell turned to Rajmahal, a town he knew personally, he could only comment that while its situation was "romantic," it was "not pleasant" because in Hindustan

> the hills and eminences being always covered with wood, that beautiful swelling of the ground, which is so justly admired in European landscapes, is lost; and the fancy is presented at best with nothing beyond a wild scene: which can only be relished by being contrasted with soft and beautiful ones.[31]

In a work that, in its use of pre-British sources, exhibited a partly Orientalist character, it is not surprising that "the tropics" did not appear in Rennell's *Memoir*;[32] nor did he employ the term "jungle" which later became so expressive of the moral and physical geography of India. Significantly, however, Rennell did invoke "the tropics" in an account of the Ganges and Brahmaputra rivers, appended to the 1792 edition of the *Memoir* but first published separately in 1781. In this article "tropical" was used to describe the violent seasonal flooding of rivers in the "tropical regions," the model being the Amazon as described by the French naturalist Charles Marie de La Condamine in 1743. "Next to earthquakes," Rennell remarked, "perhaps the floods of tropical rivers, produce the quickest alterations in the face of our globe."[33] From its base in the New World, tropicality was beginning to infiltrate Old World Hindustan.

For all its limitations, Rennell's *Memoir* nonetheless stood on the cusp of a revolution in India's physical and imaginative geography. Within five decades of his writing, India had been extensively surveyed and mapped to a degree matched in few other British colonies and on a scale surpassing that in Europe itself.[34] Although references to Arrian and Abu'l Fazl persisted well into the 1830s and 1840s,[35] it was becoming less necessary to defer to ancient authors as authorities for the geography of present-day India. But surveying and cartographic precision did not meet every representational need. Alongside the technology of trigonometric surveys there developed no less rapidly a composite language through which the landscape of India could be readily evoked and depicted. In part this language drew its terms and inspiration from an already extant British Indian vocabulary of place and travel, but one that was now greatly embellished and popularized. Even newcomers ascended *ghats*, crossed *nullahs*, skirted *jheels* and *jangals*, camped under *topes* of mango trees or sheltered for the night at a wayside *bungalow*. By the time Joseph Hooker published his *Himalayan Journals* in 1854 most of these terms were assumed to be so familiar to British readers that they were no longer italicized or explained. But India was also being represented and envisioned through a greatly enriched literary style that drew promiscuously from the Bible, Milton and Shakespeare, from novels and travelogues, from the rich stores of European Romanticism, and was further supplemented by Orientalist and tropical writing.

The rapid rise of this rich vocabulary of place, and the allusions and associations to which it leant itself, was evident in Thomas Pennant's *View of Hindoostan*, published in 1798, only six years after the revised edition of Rennell's *Memoir*. Pennant had not visited India, but he drew freely from Firishta and Bernier, as well as writers like Hodges, Rennell, Jones, and the learned contributors to the Asiatic Society's *Researches*. Pennant made effective use of the engravings of Thomas Daniell and the artist's narrative of his travels, sometimes combining picture and text to provide complementary accounts of a landscape or monument. Even for armchair visitors, India was now acquiring a visibility and a scenic complexity it had not previously possessed.[36] In 1817, when Thomas Moore published *Lalla Rookh*, his spectacularly successful poetic account of the journey of a "tulip-cheek'd" Mughal princess from Delhi to Kashmir, it was thick with literary allusions and scholarly references: to Rennell's *Memoir* and Pennant's *Hindoostan*, to the Koran, Firishta, and Hafiz, to Orientalists like William Jones and historians like Edward Gibbon and Alexander Dow, to seventeenth- and eighteenth-century travelers like François Bernier, John Baptiste Tavernier, and John Chardin, as well as to recent authors like Maria Graham and Mountstuart Elphinstone.[37] As a site for Europe's imaginative geography, India had come of age. But what kind of India emerged from this great amalgam of sources, subjectivities and sciences?

India's Orient

When, in 1978, Edward Said published *Orientalism*, he did more than fire a polemical broadside that still reverberates through colonial and postcolonial studies. By identifying Orientalism with the West's persistent and almost timeless representation of the East as its inferior and essentialized "other," he added a rich layer of meaning to an already complex term. Further, he directed attention to the representational power of an exoticized landscape (as well as the human subjects it contained) and the force of an externally generated imaginative geography within the encompassing schema of Orientalist thought.[38] Said's analysis intentionally ran counter to earlier use of the term Orientalism, current from the late eighteenth century, to describe the scholarly (and hence sympathetic or impartial) investigation of "the East" and the academic study of the languages, history, religions, and societies of the regions lying to the east of Europe. Although the Islamic Middle East was Said's main focus, "the Indian Orient" also fell within the ambit of his Orientalist critique. In the South Asian context, Orientalist scholarship has long been associated with William Jones and contemporaries like H.B. Halhed and Charles Wilkins who pioneered the Western investigation of Sanskrit and Hindu texts, with the founding of the Asiatic Society in Calcutta in 1784, and, over the following fifty years, the European "discovery" of India, especially its languages, literature, religions, and ancient history.[39]

It should be recognized, though, that for many Europeans in India at the time, and for many of those who read about India in Britain, "the Orient" as applied to South Asia had a less scholarly (and less taxing) significance. This more popular understanding is evident, for example, from the articles and illustrations that appeared in the *Oriental Annual*, published in London between 1834 and 1840. Feeding off the appeal of *Lalla Rookh* and similar works, the *Annual* sought as much to entertain as to instruct its readers through accounts of the manners and customs, arts and literature of India. Early volumes were illustrated with "picturesque" engravings by Thomas Daniell (taken or adapted from his earlier collections of *Oriental Scenery*). Later ones included scenes of Bhutan and the Himalaya drawn by Samuel Davis, who had accompanied Turner in 1783. The *Annual* also ran a series of illustrated articles dramatizing the "Lives of the Moghul Emperors," accounts of Indian topography and European travel (replete with elephants, tiger hunts, hilltop forts, and

FIG. 7. The Ruins of Etawa, Rajasthan, from T. Bacon (ed.), *Oriental Annual* (1839).
Reproduced by kind permission of the School of Oriental and African Studies, London.

moonlit ruins), and stories retelling Hindu myths or romances of Muslim court life. In this eclectic, exotic—but seldom entirely sinister—world the European experience of Indian landscape and travel mingled freely with tales of sati, episodes from the life of Aurangzeb, Heber's *Narrative*, or Southey's *Kehama*.[40] Orientalism, thus understood, might be regarded as essentializing and demeaning to its subjects, but it also represented a kind of imperial entertainment.

Too much so for the liking of some commentators. In 1844 when Henry and Honoria Lawrence set out to parody and rebuke the common British image of a "Romantic" India, they did so in terms that largely reflected an "Oriental" vision of the country.[41] "We begin life," they observed, "with splendid delusions, learnt from the Arabian Nights, and the scenic melodramas of the London stage; as we advance, the gorgeous poetry of *Lalla Rookh* stamps these delusions still more deeply on our mind." India, in this fanciful geography, was a land of "castellated elephants," proud rajas and "melodious" bulbuls, of silks, muslins, and precious gems, of "white cities," "gilded minarets," and "glittering scimitars," of "snorting

Arabs" (horses, not people) and the "dark-eyed daughters of the East." It was a place of "tall palm trees and browsing camels, rose-gardens and citron-groves."[42] It was not surprising, the Lawrences continued, that Britons were deeply disappointed when they arrived to find that the real India failed to match up to these romantic expectations. Their argument was that, beyond these glittering and superficial images, there was real romance and adventure in India, most especially, as they dutifully saw it, in selfless Christian service to the Indian people.

Despite such reproofs, India, especially the India of the urban streets and bazaars, of Mughal tombs and palaces, held—and long continued to hold—in the Western mind strong associations with Aladdin and the *Arabian Nights*. As Captain Skinner, no giddy adolescent, wrote on visiting Delhi in 1828, it was "impossible to pass through its streets without having the Thousand and One Nights constantly in the mind."[43] And, as we saw in the previous chapter with Heber, *Lalla Rookh* continued to be regarded as a reliable guide to Indian life and culture which few educated visitors neglected to read before arriving in the country. But, as Said's work would also lead us to expect, between the scholarly Orientalism of the historians and philologists and the cultural stereotypes and romantic myths of the Orient as popularly conceived,[44] there was almost constant traffic. Furthermore, although the early Orientalists directed much of their attention to the study of Hindu texts and traditions, and though the idea of the "Indian Orient" as represented in works like the *Oriental Annual* covered a great diversity of landscapes and cultures and certainly had its Hindu (and latterly, as we will see from Joseph Hooker, its Buddhist) ingredients, the trope of "the Orient" in early nineteenth-century India tended to look westward and so to align India with Persia and the Muslim Middle East. Behind this Islamic orientation lay the pervasive influence of the *Arabian Nights* and *Lalla Rookh* but also the more familiar monuments and histories of the Mughals and the ready association of dry landscapes with Oriental topographies.[45]

Just as Samuel Turner's account of his 1783 mission to Tibet provided the essential guide for almost every traveler to the eastern Himalaya over the next three-quarters of a century, so Mountstuart Elphinstone's narrative of his mission through 1808 and 1809 to the court of Shah Shuja of Afghanistan at his winter residence at Peshawar became a foundational text for Orientalist representations of Indian travel. Coming shortly after the British had gained control of the Delhi region in 1803, the mission was motivated by fears of a possible French alliance with the rulers of Persia and Afghanistan. Along with Sir John Malcolm's mission to Persia in 1808, it reflected the perceived importance of protecting British India's western frontier by diplomatic and, if necessary, military means.[46] First published in 1815, Elphinstone's *Account of the Kingdom of Cabul* represented not merely a description of a journey into a foreign land which has many of the cultural and topographical hallmarks of "the Orient," but also a journey into a past, and even latterly into a landscape, that was in many respects less alien than the India he and his companions had left behind them.

Accompanied by a military escort and a small staff of medical and military officers, Elphinstone left Delhi on 13 October 1808. Heading west, the party soon entered the Rajasthan desert, a region dotted with sand hills, "which at first were covered with bushes, but afterwards were naked piles of loose sand, rising one after another, like the waves of the sea, and marked on the surface by the wind like drifted snow."[47] Botanical observation helped plot their course through this arid terrain. The journey took them through parched, sandy, almost uninhabited plains, thinly covered with coarse grass, mimosa bushes and the "phoke" shrub, its leafless stems eaten by camels, and "peculiar to the desert and its borders."[48] The Shekhawati country through which the mission passed possessed few wells, most yielding only brackish water. They needed six hundred camels, and a dozen elephants to transport their water and other supplies, and they moved by night to avoid the intense heat of day. On 5 November they reached the town of Bikaner, which looked impressive enough but was situated within a landscape "as waste as the wildest part of Arabia."[49] Beyond Bikaner, Elphinstone's caravan entered "a wilderness," a "naked plain," with taunting mirages of lakes and rivers. As they approached Bahawalpur they found themselves in a country that—in terms of the language, dress, and physical features of the population, as well as the landscape—seemed to bring them closer to Persia (and thence to Europe) than the north Indian plains they had left behind. Here they reached the five rivers of Punjab which Elphinstone (like Rennell) knew best by their ancient Greek names and associations: "it was impossible," Elphinstone declared on seeing the "Hyphasis" (Beas), dried up though it was, "to look without interest on a stream which had borne the fleet of Alexander."[50] Continuing beyond Bahawalpur, Elphinstone's party found further testimony in the landscape, as in the people who inhabited it, that aligned this desert region with the Middle East. Thus one "cheerful and beautiful spot" was "such as one would figure in a scene in Arabia Felix." It lay in "a sandy valley, bounded by craggy hills, watered by a little stream, and interspersed with clumps of date trees, and with patches of green corn." The nearby village "stood in a deep grove of date trees," its inhabitants "Beloches and Shaikhs, of Arabian descent."[51] On the banks of the Indus, Arabia beckoned.

In a further shift in the appearance of the country, as they approached Peshawar Elphinstone and his party began to notice the presence of "English" plants—plums, peaches, willows, and plane trees—from which they had "long been estranged in the climate of India." Even dandelions, plantains, and chickweed put them nostalgically in mind of long-unseen "English weeds."[52] At Peshawar itself, which they reached in late February 1809, they could see in the distance the snow-covered peaks of the Hindu Kush, while nearer at hand were walled gardens, filled with roses and other familiar flowering plants, and trees, covered in bright foliage, "which had a freshness and brilliancy never seen in the perpetual summer of India." The sight of flowers, fruit trees, and scented shrubs set in a secluded garden was a familiar Islamic trope, but in the travelers' minds they also had an unmistakably English air about them. In orchards around the town bloomed pear, apple, plum, quince, and pomegranate trees, and the fields "were covered with a thick elastic sod, that perhaps never was equalled but in England."[53] For all its exotic setting, this "Orient" possessed a reassuringly homely quality.

Diplomatically, Elphinstone's mission was futile: Shah Shuja was deposed soon after and so ceased to be a useful ally for the British. Despite this, through his simple but elegant prose, Elphinstone helped make the lands to the west and northwest of Delhi appear close to the fabled Orient, and many of the images he invoked—deserts, camels, oases, mirages, date palms, thorn scrub and flower-scented gardens, hawking, the Middle Eastern appearance of buildings, the "Jewish" countenance of girls and the thick beards of men, even the familiar taste of apples, pears and plums—helped to establish for later writers a rich repertoire of Oriental scenes and emblems. Even though his account of Rajasthan was more redolent with Hindu associations, the desert landscapes Tod described contained many references to Elphinstone's narrative or used topographical and ethnographic tropes that similarly aligned the sandy deserts of Marwar with Arabia and the Sahara rather than with "Gangetic India."[54] Equally, although Elphinstone never entered Afghanistan, his account of the kingdom of Kabul, based upon interviews with courtiers, traders, and other informants, excited the European imagination. When the author of *Lalla Rookh* sought to invoke the sight of the "stupendous ranges" of the Hindu Kush or sought authority for the pomegranates, apples, and pears said to grow in the "thousand gardens" of Kabul, he directed readers to Elphinstone's narrative.[55]

As a traveler, Elphinstone had many successors, especially as by the 1830s and 1840s the British became increasingly involved in the politics of the Indus valley, from Sind (annexed in 1843), to Punjab (conquered within ten years of Ranjit Singh's death in 1839) and beyond into Afghanistan, the site of imperial intervention and humiliation in 1838–42. In one such account, Alexander Burnes set out in 1831 on a two-year journey from Ludhiana on the British frontier through Punjab to Kabul and Bukhara, before returning via the Indus. Not only did his journey help reconnoiter this largely unknown territory and to sketch out, in prospect, British ambitions for the region, it also reinforced many of the Orientalist tropes of earlier writers. If Lahore instantly reminded Burnes of the gardens and palaces of *Lalla Rookh*, and the mountains and deserts recalled Elphinstone, so the rivers of the Punjab propelled him back two thousand years to Alexander, whose adventures he had known of since childhood. Such were the similarities in Burnes's mind, that the people of the middle Indus still looked like those described in Arrian's *Anabaxis*, just as Ranjit Singh was "the modern Porus" (the Indian king Alexander defeated), even as his army seemingly resembled that of his ancient predecessor.[56] If the lands of the Indus already belonged to the geography of European antiquity, so the fate of Porus seemed to portend that of Ranjit Singh and his empire.

As British ambitions and territory expanded across the Indus, so this Indian Orient—part Old Testament, part Arrian, part *Lalla Rookh*—continued to flourish and to intertwine fiction and fantasy with travel, ethnography, and science. In his account of Sind, written more than forty years after Elphinstone's mission, Richard Burton displayed his own Orientalist credentials, proudly parading his insider knowledge of local culture, custom, and romance. And yet, while affecting to despise those "jungly" Europeans who failed to realize that in the East a "knowledge of language and manners is all powerful," he also identified himself with the need for "improvement" and the transforming power of European science and technology to realize Sind's economic potential and military value for the British.⁵⁷ Like Elphinstone and Burnes before him, Burton used similar topographical tropes and ethnographical markers to indicate proximity to Persia and Afghanistan and to distance Sind from what he clearly considered an effete and inferior Hindustan.⁵⁸

Burton's colleague, the surgeon John Ellerton Stocks, also on duty in Sind in the 1840s, wrote equally passionately about the botany of the province and neighboring Baluchistan, recognizing plant products sold in the bazaars (dyestuffs, aromatic gums, and pungent cordials) that linked this little-known, arid region with its famed counterparts in Persia, Syria, and Arabia.⁵⁹ As he confided to William Hooker at Kew, he dreamed of tracing the transition from tropical and subtropical to semi-desert vegetation from western India to the Persian Gulf, and of quitting his job as a vaccinator long enough to cross the Makran desert ("through which went Alexander"), to visit Muscat and the "rich" island of Socotra ("Aloes! Dragon's blood!"), and follow the botanical trail to the "*true* Garden of Arabia."⁶⁰ In Stocks's uninhibited letters one can sense how easily the fabled Orient of the *Arabian Nights* and of Alexander could mingle with zeal for new scientific discoveries. Despite critics who thought his writing repetitive and dull, Burton contrived to leave "pestiferous Sinde" behind him and become one of the most celebrated travelers—and controversial Orientalists—of his day.⁶¹ Stocks was less fortunate. He contracted malaria during one of his botanical "forays" and died in England in 1854, aged 34, his ambitions for "Oriental botany" largely unfulfilled.⁶²

Jacquemont: Between the Orient and the Tropics

Although British dominance over South Asia had been clearly established by 1817 and the possibility of French suzerainty correspondingly extinguished, French interest in India was longstanding, and, as reflected in travel writing, natural history, philology, and theology, continued well into the second half of the nineteenth century. Since Bernier in the seventeenth century, many of the most influential observers of India had been French and, for all their country's dwindling authority and commerce, this remained so into the late eighteenth century and beyond: the exercise of political control was not the only index of a colonizing engagement. Despite the growth of their imperial interests elsewhere, French scholars and novelists, travelers and scientists, continued to write and reflect on India. Even without an empire to sustain them—perhaps the freer for it—the French still dreamed of India.[63] As the involvement of many Germans also attests, the eighteenth- and nineteenth-century exploration and articulation of the tropics was a European, and not merely British, venture: like India, "the tropics" were too important—culturally, commercially, and scientifically—to be left to Britain alone. The travels of the French naturalist Victor Jacquemont in the late 1820s and early 1830s serve not only to illustrate the involvement of other Europeans in the making of science and scenery in India; they also further illustrate the contradictory tensions and expectations that existed between ideas of "tropical" and "Oriental" India.

Born in Paris in 1801, Jacquemont came from a well-connected family, and, despite the turmoil of the age, was brought up in a "cultivated and learned atmosphere."[64] His father, Venceslas, instilled in Victor a taste for intellectualism, republicanism and a rational skepticism that bordered on atheism. Despite his passion for Rossini operas (and Italian divas), the young Jacquemont was said to have deplored the emotional excesses of Rousseau and his followers. He was overtly suspicious of Romanticism, but this arguably belied his own "very impressionable and emotional nature."[65] Of his two elder brothers, Porphyre was an old soldier, who had survived Napoleon's retreat from Moscow, while Frédéric was a businessman (by some accounts, a sugar planter) in the black republic of Haiti on the island of Santo Domingo. Victor Jacquemont became interested in natural history, helping to establish the Société d'Histoire Naturelle in Paris in 1821, and traveled on botanical expeditions in France and neighboring countries. He studied at the Faculté de Médicine in Paris in 1822 and was destined for a medical career when in 1826, to cure him of an infatuation with an opera singer, his family packed him off to New York. During his American visit he spent three months in Haiti with Frédéric, an experience that was to have a profound impact upon his career as a naturalist. Back in the United States, he was invited by Georges Cuvier to investigate the natural history of India and collect plant and animal specimens for the Museum of Natural History in Paris.[66]

In 1827 he went to London to seek permission from the East India Company to visit India. As Jacquemont was well aware, the Company was very wary of outsiders visiting India, fearing that they might seek to revive Napoleonic ambitions to supplant the British or, like several foreigners under Ranjit Singh, enter the military service of Indian princes.

Even Alexander von Humboldt had been denied access to India, possibly anticipating that he might be as outspoken a critic of British rule in India as he had been of the Spanish in the New World.[67] Jacquemont was more fortunate. Befriended by several influential figures in London, notably Sir Alexander Johnston of the Royal Asiatic Society, he soon secured the necessary permission and, armed with a sheaf of letters of introduction to "all the powerful men" in India, he departed from Brest in August 1828.[68] *En route* to India, Jacquemont visited the Canaries, Rio de Janeiro, the Cape of Good Hope, Réunion and Pondicherry, before reaching Calcutta the following May. This itinerary further deepened the impression the tropics had so profoundly made upon him in Haiti two years earlier.[69]

In Calcutta Jacquemont was taken up by the Governor-General, Lord Bentinck (much as Joseph Hooker was later adopted by Lord Dalhousie), and this yielded further important contacts and connections, especially among East India Company officials. In the six months he remained in Calcutta, Jacquemont devoted his time to studying Indian botany and mastering Hindustani. He had originally intended to spend four years in India, hoping to visit Afghanistan (in the wake of Elphinstone, whose *Account of the Kingdom of Cabul* he admired) and then, at the other topographical extreme, Malabar (whose luxuriant "tropical" vegetation he knew from van Rheede).[70] In fact, Jacquemont never reached the southwest coast or the mountains of the northwest. Quitting Calcutta in November 1829 and following a fairly conventional route to North India and the Himalaya, his travels took him through Bengal to Bundelkhand and Benares, then on to Agra, Delhi and the cities of the northern Indo-Gangetic plain. He made botanical excursions into the Himalaya which took him through Kumaon to the borders of Ladakh and across into Tibet at 18,000 feet. With Ranjit Singh's consent, he then journeyed through Punjab into Kashmir (where he spent the summer of 1831, reliving Bernier's impressions of two centuries earlier), before turning southwest through Rajasthan to Bombay. By this time Jacquemont had become seriously ill with dysentery. He died in December 1832, aged 31, from an abscess of the liver "brought on by hardship and reckless exposure in pursuit of his favourite science."[71]

Jacquemont's literary and scientific reputation grew rapidly after his death. His letters to his family, published in French in 1833, were translated into English the following year. Despite being French and agnostic

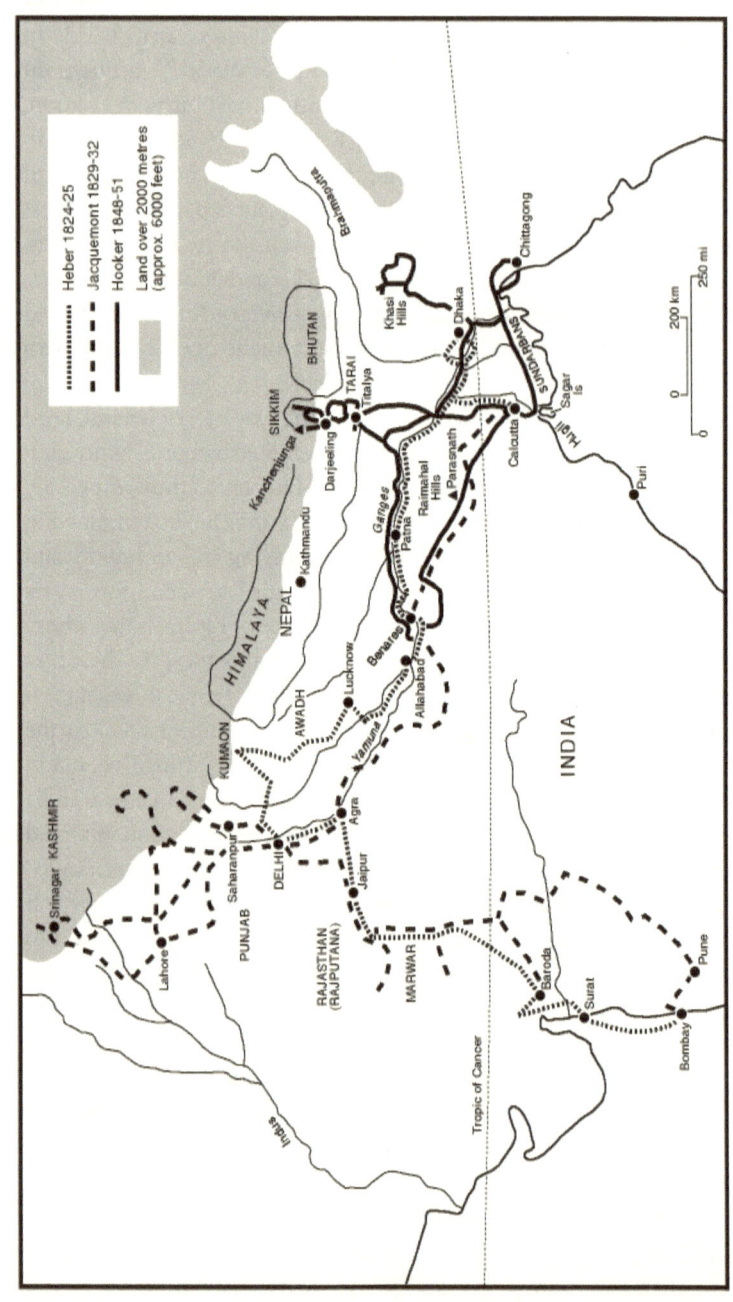

MAP. 2. The North Indian Travels of Reginald Heber, Victor Jacquemont, and Joseph Hooker.

(as much about the British presence in India as about the existence of God), Jacquemont became one of the most widely commented upon travel writers of pre-Mutiny India. Even more illuminating from a scientific viewpoint were the detailed accounts of Indian botany, zoology, and geology recorded in his journal and published in 1841. These demonstrated the remarkable range of his scientific interests and his accuracy as a natural history observer, though Hooker and Thomson later claimed that he was ill-served by the French naturalists who prepared his unrevised journals for posthumous publication, and restricted in his botany by not having access to the herbaria of Wallich and Royle that proved vital to later plant taxonomy and biogeography.[72]

A passage from Jacquemont's journal for 11 February 1831, recording his impressions of vegetation and landscape near Sirhind (between Patiala and Ludhiana in east Punjab), gives a good example of his botanical observations and how these were linked to his awareness of the local ecology. It also anticipates some of the scenic tropes and sensibilities we will turn to shortly.

> The countryside is totally flat; there are plenty of jungles along the roadside, in a number of sandy terrains. They consist of wretched bushes of *Butea frondosa* [dhak]. The leaves, completely withered and desiccated, remain on the tree until the flowers appear in the spring. I know of no more ugly tree. Elsewhere, uncultivated areas show traces of earlier cultivation. All but the very richest of soils are exhausted after two harvests of wheat or wheat and chickpeas, every year, with no fertiliser and virtually no ploughing. Eventually, these barely fertile lands become incapable of production. They are abandoned, are invaded by wild bushes and remain jungles for an indefinite period ...
>
> Babul trees [*Acacia arabica*] are common; they appear to be allowed to grow wherever they sprout simultaneously. Their very hard wood is the only type which the villagers can use for constructing their carts and ploughs. The horizon seems to end on every side in a forest of these trees. Their light foliage is of the brightest green. They become increasingly common the closer one approaches to Sirhind.[73]

Like many other early nineteenth-century naturalists, Jacquemont greatly admired Humboldt, writing to him ahead of his Indian journey to explain the purpose of his scientific mission and asking, in effect, for the great man's approval.[74] After Haiti, "the tropics" had become an enchanted place for Jacquemont. Like a scared mantra, the term occurs over and over again in his writing, as much in his scientific notes as in his personal correspondence, though increasingly in India it signified a longing, an absence, not the fulfilling consummation of a Humboldtian dream. Like Hooker twenty years later, and almost from the moment of his arrival, Jacquemont was bitterly disappointed by what he saw of India's supposedly "tropical" nature. He was certainly not alone in this. A contrast between India on the one hand and the West Indies and Brazil on the other was often made—if only because many visitors to India (like Jacquemont) had previously spent time in the Caribbean or visited Brazil *en route* to India (or, as in his case, both). For instance, William Hickey visited Barbados, Grenada, and Jamaica between 1775 and 1776 before traveling to India in October 1777 (he had briefly landed at Madras earlier, in 1769). He clearly relished his stay in Jamaica, "this terrestrial paradise" as he called it. According to Hickey, the island's gardens abounded with "fruits, tropical and European," and its "incomparable natural beauties" and scenery made it "the most romantic country in the world."[75] Hickey never wrote with such glowing enthusiasm about the landscape and products of Bengal, the country where he spent most of his working life. Maria Graham, who wrote a *Journal* of her visit to India in 1809–11, later compiled a similar account of her residence in Brazil from 1821 to 1823, and though she found much that was interesting and "picturesque" about India, her preference seemed to lie with the American tropics. In the East, she observed, the imagination was "at liberty to expatiate on past grandeur [and] wisdom": "Monuments of art and science" were met with "at every step." In the Americas, by contrast, and despite the loathsome slavery, everything, especially in nature, bore an exhilarating air of "newness."[76]

For all his reservations about effusive Romanticism, Jacquemont felt no less passionately than Hickey and Graham about tropical America and, what is more, allowed this emotional and sensory response to inform his scientific understanding. In one of his early letters home from India he wrote: "To me Santo Domingo will always be the ideal of tropical beauty: I cannot call to mind without emotion the first tropical scenes among which I found myself."[77] As his thoughts inevitably turned back to Humboldt's ecstatic initiation into the American tropics, Jacquemont wondered whether the failure to find a comparable delight in India somehow lay with himself: perhaps the pleasure he experienced in Haiti was partly from delight at seeing his brother again. Possibly, he mused, invoking the sexuality and "voluptuousness" so often associated with the tropics,[78] one's first encounter with the beauty of tropical nature was a kind of virginity, "which is soon destroyed by enjoyment." In Haiti there had been the novelty of seeing his first banana tree and his first papaya, of enjoying previously untasted tropical fruits, and seeing for the first time such dazzling, vibrant, and spectacular scenes of nature.[79] Perhaps, after this first encounter, the tropics could never be the same again: the virginity had been lost, and Jacquemont's "capacity for wonder" had "dried up." But then he recalled that not only had he "passionately admired the natural beauties of Santo Domingo" but also, on his subsequent voyage, those of Brazil and Réunion. No, he concluded, "the fault is not in myself: it lies with the things themselves, with the country."[80] India simply was not the tropics he had already seen, and continued to imagine and desire.

Jacquemont's dismay was evident almost from the outset. Traveling along the banks of the Damodar in western Bengal in December 1829 he recorded his first sighting of "jungle."

> I must confess that I was greatly disappointed. I had imagined an impenetrable forest, offering the whole wealth of form and colour of tropical vegetation, bristling with thorny trees, intertwined with bushy shrubs, with creepers growing right up to the tops of the tallest trees and descending gracefully in cascades of flowers. At Rio de Janeiro and Santo Domingo I had seen the scattered components of this picture. But far from it! I found myself among woods even more monotonous than those of Europe; beneath, a few meagre shrubs; and instead of the distant roar of tigers, the sound of the woodman's axe.[81]

As he continued his travels the appearance of the landscape did in his eyes improve somewhat, and he began to see "scenes less remote from those painted by my imagination."[82] Thus, in April 1830 as he left Delhi and plunged into the warm valleys of the Himalayan foothills, Jacquemont at last discovered vegetation in his estimation deserving of the term "tropical" and which reminded him of Haiti and tropical America.[83] But even here the experience was short-lived. A few months later, having meanwhile seen the spectacular Himalaya, Jacquemont was back in the seemingly barren plains of North India, which he repeatedly described as "miserable." In January 1831, he expressed to his father his "feelings of sadness" at being "once more on the sandy, desolate plains of Hindustan." They were "covered with high grasses, yellowed and dry, and in other parts with a wretched, bleached prickly shrub which lends the same desolate and mournful appearance to the whole of India and Persia."[84] Of course, even for Jacquemont, the tropics were not entirely idyllic. Like Humboldt and Darwin before him, he had seen the slave-holding societies of the Americas, especially Brazil's, with its deep racial divide and accompanying cruelty. But that was the fault of humankind, not nature. And despite this taint, he still retained a powerful notion of the tropics as a glowing spectacle, "*un tableau des scènes de la nature sauvage*," a vivid ensemble in which all the diverse aspects of nature—from the brilliant sky and towering trees to the luxuriant, flowering foliage at his feet, from the perfumed air wafted about him to the rich taste of tropical fruits, to the brilliant plumage of birds and painted wings of butterflies— combined to form an assemblage of sensory delight. Such was the intensity of this tropical experience that it was painful even to contemplate leaving.[85]

India did not embody the perpetual summer of the "true" tropics; conversely, neither did its seasons seem to possess the scenic pleasures and poetical charms associated with Europe's changing year. Like many other European travelers, he struggled to come to terms with a landscape that was bright, verdant, and bursting with life after the monsoons, but seemingly barren and "naked" for much of the rest of the year.[86] In the cold weather months (as Jacquemont's account, quoted earlier, of Sirhind in 1831 illustrates) the trees looked dried-up and dead. There was no vine-harvest to celebrate, no glory of leaves changing color in the fall, no frost to sharpen the wintry atmosphere and prick the senses, no animals stabled in warm stalls. There was, in short, to his alien eyes, none of the physical signs and cultural activities that made the seasons, their coming and their passing, so central to European art and experience across the ages.[87] Far from the natural wealth and plenitude of the imagined tropics, Jacquemont saw instead the grinding poverty of the Indian people. He wondered how they could survive on so little food and such scanty wages, but surmised that historical and social factors must have compounded the misery resulting from deficiencies of climate, soil, and vegetation. There might not be the plantation slavery that so offended the traveler in the American tropics, but there were in India other forms of exploitation and oppression to produce a comparable effect.[88]

Jacquemont's disappointed discovery in India of the "poor tropics" was a significant one, for it echoed the experience of the British themselves and anticipated the negative representation of the tropics by the French geographer Pierre Gourou a century later.[89] Having first glimpsed the extraordinary natural abundance of Bengal—"the paradise of India," as Robert Orme described it, echoing earlier Mughal sources[90]—the British had been surprised in their admiration and avarice by the devastating Bengal famine of 1770, in which a third of the population perished for want of food. The British had further to revise their ideas of India's innate prosperity in the early nineteenth century, notably with the 1838 famine in northern India, which a number of British travelers (including Emily Eden) witnessed first-hand.[91] Tod's depiction of the harsh landscapes of western Rajasthan (and his interest in "improving" canals) was similarly influenced by his recognition that periodic rainfall deficiencies, and not just recent episodes of plunder and rapine, were a recurring cause of drought and famine.[92]

The East India Company and its servants might decline to take responsibility for calamities which historians have been more than ready to lay at their feet, preferring to blame a capricious climate and the niggardliness of nature. But the grim spectacle of famine and its devastating impact (not least on agricultural productivity and state revenues) ensured that the famines were not forgotten: indeed, they continued to shape negative ideas of the Indian landscape and the corresponding need for "improvement." There was at least partial recognition that the productivity of India could not be either assumed or guaranteed. From the time that Colonel Robert Kyd proposed setting up a botanic garden at Calcutta in 1786,[93] it became one of the tasks of colonial botany to find ways to supplement and "improve" Indian agriculture by introducing new food crops or developing commercial products, like cotton and tea, that might stimulate trade and raise rural incomes. The recognition in India of the "poor tropics," and the absence there of the fecundity and abundance so closely identified with the tropics elsewhere, helped complicate the understanding (and darken the representation) of the tropical world as a whole and hence to anticipate later perceptions of the tropics as a site of impoverished societies in urgent need of "development."

But let us return to Jacquemont. Deeply disappointed in his hopes of finding in India the luxuriant tropics of his imagination, as he traveled, Jacquemont was more and more aware of, intrigued and absorbed by,

India's Orient. On leaving Bengal and entering the drier provinces of the north and northwest, he began to recognize the dress, the language, customs, and (in Islam) the religion of "the Orient."[94] He was struck by Agra, "the first large Moslem city" he had ever seen, "full of memorials of the recent grandeur of the house of Timur."[95] Although Delhi was not as resplendent as his reading of *Lalla Rookh* had led him to expect, its extensive ruins still caused him to reflect on India's Mughal rulers and their fate. Jacquemont took pride in his growing command of Hindustani and was correspondingly scathing about the many British officers he met who were ignorant of India's languages. He was drawn, by contrast, to William Fraser, the British Resident in Delhi, an accomplished Orientalist, whose fluent Persian and Hindustani he greatly admired.[96]

For Jacquemont, as for many of his European contemporaries, Punjab, still more than Delhi, stood at a crossroads. Culturally and commercially, it linked the Islamic lands of Persia, Afghanistan, and Kashmir with the plains of Hindustan; politically and military, it opposed Ranjit Singh, ruler of the last Indian state of any significant power, to the remorseless tide of British expansionism, and juxtaposed the advancing "civilization" of the modern West to the last remnants of India's waning "feudal" order. Appalled by the "medieval" barbarity of the maharaja's cruel and rapacious regime,[97] Jacquemont delighted nonetheless in the "picturesque" grandeur of Ranjit's court, which for him embodied the fanciful, as well as the anachronistic, Orient. As the maharaja's guest at Lahore, he was put up in a spacious building, surrounded by orange trees and jasmine bushes, that was "exactly like a magic palace in the *Arabian Nights*." Witnessing the Dussera festival at Amritsar, Ranjit's varied and colorful entourage vividly recalled scenes from Europe's age of chivalry. Now he felt he had seen "*l'Orient dans toutes ses pompes*" [The Orient in all its pomp].[98] Failing to find a tropical nature to compare with the Americas, Jacquemont found partial consolation in the spectacle of the Indian Orient.

Tropicalizing India

To some extent Jacquemont's increasingly Oriental view of India was influenced by the route he followed. Traveling to north and northwest India took him into the most conspicuously Muslim parts of India, into camel country, and the kinds of arid landscapes and semi-desert vegetation most closely identified with the Orient. Had he accomplished his ambition to journey south to Malabar, his perception of India might have changed again and the tropical attributes of South Asian scenery and botany might have become more apparent to him. Joseph Hooker, whose travel narrative was markedly less Orientalist than Jacquemont's, proceeded no further west than Benares and never visited the cities of the north Indian plains. The word "Oriental" seldom entered Hooker's vocabulary, except, in a generalized way, to designate Eastern races and places.[99] But it was not merely a question of how different itineraries might influence travelers' impressions of India. Jacquemont was also visiting India at a time when Company rule still retained something of its Mughal inheritance. Persian remained until 1835 the official language of government. Men like Fraser in Delhi, if increasingly rare, still represented a degree of cross-cultural contact and appreciation. As we have seen, the landscapes and ruined cities that Heber, Roberts, and Jacquemont observed in traversing North India in the 1820s and 1830s were strewn with the highly visible monuments of the Mughals and other pre-British rulers. However, by the time of Jacquemont's death in 1832 the Orientalist era was hastening to its close. The death of Ranjit Singh in 1839 and the annexation of Punjab ten years later, the occupation of Awadh in 1856, and the exile of the last Mughal king of Delhi in 1858, marked further stages in the decline of British interest in (and perceived necessity for) Oriental languages and learning. By that time, too, the controversy between the Anglicists and Orientalists, over the appropriate language of instruction for India, had long since found its resolution in the triumph of the Anglicists, signaled by T.B. Macaulay's Minute on Education in 1835.[100] Arriving in 1848, Hooker was entering a very different India from that Jacquemont encountered twenty years earlier.

The decline of the scholarly, semi-governmental Orientalism of the late eighteenth and early nineteenth centuries has been much remarked upon by historians. What has not, however, attracted similar attention is the way in which this reflected, or impacted upon, British perceptions of the Indian landscape. As colonial rule became more assured and feats of canal-building and railway construction began in British eyes to surpass the achievements of the Mughals and to inspire a new technological pride in empire, as the Victorians began to ditch the sentimental baggage of their predecessors and as works like *Lalla Rookh* and *The Curse of Kehama* faded from fashion, so understanding of the Indian landscape, and nature's place within it, also underwent significant change. As India's Oriental identity became eclipsed (though never entirely erased) and as the British regime associated itself more with "modern" science and technology and less with "traditional" learning and indigenous culture, so the identification of India with the tropics grew in strength.

The reasons for this shift lie not just in the political circumstances and literary tastes of the period, but in a number of other interrelated factors that the rest of this chapter will seek to explore further. As the Orientalist respect for, and engagement with, the history, languages, and cultures of South Asia waned, so a new generation of travelers, naturalists, and administrators gazed unmoved on the monuments of India's past. Either they saw India as a land of poverty, disease, and famine, whose current state of pitiful backwardness negated the extravagant claims once made by Orientalists for Indian civilization, or they turned with relief from the scorched and dusty plains to the cool delights of the forests, hills, and mountains where nature reigned. A growing sense of nature's dominance over India—whether in the malevolent form of tropical diseases or, more pleasurably, of tropical flora—was one of the ways in which the move away from Orientalism to tropicality manifested itself.

Although the concept of Orientalism was used by Said to indicate the essentializing "otherness" of the Western view of the Orient, in some respects, from the perspective of early nineteenth-century India, the Orient was all too connected with and half-familiar to Europe. Orientalism had been resonant with history—albeit a history that could roam from the Old Testament and Alexander to Akbar and Aurangzeb—and had situated India in a historical past that was impressionistically either medieval or antique. The tropics, by contrast, represented paradigmatically by Brazil, had no history: they echoed to the dawn of humankind, the Garden of Eden, where nature provided all human wants and people lived in primitive harmony with nature. As the Scottish philosopher Adam Ferguson put it: "The torrid zone, everywhere round the globe, however known to the geographer, furnished few materials for history."[101] Although India answered less readily to the picture of the primordial tropics than might some neighboring, heavily forested regions like Ceylon or Sumatra, and the evidence of its long history and civilization was difficult entirely to gainsay, it still came to share many of the primitive associations of tropical nature.

Again, while the term "Oriental" was occasionally applied to geography, botany, and medicine, it seemed largely devoid of scientific meaning. Did it refer to some ill-defined region to the east of Europe, or perhaps to the crude and anachronistic way in which "Orientals" drew their maps, named their plants, and healed their sick? The term belonged more convincingly to the arts, to language, religion, and culture. Conversely, the idea of the tropics leant itself to science in a way that the concept of the Orient did not: indeed, the trope of the tropics had itself grown to maturity during the eighteenth and early nineteenth centuries through repeated association with geographical reconnaissance and the scientific exploration of nature in the lands beyond Europe. In several scientific fields, like botany, meteorology, and ethnology, a growing knowledge of the tropics helped to shape ideas of Europe's distinctiveness and its privileged place even within the temperate portions of the globe. The tropics, as Humboldt and Jacquemont had demonstrated, were as rich in sensuous feeling and visual impressions, as dreamlike, as the Orient; but their appeal came more from nature than from culture. Partly because the tropics signified a domain of nature and a world largely uncluttered by pre-existing civilizations, these vast areas of the globe were available for science, especially for those sciences that would facilitate European mastery and exploitation. There never was, in any developed sense, an "Oriental medicine" or "Oriental botany," but the increasingly colonized tropics spawned a growing number of scientific specialties—in botany and zoology, in medicine and hygiene, in agriculture and veterinary science, in forestry and, ultimately, ecology.

As a cultural as well as scientific concept, the tropics were no less paradoxical and topsy-turvy than the imagined Orient. Associated on the one hand with Edenic islands, brilliant blue skies and luxuriant vegetation, they were also identified with the far less pleasurable side of nature. In his *Indian Zoology* in 1790, Thomas Pennant followed an alluring account of the "enchanting prospect" presented by the landscapes and animate nature in South and Southeast Asia with its less appealing "reverse." There, he declared, "you are harassed in one season with a burning heat, or, in the other with deluges of rain: you are tormented with clouds of noxious insects: you dread the spring of the *Tiger*, or the mortal bite of the *Naja* [cobra]." In the tropics, he wrote, half-anticipating Darwin and Wallace, "brute creation" was "more at enmity with one another than in other climates."[102] Indeed, the tropics were characterized by extremes of natural violence unmatched in the temperate zones. If India gave to the rest of the tropical world the emblematic term "jungle," so it received back from tropical America the Arawak word "hurricane" to describe the fierce cyclonic storms that swept up the Bay of Bengal, destroying ships in the Hugli and wreaking devastation for miles inland.[103] As the Arabic word *mausim* mutated from meaning a seasonal wind to the periodic "monsoon" rains that accompanied its arrival in India, so it acquired the sense of being a prolonged and violent "deluge" that bore no European equivalent.

No less revealing in the evolving semantics of Indian tropicality was the word "surf." Although the precise origins of the term are unclear, it has sometimes been suggested that its etymology must lie in some as yet unidentified Indian word. It seems more likely, however, that it was closely related to words like "surge" with which it was often used synonymously.[104] An Indian origin is improbable, but many European travelers, who may have acquired the term from reading Hakluyt's *Voyages* or the passage where Robinson Crusoe struggled to bring his shipwrecked bounty ashore, seemed only to recognize "surf" when they found themselves in, or on the threshold of, the tropics. Thus, "violent surf" pounded the shores of Madeira or the Cape Verde islands (which for many Europeans were the

FIG. 8. Surf at Fort St George, Madras, from R. Montgomery Martin, *The Indian Empire Illustrated* (1861).
Reproduced by kind permission of the School of Oriental and African Studies, London.

Atlantic gateways to the tropics), or crashed onto the glistening beaches of Pacific islands and atolls.[105] One of the earliest uses of the word, dating from 1685, was to describe how the "greatness" of the sea at Madras prevented Europeans from landing there, and most eighteenth- and early nineteenth-century accounts of arriving on that hazardous and unharbored shore similarly identified "surf" with the perils of being ferried ashore through foaming, shark-infested waters.[106] William Hickey, who visited the town in 1769, devoted several pages of his *Memoirs* to describing the violent "Madras surf" or "surge." It was, he recalled years later, "the most terrific thing I ever beheld."[107] In his authoritative *History of Sumatra*, the East India Company servant and naturalist William Marsden speculated on the Indian origin of the word and contrasted the violence of the "surfs of India" with the gentler waves that broke along the coast of western Ireland. He further identified "surf" as a phenomenon "so general in the tropical latitudes."[108]

Since this unbridled violence in nature was taken to characterize the "torrid zone" in general, it eased India's incorporation into the tropical world. The destructiveness of the tropics was also a recurring theme in the Indian medical and topographical literature of the early nineteenth century, which again looked in part to tropical America for its inspiration. This was a period when the connections between the East and West Indies were particularly strong. Even after the end of Anglo-French warfare in 1815, there was an extensive movement of British military, naval, and medical personnel between the two: both regions were expected to produce such "tropical" crops as cotton and sugar; and in medicine, as in agriculture, commerce, even government, the long-colonized West Indies provided a partial model for the emerging eastern empire. By the time slavery was abolished in the Caribbean in the 1830s and the West Indian connection with India faded, the impact of America's tropics had already made itself felt.

Many medical commentators in India had either visited the West Indies or read medical texts written by British and French army and naval surgeons about the diseases of tropical America, notably Benjamin Moseley's *Treatise on Tropical Diseases*.[109] India might lack some of the most representative diseases of the Caribbean canon—yellow fever, yaws, sleeping sickness—but it had in dysentery, malarial fever, hepatitis, and cholera complaints that could be directly linked to tropical conditions such as intense heat and humidity, poisonous miasmas, violent changes of temperature, and torrential rains: conditions that appeared very similar to those of the West Indies. As well as identifying "tropical" diseases, or diseases that in "tropical climates" "put on a different aspect and character,"[110] these sources also presented an unremitting account of the many natural hazards that afflicted life in the tropics, from hurricanes to scorpions, snakes, and sharks.[111]

Particularly influential in consolidating this pan-tropical connection was James Johnson, a naval surgeon who early in the nineteenth century visited both the West Indies and India. His treatise, *The Influence of Tropical Climates, more especially the Climate of India, on European Constitutions*, first published in 1813, was one of the principal medical texts used in India over the next forty years. As his title clearly indicated, Johnson saw no difficulty in situating India firmly within the tropics. He attributed virtually every Indian disease to the effects of tropical heat and humidity, while following Moseley and other West Indian writers in arguing that Europeans in the tropics needed to live "temperately" in order to survive.[112] Many other medical writers in India followed Johnson's lead, notably J.R. Martin, whose 1837 study of the climate, diseases, and topography of Calcutta extensively cited West Indian treatises. Martin was an advocate of hill-stations and sanatoria for Europeans in India, an idea partly derived from the Jamaican experience and one which emphasized the growing dichotomy perceived to exist between "tropical" plains and "European" hill resorts.[113]

The authority of Johnson's work was immense, and like Humboldt's *Personal Narrative*, it showed how texts could shape the ideas and expectations of Europeans even before they set foot in the tropics. When James Wallace, a young naval surgeon, went to India in 1821, he took four textbooks with him—Lind's *Diseases Incidental to Europeans in Hot Climates*, Clark's *Observations of the Diseases of Long Voyages to Hot Countries*, Moseley's *Treatise on Tropical Diseases*, and Johnson's *Tropical Climates*. Of these Wallace found Johnson's book so comprehensive as to make the others almost redundant. In his opinion it gave "perhaps the best view of tropical diseases that has yet been taken."[114] Other medical writers sought to capitalize on the expanding demand for works on tropical diseases and saw India as a central part of their authorial remit. In 1817 Richard Reece, a London surgeon, produced a *Medical Companion* for visitors to "tropical climates." India featured prominently in his book, even though Reece had never been there: knowing something of the West Indies and consulting sources at the East India Company's headquarters in London was apparently sufficient for the purpose.[115]

More generally, though, a significant feature of the tropical medical literature emerging in and about India at this time was the claim to authority based on personal observation and experience. J.P. Wade, writing in the 1790s and one of the first India-based physicians explicitly to identify Bengal with the tropics, scorned those authors who wrote "large treatises on the diseases of warm climates from the warm climate of a chimney corner in Europe."[116] This view was widely held by the growing band of medical practitioners in India. While clearly wishing to remain part of the wider medical and scientific community and contribute to its store of knowledge, they stressed the indispensability of their own, hard-won, local expertise. It was repeatedly stated that "the diseases of warmer latitudes differ very materially from such as afflict the inhabitants of cold climates," and that on-the-spot experience dictated that therapeutic methods must differ accordingly.[117] Perceptions of tropical difference (and the professional capital invested in such a concept) increasingly informed the distinctive nature of tropical medical practice.

Even with such an influential advocate as Johnson, India's incorporation into the medical topography of the tropics was not accomplished without some resistance. In a medical treatise of 1828, based on a quarter-century of medical practice in Madras, James Annesley wrote non-specifically of India's "inter-tropical" location, and, while making respectful reference to Humboldt on tropical America, he generally adhered to the older idiom of "warm climates" and their diseases. He drew upon a wide medical geography that included Mediterranean Europe and the southern United States as well as India, and when he wrote of the miasmas that emanated from swampy deltas his examples ranged from the Danube and Mississippi to the Orinoco, Indus, and Irrawaddy. In his view, the diseases of warm climates were still essentially those to be found during warm seasons in cooler northern lands.[118] Similarly in 1832 William Twining in Calcutta made scant reference to the tropics in his medical treatise on Bengal and observed that the fevers of the province "do not materially differ from the severe febrile diseases of unhealthy seasons in Europe."[119] Three years later, however, in a revised edition of his work, Twining included a new section on "tropical hygiene," added a discussion of hill-stations, and advised, after the manner of Moseley and Johnson, that for Europeans to preserve their health in a "tropical climate" it was important to live "temperately."[120] By the 1840s the representation of India's diseases as "tropical" or the products of a "tropical climate" was so commonplace as to require little explanation.[121]

Tropical Orientations and Tastes

It was not only the representation of "tropical" climate and disease that helped fashion India's emergent tropicality. Botany too was influential, and since many of India's botanists were also Company surgeons, one disciplinary perspective tended to reinforce the other. As botany moved toward the more systematic identification and classification of plants (and of those orders and genera that appeared most characteristic of tropical lands), so travel narratives and literary works exploited expanding plant knowledge to reinforce the wider representation and characterization of the tropics.

Plant taxonomy and physiology had their historic roots in Europe, where the "relative simplicity of temperate floras" made it possible for botanists to perceive patterns and devise viable schemes for the organization and identification of plants. However, increasing exposure to the tropics, or to plant specimens drawn from the tropics, forced European botanists to expand their understanding to accommodate "the incredible profusion and diversity of tropical plant life."[122] As one modern botanist has put it:

> The impressions of even a botanically trained person, on first visiting the tropics[,] are those of overwhelming astonishment. The myriads of unfamiliar kinds of plants, whole new families, woody members of "herbaceous" families ... numerous vines ... tree ferns, [and] profusion of epiphytes, all build a picture of strangeness and hopeless complexity ... The number of kinds of plants seems endless and it takes a great mental effort to fit what one sees into a framework developed to accommodate the temperate plant world.[123]

By the 1850s botanists could already look back on some two hundred years of European exploration of tropical flora, no small part of it carried out in South and Southeast Asia.[124] It was not surprising, therefore, that many naturalists began to see the tropics as having a floristic identity distinct from that of Europe or as possessing plants that symbolized the differences between the tropical and temperate zones of vegetation. Thus, for Humboldt, palm trees were particularly noble and emblematic representatives of tropical flora, just as bananas (or plantains) epitomized the fruitful, life-sustaining abundance of the "torrid zone" and provided the tropical equivalent of the cereal crops of Europe and western Asia or the rice of monsoon Asia.[125] Echoing Humboldt but writing specifically of India, J.F. Royle further remarked in the 1850s how bananas and plantains were "from their luxuriant-growing and large over-hanging leaves ... among the most characteristic forms of tropical vegetation." Palms, too, were very "conspicuous in tropical countries," the coconut palm being "one of the greatest ornaments" of tropical shorelines.[126] The form as well as the function of such emblematic plants helped define the tropics and so India's place within the tropics.

Significantly, one of the earliest and most enduring uses of the adjective "tropical" was to describe fruit.[127] In the days before supermarkets in Europe and North America stocked bananas, mangoes, pineapples, and papayas, such fruits could only be seen and tasted in the tropics themselves (apart from those aristocrats who could afford to grow pineapples in heated greenhouses or sailors who spiked pineapples on their gateposts to announce their return). The intra-tropical dissemination by the Portuguese and other European voyagers of fruit-bearing plants (along with other food crops), particularly from tropical America, emphasized the commonality of the tropics, as did the pan-tropic dissemination of such decorative trees and shrubs as jacaranda (from Brazil), hibiscus (from India) and bougainvillea (from the South Seas). By the early nineteenth century pineapples and guavas grew almost as plentifully half a world away in South Asia as they had in their original American habitats, just as Indian mangoes and (thanks to the persevering Captain Bligh) Tahitian breadfruit flourished in the West Indies. Tropical fruits and the plants that bore them helped delineate difference between the tropics and the temperate zone. In the realm of the senses, the tropics not only looked, but smelled and tasted, very different from Europe. Fruit articulated and symbolized important geo-cultural distinctions: the sight and taste of "European" fruits—apples, pears, cherries, raspberries, and strawberries— immediately made the European traveler nostalgic, just as durian, jackfruit, and guavas signaled the strange and sensual tropics. No wonder that

Jacquemont's first sight of banana and papaya trees in Haiti produced such ecstasy or that Moore, striving for the exotic in *Lalla Rookh*, remembered Marsden and invoked "Malay's nectar'd mangusteen."[128]

Within the fructiferous tropics, India had an assured place. Few visitors—or, indeed, conquerors—failed to remark on its fruits.[129] But early travelers often struggled to find a language to describe the unfamiliar produce of the tropics: for Edward Terry the taste of a plantain resembled a "Norwich peare," mangoes were "like to our apricots, but more luscious," and the flavor of the "ananas" or pineapple was a "pleasing compound made of strawberries, claret-wine, rose-water, and sugar, well tempered together."[130] By the early nineteenth century it was customary to list the abundance of tropical fruits that greeted the new arrival and to pass judgment on their merits.[131] Many enthused over the mango which, Hooker observed, "is certainly *the* fruit of India", though he was not alone in maintaining that India produced neither "tropical" nor "European" fruits of a high standard.[132] Heber, whose Romantic tastes did not extend to tropical fruits, was also unimpressed by what India offered, finding the plantain like "an indifferent mellow pear" and the guava "an almost equal mixture of raspberry jam and garlic."[133] Like so much else in the tropics that appeared superficially pleasurable, fruit was also a potent source of danger. The young and beautiful Rose Aylmer allegedly died in Calcutta in 1800 from a surfeit of that "mischievous and dangerous fruit, the pine-apple," despite Hickey sternly warning her to desist.[134] Fifty years later Dalhousie similarly attributed dysentery among British soldiers in Burma to excessive consumption of cheap, half-ripe pineapples.[135]

While the British were drawn toward "the Orient" by their diplomatic and military engagements in Sind, Afghanistan, and Persia, they were also being lured in the opposite direction by "tropical" Southeast Asia. The impetus for this came partly from the Napoleonic wars and British occupation of the Dutch East Indies. Until the war ended Java and Sumatra were major areas not only of British military and naval activity but also important sites for the archeological, historical, botanical, and ethnographical investigation of island Southeast Asia. Even after the Indonesian islands were returned to the Dutch, the takeover of Singapore in 1817 and retention of Malacca kept open an important scientific conduit between India and the Malaya world. The poet and linguist John Leyden, the naturalist William Jack, and the botanist William Griffith were among several Company surgeons who worked and died there. Contact across the Bay of Bengal was further extended by British expansion into Burma, beginning with the war of 1824–5. As elsewhere in South and Southeast Asia, military, diplomatic, and commercial activity stimulated scientific reconnaissance, but also encouraged the British to think of India in a wider geographical context. As early as 1769, Pennant's study of "Indian" zoology embraced a broad and brightly colored tropical world from the Ganges to New Guinea.[136] Marsden's *Sumatra*, with its frequent references back to India and its detailed depiction of tropical vegetation and climate, further extended the scientific frontier of British India across the Bay of Bengal, just as Jack's correspondence with Nathaniel Wallich in Calcutta helped strengthen the botanical connection and made Calcutta, for a generation or two, the capital of tropical South and Southeast Asia. Until other societies in Singapore and Penang began to usurp its sway, the Asiatic Society in Calcutta heard and published papers that commented upon the culture, antiquities, and natural history of Southeast Asia. And, as late as 1855, Hooker and Thomson's *Flora Indica* treated "Hindustan" as only one of the several botanical regions (along with the Himalaya, Afghanistan, and Ceylon) within their broad "Indian" remit.[137]

In 1820 John Crawfurd, another East India Company surgeon with experience of Burma, Siam, Penang, and Java, published his three-volume account of the *Indian Archipelago*. This repeatedly invoked the "high authority of that enlightened philosopher Baron Humboldt" and his depiction of tropical America, while boldly proposing Southeast Asia as "another new world, richer and more interesting than America." From Sumatra to New Guinea, the islands of Southeast Asia indisputably belonged, Crawfurd argued, to the tropics: they possessed barely inhabited "deep forests of stupendous trees" and had in abundance the "common characters of other tropical countries—heat, moisture, and luxuriant vegetation."[138] Except where India or China held sway, this was a portion of the globe in which literate civilizations seemed to have played little part. In the Malay tropical world, as in Humboldt's equatorial America, nature reigned. If that nature seemed more exuberant and preponderant in Southeast Asia than in India itself, the latter was nonetheless implicated in the tropicality of the former by dint of geographical proximity, the continuities of scenery, climate, and vegetation, and the administrative, commercial, and scientific ties that linked them together. What applied to Burma or Sumatra might apply willy-nilly to mainland India as well.[139]

That India belonged to the tropics by association and by expectation was no less evident from accounts of Ceylon. By the 1840s many European travelers to India touched first at Ceylon and had their tropical anticipations of India reinforced by their impressions of the adjacent island. The young German physician and naturalist W. Hoffmeister, accompanying Prince Waldemar of Prussia to India in 1844, arrived at Point de Galle by steamer from the Red Sea and was immediately dazzled by all he saw—by plantains, breadfruit, papaya and "a profusion of tropical fruits new to me," by "the magnificence of tropical nature," by coconut palms, hibiscus shrubs, myna birds, and parrots, and by the apparently carefree contentment of the islanders.[140] "It is impossible," he declared, "to describe the wondrous impression made upon the traveller by the luxuriance of tropical nature; the warm, humid, heavy air, laden with the perfumes of spices and of cocoa-nut oil, and the fairy-like glancing of the light... through the palmy crests above." "Everything," he added, "produces an impression of dreaminess and repose."[141]

Joseph Hooker's impressions of Ceylon, which he also visited *en route* to Calcutta three years after Hoffmeister were remarkably similar to the German naturalist's and almost equally enthusiastic.[142] But visiting India after the "voluptuous verdure of Ceylon"[143] proved for both men to be a profound shock. Arriving in Calcutta shortly after leaving the island, and visiting its famed botanic garden, it was at first not difficult for Hoffmeister to see Bengal, too, as a "perfect Paradise;" but, as he moved up-country with his prince, his mood rapidly changed. His disappointment grew as he no longer saw the enchanting tropics, only something more akin to the "monotony of the arid desert."[144] India might be deemed tropical by association with its neighbors—Burma, Sumatra, and Ceylon especially—but the actual experience of visiting the country might engender the contrary impression, that, while much of India lay technically within the tropics, it was largely devoid of the scenic, sensual, and scientific expectations that the idea of the tropics had come so powerfully to represent in European minds.

5
NETWORKS AND KNOWLEDGES

PREVIOUS CHAPTERS HAVE FOCUSED ON TRAVEL WRITING AND LITERARY representations of the Indian landscape. This chapter takes up for more detailed consideration the ways in which nature was represented through science, and particularly through botany, one of the principal fields of scientific activity during the Company period. It examines the personal and professional context of botanists' engagement with the plant-life of the region, the networks of communication and patronage that helped sustain them, and the systems of knowledge they employed in their work. In turning to the professionalization of nature, this chapter does not thereby abandon earlier themes: rather, it offers further perspectives on the part that the tropics and the traveling gaze played in the constitution and articulation of colonial science. As one of the sciences most widely practiced and institutionally grounded in the early nineteenth century, botany was influentially involved in the scenic depiction as well as the scientific investigation and material exploitation of the country.

How a science like botany functioned in a colonial setting, how (or how far) it succeeded in straddling the spatial and epistemological divide between Europe and India, has been a critical issue in emerging debates about science and empire. There is less of a presumption now that science in the colonies meekly followed or imperfectly replicated metropolitan science, or that science in the "periphery" was little more than empiricist fact-finding and specimen-collecting, a second order activity compared to more intellectual, trail-blazing enterprise of science at the "core." And yet, if old and unsustainable shibboleths have crumbled, the exact nature of the relationship between metropole and colony remains in many respects insufficiently explored and imperfectly conceptualized. Recent literature on the history of science, for India as elsewhere, still suggests a wide spectrum of possibilities. These range from the wholesale transfer of European scientific personnel and practices to the colonies with little evident departure from metropolitan methods and institutional precedents, through the parallel evolution of distinctive scientific priorities and specialties resulting from colonial needs and opportunities, to the selective (or even substantial) incorporation of vernacular knowledge into metropolitan science and the mutual constitution of science as much through local, extra-European inputs as through metropolitan initiatives and networking.[1]

This lack of consensus is not surprising given the diversity of scientific fields involved, the varied and changing nature of the colonies themselves, and the differing degree to which pre-existing knowledge systems had the ability or opportunity to influence European scientific ideas and practices. But, it might be asked in the context of early nineteenth-century India (unquestionably one of the most important sites of scientific activity outside Europe), how far, by what routes, and to what effect, did a science like botany *travel*—whether between India and Europe, or between Indian and European systems of knowledge? To what extent was botany as practiced by Europeans influenced by, or even predicated upon, indigenous knowledge and agency, or, conversely, how far did it seek to distance itself from them?

Although travel thus remains a continuing theme in this discussion, the present chapter is as much concerned with the interconnectedness of scientific lives and botanical texts as previous ones have been with overlapping itineraries and intersecting travelogues. The pursuit of botany in early nineteenth-century India is particularly seen here from the vantage point of William Hooker. Hooker was one of Britain's most eminent and, especially once he became director of Kew Gardens, most influential and well-connected botanists: his contacts and exchanges with India yield valuable insights into the multiple functions of colonial science at the time. His enthusiastic but distant engagement with South Asia in turn forms a basis for discussion in the following chapter of his son Joseph Hooker's botanical expedition to India and the Himalaya in 1848–51.

Hooker, Wallich, and Tropical Botany

Born at Norwich in 1785, William Jackson Hooker's interest in South Asia long pre-dated his son's arrival there in the closing weeks of 1847. Nearly forty years earlier, in 1808, Sir Joseph Banks (his patron and president of the Royal Society in London), had proposed that William Hooker should visit Ceylon to investigate its natural history. The flora of the island had received some attention from earlier botanists, but its recent acquisition from the Dutch created new possibilities for the British: the island, renowned for its cinnamon, seemed to offer British commerce the opportunity to develop other tropical products. As an adviser to the East India Company, Banks was already familiar with the activities of several botanists working for the Company in Madras and Bengal, including Johan König, formerly attached to the Tranquebar Mission in South India, who had entered Company service in 1778 but died seven years later, and William Roxburgh, who succeeded Robert Kyd as superintendent of the Calcutta botanic garden in 1793.[2] In practice, events (including the resumption of international warfare) intervened and William Hooker, unable to execute his "projected voyage to a tropical climate," settled instead for Iceland, a country Banks had also visited in 1772.[3] Almost at the opposite climatic extreme from Ceylon, Iceland proved nonetheless to be botanically significant. The substitution of a cold, almost treeless island in the North Atlantic for one basking in the Indian Ocean and teeming with tropical life is indicative of the way in which European botany at the time was actively seeking to expand its frontiers of knowledge, whether by pressing northwards toward the Arctic Circle or by venturing south into the "torrid zone."

If Banks provided the young William Hooker with one important source of patronage, his marriage to Maria Turner in 1815 gave him a further prop. His father-in-law, Dawson Turner, was a keen botanist as well as a prosperous Norfolk banker. Marriage gave Hooker access to a degree of family wealth and a social standing he might not otherwise have attained. It enabled him to become a professional botanist rather than a dedicated amateur; but in return, and virtually until his death in 1858, Turner expected to advise William (and later Joseph) and have a say in their botanical careers.[4] He, like the Hookers, was also an indefatigable correspondent, thinking nothing of writing twenty letters in an evening and he regularly read out the correspondence he received to his family

FIG. 9. Sir William Hooker, photograph, c. 1855.
Reproduced by kind permission of the National Portrait Gallery, London.

and visitors.[5] When his son Gurney Turner (sixteen years Maria's junior) left home to join the Bengal Medical Service in 1839, his accounts of life and work in India were regularly passed on to the Hookers.[6] There was a further family connection with India through W.J. Palgrave, a son of Maria's younger sister Elizabeth, who joined the Bombay Army in the 1840s, though his great enthusiasm was hunting, and not, as the "unworthy nephew" confessed to his uncle, botany.[7] Thus, when Joseph Hooker arrived in India in January 1848, he, like many other well-connected members of the British middle classes, already had relatives installed in the Indian services.

After Iceland, William Hooker made no further attempt to visit India or Ceylon; his career led him elsewhere. But the exchange of letters, at a personal as well as a professional level (between fellow naturalists), did much to make India accessible to those like Hooker who had never been there in person. The empire of affect and the empire of science repeatedly intersected in the Hooker household as they did across early Victorian Britain as a whole. Janet Browne has remarked on the way in which Charles Darwin assiduously used his extensive network of correspondents in Britain and abroad as a means of tapping the knowledge of other naturalists and gaining access through letter writing to the wealth of "international intellectual endeavour." His achievements, she argues, especially with regard to the theory of evolution, "were manifestly the product of a highly efficient Victorian communication system, firmly embedded in what can be called knowledge-producing relationships."[8] The Indian correspondence and contacts of first William Hooker, and then Joseph, reveal a not dissimilar pattern of "knowledge-producing relationships" at work.[9]

In 1820, through the influence of Banks shortly before he died, William Hooker consolidated his position as a rising botanist by appointment to the newly created chair of botany at Glasgow University. Knighted in 1836, he outmaneuvered his closest rival, John Lindley, Professor of Botany at University College London, by moving to Kew as Director of the Royal Botanic Gardens in 1841.[10] During his twenty-one years in Glasgow (building in part on his Banksian connections), Hooker created one of the finest private herbaria in Europe. Not only did it include large numbers of North American and Arctic species, but Hooker also began to correspond with Europeans in India and in other parts of South and Southeast Asia who were willing to send him specimens from their own collections or gather them for him. By the 1840s the range of his India correspondents was remarkable, a tribute both to his personal standing as one of Britain's leading botanists and also to his tireless letter writing and his skill in nurturing the botanical enthusiasm of those he communicated with.

As in Britain, where the court and nobility remained influential patrons, Hooker made contact with aristocrats who held high positions in India. In 1833, while still in Glasgow, he was approached by Lady Dalhousie, wife of the ninth Earl, who sought help in identifying the plants she had collected including a number of Himalayan plants gathered near Simla during her husband's term as commander-in-chief of the Indian Army.[11] When she died in 1839, she bequeathed part of her collection to Hooker.[12] In August 1847, when Joseph Hooker was planning his Indian expedition, William contacted the tenth Earl, who was about to take up the governor-generalship, to remind him of his mother's interest in Indian botany and to seek his influential assistance for his own son. Dalhousie obliged by inviting Joseph to accompany him to India and (for the second stage of the journey from Egypt) to join his personal suite.[13]

Not all the Hookers' contacts occupied so elevated a place in colonial society. Most were practicing (but not always professional) botanists, and though many were employed by the Company in its medical, military, and administrative services, Hooker's correspondence frequently bypassed the formal structures of the Indian administration. One of William's earliest, most valued and enduring, contacts was with Nathaniel Wallich. Born in Copenhagen in 1786, Wallich entered the Danish medical service and was sent to Serampore in Bengal as a surgeon. When the British annexed the Danish enclave in 1809, he became first a prisoner and then a surgeon under the English Company. It was, however, as a botanist rather than as a physician that Wallich flourished, and in 1817, on Banks's recommendation, he was appointed to succeed Francis Buchanan (the acting superintendent) at the Calcutta botanic garden. He gratefully repaid his patron by sending him Indian, Himalayan, and Southeast Asian plants for Kew.[14] Wallich cultivated successive governors-general and their families, including the Amhersts, naming the glorious scarlet flowered *Amherstia nobilis* after Lady Amherst and her daughter, and the Aucklands, for whom he obligingly laid out a garden at Barrackpore. Some of these aristocratic families were genuinely interested in botany. Others, like many of Calcutta's European elite, merely regarded the botanic garden as a convenient pleasure park in which to picnic and escape from the city's heat and bustle.[15]

Despite Jacquement's dismissive description of him as "a rather inferior Danish botanist,"[16] Wallich was a loyal and enterprising servant of both botany and the Company. From 1825 to 1827 he undertook a survey of teak trees in Burma, which was later seen as laying the foundations for forest conservation in India; he likewise reported on the forests of Awadh and the northwest.[17] As superintendent of the Calcutta garden, he inherited from Roxburgh and Buchanan an enormous collection of plants, drawn from different parts of the subcontinent, and to these he added further by his own plant-collecting expeditions, notably to Nepal in 1820–2 (previously visited by Buchanan in 1802–3), where he acquired more than 2,500 species. Travel, whether by botanists themselves or by proxy, through "native" collectors, was the indispensable means of unlocking the plant wealth of southern Asia, especially as many of the most botanically interesting and attractive plants were to be found not in the more accessible plains but in remoter upland areas, like the Nilgiri and Palni hills in the south and the Himalaya and Khasi hills in the north and northeast.[18] Wallich was one of the first naturalists to benefit from the

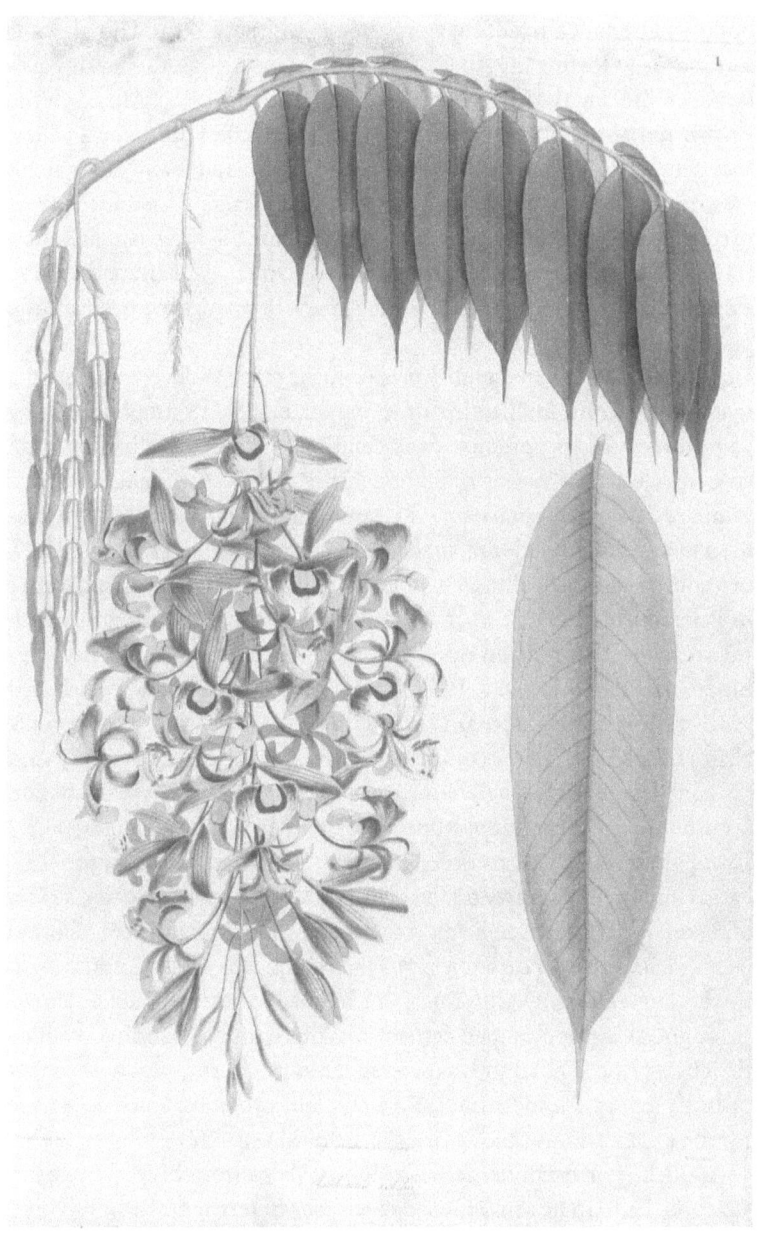

FIG. 10. *Amherstia nobilis*, from Nathaniel Wallich, *Plantae Asiaticae Rariores*, vol. 1 (1830), drawn by Vishnu Prasad.

botanical bonanza resulting from the opening up of the Himalaya to Europeans following the Anglo-Gurkha War (as he was, too, of Burma's botany following the first stage of its annexation in 1825). Although the British remained restricted by the Nepalese to the Kathmandu valley, they sent out collectors to gather plants for them and many of Wallich's "discoveries" were made in this way. These botanical finds included plants used locally for timber, dyestuffs, and medicines, as well as magnolias, rhododendrons, alpines and others whose ornamental qualities, including elegant shapes and attractive flowers,[19] made them highly prized among plant connoisseurs in Europe.

Access to such a vast quantity of specimens made Wallich an influential figure in the commodification of Indian plant-life. Although monetary gain was seldom the foremost consideration (the pursuit of botany often cost India's naturalists far more financially than it ever repaid them), it was hard for contemporaries not to think, if only metaphorically, of access to so many exotic and desirable species as a form of tangible wealth. Thus, in a common turn of phrase, in reporting his recent botanical discoveries in Penang in 1819, Jack wrote to Wallich, "I am . . . overwhelmed with the treasures that pour in upon me."[20] In similar fashion, shortly after his friend's death in 1854, William Hooker observed that Wallich had "such means at his disposal for studying and dispensing the vegetable riches of India and other countries, as have never been at the command of any single individual before or since."[21] By 1827 Wallich had accumulated a herbarium estimated at between 6,500 and 9,000 species (compared to the 2,000 recorded in Roxburgh's *Flora Indica* twenty years earlier and the 14,500 eventually incorporated into Joseph Hooker's *Flora of British India*). The publication of his Nepalese flora in 1826, followed by his *Plantae Asiaticae Rariores* (1830–2), combined with the distribution in the late 1820s of large numbers of plant specimens to botanists throughout Europe, helped cement his international standing. Wallich thereby advanced not only his own reputation: he further established that of India, broadly understood, as a rich plant province, a privileged site for the exploration of the "glories of tropical vegetation."[22]

Wallich's correspondence with Hooker dates from his early years in Calcutta. In 1818 he sent Hooker specimens of ferns, mosses, and other "invaluable treasures" collected by the British Resident, Colonel Edward Gardner, in Nepal, "that inexhaustible mine" as Wallich termed it.[23] In return for Himalayan plants, Hooker sent Wallich samples of his own wares—including copies of his botanical publications—and promised to publicize Wallich's discoveries in British journals. Wallich also introduced Hooker to other botanists keen to correspond with him and to exchange plant specimens, articles, and information. These included John Forbes Royle, superintendent of the Company's Saharanpur botanic garden from 1823 to 1831, who was interested in acquiring both tropical and temperate species,[24] and William Carey, the Baptist missionary. Carey was delighted to send Hooker some dried plants as a way of advancing "the study of a science which has always been to me a source of pleasure." Repaid with four volumes of his correspondent's *Flora Exotica*, Carey's modest request was for geranium and helianthus seeds to grow in his own extensive garden at Serampore.[25]

Wallich was no grand theorizer. He showed little interest in plant geography or anatomy, or in the more "philosophical" issues of the distribution and variation of species that later intrigued Joseph Hooker and fueled his discussions with Darwin and Lyell. Wallich's significance was as a key figure in the patronage networks that surrounded botany in the East India Company's territories, and as a scientific entrepreneur, the man who, more than any other single individual, controlled and delivered to the West, India's vast botanical "riches." The "great Wallichian herbarium" rapidly became "one of the foundations of Indian botany" and an indispensable source of reference for all subsequent studies of South Asian flora.[26] He thereby brought to Europe's attention the extraordinary wealth and diversity of plant-life in India and neighboring lands, from the mosses and magnolias of Nepal to the flowering trees and stately palms of Burma and Malaya. In 1828 Wallich transported to London a large part of Calcutta's accumulated plant booty; he spent the next three years there distributing specimens, inviting metropolitan experts like Hooker, Bentham, and Lindley, and visiting savants like Alphonse de Candolle, to examine his botanical hoard and help classify plant species. He was delighted when the Court of Directors agreed to present the bulk of his collection to the Linnean Society, thereby assuring him a prominent place in metropolitan science.[27]

It was during these years, through a decade of correspondence, that Wallich and William Hooker (still in Glasgow) became close friends, exchanging, often by post, botanical information and a great deal of personal and professional gossip. When in 1832 the Court of Directors insisted that Wallich return to Calcutta, he expressed his deep dismay to Hooker: he was, he wrote, already (at 46) an old man and his ruined constitution (undermined by malaria contracted in Nepal ten years earlier) could not survive further exposure to India. "My distress is beyond all utterance," he wrote to Hooker as he left to take ship for India; "it is almost beyond endurance."[28] In fact, despite nagging ill health, Wallich survived in Calcutta for another nine years. When he finally retired to London in 1846, he resumed his frequent—at times almost daily— correspondence with William Hooker. He died in 1854, aged 68, having five years earlier become a vice-president of the Royal Society, a scientific honor and sign of metropolitan esteem he had long sought. For the Hookers, Wallich remained, even in retirement, an invaluable link with the East India Company and the botany of its eastern possessions. Not only did William Hooker think highly of the "indefatigable" Wallich; he also regarded his "tropical experience" as "probably greater than that of any other botanist" of his day.[29]

Networking India

Although by the late 1830s William Hooker was keen to leave Glasgow and return to England,[30] as far as Indian botany was concerned, his Scottish sojourn was invaluable. It facilitated connections not just with Scottish aristocrats like the Dalhousies but also with the many Scots in the Company's service, particularly surgeons who had received their medical training at Edinburgh or Glasgow.[31] To take one example, Hugh Falconer, who graduated from Edinburgh University in 1829, had become interested in botany as a student and boasted of having a copy of Hooker's *Flora Scotia* with him in the "marching library" he took to the Himalaya and Saharanpur, where he succeeded Royle as superintendent. Keen to contact a metropolitan expert who might keep him abreast of current science and publish the results of his labors, Falconer wrote to Hooker in 1837, offering as bait his interest in the *Orchideae*, "if I mistake not ... a favourite family of yours."[32] Though Hooker responded, Falconer proved a poor correspondent. Despite extensive plant collections made in Kashmir, Kumaon, and Punjab, Falconer's reputation was established not through botany but as co-discoverer of the momentous Siwalik fossils, which revealed the rich faunal life of the tertiary sub-Himalaya.

Like Wallich, Falconer took most of his scientific treasure trove with him to London in the early 1840s. He thereby left India the poorer,[33] but

in this age of booty-laden returning naturalists—nature's nabobs—
scientific circles in Britain offered a far more prestigious forum for
exhibiting accumulated "riches" than Saharanpur or Calcutta. The earlier
association of India with fabled wealth and easy plunder may have receded
and been overshadowed by images of poverty and famine, but, like the
Wallichian herbarium, the Siwalik fossils demonstrated to metropolitan
science the extraordinary wealth of natural objects India possessed and
the rich scientific tribute it could pay its imperial masters. Falconer became
a prominent figure in geological circles in London: he was befriended,
among others, by Darwin and Joseph Hooker. But his presence in London,
like that of Wallich, also created reciprocal opportunities for metropolitan
naturalists to establish or develop their colonial connections. Thus, it
was Falconer who directed Joseph Hooker to the relatively unexplored
northeast Himalaya and Darjeeling ("the *richest* and least explored
botanical station of India"),[34] rather than Kumaon or Assam, areas already
extensively botanized by Jacquemont, Griffith, and others.[35]

Bound by his terms of service to the Company, Falconer grudgingly
returned to Calcutta in 1848, showing as much reluctance as Wallich
had sixteen years earlier; he was to take charge of the botanic garden and
teach botany at the city's medical college. Despite having mixed with
the leading naturalists of his day in London, Falconer brought little by
way of scientific innovation or inspiration back to India with him. Being
sent like Wallich before him to investigate the teak forests of Burma did
nothing to improve either his health or his humor.[36] Even so, as a
prominent—if often ill and irascible—figure in Calcutta's small scientific
community,[37] and superintendent of the botanic garden, Falconer's
assistance and expertise (and perhaps even more that of his able Bengali
deputy Kali Kumar Mukherji) proved invaluable to Joseph Hooker.
Although Hooker raged over his friend's "dilatoriness" and erratic
correspondence, fearing that his precious collections would be left to rot
in Calcutta, it was through Falconer that Hooker's vast Himalayan haul—
packets of seeds, boxes of dried plants, sealed tins and glazed cases full of
roots and cuttings, as well as crates of curiosities from porcupine quills
to Tibetan prayer wheels—was sorted, packed up and sent on to Kew.[38]
In return, Falconer asked William Hooker for any tropical, especially
West Indian and South American, plants that Kew could spare.[39] Falconer
finally left India in 1855, resuming the life in British science he had
unwillingly quit seven years before; he died in 1865.

As the London careers of Wallich and Falconer show, direct personal contacts were important; but botany, especially colonial botany, relied as heavily upon letters, the exchange of plant specimens, and the circulation of printed texts. Where other metropolitan botanists proved too self-absorbed to invest much time in writing to far-away botanists craving metropolitan approval, William Hooker was extraordinarily painstaking in his correspondence. Although few of his letters to India survive,[40] it is clear from the generally enthusiastic responses he received from correspondents that he wrote frequently and responded in patient detail to their taxonomical queries, encouraging novices to persevere with their collecting, to send him specimens and drawings, and to write up their observations for publication in his journals. This careful nurturing of botanical relationships can best be seen through his correspondence with John Ellerton Stocks. Born near Hull in 1820 and a former pupil of Lindley's at University College London, Stocks began writing to William Hooker at Kew soon after he joined the Bombay Medical Service in 1847. Stocks quickly cast diffidence aside and began to write Hooker long, ebullient letters, full of exclamation marks and underlining, revealing his growing passion for botany, his undisguised delight in new plants discovered in Sind and Baluchistan, and his frustration at administrative duties that stopped him from collecting even more plants.[41] Stocks clearly relished Hooker's "kindness & remembrances," just as he "treasured" the detailed taxonomic advice, which saved him, he cheerily acknowledged, from "adding to the Botanical Dungheap made up of synonyms."[42]

Hooker displayed an almost parental concern for his correspondents. For many of them—lonely, often unmarried, anxious to escape the isolation and tedium of their posting and make some mark on the world—Hooker was more than a scientific patron and mentor. At the least, his correspondents found his letters "interesting and instructive;" others, less guardedly, regarded letters from such a "kind and generous friend" as a source of "both pleasure and profit." They were overjoyed to receive books, to see their botanical notes (judiciously culled by Hooker from their letters) appear in print, or, like Stocks, to have species, even genera, named in their honor.[43] Perhaps Hooker tapped into a deeper emotional vein than he consciously realized. Botany was certainly not incompatible with marriage: from the days of William and Anna Maria Jones onwards, botany in India had often been a companionable husband-and-wife pursuit. But many of the botanists of the early nineteenth century (including

Falconer, Stocks, and Thomson) never married, or like Griffith and Wight did so late in their Indian careers, or (like Royle) only after leaving India, and this at a time when liaisons with Indian women, once commonplace, had become unacceptable among the imperial race. As a male occupation and recreation, botany, with its acquisitive drive and ardent pursuit of "rare beauties," served (in one of its many registers) as a surrogate, if not for sexual satisfaction, then at least for the intimacy of missing family relationships.

By the 1840s Hooker had more than twenty regular correspondents in India, ranging from the superintendents and head gardeners at botanic gardens, through Company surgeons and army officers, to civil servants and missionaries. His contacts were strongest in North India and Bombay, but they ranged across the subcontinent from Sind to Ceylon, from the Nilgiris to Assam. About half of these contacts had initially been made through Wallich. In moving to Kew, Hooker assumed even greater stature in the eyes of India-based botanists, just as he redoubled his efforts "to be put in communication with any person who has a taste for botany."[44] Many of his correspondents felt that by sending plants to Kew they were fulfilling an imperial duty and helping to assure India its rightful place in the wider conspectus of science and empire. One of Hooker's best-placed contacts was Major F. Jenkins, Commissioner for Assam. In addition to keeping Hooker informed about the progress of the tea industry, Jenkins regularly supplied him (via his own collectors) with orchids and other plants from one of the most botanically bountiful provinces of India. Jenkins explained in 1846 that he saw this "not only as a point of duty in one of H[er] M[ajesty's] subjects having the opportunity of adding to our national stores in any way, but especially for the pleasure of seeing the plants of this Province done justice to."[45]

"Indian Botany," remarked William Hooker in 1848, "has always charms for me."[46] By mid-century, he had amassed by purchase, gift, and exchange, an enormous collection of Indian plants.[47] Given his growing stature and influence, however, it was inevitable that he should also dabble in the patronage politics of British India and thereby seek to promote those botanists whom he thought most deserving or most in tune with his own outlook and ambitions. One of the most significant recipients of his attention was Thomas Thomson. Born in 1817, Thomson was the son of one of William Hooker's professorial colleagues in Glasgow, a boyhood friend of Joseph's, and one of his own students. He qualified with a Glasgow MD, and joined the Bengal Medical Service in 1839, at the same time that Joseph set out for the Antarctic. Confident of Thomson's potential as a botanist, William Hooker kept in touch with him, though he proved to be one of the most self-effacing of his India correspondents. In 1841 Thomson was sent to Afghanistan as part of the British invasion force: besieged and taken prisoner at Ghazni, he was about to be sent to Bukhara to be sold as a slave when his captors were bribed to release him and his fellow captives into the hands of the British relief force. Like many other victims of this disastrous war,[48] Thomson wrote a painful account of his ordeal (which Joseph later read).

As well as seriously affecting his health and sending him into "a fit of deep depression," Thomson lost most of his possessions in Afghanistan, including his botanical collections and microscopes. But William Hooker had not lost faith in his young protégé: "My father," Joseph Hooker later confided to Brian Hodgson, "whose heart is set on Thomson," was determined to advance his career in any way he could.[49] In 1847 he lobbied unsuccessfully for Thomson to be given temporary charge of the Calcutta botanic garden,[50] and then, shortly before Joseph's arrival in India, he helped secure for Thomson a prestigious place as naturalist on a three-man expedition to Kashmir and Tibet. This temporarily freed Thomson from army duty and enabled him to rebuild his botanical collection. Hooker printed extracts from Thomson's letters in his journal and encouraged him to publish his narrative, which he did in 1852.[51]

At the end of December 1849 Thomson joined Joseph Hooker in Darjeeling, the start of a period of collaboration they had planned since boyhood.[52] Hooker recognized that Thomson's knowledge of Indian flora neatly complemented his own, being especially strong for North India and the western Himalaya, regions Hooker had not visited. For his part Thomson had decided to refuse any appointment that might interfere with his "scientific pursuits" and regarded collaboration with Joseph Hooker as more than a matter of friendship: "Being associated with so eminent, enthusiastic & laborious a man is not," he informed his father, "a prospect to be willingly relinquished."[53] Although it cost Thomson a year's furlough, the two botanized together in the Khasi hills, East Bengal and Chittagong, and decided to pool their expertise to produce the definitive flora India still lacked.

Thomson's contribution to this joint enterprise (the *Flora Indica*, of which only the first volume ever appeared) was indispensable, but

Hooker, a stern judge even of his friends, frequently lost patience with Thomson's "excessive scrupulosity," "natural slowness," and "matchless procrastination."[54] Yet in 1854 when Falconer informed William Hooker of his impending retirement as superintendent of the Calcutta garden, the latter again pressed Thomson's claims and it was agreed that they should "secure the appointment" for him, even though William Jameson (another surgeon-naturalist, then at Saharanpur) had greater seniority.[55] In 1855, the same year that Joseph Hooker became his father's deputy at Kew, Thomson took over as superintendent in Calcutta. Like the *Flora Indica* of that year, Thomson's appointment underscored the value of collaboration between botanists in colony and metropole, and on his return to India Thomson appealed to botanists in India to assist in collecting the data that could alone make the publication of further volumes of the *Flora* possible.[56] But at the same time the appointment of Thomson, the Hookers' protégé and collaborator, also signaled the growing dominance of Kew over the botanical establishment in India.

Economic Botany

In considering more closely the development of botany and colonial science in India in the early nineteenth century it is necessary to distinguish between the East India Company and its scientific servants. The Court of Directors in London prided itself on being a patron of science, if only to remind the British public and government that the Company had more than a narrowly material interest in India. Naturalists in the Company's service in India, recognizing that their careers and the active pursuit of science depended heavily upon the Court's favor, appealed to the Directors' vanity by praising their "munificence" and "liberality," hailing them as "the enlightened and liberal patrons of botanical science."[57] Privately, however, they muttered about the Court's ingratitude, its capricious whims and meager purse, especially when it came to subsidizing expensive volumes of natural history. Prestigious and lavishly illustrated works, like those of Roxburgh, Wallich, and Royle on Indian botany, fulsomely dedicated to the Court of Directors, proclaimed the Company's ownership over India and impressed upon readers the extent of British knowledge and, by implication, power. But in the main the Company supported science for the material benefits it was expected to bring and as an aid to conquering, administering, and taxing its territories.

From the Company's perspective, botany clearly had its utilitarian value—or potential value. Since the 1770s, following the path blazed by Banks as an adviser to the Company, botany had been closely identified with practical needs and commercial opportunities. Economic botany in India was concerned with identifying and establishing the properties of plants used as vegetable dyes or tanning materials, of timber suited for construction or fibers for sacking and cordage. It was also committed to the introduction and dissemination of new or improved varieties of such "tropical" crops as cotton, tobacco, and sugarcane. Calcutta's botanic garden had explicitly been established with such practical purposes in view and Roxburgh, as its first professional botanist, dedicatedly pursued this agenda during his tenure as superintendent.[58]

A related concern, no less important in motivating the Company's patronage of botany, was *materia medica*, identifying plants known to have therapeutic properties (or which, conversely, might be dangerous to use medically) and establishing whether they might replace the use of expensive imported drugs. By the 1840s and 1850s, through a combination of indigenous knowledge and European botanical research, India's medicinal plants had been extensively cataloged, and though many remained, from a Western perspective, untried, others had found their way into the European pharmacopoeia.[59] However, even in this regard the Court of Directors could be remarkably shortsighted. It failed to act, for instance, when Royle proposed in 1839 that cinchona, native to South America, be grown in India to provide quinine for use against malaria, even though this disease was one of the main causes of sickness and death among its servants and in the population at large. Cinchona only began to be cultivated in India in 1860.[60]

As William Hooker's correspondents frequently wrote, the aims, interests, and personal enthusiasms of individual botanists in India were not always identical to, or even reconcilable with, the Company's own priorities or vacillating concerns. However, the career of John Forbes Royle illustrates how a personal commitment to botany could be broadly compatible with Company service and, further, how botany as practiced in India could yet find a recognized place in wider scientific circles. The son of a Bengal Army officer, Royle was born at Kanpur in 1799. Educated in Edinburgh, he acquired a stronger taste for botany than for military service, but, since there were few opportunities at the time for professional botanists, he joined the Bengal Medical Service as an assistant surgeon in 1819. In 1823 he was appointed to Saharanpur where for the next eight years he supervised the Company's botanic garden, which he described to William Hooker as being both "highly ornamental" and "a very useful institution."[61] Although scholarly attention has mainly focused on the Calcutta garden, Saharanpur, a thousand miles to the northwest, had an equally important role in the development of India's botany and in the increasing delineation of its tropical, as opposed to temperate, climatic zones and flora.

In 1839, after retiring from the service and returning to Britain, Royle published his *Illustrations of the Botany ... of the Himalayan Mountains*, based on material collected at Saharanpur. This was followed by a number of works—on *materia medica*, fibrous plants, cotton cultivation, and the plant resources of India in general—that extended his own research or summarized recent progress in applied botany.[62] Elements of indigenous knowledge surfaced in Royle's work, notably in naming plants and identifying their therapeutic and other uses. But his practical interest in plant geography, involving temperate/tropical differences, and in the results of recent experiments in "improving" Indian agriculture, made him far more than either a recorder and recycler of Oriental knowledge or a passive instrument of metropolitan scientific enquiry. One of Royle's ambitions was to remove the "unaccountable discrepancy" between the apparent fertility of India's soil and the poor quality of its natural products. In so doing, he hoped to help develop the country's "immense resources" for the benefit of India and Britain alike. Since the "Hindu cultivator" needed to be taught "by example rather than by precept," it was one of the tasks of economic botany to introduce and disseminate "tropical" and "extra tropical" plants that would contribute to the progress of Indian agriculture.[63]

Royle had long been interested in connections and correspondences over time as well as across geographical space. In his work on medicinal plants, he tried to relate India's *materia medica* to that of the Greeks and Arabs, thereby establishing the antiquity of "Hindu medicine" and its links with early Western medicine.[64] But the spatial dimensions of Royle's work steadily assumed more importance than the temporal, propelling him away from the concerns of Orientalist scholarship and closer to India's nascent tropicality. In his *Illustrations* in 1839, Royle firmly aligned

India with the tropical world: its coasts were "washed by tropical oceans," and between the sea and the Himalaya much of the vegetation was said to be "of a tropical nature." It followed that across India as a whole, the "valuable products of tropical countries"—such as cocoa, nutmeg, and cashew—might usefully be "acclimed."[65] At Saharanpur, within sight of the Himalaya, the climate was "tropical at one season, and partially European at another,"[66] and this experience encouraged Royle to see a practical value in differentiating between India's predominantly tropical conditions and its more temperate areas. He drew up a table of correspondences between India and those parts of the globe that might provide it with "useful" plants. The most clearly "tropical" regions of India (Travancore, Malabar, Chittagong, Bengal, and lower Assam) he equated with the East Indies, Brazil, the West Indies, and Florida; the "extra tropical" localities of northern India (including Saharanpur and the northern Doab) corresponded to South Africa, Australia, and South America (below the Tropic of Capricorn); and "temperate" India (the Nilgiris, upper Assam, and the Himalaya) approximated to China, Japan, and the Andes.[67] In making these biogeographical connections, Royle cited Humboldt, arguing that the factors—climate, altitude, aspect—affecting the natural distribution of plants in the Himalaya closely corresponded with those given by Humboldt for vegetation on the slopes of Mt Chimborazo.[68]

The *Illustrations* established Royle as a leading authority on India's economic botany. Following his return to Britain in 1831, he was appointed professor of *materia medica* at King's College London, and in 1838 took charge of the plant collections at India House, the Company's headquarters in London. He thus became the Court of Directors' principal botanical adviser, a position of patronage and authority he jealously guarded both in his dealings with surgeon-botanists in India and with naturalists like Lindley, Bentham, and Hooker in Britain.[69] The Hookers found him uninspiring and self-important (Joseph once described him as "flatulent"), but he had become too powerful and well connected for them to ignore. Many of the plant specimens William Hooker received from India came via Royle at India House,[70] and in 1849 he diplomatically named one of his son's newly discovered rhododendrons after Royle.[71] Royle may not have inspired much affection among fellow botanists, but he was relatively successful in bridging the gulf between colonial and metropolitan science, bringing, through his books, articles, lectures, and involvement in the Great Exhibition of 1851, an enhanced appreciation in Britain of India's natural resources and the contribution its botany could make to trade and empire.

However, to a "philosophical" botanist like Joseph Hooker, Royle's observations on plant geography appeared somewhat superficial. Reverential references to the "illustrious" Humboldt abounded in India's scientific literature, the lack of a naturalist of comparable stature having long been regarded as one of the country's greatest deficiencies. Royle came closer than many of his contemporaries to filling this lacuna, but his biogeography remained limited in both conceptual scope and empirical detail. To his critics, Royle's work on Himalayan flora was an assemblage of "valuable and curious" details but it lacked a more analytical purpose. There was a "vast amount of ... miscellaneous matter," but too little attempt to structure it schematically, and the taxonomy was flawed by the mistaken assumption that many of the plants described were new to botany. Perhaps his commitment to economic botany and to the Company's material interests made it difficult for Royle to persuade metropolitan science that he was a botanical innovator and interpreter rather than a glorified collector. Colonial botany, as represented by Royle, appeared to its critics to be "laborious," unimaginative, and excessively practical—as if plants that were "useful" were necessarily more important to botanical science than those that were not.[72]

Further, unlike Humboldt, Royle was no great traveler. His personal knowledge of the tropics was confined to India, and although he made some plant-collecting forays into the Himalaya (one in Jacquemont's company), his duties at Saharanpur precluded more extensive travel. His observations on Himalayan flora were heavily reliant on specimens purchased in Indian bazaars, brought to him by Kashmiri merchants or gathered by gardeners from Saharanpur.[73] It was not always possible, therefore, for Royle to know exactly where individual plants had originated or the conditions in which they grew in the wild. Nor, without greater personal experience of the region, could he more accurately relate the complex topography of the Himalaya to its varied plant forms.[74] Clearly, not all colonial scientists were travelers, profit though they might from the travels of others. Moreover, Royle tended to see Himalayan flora in terms of analogy between this and other temperate and alpine regions rather than recognizing the actual connection between European and Indian botany and the important questions of plant distribution and variation this raised.[75]

Though the prominence he eventually attained was exceptional, Royle nonetheless represented a more general trend among Company botanists. While many botanists were personally attracted to other, less obviously utilitarian, aspects of botany, few failed to take economic botany seriously. This was partly because they dutifully accepted the Company's economic agenda as their own (and their passport to preferment). But it was also that they subscribed to the doctrine of "improvement" and shared the belief that one of the principal functions of botany was to investigate medicinal and commercially "useful" plants and so contribute to India's material well-being. It was for this reason that botanists supported the Agricultural and Horticultural Society of India and that zealous surgeons like Stocks filled their letters to William Hooker at Kew with accounts of tanning bark, dyestuffs, and little-known vegetables,[76] knowing that he, too, had a political and professional interest in promoting botany in the service of industry and empire.

The Pursuit of Botany

Even when the germ of botanical enthusiasm had been planted, many Company surgeons found that their official duties, far from favoring their scientific interests and ambitions, actually thwarted them. One of the most significant contacts William Hooker made during his Glasgow years was with Robert Wight. Born in East Lothian in 1796, Wight gained an MD from Edinburgh in 1819 and joined the Madras Medical Service. Although he arrived in South India with "no more knowledge of Botany than usually falls to the lot of a well-educated medical man,"[77] like many other surgeons, Wight soon became fascinated by the subject and, conscious of his own inexperience, sent dried plants back to Britain for expert identification. His first consignment, sent to Dr Robert Graham at Edinburgh University, was lost at sea off the Cape of Good Hope. Undeterred, in 1826, Wight began to send further installments of plants from his extensive travels as an army surgeon to Hooker and other British contacts. Although Wight collaborated principally with G.A. Walker Arnott in Glasgow, with whom he produced the first (and only) volume of his *Prodromus* of south Indian plants in 1834, Hooker remained a valued friend and mentor.

Like many Company surgeons, Wight frequently complained to Hooker about the lack of consistent official support for his research.[78] He was at first encouraged to develop his botanical interests by being appointed "naturalist" to the Madras government in 1826. During a nine-month collecting trip he amassed 2,000 plant species, but his post was abruptly abolished in 1828 and he was sent back to regimental duties at Nagappattinam, a coastal town devoid of botanical interest. Without government support, botany for surgeons like Wight was heavily dependent not only on personal dedication but also on fortuitous events. Griffith's botanical excursion into Afghanistan in 1839 was only made possible by his being attached to the invading forces, and even then his attempts to collect specimens was "cramped by moving with an army through hostile country, when it was madness to stir 200 yards from camp."[79] Two "small wars" broke out in the northern hill tracts of the Madras Presidency at about the same time, but, Wight ruefully noted, "unfortunately there was not a botanist with either of our armies, so that both opportunities of investigating these districts were lost." No wars came Wight's way, and his main opportunities to botanize occurred when he marched with his regiment from one station to another. Route surveys may have been superseded by trigonometry among surveyors, but for botanists they were frequently the only means of examining the flora of a previously unknown country. However, in moving from place to place, Wight often had to leave his books and plant collections behind, though without them he greatly felt the want of these "silent monitors."[80]

Like most other botanists in India, Wight had to meet the considerable expenses involved in drying and preserving plants (never a cheap or easy task in the Indian climate), and of transporting them and sending specimens to Europe, from his own pocket. He also paid for Indian plant collectors to visit areas he was unable to reach or visit for long enough himself. The towns in the Tamil plains where he spent much of his early career offered little of botanical interest, and as his fascination with the upland flora of South India grew, Wight employed two collectors to scour the Courtallum, Palni, and Malabar hills on his behalf, and paid Indian illustrators to record his specimens.[81] In 1836, shortly after his return from home leave, Wight was appointed to investigate the vegetable products of the Madras Presidency. Thus, although Wight had a strong personal interest in the temperate plant-life of the southern hills and mountains, his professional duties propelled him in the direction of economic botany and "tropical agriculture." Even more than Royle at Saharanpur a decade earlier, Wight became an expert on the introduction and cultivation of new commercial crops: as superintendent of the government cotton farm at Coimbatore (1842–50) he oversaw the adoption of new (particularly American) strains of cotton.[82] But Wight was able to carry this practical plant knowledge to a higher analytical plane than Royle. For all the disadvantages of his situation, he built upon the combined expertise of British taxonomists like Arnott and unnamed local plant collectors to situate Indian botany within a wider scientific and geographical field. The idea of the tropics, as perceived in the value of pan-tropic exchanges or in the possible acclimatization of exotic species to India's "tropical" conditions, greatly influenced his work as an economic botanist. But the same broad schema informed his taxonomic studies, as he identified Indian plants according to their geographical distribution and distinguishing features as belonging principally to either tropical or temperate orders.[83]

Wight was not alone either in the considerable difficulties he faced in his cherished pursuit of botany, or in bemoaning the lack of official support for his researches. Even the superintendents of the botanic gardens, regarded as among the important scientific establishments in the country, were saddled with a host of other responsibilities. Saharanpur's superintendent was still in the 1840s required to perform the "duties of Accoucheur to the Civilians' wives ... and of Body Surgeon to the convicts of that station."[84] His counterpart in Calcutta was obliged to teach botany to students at the city's medical college, a task both Falconer and Thomson considered an irksome and time-consuming distraction from their scientific research and administrative responsibilities. Apart from the frequent changes of station and the recurrent burden of ill health (which left individuals like Falconer or Stocks incapacitated for months at a time), there were further reasons why colonial botanists often felt themselves distinctly disadvantaged compared to their *confrères* in Europe. Although to envious outsiders India under the Company may have appeared generously endowed with scientific appointments, residents were only too aware of how small and scattered their scientific community actually was. It was difficult to maintain meetings even of established and prestigious organizations like the Asiatic Society in Calcutta or find enough subscribers for learned journals and natural history publications. Even among Europeans, an interest in science was by no means universal. Wight was incensed (though thereby goaded into renewed activity) to discover, when stationed at the small town of Palayamkottai, "the eternal frivolous conversation about hunting, shooting, dogs, horses, &c, to which I am exposed in the limited society of this place."[85] Although some naturalists in India were able to place articles in the main scientific journals in London and Edinburgh, most were not, or felt too provincial to try, and looked instead to the *Journal of the Asiatic Society of Bengal* or short-lived publications like the *Calcutta Journal of Natural History*, which had a small circulation even in India. It was a common complaint among those who hoped to reach a wider audience that such journals were slow to reach Britain and not widely read there.[86]

The vast distances within the subcontinent made even Calcutta, India's scientific capital, appear to naturalists like Wight, a thousand miles away in South India, as remote as London, making effective communication and the sharing of scientific knowledge highly problematic. The failure in the 1830s to establish a Calcutta branch of the British Association for the Advancement of Science[87] compounded the inherent weakness of the scientific community in India and highlighted the lack of organizational links with Britain as well as inside India. The want of standard reference works, up-to-date journals and accessible herbaria for consultation, figured repeatedly in the litany of complaints made by Wight and many of William Hooker's other correspondents.[88] It was not therefore surprising that they eagerly sought his guidance and were so appreciative of the books and articles he sent their way. Science undoubtedly traveled between metropole and colony, but, from the perspective of many botanists in India, who craved reciprocity, it all too often appeared a one-way traffic.

It was necessary, therefore, for colonial botanists to travel in person, armed with whatever India had given them, to seek recognition and assistance directly from experts in Britain. One of the reasons why Wight sought Arnott's collaboration was that he had published an article in the *Encyclopaedia Britannica* on the principles of plant classification according to the Natural System that had caught Wight's attention: he was keen to follow this, rather than the outmoded Linnaean system, in his own work.[89] Despite the hardships of colonial botanists, perseverance sometimes brought its eventual rewards. Wight and Arnott's *Prodromus*

Florae Peninsulae Indiae Orientalis, published in 1834, was hailed by Hooker and Thomson twenty years later as a unique contribution to Indian botany, invaluable for its accuracy, scrupulous attention to detail and "truly philosophical views of the limits of genera, species, and varieties." A product of colonial-metropolitan collaboration, not unlike their own, it was a work "with few rivals in the whole domain of botanical literature, whether we consider the accuracy of the diagnoses, the careful limitation of the species, or the many improvements in the definition and limitation of genera and the higher groups of plants."[90] Wight was also one of the few colonial botanists to persist, with William Hooker's encouragement, in having plant illustrations produced in India, even though his *Icones Plantarum Indiae Orientalis* cost him fifteen years' labor and a considerable slice of his income. Begun in the late 1830s, the series covered more than 2000 species, though the relatively poor quality of lithographic production in India and the lack of color plates (so crucial to botanical illustration for purposes of reference and comparison) limited its ultimate utility. Like the *Prodromus*, and for all its flaws, Wight's *Icones* was said to demonstrate his "wonderful energy" and to show what could be "accomplished by perseverance under apparently insurmountable obstacles."[91]

Even for its most dedicated practitioners, botany in India was an uphill struggle. When he left India in 1853 it was, Wight wearily informed William Hooker, "without regret or rather I should say with pleasure as my sojourn within the Tropics has been a long one."[92] He settled near Reading and, until his death in 1872, made occasional visits to Kew.[93] William Hooker valued Wight's scientific contribution to Indian botany even more than Wallich's, dubbing him "this modern Roxburgh," praising his "accurate and sound view of structure, system, and nomenclature," and hailing his *Icones* as "one of the most valuable contributions to Botanical science that has ever appeared in any country."[94] Few among India's colonial botanists received such unstinted praise.

Collaboration and Conflict

The converse of metropolitan collaboration, patronage, and praise was a common feeling that the deserving labors of colonial naturalists passed unnoticed or without due appreciation of the unique contribution they could make. There was, in fact, a strong argument that local expertise, grounded in years of patient observation and diligent collecting was as important, and in some respects even more valuable, than the contribution made by those metropolitan savants who had never visited the countries they described or seen its nature *in situ* for themselves.

Brian Hodgson, Joseph Hooker's host at Darjeeling in 1848–50, struggled unsuccessfully in the 1830s and 1840s to find a collaborator among those whom he described as "the Ministers and interpreters of Nature" in London, to help him catalog and publish the huge number of bird and mammal species he had collected during his twenty years in Kathmandu.[95] A self-taught naturalist, Hodgson hoped that the publication of his work could be the "joint product of European science" and "local science." Writing in 1835 to Sir Alexander Johnston, the man who had helped Jacquemont on his visit to London a few years earlier, Hodgson dwelt on the "unique opportunities" he had enjoyed during his long sojourn in Nepal, at a time when that country was otherwise closed to Europeans. The skill of his "native artists," carefully trained to the "strict observance & delineation of the significant parts" of fresh zoological specimens, had, he explained, been augmented by his own observation of birds and animals in their natural surroundings and at different times of the year. He argued that there had hitherto been a "disconnection between local facilities" in places like Nepal and "the knowledge [needed] to turn them to the best account." Itinerant collectors had "either been wholly inexpert in science" or were "rapid passengers through the field in which they had to reap." Either way, he continued, it was obvious that such modes of investigating inanimate nature were subject to "the most serious drawbacks." So, too, were the investigations of naturalists in Europe who had no first-hand experience of the regions concerned and relied entirely on dried and often incomplete specimens.[96]

> Our Jacquemonts have been few and far between [Hodgson declared], and even *they* have been too much hurried to study with effect, or to collect materials for the study of the perishable, varying, and complex peculiarities of living beings—which peculiarities change with age, with sex, and with season, & consequently require continuous attention and repeated opportunities of observation, such as time only and residence can supply the means of.[97]

Not all Hodgson's strictures applied with equal force to botany, but many did, and the underlying argument about the need to recognize local expertise was widely shared. William Griffith similarly railed at the arrogance of metropolitan experts who had little or no direct acquaintance with the countries on whose flora and fauna they presumed to pronounce. Writing to a fellow botanist, William Munro, in 1844, he declared that botany would only be advanced by men actually living in the tropics and not by those "who never leave Europe and prefer dried to living plants."[98] Like those Company surgeons who argued for the indispensability of local experience in the identification and treatment of India's tropical diseases, many botanists (themselves also surgeons) used their hard-earned tropical expertise to imprint their authority and command metropolitan respect.

Griffith's brief career in Indian botany merits further comment, for it illustrates some of the underlying conflicts within the scientific community in India and in relation to metropolitan figures such as the Hookers. Like Stocks, a pupil of Lindley at University College London, Griffith initially came to the attention of Wallich during the latter's stay in London in the late 1820s. Griffith had already as a student shown a keen interest in plant anatomy and Wallich invited his "young friend" to prepare some of the section drawings for his *Plantae Asiaticae*. Praising Griffith's "botanical skill," Wallich remarked, just as Griffith was about to leave England to join the medical service in India, that his "future exertions, if equal to the early display of his talents and zeal, will shed much additional light on the botany of that country."[99] Griffith was quickly taken up by Wallich and Auckland and assigned to a series of postings and expeditions that took him in rapid succession to Assam, Bhutan, Sind, Afghanistan, Burma, Calcutta, and Malacca. During his travels he accumulated a collection of nearly 9,000 species—"by far the largest number ever obtained by individual exertions."[100]

Unlike Royle and Wight, Griffith showed little interest in economic botany,[101] and where many of his contemporaries were content to collect and name "novelties," Griffith strove for innovation. A talented microscopist, he investigated plant anatomy in a fashion then rare in India. Griffith never became one of William Hooker's protégés, but when they did start to correspond in 1840 he apologized for being able to offer little in return, fearing, as did many peripatetic Company naturalists, that "my rambling life will hinder me from attempting anything precise." His hope was to "amass materials for future study, that is, at a time when residence in Europe may enable me to avail myself of its splendid libraries

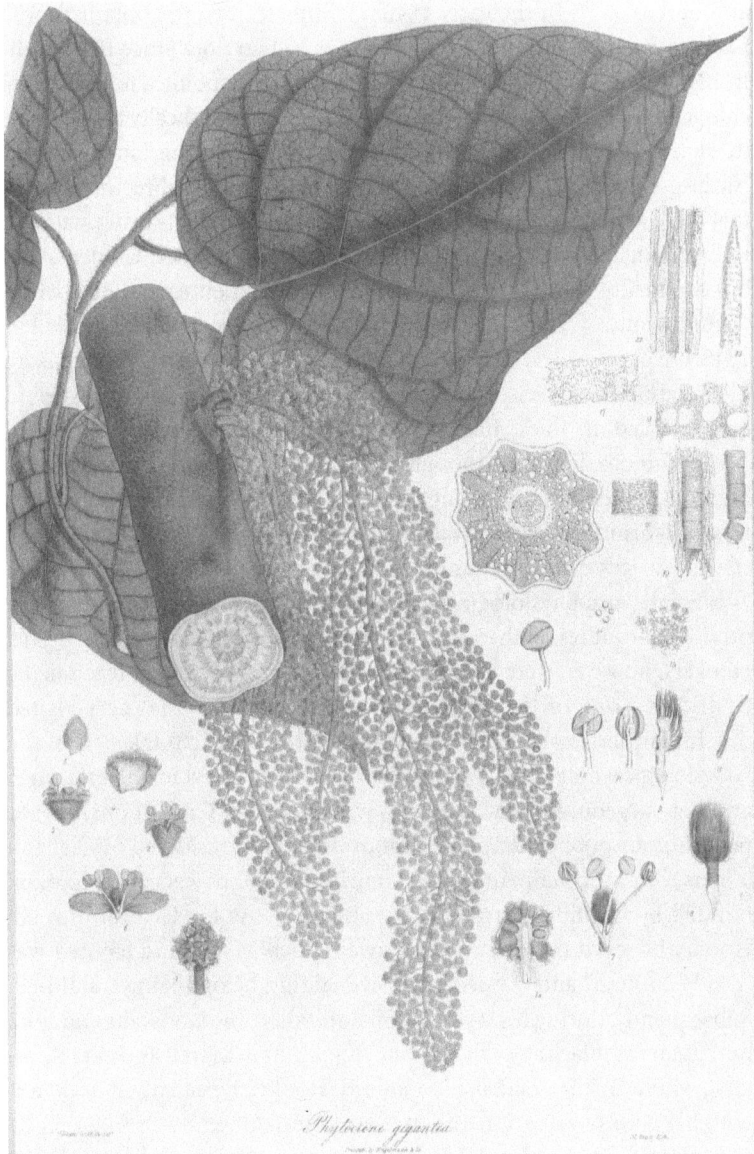

FIG. 11. *Phytocrene gigantea*, from Nathaniel Wallich, *Plantae Asiaticae Rariores*, vol. 3 (1832), drawn by Vishnu Prasad, with anatomical sections by William Griffith.
Reproduced by kind permission of the Royal Botanic Gardens, Kew.

and herbaria."[102] In the early 1840s Griffith seemed the botanist most likely to produce the first comprehensive Indian flora since Roxburgh. In 1843 when Griffith (rather than Thomson) was appointed to temporary charge of the Calcutta botanic garden, he set about radically redesigning it, planning a series of plots laid out according to the Linnaean and Natural systems. He informed William Hooker, now director at Kew, that there was "no garden" at Calcutta at present, "the plants being scattered indiscriminately over the large area... It is not a Botanical Garden at all, but a pleasure ground, and not very ornamental either."[103] But before Griffith could do more, he was transferred to Malacca, where he died in 1845. On his deathbed he hoped that his collections, at least, would ensure his "reputation as a Scientific Botanist, which I hoped a longer life would have enabled me to establish."[104]

Griffith dazzled. Even though little of his work was published in his lifetime, his reputation among botanists in India (and even in Britain) was extraordinarily high. Wight claimed that Griffith was a quarter of a century in advance of botanical science as a whole, and his work as a "systematic and physiological botanist" was warmly commended in the presidential address at the 1847 meeting of the British Association.[105] The Hookers, however, were more parsimonious in their praise, recognizing Griffith as "one of the most promising Naturalists that ever visited our Indian territories," but believing that his principal talent was as a "physiological botanist."[106] Joseph Hooker, who arrived in Calcutta when another surgeon, John M'Clelland, was preparing Griffith's papers for posthumous publication, was unimpressed. He considered M'Clelland a "persevering Scotchman without much ability or powers of perception, blinded by Griffith's extraordinary ability."[107] As for Griffith himself, Hooker believed that the material over which M'Clelland labored was "crude enough" and needed extensive editing before being published. Subsequently, during his travels in Sikkim, where the landscape and flora bore many similarities with neighboring Bhutan, as well as in the Khasi hills, where Griffith had also botanized, Hooker repeatedly found fault with his poor observation and careless note-taking.[108]

Hooker further believed that Griffith had wrecked the Calcutta gardens during his short tenure there, selling off some of the most valuable trees for timber (at an absurdly low price) and spoiling its visual appeal as well as its scientific standing. Not the least of Griffith's sins, in Hooker's eyes, was his failure to preserve the botanic garden as a tropical showpiece.

When he visited the gardens in January 1848, he found that Griffith had removed most of the palms, along with many of its other "tropical features." In particular, the avenue of cycads "once the admiration of all visitors, and which for beauty and singularity was unmatched in any tropical garden, had been swept away by the same unsparing hand which had destroyed the teak, mahogany, clove, nutmeg, and cinnamon trees."[109] There remained "nothing . . . of its former beauty and grandeur," only "a few noble or graceful palms rearing their heads over a low ragged jungle."[110] With his father widely praised for improvements at Kew, Joseph Hooker took a distinctly proprietorial attitude toward its poor relation in Calcutta. Finding so much "devastation" and blaming Griffith's "want of judgment,"[111] Hooker sketched out his own plans for the garden's rejuvenation. Pleased though he was that Falconer was taking charge of the garden, Hooker wondered whether he was equal to a task that required good taste as well as sound botanical knowledge.[112] It was in matters of taste as much as expertise that Hooker often found India's botanists seriously wanting.

A vast herbarium, unedited papers, and the ruined state of the Calcutta garden were not Griffith's only legacies. Despite the encomiums, he had a reputation for being "violently opinionated," and Joseph Hooker, who had never met him, rapidly formed the impression that Griffith had been "overbearing, insolent & rude." The bitter infighting among India's naturalists, to which Griffith had so substantially contributed, disgusted Hooker and offended his sense of how professional scientists should behave.[113] Both he and his father deplored Griffith's open contempt for his colleagues and lamented that "some of the hostile and bitter feelings" which had "so much tended to injure [his] good fame," appeared unedited in his posthumous works.[114]

Behind these remarks lay Griffith's bitter feud with Wallich, his former patron.[115] In 1836, when Wallich, Griffith, and M'Clelland were sent to Assam to investigate tea trees, Griffith regarded this as an opportunity to botanize *en route*, while Wallich, anxious about his health, was keen to complete the task quickly and return to the relative safety of Calcutta. Griffith alleged that the "theatrical" Wallich was jealous of his success in finding new plants, and wanted, as the senior botanist, to claim them as his own. Tempers flared and within days they were barely on speaking terms.[116] Apart from a possible undercurrent of anti-Semitism (Wallich had been born a Jew though by the 1830s he was an active Freemason), there was a significant generational difference between the two men. Wallich, twice Griffith's age, had been raised in the Linnaean system of classification. He needed help in London to classify his plants according to the Natural System that by the 1820s and 1830s had gained ground among more up-to-date practitioners like Royle and Wight.[117] Griffith was savage in his contempt for anyone he did not consider a proper botanist—the list included Falconer and, less deservingly, Royle[118]— and regarded himself as uniquely qualified to propel Indian botany into a new scientific age. That he redesigned the Calcutta garden over which Wallich had presided for so many years (and to which Griffith still expected him to return), and planned a new layout according to the Natural System, might thus be construed as a deliberate gesture of defiance toward his erstwhile patron and disdain for his more ornamental vision of tropical botany.[119]

Whatever the precise cause, the upshot was that the "Griffithian affair" deeply divided the botanic community in India and it rumbled on long after its originator's death.[120] For his part, Wallich was determined to clear what he regarded as his besmirched reputation. His wooing of the Hookers and other metropolitan naturalists and his sense of triumph at becoming a vice-president of the Royal Society were part of his quest for vindication before botany's highest courts of appeal. The affair also showed how difficult it was for India's botanists to work together and pool their expertise, or speak with a single authoritative voice and exert combined pressure on the administration. To those like Joseph Hooker, who seemed, from a position of metropolitan superiority, predisposed to view the pursuit of botany in India critically, the bitterness of the feud further fueled doubts about how professional science could be in such an embittered setting.

Subaltern Science

As fundamental as the nature (and alleged shortcomings) of colonial science was the issue of indigenous knowledge. In recent years there has been a significant reappraisal of the place of India's indigenous science and naturalist knowledge. Having been relegated to marginality by writers of the colonial era, indigenous knowledge is now sometimes credited with having a far more substantial and creative role. But academic opinion remains deeply divided. Some writers see indigenous knowledge as contributing directly to the formation of Western science from the sixteenth century onwards, as preserving alternative systems of thought and practice that rivaled (or remained independent from) those of the West, or as leading to the creation of a hybrid colonial science in which Indian ideas and agency remained as vital as those of the colonialists themselves.[121] Others have argued, conversely, that the colonial era was characterized by a high level of "epistemological violence," directed against indigenous norms and systems of knowledge.[122] It would be reckless to generalize across the whole range of scientific activity in British India and the entire colonial period. But botany is one of the fields where the question of indigenous agency and knowledge has been most extensively debated and remains most problematic.

As in many other fields, there was an early engagement with Indian botany through the Orientalist investigation of indigenous texts. William Jones typifies this late eighteenth-century trend. Among his many other activities, he was interested in exploring Sanskrit texts to discover what they might say about the "virtues" or properties of Indian plants and their "uses in medicine, diet, or manufactures," and, further, how this might connect with the more familiar knowledge systems of the Bible and Europe's classical antiquity. Jones, though, was generally unimpressed by what he found, which seemed to consist largely of lists of plant names and to compare poorly with what he knew of Linnaean botany.[123] Unlike astronomy or mathematics, there seemed to be few Indian works devoted entirely to botany and little by way of systematic thought on the subject.

An alternative route into Indian epistemology lay through indigenous categories and descriptions of landscape and vegetation. The surgeon-naturalist Benjamin Heyne in early nineteenth-century South India was one of those who explored this route. In his discussion of the *Kalpastanum*, a Telugu edition of an earlier Sanskrit work, he identified three kinds of countryside as depicted in classical Hindu texts—the *jangala desam*, or dry, elevated country, characterized by thorn scrub and large trees; the wetter and more fertile *anopa desam*, or low country, with rich, luxuriant vegetation, including palms; and the intermediate zone, *sadaranam*, which combined elements of the other two. Each of these divisions had its associated diseases as well as plants and was differently affected by the changing seasons.[124] But Heyne did little more than note the existence of such ideas. Apart from adopting "jangal" in a manner close to its original sense, as signifying "a barren, stony ... desert,"[125] he does not appear to have incorporated other indigenous terms and concepts into his botanical and topographical thinking. Indeed, he grew increasingly impatient with a text he eventually dismissed as a "banquet of absurdity."[126]

Twenty years after Heyne, James Tod showed a greater enthusiasm for Indian categories and concepts in his discussion of the "physiognomy" of Rajasthan. He employed local terms not only to give added authority to his topographical understanding—for instance, as noted in Chapter 2, of Marwar as *Maroost'hali* (a "region of death")—but also to differentiate between different kinds of desert scenery, thus distinguishing the *t'hul*, or bare desert, from the *rooé*, with its more extensive vegetation.[127] Citing indigenous names for trees and shrubs and recording their local uses helped Tod typify the landscape (thus *j'hal, babool* and *khureel* were noted as "the characteristic shrubs of the *t'hul*") and to demonstrate his knowledge of (and empathetic engagement with) the country and its people.[128] To an "improving" mind, too, ethno-botany might have its practical uses, as a guide to how the resources of the region might be more fully utilized; but it also marked Tod out as a knowing and accomplished traveler, able to move with cosmopolitan ease from Byronic Romanticism to the local names and uses for each wizened desert shrub. This recognition and use of vernacular terms lived on in revenue surveys and ethnographic descriptions well into the late nineteenth century and beyond, but even by the 1830s it was being replaced by a less compromising, less empathetic, language. The rise of medical topography and statistical reports increasingly emphasized external perception, economic utility, and scientific objectivity: such works cared far less than Tod for local names and indigenous topographical markers.[129]

Apart from topography and vegetation, the other main route into vernacular knowledge was through the study of *materia medica*, a field of evident practical importance to the British, and it was in this utilitarian domain that the investigation of indigenous knowledge was most systematic and sustained. However, it was no uncritical encounter and much of the indigenous knowledge of medicinal plants was treated with skepticism (until it could be "proved" by science), or hedged around with uncertainty as to exactly which plant (or part of a plant) was intended for use and for which ailment. In Nepal in 1802–3, Francis Buchanan deplored the "miserably defective" naming of Indian medicinal plants, such as aconitum: the man he sent to collect plants for him returned with samples of a species that, far from having healing properties, yielded a deadly poison.[130] Thirty years later, J.F. Royle noted continuing confusion over the identity, properties, and uses of this powerful drug.[131] The problem of an agreed and appropriate nomenclature greatly added to the complex task of identification. Jones believed that Linnaeus would have favored the use of "Indian appellations," particularly Sanskrit plant names, as those most fitting to their country of origin.[132] Later naturalists demurred, especially as the experience of travel revealed the absence of any India-wide system of plant names. As Buchanan complained repeatedly during his south Indian journey of 1800–1, vernacular names varied enormously from one locality to another or were too vague to serve any reliable scientific purpose: their use could only result in confusion.[133]

As well as questioning the reliability of Indian plant knowledge, colonial botanists squabbled over each other's taxonomic practices. Buchanan complained in 1821 that Roxburgh's names in his *Flora Indica* were "grievously barbarous, owing chiefly to his ignorance of the Latin language," and that he had made many mistakes in identifying and describing plants.[134] Wallich in turn criticized Buchanan's use of "vague native name[s]" for Nepalese plants, suggesting, with some condescension, that he had must have done so only "on the spur of the moment, in the hurry and inconvenience of travelling, for the purpose of easier reference," and not as permanent designations. Like many of his contemporaries, however, Wallich's main criticism was directed at local informants. "No nation on earth," he declared, "is more fertile in the production of names of plants than those of India ... This evil is often compounded by the people inventing names on the spot." "If," he conceded, "a specific or generic appellation is to be derived from any native language, which can never be necessary, and can rarely prove expedient, the Arabic or Sanskrit ought to be the only source from whence they are to be derived."[135]

Such doubts and disagreements encouraged the view that botany in India was chaotic, even anarchic. In their *Flora Indica*, Hooker and Thomson paid tribute to the pioneering figures of Wallich, Wight, and Royle, but were otherwise highly critical of the "backward state" of Indian botany.[136] One of the principal reasons for their strictures was the "perfect chaos of new names for well-known plants, and inaccurate or incomplete descriptions of new ones"—a state of confusion to which even Jacquemont and Wight had contributed. By their reckoning, "more than one-half of the recorded species of Indian plants are spurious," and though the problem was not confined to India alone, the "difficulty of determining synonymy" had become "the greatest obstacle to the progress of systematic botany."[137] Significantly, Joseph Hooker carefully noted local plant names during his Indian and Himalayan travels, drawing his information either from the plant collectors and porters who accompanied him or from knowledgeable villagers and Buddhist monks. He later cited vernacular (especially Lepcha and Bhotia) plant names in his *Himalayan Journals*. These gave local color and the authority of travel to his narrative and they helped distinguish between different plant species and their uses (as, for instance, between the many different kinds of bamboo).[138] This practice was, however, of little use with plants for which the local population had no great practical or ritual use. In particular, the many different species of rhododendrons he recorded and whose varieties were of such enormous scenic and scientific importance to him, were known only by a single local name, *guras*, sometimes qualified according to the color of the flower.

To Hooker, who personally found the "Babel of tongues" in Sikkim "very distressing,"[139] the use of "native appellations" as species names was very unsatisfactory. "These are in general very uncouth, and disagreeable to those who are unfamiliar with Indian languages" (as he was). They were also "quite unpronounceable without special education in the mode of spelling." Moreover, linguistic provinces seldom corresponded to botanical ones. The names given to plants were merely local ones, "confined to a single dialect of one of the many languages of quite different roots spoken over the area the plant inhabits."[140] The issue of nomenclature, and of taxonomic confusion in general, thus presented colonial botany in a negative light, tainted rather than enlightened by its local associations.[141] In this sense local knowledge might be considered to be doubly subaltern—subordinate to an often censorious colonial system of knowledge that was itself in turn seen as unsystematic, even amateurish, by metropolitan experts.

After the era of Jones and high Orientalism, surgeon-botanists tended to move away from interrogating texts (which required a demanding level of language skills and seemed scientifically unrewarding) to the questioning of Indian informants or the observation of indigenous plant practice. The "scientific auxiliaries" to whom the botanists turned included *hakims* and *vaids* (as practitioners of indigenous medicine the source of much information about medicinal plants), but also merchants, gardeners, and others who might possess a practical knowledge of plants and their products. For instance, the glorious *Amherstia nobilis*, which became one of the flowering trees most prized by Wallich and his successors at the Calcutta botanic garden (see Fig. 10), was first "discovered" in 1826 growing in a Burmese temple, where its flowers were presented as daily offerings to the Buddha. The subsequent search for an *Amherstia* growing in the wild proved futile.[142] There was also the evidence of the bazaar. Royle was one of several botanists who extensively utilized bazaar knowledge, cross-referencing what he could discover of plants sold there with those grown at Saharanpur or brought in by traders from Kashmir.[143] In Sind, Stocks followed a similar strategy: much of his initial knowledge of (and curiosity about) aromatic gums, medicinal drugs, and tanning bark came from examining substances displayed in Karachi's bazaars.[144] Driven by the Company's utilitarian agenda, early texts like Roxburgh's *Plants of the Coast of Coromandel* also made frequent reference to local knowledge about how to prepare dyestuffs or which fibers or timbers were best suited for specific purposes.[145]

This turning away from elite to local commercial or artisanal knowledge signaled the dwindling authority of scholarly Orientalism and the increasing emphasis upon Indians as repositories of empirical knowledge. It can be argued, from a present-day perspective, that the "divide" between "indigenous" and Western or "scientific" knowledge is artificial, given the changing nature of all "knowledges" and the frequent connections and borrowings between them. It thus represents a "sterile dichotomy" that needs to be erased.[146] While this fluidity and eclecticism might be a fair representation of how knowledge actually flowed and evolved, even in a colonial situation like that of early nineteenth-century India, it was clearly the intention of colonial, and even more of metropolitan, naturalists to deny such an apparent freedom of movement and to hierarchize knowledge in such a way as to privilege, as the science of a superior civilization, their own attempts to understand and order the natural world.

That said, though, without actually elevating it to the level of science, there could be genuine botanical appreciation for the practical knowhow that Indians possessed. Stocks described encountering a villager in Baluchistan who knew not only how to distinguish male from female date trees, but also fertilized his palms by extracting the male inflorescence from an unopened spathe, cutting it into pieces, and "wedding" it to the female flowers. The cultivator had clearly inherited his knowledge about how to fertilize date palms: "But," Stocks wondered, "how *did* his fathers first find out?" "Probably just as the superintendent of the commissariat garden at Kurrachee, who noticed that *Dodonoea* (female), never ripened its seed till this year, when accidentally he transplanted another plant of it (which happened to be male), and brought it from a distant part of the gardens near the other."[147] As this observation implicitly recognized, colonial botany might be no less empirical than its indigenous counterpart, and yet it still maintained its superior ability to comprehend, classify and ultimately to control nature.

Collecting and Illustrating

One of the most fraught issues in colonial botany were the merits, or otherwise, of using collectors. Some botanists, like Royle, were able to use other Europeans, themselves naturalists and travelers, to enlarge their collections.[148] European collectors (often working for aristocratic employers in Britain) were also active in botanically rich provinces like Assam. But more often it was to Indians that colonial botanists turned.

Citing difficulties of climate and transport, Heyne argued early in the century that it was almost impossible to pursue botany in India without Indian collectors. For a European, botanizing in person for any length of time was "quite out of the question." Besides, Indians could be adequately trained to do the work: "I have some collectors," Heyne declared, "who have made such progress in the Linnaean system as to be able to distinguish male flowers from female in the Dioecious class, in plants which they have never seen before."[149] In Nepal, where Europeans enjoyed little freedom to roam, Buchanan and Wallich employed "native collectors" to gather plants outside the Kathmandu valley, though Wallich stressed the superior value of seeing plants *in situ* and regretted that his only knowledge of what some plants looked like in flower came from collectors.[150] Despite complaints about the unreliability of some individuals (who returned with rain-sodden specimens or plants that were already well known), Robert Wight and Joseph Hooker also made extensive use of collectors. In Wight's case this was because he seldom had the time to collect plants himself, or at the most desirable season; in Hooker's because it helped him maximize his collecting at a given time and place or freed him to perform other tasks, such as preserving specimens or writing up his botanical notes.[151] But these collectors were seldom identified by name (except generically, as in Hooker's case, as "Lepchas") and while some were kept under close supervision, others were given almost complete freedom as to where and what they collected.[152]

But while the need for plant collectors was widely accepted, the importance of their contribution to plant acquisition and knowledge was seldom adequately acknowledged. When Hooker and Thomson spoke of "Indian botanists" they had only Europeans in mind, just as when they wrote about the history of "modern Indian Botany" they began with König and Roxburgh.[153] Very few Indians were thought to merit the title of "botanist," as opposed to the humbler term "collector." Edward Madden in the 1840s identified one, Murdan Ali, a munshi at Saharanpur, whom he described as a "very intelligent and respectable Syyud, the first of his race, perhaps, who addicted himself to Natural History, or any useful knowledge, and in whose honour Dr Royle established the genus Murdannia." Instructed by Falconer and Edgeworth as well as Royle, Murdan had "attained a considerable proficiency in Botany" and was said to be preparing a vernacular flora of North India and the Himalaya using the Natural System. The manuscript (presumably in Urdu) remained unpublished, however, "the expenses of printing being beyond the author's means."[154]

One of the areas in which Indians were valued (and most likely to be named in colonial texts) was as illustrators. The use of Indians for this purpose dated back at least to Roxburgh in the 1780s and arose partly from the non-availability of European artists to depict plants, many of which were highly perishable in the Indian climate or whose original appearance could not be reliably determined from the desiccated specimens that reached Europe.[155] However, the common refrain was that while Indians had a flair for decoration they failed to match the exacting standards of perspective and plant anatomy required in scientific illustration—though some commentators clearly thought this criticism unwarranted. When Maria Graham visited the Calcutta botanic garden she paid warm tribute to the artists' work, declaring that "they are the most beautiful and correct delineations of flowers I ever saw. Indeed, the Hindoos excel in all minute works of this kind."[156] The ablest artists were highly prized for their work, and some like Vishnu Prasad (see Fig. 10 and 11) moved from one botanist to another, even traveling from Calcutta to Saharanpur to ply their expert trade.[157] J.F. Cathcart, in his Himalayan retreat, employed between two and six illustrators, who completed about three drawings a week between them, and produced in all nearly a thousand illustrations. Joseph Hooker, who saw them at work in Darjeeling, was as much impressed by their cost as by their craft, noting that their wages amounted to "more than all my pay together."[158] Wight also placed great reliance on his artists, even naming a species after one of them, Govindoo, whose "skill in analytical delineation" was "as yet quite unrivalled among his countrymen, and but for his imperfect knowledge of perspective, rarely excelled by European artists."[159]

Yet, valued though these artists were locally, in the wider world of botany their work was often regarded as second best. From Joseph Banks to William and Joseph Hooker, botanists in Britain complained that the work even of trained Indian artists was inaccurate or unscientific. When Wallich published his *Plantae Asiaticae Rariroes* in London in the early 1830s he prefaced the work by apologizing that the 1,200 illustrations had been made by Indian artists in Calcutta, adding that "this will at once explain any imperfections in the figures."[160] In several cases, as with Roxburgh's Coromandel flora in the 1790s and Cathcart's Himalayan plants sixty years later, the illustrations were redrawn by artists in London. For the Cathcart volume the work was done by W.H. Fitch, the Hookers' favorite illustrator, who was called upon to correct "the stiffness and want of botanical knowledge shown by the native artists who executed most of the originals" (cf. Figs 2, 15).[161] Despite the considerable skill, labor, and cost involved in producing botanical illustrations in India, their existence seemed merely to confirm the prevalent impression that colonial botany was inferior to its metropolitan counterpart. The contribution of Indians was in this respect, as in many others, more valued in India than in Britain, but even in India they were seen mainly as a subordinate agency rather than as making an original—or truly scientific—contribution to plant knowledge.

6
BOTANY AND THE BOUNDS OF EMPIRE

JOSEPH HOOKER'S VISIT TO INDIA AND THE HIMALAYA (JANUARY 1848 to January 1851), and the spectrum of published work that emerged from his travels, constitute a high point in early and mid-nineteenth-century travel writing about India, in the natural history of the region, and in the representation of South Asian landscape and scenery. His *Himalayan Journals*, published in 1854, represent one of the few and certainly one of the most accomplished examples for India of a scientific travel narrative comparable to those of Humboldt, Darwin, and Wallace. And yet the *Himalayan Journals* also signal the beginning of the end of an era for Indian botany, the decline, as the railway age loomed, of the once prolific genre of travel writing about India, and the waning of travel's centrality to colonial science.

This was not the only sense in which Hooker and his *Journals* were pivotal. Despite his strong—one might say ancestral—roots in metropolitan science, travel made Hooker, for a time at least, into a more eclectic figure. Even though he was an outsider to the East India Company and its administrative establishment, and was often scathing about scientific practice in India, he saw the country with more than merely metropolitan eyes—or solely from a distance, like his father, through correspondence.[1] His stay in India and the Himalaya was of sufficient duration and his contacts with colonial naturalists close and informative enough for him to profit handsomely from accumulated colonial (and even, to a degree, indigenous) knowledge.[2] As well as his own insights and observations, Hooker was able to synthesize and incorporate into his work a great deal of the research into natural history that had been conducted in India under the Company over the previous half century.

Moreover, although in some respects his understanding of India and of Indian botany anticipated, and contributed to, the dawning of a new scientific era, the nature of Hooker's investigations and the manner in which he represented his encounter with India also looked back: to Humboldt, to scientific Romanticism, and to the scenic sensibilities of an earlier age. In this respect, the *Himalayan Journals* represent a kind of retrospect, a summation of what had gone before, even while physically and intellectually Hooker was pushing into new territory. And, while illuminating the complex and evolving relationship between science and imperialism, Hooker's travels further helped to strengthen, publicize and to give added scientific credibility to ideas of India's tropicality.

The "Fortunate Traveler"

Like his father, and like so many of the British middle classes, by the mid-1840s Joseph Hooker was already well acquainted with India without ever having been there. His boyhood reading had included not only Cook's Pacific voyages and Mungo Park's African travels, but also Turner's journey to Tibet (a work Joseph used, more than fifty years after its publication, as a guide to his own Himalayan wanderings). He had heard, too, family reports about his uncle Gurney Turner's career in the Bengal Medical Service, as well as, mainly via his father, of the activities of Company botanists, including his childhood friend Thomas Thomson. As he discovered somewhat to his surprise when he arrived in India in 1848 and traveled upcountry, through family connections, his father's former students and botanical contacts, and his own circle of acquaintances, he already knew a remarkable number of Europeans based in India: at Bhagalpur he even ran into the son of the tobacconist he bought cigars from in Charing Cross.[3] Conscious of being a "griffin," and in some ways perplexed by so strange a country, Hooker yet found India already half-familiar.

Despite his youth, in 1848 Joseph Hooker was "on the threshold of a career as one of Europe's most noted botanists."[4] Born at Halesworth in Suffolk in June 1817, he moved to Glasgow in 1821 when his father was appointed to the chair of botany at the university there. He qualified as an MD in 1839, but, while his degree gave him a scientific training, his heart was never in medicine. His principal interest was in natural history and, following his father, in botany. As his biographer Leonard Huxley observed, Joseph "did not so much learn botany as grow up in it."[5] Access to his father's library and herbarium was one of his greatest assets in embarking on a botanical career: by the early 1850s the Hookerian herbarium was "the richest and best-named herbarium in the world" and "especially rich in Indian plants."[6] The death of his elder brother William from yellow fever in Jamaica in January 1840 (shortly after he had been sent there to cure him of the tubercular complaint that affected most of the Hooker children and eighteen months later claimed the life of one of his sisters) increased family expectations that Joseph, the only surviving son, would make a name for himself in science.[7] William's death fueled subsequent anxiety, too, that a family which had already sacrificed one son in the West Indies should not forfeit another in the East.

Hooker's four-year voyage (1839–43) with Sir James Ross to investigate terrestrial magnetism in the southern hemisphere, during which he served as naturalist on board HMS *Erebus*, took him to Tasmania, New Zealand, and the Falklands as well as the edge of Antarctica. The publication of

FIG. 12. Joseph Hooker, daguerreotype, c. 1852. National Portrait Gallery, London. Reproduced by kind permission of the National Portrait Gallery.

the botany of that voyage, the first parts of which appeared in 1847, helped establish Hooker as a talented botanist in his own right (it was a work, he was thrilled to discover, known even to his hosts in India).[8] It showed his capacity for accurate observation in the field alongside his interest in trying to theorize about the factors affecting plant distribution across vast areas of land and sea.

By the time Hooker returned to Britain in September 1843 his father had left Glasgow to take up the directorship at Kew. In the eyes of the envious, Hooker was "a fortunate as well as an enterprising traveller," advanced by his father's unique position as much as by his own accomplishments.[9] But, without the private means to maintain him as a man of science,[10] Joseph (and his father) remained deeply anxious about his prospects. Egged on by his family, in 1845 he applied for the vacant chair of botany at Edinburgh University. Although he was supported by glowing testimonials from many of the leading scientific figures of the day, including Humboldt, John Stevens Henslow (his future father-in-law), John Lindley, and Charles Lyell,[11] the politics of the selection procedure told against him and Joseph was unsuccessful. The family felt the snub more keenly than Joseph, who felt that he was not cut out for academic life and that it would allow him few opportunities to travel: essential, as he saw it, for expanding his botanical expertise.

Apart from writing up the botany of the Antarctic voyage, Hooker was employed at the Geological Survey, researching the paleobotany of English coal seams. This work gave him an additional interest in geology and, through the supposed resemblance of the plant fossils found in the coal seams to present-day tropical ferns and other plants, it further stimulated his interest in tropical botany.[12] It was in these years, too, sandwiched between the Antarctic and India, that Hooker became a close friend and confidant of Darwin, a relationship that had a profound influence on his own intellectual agenda. In the summer of 1847 he became engaged to Frances Henslow, daughter of the Cambridge botanist, but he seemed loath to settle down or felt he lacked the means to do so. Conscious of how much he remained dependent on his father for his financial support and scientific standing, Hooker was anxious to find ways to advance his own career. He was already planning an expedition to India before his engagement: marriage had to wait four years until his tryst with the tropics was over.

Concern for his future prospects was a recurring theme in Joseph's letters to his father from India, his ambitions centering on a scientific career in Britain, preferably at Kew. "A position like my father's is the only thing I am cut out for except travelling," he confided to George Bentham.[13] Foreign travel, as he explained to his patient fiancée, was the only way for a young man in his line of work to get a "really good opening." Contrary to what some in his family (especially his grandfather, Dawson Turner) might think, it was "worth ... sacrificing a few years to it."[14] Hooker toyed with the idea of seeking employment under the East India Company— if not as a botanist, then, knowing the Company's interest in coal, as a geologist. Despite declaring himself to be "no Geologist" and insisting "Botany is my first object,"[15] Hooker's Indian notebooks and letters are filled with geological notes and observations, especially on the geomorphology of the Himalaya. This, rather than the flora, formed the principal subject of his letters to Darwin,[16] and the subtitle given to his *Himalayan Journals*—"Notes of a Naturalist"—further suggests his desire to be seen as more than a mere botanist.

Having traveled widely in the southern temperate zone, Hooker was keen to see more of the tropics. He wrote to the doubting Dawson Turner in July 1847, "I shall be ready to make any sacrifice to get to the tropics for a year, so convinced am I that it will give me the lift I want, in acquiring a knowledge of exotic Botany."[17] He had already glimpsed something of the botanical interest and scenic splendors of the tropics. Outward bound with Ross in 1839, he had his first taste of "tropical verdure" at Madeira and on the return voyage stopped briefly at Rio de Janeiro.[18] Although Joseph contemplated emulating Humboldt by investigating the Andes, advice from Hugh Falconer and the evidence of the Wallich herbarium suggested that India, more accessible and better known to British naturalists, offered greater opportunity to explore tropical vegetation and against the spectacular backdrop of the Himalaya. At first constrained by the belief that the region was being fully investigated by Company naturalists, Hooker soon became convinced that there were areas where they had not yet ventured or made the best scientific use of their privileged location.[19]

When, however, William Hooker consulted his India correspondents many proved less than enthusiastic about Joseph's proposed itinerary. As if to underscore the still contested status of India's tropicality, J.S. Law, one of William's principal contacts in Bombay, warned that if Joseph were to visit western India he was likely to be "very disappointed" with the local vegetation, for "There is nowhere to be found the tropical luxuriance & varied assemblance of numerous species of which we hear in Brazil & the Eastern Islands."[20] Stocks was equally discouraging and customarily forthright. Hooker might be right in believing that the luxuriant vegetation of the Malabar coast would "repay investigation," though Stocks knew nothing of the area personally. "The worst of the Botany of *Deserts* (which alone I have seen in my short stay in India) is the paucity of *species*," he lamented. With little or no rain in the previous two years, Sind was so parched and bare that he "might as well have botanised down Piccadilly."[21] When the elder Hooker sought William Munro's advice about the Himalaya, the response of the soldier-naturalist was equally negative. His personal knowledge was confined to the drier western part of the mountain range: Darjeeling was "not on my map." He added: "I almost fear your son will be disappointed with Darjeeling. It is the only part of his visit that will not repay him in my opinion."[22] Fortunately for the career of Joseph Hooker and for the future of Indian botany, Munro's advice went unheeded.

Humboldt's influence and example also dissuaded Joseph Hooker from bowing to skeptics. Hooker had met Humboldt in Paris in 1845 and found him, then in his seventies, "still a most wonderful man."[23] Even though the great German naturalist had never been permitted to visit India, having to be content with Central Asia and Siberia instead, the country had a deep and lasting appeal for him. Humboldt had written influentially about the structure of the Himalaya and the factors affecting the height of its snowline. But his vision of India (influenced by his Indologist brother Wilhelm) was also of a rich and luxuriant landscape whose tropical vegetation had so deeply moved the incoming Aryans that it generated in them a profound, almost proto-Romantic, feeling for nature and inspired the poetic and religious works of early Hindu civilization.[24] Humboldt never visited India in person, but his ideas (as evinced by J.F. Royle's work) had traveled there regardless and had a powerful impact upon its natural sciences.

As Hooker's plans took shape, Humboldt wrote to encourage him in his "botanical mission" to India, urging him to pursue questions he had himself raised about the configuration of the Himalaya and the mountains' impact on vegetation and climate. He understood the ambitious scope of Hooker's itinerary by remarking "*Je suis avide de vos Galapagos*" (I am eager for your Galapagos) and sending his regards not just to William

Hooker but also to Joseph's "spirituel ami," Darwin.²⁵ Hooker (like Darwin) greatly admired Humboldt and sought to emulate his exploits both as a naturalist and as a traveler. In August 1849, camped high up among the mountains of northern Sikkim, Hooker described Humboldt in a note to Brian Hodgson as a "model man." Although he regarded his recent *Cosmos* as "a great falling off," the *Narrative* of his South American journey had been "truly a wonderful book," full of taste, energy and descriptive power. Humboldt seemed to possess great "mental & bodily vigor," to be "indifferent to fatigue, heat, cold, exposure, direct rays of a tropical sun, seasickness & freedom from all the evils flesh is heir to." This, combined with his scientific erudition, his delightful manners and amiable temperament, made him "decidedly the greatest man of his day."²⁶ Later generations might disparage Humboldt as a "shallow man," but Hooker long regarded him as one of his "Gods" and one of the greatest of all "scientific travellers."²⁷

Biographers and historians have tended to see Hooker's Antarctic and Indian travels as pointing forward to his collaboration with Darwin and the theory of evolution;²⁸ but Hooker appears at the time of his Himalayan expedition to have been constantly glancing over his shoulder at Humboldt. Humboldt not only helped inspire Hooker's visit to India, but also informed (to a greater degree than the passing references in the *Journals* to the "illustrious" German might suggest)²⁹ his expectations of what he would find there and the manner in which he interpreted what he observed and experienced. The climax of Hooker's Himalayan journey came on 9 September 1849, a month after his eulogistic note to Hodgson, when he reached a height of 19,300 feet on the Donkia Pass, thereby matching (perhaps surpassing) Humboldt's ascent of Chimborazo fifty years earlier.³⁰ Not content to be a stay-at-home naturalist, Hooker believed that he had to travel for his science and to endure the physical hardships this entailed. He aspired, in short, to be a great "scientific traveller" like Humboldt.

In visiting India, Hooker was the beneficiary of more than Humboldt's good wishes: he was able to build on his own contacts and reputation as well as his father's. The Antarctic expedition had brought him a number of Admiralty connections, including Lord Auckland, who had been governor-general of India before becoming First Lord of the Admiralty. Like many colonial viceroys and governors, Auckland was a keen plant collector: his early contacts had been with Lindley at University College, but William Hooker was more assiduous in cultivating his interest and solicited his help for Joseph's naval and botanical career. Auckland secured for Hooker two years in India on Admiralty half-pay, and, in the interconnected world of family and empire, he provided a valuable introduction to his nephew Sir James Colvile in Calcutta. Advocate-general of Bengal as well as president of the Asiatic Society, Colvile was well placed to advise and assist Hooker, especially in planning his upcountry travels.[31] He furnished Hooker with other contacts, notably with Brian Hodgson, by then living as a semi-recluse in Darjeeling.

Botany, too, opened many doors. With the assistance of William Munro and others, Joseph arrived in Calcutta armed with a sheaf of letters of introduction, and William Hooker equipped his son with the names of individuals known to him through the confederacy of plant lovers, including Sir Lawrence Peel, a cousin of the former prime minister Sir Robert Peel, and chief justice of the supreme court in Calcutta. Hooker stayed part of his time in Calcutta with Peel, who owned one of the finest private gardens in Bengal. President at that time of the Agricultural and Horticultural Society, Peel was well placed to commend Hooker to other "improvers"—civil servants, planters, army officers—in upcountry stations.[32] Though he was at times snobbish toward colonial naturalists and organizations like the Asiatic Society, Hooker rapidly came to appreciate the value of such contacts, if only to secure transport, accommodation and other facilities: "things in which the traveller is more dependent on his fellow-countrymen in India, than in any other part of the world."[33]

No less important to the success of Hooker's mission was his arrival in the company of Lord Dalhousie. Old India hands like Wallich noted with admiration, touched with envy, how "extremely kind & attentive" the new governor-general was toward his new friend.[34] Hooker, who also struck up good relations with Lady Dalhousie (and later named one of his most glorious rhododendrons after her: see Fig. 15) was invited to stay at Government House whenever he was in Calcutta. Even though Hooker's "botanical mission" was not officially supported by the Company, the governor-general's favor was bound to ensure Hooker the assistance of officials throughout India. For his part, though, while recognizing the value of Dalhousie's patronage, Joseph did not take readily to the Dalhousies' "aristocratic gossip."[35] He was disappointed to discover how little the former president of the Board of Trade knew or cared about science and how difficult it was to interest him in the scientific objects of his expedition. He attributed this to the defects of an Oxford education and a political career that had left Dalhousie "as ignorant of the origin & working of our most common manufacturing products & arts as he is well informed on all matters of finance, policy &c."[36] Hooker tended to despise those who failed to share his scientific preoccupations, but, even if Dalhousie did not "care a fig for science," it seemed sensible to hang on to the governor-general's coat-tails in the hope, as Joseph put it to his father, that "he will drag me on."[37]

The Himalayan Tropics

Like many travelers before him, Hooker was at first deeply disappointed by India. Having reveled in the delights of Ceylon, with its "forests of tropical trees of the greatest beauty" and with Humboldt and *Paul and Virginia* foremost in his mind,[38] the first sight of Bengal filled him with dismay. The approach to Calcutta through the creeks and swamps of the Sundarbans was "exceedingly disappointing," yielding no evidence of "tropical luxuriance."[39] The city itself proved welcoming, but, apart from the ravaged botanic garden, of scant scientific interest. In late January 1848, after barely two weeks in the city, Hooker began his travels, accompanying the geologist D.H. Williams to the Damodar valley in western Bengal. Here, too, disappointment reigned. The dry-season landscape appeared parched and bare, causing Hooker to think more of bleak English moorlands than stately tropical forests. There were occasional palms, bamboos, and fruit trees, but mostly only "low stunted jungle" of dhak and acacia. Occasionally Hooker observed "picturesque" scenes with noble trees that might grace an England park; but otherwise the landscape was "tame" and the "prime elements of a tropical flora" were "wholly wanting."[40] This was a land without either "luxuriance" or "novelty," and in three months' rambling before he reached the Himalaya, he collected only a thousand species, a miserable hoard for an ambitious botanist. The country, Hooker reported, was "altogether ... as unlike what I had expected to find in India as well might be."[41] Only when he climbed to the summit of Parasnath, a hill rising more than 4,000 feet above the plains of Bihar, did he find anything to whet his botanical appetite: with increasing altitude the vegetation grew more luxuriant, until near its summit it supported "a more tropical flora than its base."[42] Although Hooker did not visit those areas of northwest India that were beginning to show the worst consequences of deforestation and rainfall decline, he noted similar effects in parts of eastern India.[43] In general, though, Hooker believed that the bare landscapes of the Gangetic valley were more natural than man-made, the effect of a dry climate rather than deforestation, and had never been heavily wooded like the plains of South America.[44]

In mid-April 1848, when Hooker reached Siliguri, at the edge of the Tarai, the landscape at last began to change. The first mountain peaks became visible through the mist, and, as the air grew moister, the dry vegetation of the plains yielded rapidly to that of the sub-Himalaya. Bamboos of greater girth and variety than in the plains, began to appear, wild banana trees sprouted up in profusion and the screw-pine made its distinctive, tousled appearance. Three thousand feet above sea level in this "foreshortened tropical forest," creepers festooned the trees, epiphytes burst from limbs and branches, and beneath, in the moist undergrowth, ferns sprang up "luxuriant and handsome" (see Fig. 13).[45] Looking back over the "sea-like expanse of the plains" below him, Hooker was able, for the first time, to visualize India's vastness and the dynamic interdependence of its constituent elements.

He also found the Humboldtian language to match. In a passage that displays many characteristics of his prose style (its pictorial qualities and repeated emphasis upon light, color, and form), Hooker described how he could make out the distant Cosi and Teesta rivers, "the great drainers of the snowy Himalayas." The "ocean-like appearance" of this southern prospect was

> even more conspicuous in the heavens than on land, the clouds arranging themselves after a singularly seascape fashion. Endless strata run in parallel ribbons over the extreme horizon; above these, scattered cumuli, also in horizontal lines, are dotted against a clear grey sky, which gradually, as the eye is lifted, passes into a deep cloudless blue vault, continuously clear to the zenith; there the cumuli, in white fleecy masses, again appear; till, in the northern celestial hemisphere, they thicken and assume the leaden hue of nimbi, discharging their moisture on the dark forest-clad hills around. The breezes are south-easterly, bring that vapour from the Indian Ocean, which is rarefied and suspended aloft over the heated plains, but condensed into drizzle when it strikes the cooler flanks of the hills, and into heavy rain when it meets their still cooler summits. Upon what a scale does nature here operate! Vapours, raised from an ocean whose nearest

FIG. 13. Punkabaree Bungalow at the Foot of the Himalaya, from
J.D. Hooker, *Himalayan Journals*, vol. 1 (1854), based on a sketch by Hooker.
Reproduced by kind permission of the School of Oriental and
African Studies, London.

shore is more than 400 miles distant, are safely transported without the loss of one drop of water, to support the rank luxuriance of this far distant region. This and other offices fulfilled, the waste waters are returned, by the Cosi and Teesta, to the ocean, and again exhaled, exported, expended, re-collected, and returned.[46]

As Hooker continued his ascent, the fleeting vision of "tropical" India was rapidly replaced by a very different kind of landscape and vegetation. Above 4,000 feet, and as he neared Darjeeling at 7,000 feet, his brief passage through the tropics ended and he began to observe, as had so many visitors to the Himalaya before him, the appearance of "European" plants—at first a "very English-looking bramble," then, as the wind blew colder and moss and lichen began to carpet the wayside, there followed oaks, birches, violets, geraniums, and other trees and flowers that "vividly recalled" an English spring. In the space of a day or two's journey and a few thousand feet in altitude, Hooker had left the "winter of the tropics" for the "spring of the temperate zone." The paradox of finding tropical and temperate plants nestling in close proximity was not lost on Hooker.

Many of these flowering plants were "so notoriously the harbingers of a European spring that their presence carries one home at once," and yet they were accompanied, even at 5,000 feet, by tree-ferns, bananas, palms, figs, epiphytical orchids "and similar genuine tropical genera."[47] North of Darjeeling, in the warm trough of the Teesta valley, the heat and the humidity created by winds sweeping in from the distant ocean carried "tropical vegetation" far into the interior, to within a day's journey of the perpetual snowline. Here, beneath the yak pastures and the peaks, was a landscape "luxuriantly clothed with ... tropical plants."[48]

Over the course of the eighteen months following his arrival in Darjeeling, Hooker's travels took him to nearby Sinchul and Tonglo and down the Teesta valley into Sikkim, and on two major expeditions. The first, beginning in October 1848, took him to eastern Nepal, around the slopes of Kangchenjunga and onto the edge of the Tibetan plateau. The second, starting in May 1849, led him into northern and eastern Sikkim as far as the Donkia Pass and Tibetan border (for Hooker's travels, see Map 2). The diversity of this landscape was extraordinary and, as one reviewer remarked, Hooker's account of his travels gave the impression that this was a vast area when it was actually no larger than a couple of Swiss cantons.[49] Through his often arduous journeys and through close observation, Hooker was able to show how tropical genera, like palms, bananas, and figs, could reach remarkably high altitudes, where they mingled freely with typically temperate trees, shrubs, and flowers, such as oaks, birches, rhododendrons, and firs, before they too, at the highest elevations, yielded to the alpine vegetation of the high passes and Tibetan plateau.

At times the representative flora of the tropical, temperate, and alpine zones, instead of being geographically distant and distinct, could be seen simultaneously from a single vantage point or found entangled in jungles that were, botanically speaking, tropical and temperate at the same time. On his excursion to Tonglo in May 1848, Hooker observed fig trees growing at surprisingly high altitudes, "one species of this very tropical genus" ascending to almost 9,000 feet on the outer ranges of Sikkim.[50] In the Tambur valley of east Nepal in November that year (see Fig. 14), he passed through vegetation that was "entirely tropical" (including sal trees and acacias), but then, from a neighboring viewpoint, he could observe "black mountains of savage grandeur" towering above him, their "rugged, precipitous faces ... streaked with snow," while the lower outcrops were

FIG. 14. The Tambur Valley, Nepal, from J.D. Hooker, *Himalayan Journals*, vol. 1 (1854), based on a sketch by Hooker. Reproduced by kind permission of the School of Oriental and African Studies, London.

crowned with silver firs. At the same time he could see the "tropical luxuriance" of vegetation in the valley far below.[51] Six months later, in the Lachen-Lachoong valley of northern Sikkim, Hooker was struck by how, at more than 4,000 feet above sea level, typically "European" trees (birch, willow, alder, and walnut) grew side by side with wild plantains, palms, figs, and gigantic bamboos, climbing vines mixed with brambles and speedwell, and English strawberries flourished alongside orchids growing on the trunks of oak trees.[52]

Hooker's powers of descriptive writing were directed at depicting the varying nature of the vegetation, the species that typified particular elevations, and their visual impact. This was particularly significant for the rhododendrons, which in many locations grew in such profusion as to form the dominant plant-life. No less impressive was the variety of rhododendron species and their distribution, ranging from *R. argenteum* at 8,000 to 9,000 feet to *R. nivale* at alpine heights of about 17,000 feet.[53] Along with the magnolias, the rhododendrons created some of the most stunning sights of the Himalaya. "In the months of April and May," Hooker wrote of the view from Sinchul, "when the magnolias and rhododendrons are in blossom, the gorgeous vegetation is, in some respects, not to be surpassed by anything in the tropics," even if the effect was often "marred by the prevailing gloom."[54]

> The white-flowered magnolia (*M. excelsa*, Wall.) forms a predominant tree at 7000 to 8000 feet; and in 1848 it blossomed so profusely, that the forests on the broad flanks of Sinchul, and other mountains of that elevation, appeared as if sprinkled with snow. The purple-flowered kind again (*M. Campbellii*) hardly occurs below 8000 feet, and forms an immense, but very ugly, black-barked, sparingly branched tree, leafless in winter and also during the flowering season, when it puts forth from the ends of its branches great rose-purple cup-shaped flowers, whose fleshy petals strew the ground. On its branches, and on those of oaks and laurels, *Rhododendron Dalhousiae* grows epiphytically, a slender shrub, bearing from three to six white lemon-scented bells, four and a half inches long and as many broad, at the end of each branch. In the same woods the scarlet rhododendron (*R. arboreum*) is very scarce, and is out-vied by the great *R. argenteum*, which grows as a tree forty feet high, with magnificent leaves twelve to fifteen inches long, deep green, wrinkled above and silvery below, while the flowers are as large as those of *R. Dalhousiae*, and grow more in a

cluster. I know nothing of the kind that exceeds in beauty the flowering branch of R. *argenteum*, with its wide spreading foliage and glorious mass of flowers.[55]

Higher still, the blood-red blossoms of R. *fulgens* formed the "richest ornament" of the alpine zone.

The foliage is perennial, and gives a singular hue to the bleak snowy mountain-faces immediately overhung by the perpetual snow, contrasting in August in broad masses or broken clumps with the bright scarlet of the Berberry, the golden yellow of the fading Birch and Mountain Ash, the lurid heavy green of the perennial Juniper, and the bleak raw brown of the withered herbage. Whether then, for the glorious effulgence in spring of its deep scarlet blossoms, which appear to glow like fire in the short hours of morning sunlight, or the singular tint it at other seasons wears, this is among the most striking of the plants which lend to these inhospitable regions the varied hues which are denied to the comparatively habitable but gloomy forests of the temperate zone of the same mountains . . .[56]

As these passages further indicate, and complex though the plant ecology of Darjeeling and Sikkim clearly was to his eyes, Hooker did not abandon the idea of characteristically tropical, temperate, and alpine genera. On the contrary, such seemingly bizarre occurrences as the presence of "tropical" monkeys, butterflies, and grasses in "temperate" settings, displayed against the backdrop of the highest mountains in the world,[57] encouraged Hooker to push the idea of the tropics (and hence of India's tropicality) to its extremes. The fact that there could be wild bananas at 7,000 feet or that even oaks, the pride of temperate woodlands, could be "very tropical plants," helped in his view to disturb "preconceived notions of the geographical distribution of the most familiar tribes of plants."[58]

Plants, too, could travel. As late as the introductory essay to the *Flora Indica* in 1855, Hooker still adhered to the Lyellian view that species were "definite creations," but his Himalayan experiences (coming on top of his Antarctic observations) showed that species were capable of considerable geographical mobility and (prefiguring Darwin) needed to be versatile in order to survive in such a hostile and competitive environment.[59] Species might not mutate to form new species, Hooker believed, but there could be enormous variation within species—not least, as any widely traveled naturalist soon realized, under the influence of climate and elevation.[60] Such views, combining precise local observation with a keen sense of global biogeography, fueled Darwin's own evolutionary thinking and suggested the possibility that in the remote past some temperate species might have migrated via the mountain regions of the tropics from the northern to southern temperate zones.[61] As far as Hooker himself was concerned, however, the Himalayan flora did not seem to support the idea of transitional forms, or of natural hybrids (though he kept an open mind on that point), by means of which one species changed into another.[62] Rather, the essential characteristics of a species persisted despite occurring in very different physical conditions, just as certain genera did not cease to be "tropical" even when they grew high up in the Himalaya. The alterity of the tropics was not undermined (but rather strengthened) by the fact that plants proved to be unexpectedly mobile not only within, but also between, different climatic zones.

For Hooker, as for many of his naturalist contemporaries, the idea of the tropics operated at three different, if closely interconnected, levels of perception. At the most general level, the tropics were a familiar visual and literary trope, well known from childhood reading of romances and adventures. The tropics existed in the vast repertoire of images, allusions, and associations that Hooker, his friends, and correspondents could readily summon up out of their own cultural world. And yet Hooker could contribute even to this popular envisaging of the tropics, through the striking image of rhododendrons blooming amidst semi-tropical vegetation or glowing blood-red beneath the snow-capped Himalayan peaks.[63]

At a second level, the idea of the tropics required a more precise signification. Artistic and literary associations might provide useful reference points for the non-specialist, but the specific properties of the tropics, as classified, mapped, and measured by resident or itinerant naturalists, called for close attention to the details of climate, landscape, plant and animal life, even ethnography. This more explicitly scientific approach, in part pioneered by Humboldt, was very evident in Hooker's more technical writings, as he tried to trace, through changes in temperature, humidity, elevation, and aspect, the subtle shift from tropical to temperate. And yet even here the tropical experience, as Humboldt had also persuasively shown, was not simply reducible to mapping and measurement, but called for a keen sense of aesthetics in order to comprehend and communicate the vibrant totality of tropical nature. The changing moods of the sky, the brilliant colors in the landscape, the taste and smell of exotic fruits—these were too important to be left to poets or painters, though their insights and expressiveness might further enrich the science of the tropics.

Thirdly, as an accomplished field botanist Hooker used the idea of the tropics in a still more precise fashion, to categorize particular plant species, genera, and orders and so to typify the landscapes and climatic zones in which they occurred. As Wight and others had already established, some plant families were most characteristic of (or found only in) temperate lands, where they were most widely distributed and exhibited the greatest variety of forms, just as others were predominantly (or exclusively) found in tropical or alpine regions.[64] Tropical species might, as Hooker showed, be found far from tropical lowlands: they might even flourish several thousand feet up among the world's highest mountains. But they did not thereby lose their inherently tropical characteristics. Used thus, "tropical" served as scientific shorthand for the home territory of a plant, and yet it remained suggestive of other properties—the bright coloration and strong scent of its flowers, the size of its leaves, even those cultural associations that made an orchid or palm emblematic of the tropics in the same way that an oak remained ineluctably "English" even when it grew in the warm, wet forests of the sub-Himalaya.

Regions of Romance

In writing about India and the Himalaya, Hooker aspired to do more than simply describe plants and enumerate new species. In seeking to "stand unrivalled amongst Indian travellers,"[65] and to emulate the travel narratives of Humboldt and Darwin, Hooker sought to represent both the nature of the landscape he observed and the experience of travel itself. Free from the practical limitations and material requirements that constrained so much Company science, he sought to combine the technical demands of botanical science with a high level of aesthetic sensibility. Dour, even donnish, to all but his most trusted friends, Hooker may not have been a natural Romantic, but he strove to enthuse his narrative with emotion and to attend to the senses. Like Humboldt and Darwin before him (though more self-consciously and less successfully) he tried to operate on two registers: to present a coherent and scientifically rigorous account of natural phenomena based upon close observation, careful measurement and accurate recording of empirical data; but also, after the Romantic manner, to revel in solitude and to indulge in reflective reverie, to employ imagination, association, and sentiment in the service of science, and to explore the aesthetic and emotional qualities landscape and nature stirred in the sentient observer.[66]

Religion, however, played little direct part either in Hooker's personal notes and correspondence or in his published journals: "Providence" occurs occasionally, "God" almost never.[67] Inasmuch as Hooker had any "gods" they were fellow naturalists and travelers, Humboldt the Jove among them. It is clear, though, that Hooker's attitudes toward India and his feelings for nature were influenced either by underlying religious convictions or by the perceived relationship—harmonious or discordant—between religion and nature. He may not have been as openly hostile as the evangelicals had earlier been to Hinduism and their conflation of a "cruel" religion with a "heathen" landscape, but he undoubtedly shared many of his contemporaries' antipathies. When, *en route* to the Himalaya, he visited the Jain temples of Parasnath, his response was to regard them as representative of a "less impure form of Heathen worship" than Hinduism. "Idol worship" though this religion might still be, "it was gratifying to find it taking possession of this lovely spot, to the exclusion of the abominations of Brahminism, which shock the eye as much as the senses."[68] When he reached Benares his repugnance for Hinduism intensified: he described a temple he visited there as "a horrid place for noise, smell, and sights—*Devilish* in every sense of the word."[69] His loathing extended, too, to the denizens of the torrid plains as a whole: Hindus were "cruel and vindictive," Bengalis "lazy dogs." By contrast, he found the "timorous" Lepchas whom he came to know at Darjeeling far more acceptable. They proved to be "excellent travelling companions," and he developed for them a degree of Romantic attachment and paternalistic concern.[70] Hearing Lepcha coolies playing flutes in his camp one evening, he observed how the sound of their instruments was

> sweet and melodious; . . . it is so soft, musical, and sylvan, that one can listen to it long and with pleasure. It seems to harmonize with the solitudes of these primeval forests. What a contrast to the hateful tom-toms of the Hindoo of the plains! which used to drive me almost distracted on the Ganges.[71]

Elsewhere in the hills Hooker was struck by the melancholy appearance of the "weeping cypress" (which he duly identified as *Cupressus funebris*), its long limbs and wispy foliage drooping "picturesquely" over Buddhist temples and chaits (chortens). Chortens—memorials to the dead— often stood on hillsides in a "commanding and romantic position," overlooking silent valleys. The "funereal" cypresses enhanced the wistful effect, while the fact that they were not native to Sikkim, but apparently introduced from Tibet or China, added to their botanical as well as scenic interest.[72]

Although Hooker knew little about Buddhism until he reached Darjeeling and came under Hodgson's tutoring, the religion (and its apparently harmonious relationship with the surrounding landscape and plant-life) evoked positive associations for Hooker in a way that Hinduism and its "obscenities" clearly did not. In one passage, which typically moved from religious geography to reflections on his own senses and associations, he remarked:

> I could not but gaze with a feeling of deep interest on these emblems of a religion which perhaps numbers more votaries than any other on the face of the globe. Booddhism in some form is the predominating creed, from Siberia and Kamschatka to Ceylon, from the Caspian steppes to Japan, throughout China, Burma, Ava, and a part of the Malayan Archipelago. Its associations enter into every book of travels over these vast regions, with Booddha, Dhurma, Sunga, Jos, Fo, and praying-wheels. The mind is arrested by the names, the imagination captivated by the symbols; and though I could not worship in the grove, it was impossible to deny to the inscribed stones such a tribute as is commanded by the first glimpse of objects which have long been familiar to our minds, but not previously offered to our senses.[73]

There was a similar character, too, to many of Hooker's descriptions of Himalayan scenery, combining observations of color and form in nature with personal feelings and associations. One of the passages commended by many reviewers of the *Himalayan Journals* described his visit to the Choonjerma Pass on the Nepal–Tibet border in December 1848. It was, like some of Darwin's descriptive passages in *The Voyage of the "Beagle"*, an attempt to combine science with emotion and to capture in words "the complex sense impression" of a "striking moment of experience in physical nature."[74] Evening overtook Hooker and his coolies while still above the snowline. As the sun sank,

> The snow at our feet reflected the most exquisitely delicate peach-bloom hue; and looking west from the top of the pass, the scenery was gorgeous beyond description, for the sun was just plunging into a sea of mist, amongst some cirrhi and stratus, all in a blaze of the ruddiest coppery hue. As it sank, the Nepal peaks to the right assumed more definite, darker, and gigantic forms, and floods of light shot across the misty ocean, bathing the landscape around me in the most wonderful and indescribable changing tints. As the luminary was vanishing, the whole horizon glowed like copper run from a smelting furnace, and when it had quite disappeared, the little inequalities of the ragged edges of the mist were lighted up and shone like a row of volcanoes in the far distance.

Reflecting on this scene, Hooker continued (in a passage extensively reworked from his original notes):

> I have never before or since seen anything, which for sublimity, beauty, and marvellous effects, could compare with what I gazed on that evening from Choonjerma pass. In some of Turner's pictures I have recognized similar effects, caught and fixed by a marvellous effort of genius; such are the fleeting hues over the ice, in his "Whalers," and the ruddy fire in his "Wind, Steam, and Rain," which one almost fears to touch. Dissolving views give some idea of the magic creation and dispersion of the effects, but any combination of science and art can no more recall the scene, than it can the feelings of awe that crept over me, during the hour I spent in solitude amongst these stupendous mountains.[75]

A passage that begins with Hooker among his coolies quickly turns inward to focus on his own observations and reflections until he finds himself, paradoxically, in "solitude." A scene the whole party shares rapidly travels in Hooker's imagination far beyond India and the Himalaya and becomes attached to distant images of industrial smelting and artistic associations with a painter (J.M.W. Turner) whose work Hooker had seen exhibited in London.[76] The exercise of Hooker's Romantic sensibilities not only brought experience and feeling to scientific narration; it also annexed an alien scene to the high culture of a far-away nation.

Hodgson and the Himalayan Frontier

Hooker's achievements as an itinerant naturalist were not the result of his labors alone. They relied to no inconsiderable extent on the work and support of others, particular Brian Hodgson, whom Hooker met for the first time in Darjeeling in the spring of 1848. Between June of that year, when Hooker accepted Hodgson's invitation to stay with him at "Bryanstone," with its commanding views of Kangchenjunga and the "grandest... landscape of snowy mountains in the Himalaya, and hence in the world,"[77] and Hooker's final departure from Darjeeling in May 1850, he returned to the bungalow several times from his botanical expeditions into Nepal, Sikkim, and Tibet. In all he stayed for ten months as Hodgson's houseguest and companion. As Huxley remarked, "If the friendship with Lord Dalhousie provided the key that opened official barriers and made Hooker's journeyings possible, the friendship with Hodgson more than anything else made them a practical success"— though one might add, in fairness to Hodgson, that his contribution was intellectual, not merely "practical."[78] Their relationship, personal and scientific, was of great significance to both men, but it was, in many ways, a surprising friendship.

In 1848 Hodgson was, by seventeen years, the older man, and at the age of 48 could look back on thirty years as an administrator and scholar. The son of a "broken gentleman," Hodgson joined Company service in 1818. After a brief spell in Kumaon, he was sent in 1820 to Kathmandu as Assistant Resident, becoming Acting Resident in 1829 and Resident four years later. Until the arrival of Honoria Lawrence in 1844, no white women were permitted to enter Nepal, and Hodgson, plagued by ill health, felt his isolation acutely. Initially to escape loneliness and tedium, he began to collect Buddhist manuscripts and natural history specimens; within a few years these had become his passionate interests (though in the mid-1830s he began to cohabit with a Kashmiri Muslim woman, with whom he had two children). As Resident, Hodgson played an active role in the court politics and diplomacy of Nepal. He was, however, sometimes regarded by his superiors as far too interventionist and apt to overstate his case. In 1843 he was dismissed from the Residency by Auckland's successor, Lord Ellenborough (1842–4), who was intent on asserting his own authority over Anglo-Nepalese relations and curbing the independent tendencies of political agents like Hodgson. Hodgson accordingly left

Kathmandu and resigned from the civil service in December 1843, but within two years he was back among his beloved mountains. Denied entry to Nepal, he settled instead at Darjeeling, appropriated by the British in 1835 from the Raja of Sikkim. From 1845 until 1858, he lived the life of a semi-exile, albeit on a comfortable pension of £1,000 a year, pursuing his interests in Himalayan geography, zoology, and ethnography and still hoping to publish his illustrated account of the birds and mammals of Nepal.[79]

Hodgson was a self-taught naturalist. In an age in which professional scientists were gradually emerging from the chrysalis ranks of gentleman amateurs, this was by no means exceptional. But Hodgson had received no scientific training at all, not even the medical education through which many Company surgeons were first initiated into botany, zoology, and geology. Nor was Hodgson much of a traveler: neither his health nor the restrictions imposed by the court allowed for this, but he avidly collected verbal and written reports from Nepali, Kashmiri, and other travelers and based much of his understanding of geography (and even ethnography) on the information thus gleaned.[80] This surrogacy and his long sojourn in Kathmandu, his appetite for hunting and collecting animals and birds, and his prolonged contact with the inhabitants of Nepal and later Darjeeling, substituted for a more formal apprenticeship. His time at the Residency had, he believed, given him a unique "store" of information that needed only the guidance and support of metropolitan science to attain its full worth.[81]

Hodgson freely acknowledged the limits of his scientific knowledge and (like many botanists) his reliance upon a small number of textbooks. An article he published in 1833, announcing the discovery of a new species of Indian hornbill, closed with the characteristic disclaimer: "having no extensive or scientific knowledge of Ornithology, I have been obliged to rely for the materials of the above description upon untutored eyes and ears, sedulously employed and assisted by careful reference to Shaw's *Zoology*."[82] By the time Hooker joined him Hodgson had published well over a hundred articles on the birds and quadrupeds of Nepal and adjoining regions and donated hundreds of specimens and drawings (by local artists) to the British Museum in London. He had been made a fellow of several British and Continental naturalist societies,[83] yet he still sought in vain the active assistance of metropolitan science.

Despite Hodgson's reputation for being quarrelsome and difficult, he and Hooker hit it off from the start. Hooker found his host "gentlemanly and agreeable," a "clever person" who could also be "wickedly sarcastic."[84] Struggling to fund his travels and knowing he could count on no financial assistance from the Company, Hooker was delighted to find Hodgson "a miracle of liberality,"[85] who fed and housed him for months without any expectation of payment. In his *Himalayan Journals*, Hooker paid handsome tribute to this generosity, but he also praised Hodgson's "high position as a man of science," hailing him as the man who had "unveiled the mysteries of the Boodhist religion," "chronicled the affinities, languages, customs, and faiths of the Himalayan tribes," and "completed a natural history of the animals and birds" of the region. "To be welcomed to the Himalaya by such a person," Hooker declared, "and to be allowed the most unreserved intercourse, and the advantage of all his information and library, exercised a material influence on the progress I made in my studies, and on my travels."[86]

This was no less than the truth. Before he went to India, Hooker knew practically nothing of Buddhism, or the zoology and ethnography of the Himalaya, or even of Hodgson's work: his friendship with Hodgson enabled him to appear far more knowledgeable on these subjects than he actually was and to embellish his botanical observations with authoritative remarks on the natural history, religion, and society of the Himalayan region. As an Orientalist as well as naturalist, Hodgson was singularly well placed to help Hooker. He sensibly pooh-poohed Hooker's suggestion that, because there were superficial similarities between Buddhist and Roman Catholic rituals, the Lamaism of Sikkim must have been influenced by Nestorian Christians or Jesuits.[87] When they traveled together in the Tarai in March 1849, Hodgson not only took pains to point out birds and animals to his zoologically challenged companion but also penciled into Hooker's journal annotated lists of what they had seen.[88] At times he fed him more Sanskrit and vernacular vocabulary than Hooker could possibly absorb, though some of it found its way, unacknowledged, into the *Himalayan Journals*.

There was much else that Hooker stood to gain from Hodgson. As late as September 1849, after almost eighteen months in the hills, Hooker confessed that his Hindustani was "notoriously bad" and that he had only "a smattering" of Bhotia and Tibetan. "It is true," he told his father, "that this ignorance of languages does not stand in the way of Botany" (further confirmation of how little Hooker thought of the indigenous input into botanical science), "but in every other respect it is a fearful drawback."[89] Hodgson and others obligingly supplied that linguistic facility for him. It was also Hodgson (drawing upon his own strong belief in the indispensability of local expertise) who impressed upon Hooker, who had originally planned to spend only two or three months in Darjeeling, the value of remaining long enough in one place to know its natural history well. As Hooker put it to his father in February 1849: "Hodgson dwells strongly on the simple fact that it is better to explore one district well than to wander."[90]

There was, therefore, a strongly reciprocal element in the Hooker–Hodgson relationship. Hooker genuinely respected Hodgson's local expertise and admired his formidable library and collections. Hodgson, he informed Darwin, was "so complete a Himalayan Naturalist" that he felt it necessary to pay "little other attention to Zoology than bottling beetles & applying to my host for information on all other branches."[91] He appreciated, too, that however highly regarded Hodgson's science might be in India, he still stood on the margins of the wider scientific establishment, a remarkable collector and recorder perhaps but not a theorizer or an original scientific mind. Darwin had "long been familiar with his name,"[92] but the Indian journals Hodgson published in were hard to come by in Britain, and Darwin had apparently not read any of his articles (but then Hodgson had not even perused *The Voyage of the "Beagle"* until Hooker persuaded him to read it). When Darwin wrote to Hodgson, at Hooker's request, the "hermit of Darjeeling" was "in great glee." Hooker explained to Darwin, with more condescension than he perhaps intended, "really you little know how prized a valuable scientific correspondent in England is, to the *jungle fowl* in India."[93] Through Hooker, Hodgson even began to correspond with Humboldt about an atlas of physical geography for use in Indian schools (which never materialized). For years Hodgson had been asking to be put into "effectual communication" with one of the "Ministers and interpreters of Nature."[94] Perhaps at last, through Hooker, that cherished goal had been realized.

There was more, though, to their relationship than scientific reciprocity. Hooker felt relaxed in Hodgson's company, at ease in his hospitable household. He was aware that Hodgson could be "haughty, proud and ambitious," but believed, so he told his father, that "I shall always regard [him] as one of my dearest friends on earth."[95] Shortly after leaving Darjeeling in October 1848 on one of his expeditions, Hooker wrote to

"My dear H" to tell him how badly he missed his company.[96] He began a journal, entrusted by installments to Hodgson's safekeeping, as a means of keeping in almost daily contact. When they met up again, the following February in the plains, Hooker was delighted to receive "the affectionate welcome I was long anticipating from Hodgson . . . we all but hugged and retired to the bungalow for an excellent chat."[97] Hooker later confessed that his "protracted wanderings in solitude" had been "rather dull." For eleven years he had been a traveler, "and never once with a soul who cared a reed for my pursuits." It was accordingly a delight to travel with Hodgson in the Tarai and to "bring in my flowers to some one who cared to see them, for their own sake as well as mine."[98] For his part Hodgson treated "dear Joe" like a younger brother, writing to tell Sir William and Lady Hooker how well their "boy" was doing and praising his "zeal, industry, energy, . . . steady head & . . . affectionate disposition." He even wrote to William Hooker for no better reason than to let him know "how I love and esteem your son."[99]

Despite their very different backgrounds—Hooker the "griffin," Hodgson the old India hand—the two shared a number of interests and ambitions that say much about the complementarity and interdependence of metropolitan and colonial science. At the core of this was their mutual interest in what Hodgson termed the "organic distribution" of plants, animals and other livings things.[100] Following in part in Humboldt's footsteps, but also drawing upon Hooker's Antarctic and antipodean knowledge of the effects of glaciation, and Hodgson's familiarity with Himalayan topography and natural history, the two saw a mutual interest in combining their expertise to create a systematic biogeography of the eastern Himalaya and an integrated understanding of the region that encompassed geology, meteorology, botany, zoology, and ethnography.

But even in this, Hooker and Hodgson were not alone. Despite their seeming inaccessibility, by the 1840s the Himalaya had become the subject of eager and extensive scientific scrutiny. This included investigation of the physical geography of the region and the course of its rivers, surveys of its geology and mineral resources, the discovery of the Siwalik fossils, and, through the Trigonometrical Survey, remarkably accurate calculations of the height of the main Himalayan peaks. By the 1830s it had been conclusively established that the mountains contained several summits higher than the Andes and when Hooker published his *Himalayan Journals* in 1854 it was still in the belief that Kangchenjunga (reckoned at 28,178 feet) was the tallest mountain in the world. Within months, however, (and rather to Hooker's chagrin), the peak the British called Everest had supplanted it.[101] Pioneering investigations were also undertaken, principally in the western Himalaya, into zoology and botany by Madden, Thomson, and the Stracheys, which helped to situate animal, plant, and human life within the context of the region's complex geography, geology, and climate.[102] And though Hodgson was the acknowledged leader, others were beginning, too, to investigate the elaborate ethnological and linguistic mosaic that straddled the Himalayan frontier.[103]

One outcome of this collective endeavor was to see the Himalaya less as a remote annex to the Indian plains than as the source for many of the physical factors that fashioned—or had once fashioned—almost the entire subcontinent, or as an arena in which the combined natural history of every near and adjacent region (from Europe to China, Siberia to Malaya, Africa to inner Asia) met and mingled in remarkable ways. The Himalaya seemed to contain more essential clues to India's remote past, to the origins of its climate and physical configuration, its plants, animals, races, and languages—than could be found in the barren plains below or in the records of scribes and pandits.

Hodgson was not naturally disposed to try to convert his wealth of local information into some challenging hypothesis or grand synthesis. But, with Hooker's encouragement, his expertise could contribute to the advancement of "philosophical" science. In a letter to Darwin, Hooker described their joint efforts to create (after the manner of Humboldt's biogeography of Chimborazo) a "transverse section of the Himal. from the Snow to the plains ... with rocks plants & climate & the zoology by Hodgson, projected on a chart."[104] Something of this joint endeavor surfaced as an appendix on the "Physical Geography of the Sikkim Himalaya" in Hooker's *Himalayan Journals*.[105] But Hodgson's own contribution to this exercise—and his own, more empiricist, frame of mind—can be gleaned from his essay on the physical geography of the Himalaya, published in 1849.

Some of this material Hodgson had sketched out as early as 1846, before meeting Hooker, but its final form testified to their collaboration and the synoptic project in which they were engaged. Hodgson began by stating the need to provide a "clear outline ... of the principal natural divisions of the Himalaya," both as an objective of value to geography and as a basis for other physical sciences. He argued that, even though knowledge of Britain's Himalayan possessions was incomplete, it was undesirable to wait until Nepal, Sikkim, and Bhutan became "thoroughly accessible to science." Having been "for several years a traveller in the Himalaya," personal experience told him how hard it was to stand back from "this stupendous scenery" and the "mighty maze" of mountains, seemingly without plan or order, to establish "the grand features" of its physical geography and without straying from "facts" into "theory."[106]

Despite the broad geographical and scientific scope of his article, which extended well beyond the "physical geography" of its title, Hodgson did not range far beyond assembling the "facts." Having established the complexity of the Himalaya, he moved on to consider its geology, botany, ethnography, and zoology, before finally returning to the problem of its river systems. Significantly, before 1848 Hodgson seldom used the terms "tropical," "temperate," or "alpine" in his work, perhaps because they appeared less pertinent to zoology than to botany.[107] Instead he employed descriptive terms such as "eastern Tibet," variants of indigenous topography, such as "Tarai" and "the *Hemalaya*" (with their meaning explained), or, drawing upon his classical education, he distinguished between "cis-nivean" and "trans-nivean" tracts. However, under Hooker's influence, he shifted his vocabulary to accommodate the idea of a globe divided into tropical, temperate, and alpine zones and incorporated this into his revised essay, dividing the entire Himalayan region, along with its climate, vegetation, bird and animal life, and ethnography, from the Tarai to the snowy peaks, into these three zones. Hooker may have been beholden to Hodgson for much of his local knowledge; but Hodgson derived from Hooker a new way of thinking about and presenting his local data.

From Plants to Empire

The Himalaya constituted a political as well as a scientific frontier, though the two were often inextricable one from the other. Following the Anglo-Gurkha War and the Treaty of Sagauli in 1816,[108] the Nepalese lost a third of their former territory, including Kumaon and the western portion of Sikkim. Thereafter, the British sought to contain Nepal, preventing any further expansion of its boundaries, while maintaining cordial relations with Kathmandu and especially, from the mid-1840s, with the astute and powerful Jang Bahadur, the prime minister and *de facto* ruler of Nepal.

Sikkim served as a convenient buffer between Nepal and Bhutan, another potentially aggressive kingdom, and between British India and China. At the same time, however, there was some interest in promoting British interests by advancing trade and political influence across the Himalaya and into Tibet and China. Both Hodgson and Hooker believed, in an era of free trade and in the aftermath of the Opium War of 1839–42, that China could be made more accessible to the West if the Himalayan passes were opened up as a backdoor trade route. Long after returning from India, they lobbied through Parliament, the India Office and the press for the expansion of trade in, and through, the eastern Himalaya.[109]

Hodgson and Hooker also shared a belief that Darjeeling and the surrounding hills not only made a suitable sanitarium for European invalids from Calcutta and the plains (the purpose for which it had been acquired from the Raja of Sikkim in 1835), but might also form one of several upland locations where Europeans could settle permanently, supporting themselves through farming and trade and constituting a military reserve in the event of a Russian invasion or Indian insurrection. The revolt of 1857—and the virtual immunity of hill-stations from attack—made this strategic role appear all the more urgent.[110] That so much of the vegetation of the hills was "English" suggested to Hooker that the region might be as well suited to British constitutions as it was to "European" plants.[111] Hooker saw Darjeeling as analogous to the fledgling British settlements he had visited in Australia and New Zealand, communities that were models of enterprise and "improvement," and were spreading Western civilization into regions previously little better than barbarous.[112] While Hooker was charmed by the Lepchas he considered the Bhotias "as uncouth a race (short of savages like the Australian or Fuegian) as I ever beheld."[113] He likewise remarked that eastern Nepal was "by nature" a "highly favoured country ... & well peopled," but "such an unimproved and unimproving people I never met."[114] In other words, they scarcely deserved the land they lived in.

From the time of his arrival in Darjeeling in the spring of 1848, and possibly even before he had left Calcutta that January, Hooker took the view that, in his pursuit of science, he was entitled not only to visit Sikkim, technically an independent kingdom, but also to pass through it without hindrance and as far as the Tibetan frontier. Despite approving of his expedition in other respects, Dalhousie had always been wary about this part of Hooker's travels, fearing that it might provoke conflict with Sikkim and with the Chinese who, in claiming suzerainty over Tibet, also held shadowy claims to the more southerly regions where Tibetan Buddhism prevailed.[115] Hooker declined to be dissuaded and his growing acquaintance in Darjeeling with Brian Hodgson and Archibald Campbell, the British superintendent at Darjeeling and political agent for Sikkim, encouraged him to believe in his scientific entitlement to roam virtually at will. The Sikkim raja (the Chogyal Namgyal) and his durbar (court) had already proved hostile to British surveyors and naturalists, claiming that the gods of their country (pre-eminently the spirit of Kangchenjunga, the great snowy peak that presides over the region) or that the Chinese authorities in Lhasa would be offended by such intrusions. Either way, evil consequences would follow.[116]

Although the treaty of 1817 assured the raja of "full and peaceable possession" of the territory restored after the Anglo-Gurkha War, Hooker took the view that he was not entitled to such unilateral acts of exclusion. In his view, the British, acting through the East India Company, had recovered Sikkim from the Gurkhas and restored the king to his throne: Sikkim was accordingly a British protectorate in all but name. Moreover, in the opinion of Hooker and many of those he spoke with in Calcutta and Darjeeling the raja was a "mock sovereign,"[117] who had no right to stand in the way of the British, of free trade and "improvement," and the advancement of science in such a botanically rich and geographically important region. Hooker believed that the raja should be subjected to a "very firm, but conciliatory policy," and "brought to his bearings, if not to his senses." He might remain "dissatisfied, grasping, insolent and overbearing, " but he would be forced to "acknowledge himself benefited by our proximity."[118]

Hooker's determination to reach "the Snows" and his private resolve to cross the Tibetan border far enough and for long enough to observe the landscape and vegetation of that region, still little known to Western science, ran into a series of obstacles. One was the Sikkim durbar. Hooker's supposedly innocent request, relayed to the raja by Campbell in September 1848, to be allowed to wander freely in the cause of botanical science and for the sake of friendship between the raja and the governor-general, was met with a firm rebuff, the raja observing that if Dr Hooker wished to examine Sikkim's trees and flowers he would be pleased to have samples sent to him.[119] Fearing that Hooker's visit would further erode the fragile independence of Sikkim, the raja was no doubt politically inspired in his response. But nothing was more likely to offend Hooker in his quest to see the landscapes and plant-life of the Himalaya for himself than the proposal that he be content with a bunch of desiccated specimens of indeterminate provenance. Uncowed, the raja and his court responded by stating their grievances against the East India Company, from the takeover of Darjeeling (which they had only reluctantly accepted) to the sanctuary given there to runaway slaves and dissidents. Hooker further came to believe that it was not so much the aged raja who was his principal adversary as the scheming diwan (chief minister), a Tibetan Bhotia who wished to cultivate close ties with the Chinese and to promote trade through the Himalayan passes for his own financial advantage— or, as Hooker put it, "a man unsurpassed for insolence and avarice, whose aim was to monopolise the trade of the country, and to enrich himself at its expense."[120]

But the other impediment Hooker faced was the Government of India and its agent, Archibald Campbell. As early as June 1848 Hooker described the conduct of the government and its agent as "weak to a degree and prejudicial to the interests of the country."[121] There was, however, a feeling in Calcutta that Sikkim was not worthy of greater attention. In the wake of the Afghanistan debacle, the government had begun to feel that British rule had reached what Ellenborough described as "the limits nature appeared to have assigned to its empire."[122] Barely a decade later, Dalhousie appeared to take a contrary view, favoring expansion in Burma, Punjab, and Awadh and observing in 1850 that "in the exercise of a sound and wise policy the British Government is bound not to put aside or neglect such rightful opportunities of acquiring territory or revenue as may from time to time present themselves."[123] But the tiny, mountainous state of Sikkim held out scant prospects for trade and revenue and there was the risk of antagonizing the Chinese (and perhaps the Nepalese) by attempting to bring it under closer British control. Dalhousie was content to urge the raja to afford Hooker "every facility and security," threatening to remove the annual subsidy paid to him by the Company for the secession of Darjeeling if he did not comply, adding airily, "The Sikkim Savage will be brought to his senses someday."[124] Whatever personal sympathy and support he might command, Hooker was not the responsibility of either the Company or the Calcutta government, and, with the struggle in Punjab reaching its bloody climax, there were other, more pressing, concerns. Hooker, keen to move "the Himalayah to within our reach,"[125] never fully understood how Dalhousie could warm to his botanical pursuits (even asking for some of his new rhododendrons to send to Queen Victoria) and yet be so indifferent toward Sikkim. In this respect, Hooker the itinerant naturalist and outsider appeared more imperialistic than Dalhousie, so often vilified as a remorseless expansionist.

Hooker's relations with Campbell are as illuminating (and as curious) as those with Hodgson. Having entered the Bengal Medical Service in 1827, Campbell served as physician and political assistant to Hodgson in Kathmandu, where he had used his medical training to dissect the Resident's bird and animal specimens, before moving to Darjeeling as superintendent in 1840.[126] Campbell was also, in a rather amateurish way, a naturalist, publishing accounts of Himalayan geography and meteorology, and ethnographic descriptions of the Lepchas and other hill tribes, as well as articles on the "natural products" of Nepal and Darjeeling that firmly identified him with the cause of "improvement."[127] One of his greatest achievements as superintendent of Darjeeling (certainly in Hooker's view) was to initiate an annual fair at Titalya where traders and farmers from the hills and plains could meet to exchange goods and where prizes were offered for the finest plough bullocks and the "best Darjeeling cow."[128]

Hooker found Campbell a mine of local information and a willing source of practical assistance: he provided Hooker with coolies, guides, and supplies for his travels, and shared botanical and geographical information with him. While Hodgson, pleading ill health, usually stayed at home, Campbell on several occasions joined Hooker on his mountain treks and afforded him the European companionship he often desperately craved. When Hooker was encamped in remote parts of Sikkim, the obliging and "amiable" Mrs Campbell sent him plum cake, mince pies, and sherry to cheer him up; and when he remarked on the suitability of Darjeeling for European children, it was the rosy-cheeked Campbell children he had in mind. And yet, Campbell, coming from a poor Scots family, was conscious of not having the social and scientific advantages Hooker had long enjoyed. Campbell's learning was not the equal of Hodgson's, nor his science more than a pale shadow of Hooker's. Hoping one day to follow Hodgson as the Resident in Nepal, Campbell's career as a political agent had already brought him to the critical attention of the authorities in Calcutta and he was nervous of making trouble by pushing the Sikkim raja too far.

Driven, almost hounded, by Hooker, Campbell secured the raja's reluctant agreement that Hooker be allowed to botanize in Sikkim and to travel as far as the Tibetan border (though not to cross it). But almost from the time he set out on his journey north in May 1849, Hooker encountered what he thought was deliberate obstruction, orchestrated by the raja and the diwan. Local chiefs made every effort to delay or deceive him, or coax him into going back. Villagers would not provide him and his large party of coolies with food (which had to be ferried up from Darjeeling), and the frontier was said to be much further south (and so further from the Tibetan plateau) than Hooker was prepared to accept. But he also blamed Campbell for failing to do more to exercise his powers and bring the "insolent" raja and the "scoundrels" who supported him to heel. While recognizing Campbell as "the essence of kindness & friendliness," he repeatedly railed against his "torpid energies" and lack of firmness.[129] Believing himself trapped between "a weak functionary & a deceitful Rajah," in August 1849 he gave Campbell a "horrid wigging." And when the hapless agent wrote to explain his course of action, Hooker dismissed his note as "the "d—dest shilly-shally & nonsense that ever was penned by man."[130]

Hooker was determined to press on to his goal—to reach "the snows" and Tibet, "the fondest dream I ever harboured as a traveller and botanist."[131] As he told Hodgson, he did not intend to throw away the kind of "opportunity for which you would give gold."[132] In the first week of September 1849, Hooker achieved his ambition, crossing over the Donkia Pass into Tibet and observing the "howling wilderness" beyond. But, such was the paradoxical nature of his situation (and character) that he greeted Archie Campbell with "unspeakable joy" when the agent—the first "white face" he had seen for five months—joined him shortly afterwards and they set out to explore the passes of eastern Sikkim together.[133] On 7 November, in the course of one of these joint excursions, to the Chola Pass, Campbell was taken hostage by followers of the diwan, who hoped that this would force the Calcutta government to take the grievances of the Sikkim durbar seriously. From a sense of outrage and loyalty, Hooker chose to join Campbell in his "captivity" and the two were taken back to the capital, Tumloong. Here they were held for six weeks, at first separately and then confined together in a one-roomed hut. Campbell was roughly manhandled, and it was rumored that their murder was "contemplated & openly suggested at [the] Durbar." The Lepcha coolies who had accompanied Hooker from Darjeeling were also threatened, harassed, and "barbarously treated."[134]

News of Campbell and Hooker's seizure soon reached Calcutta and provoked widespread European indignation. As the secretary to the Political Department put it, "we do not do half enough to extend our geographical knowledge on the frontiers" and "petty potentates" and "barbarians" like the Raja of Sikkim who stood in its way should be taught a lesson, if necessary by force.[135] But overall the governor-general and his council favored caution, persuaded, despite the "outrage," that no "extreme measures" had befallen the captives and anxious to avoid a more serious incident.[136] Troops were, however, dispatched to Darjeeling and an invasion of Sikkim threatened, until the raja and diwan capitulated and Hooker and Campbell were finally released. They reached Darjeeling on Christmas Eve: there they were anxiously awaited by Thomson, whose own experience of captivity in Afghanistan had been infinitely more grueling. Sikkim was punished by having to further forfeit its southern territory and by the cancellation of the annual allowance paid to the raja since the annexation of Darjeeling. Hooker was indignant that sterner action had not been taken: he wanted the whole of southern Sikkim to be annexed and the detention and trial of those responsible for their seizure.[137]

Throughout Campbell and Hooker's "captivity," Hodgson had remained in Darjeeling. As news began to filter back to the hill-station, along with rumors that the prisoners might be killed or thrown into the icy waters of the Teesta, Hodgson bestirred himself, directing Campbell's deputy to prepare Darjeeling for an invasion (possibly, it was suggested, by the combined armies of Nepal, Bhutan, and Sikkim) and writing urgently to Dalhousie in Calcutta to demand prompt military and diplomatic action. At first, Hooker and Campbell thought of Hodgson as their "Good Angel,"[138] but in a letter that reached Hooker in Tumloong (and which he subsequently destroyed) Hodgson suggested that the young naturalist had been partly to blame for the affair by his insistence on reaching "the snows" and entering Tibet in defiance of the durbar's wishes. Hooker was furious at this, insisting that "the outrage" was "unconnected with my travels," and solely arose from the durbar's longstanding grievances against Campbell and the government. Hodgson's complaint was far from groundless, but such was Hooker's anger he was forced to retract and apologize. By mid-December Hooker was again writing to "Dear old Brian" to urge that "the recollection of anything unpleasant having ever happened between us be obliterated root & branch."[139] Yet when Hooker returned to Darjeeling he discovered that Hodgson had alarmed not only Calcutta but his family at Kew, deluging them with letters about the fate that had befallen their "dear boy" at the hands of the "Sikkimites" (the term made them sound like a vengeful Old Testament tribe), hinting that the captives were about to be put in a cage and sent off to Lhasa or Beijing. In a misguided attempt to reassure the Hookers, he told them that he was "an old Diplomatist" and that they should not distress themselves unduly, "for I am used to politics & Himalayan politics especially; & our safe and cautious Government is not likely to act against my healing counsels."[140] Writing to his father a week after his release, Hooker observed that Hodgson "seems to have misapprehended the whole thing." He had made a "great mess" of the political situation, driven the government frantic with letters "of the most extraordinary description," and thrown Darjeeling into a "most disgraceful panic." "That Brian was at bottom actuated solely by love of us we know full well," Hooker continued, but he "must have been mad" to send such letters to the Government of India.[141]

In May 1850 Hooker left Darjeeling for the last time, having failed, in the wake of the Sikkim affair, to gain permission to botanize in eastern Nepal and obliged, instead, to accompany Thomson to the Khasi hills. Hooker had by now despaired of Dalhousie's good offices, and his relations with Hodgson also remained cool for some time. It is clear, though, that a great deal of mutual respect and affection still existed, as the passages quoted earlier from Hooker's *Himalayan Journals* indicate. They—and Campbell, who retired in 1862—kept in touch long after Hodgson's return to England in 1858, and the three of them communicated from time to time about botany, geography, and the prospects for trade and European settlement in the northeast. Hooker even named his third son, born in 1860, Brian Harvey Hodgson Hooker in his old friend's honor. Naming, and the associations it carried, was clearly important to Hooker. While he spurned the use of "native appellations," he named one of his most treasured botanical discoveries, a genus of climbers with vivid white and yellow flowers, *Hodgsonia*, just as he named other equally spectacular plants after, among others, the Campbells, Cathcart, Falconer, Madden, Peel, Thomson, Lord Auckland, and Lady Dalhousie (see Fig. 15). Some of the most dramatic botanical "finds" in Darjeeling and Sikkim were

FIG. 15. *Rhododendron dalhousiae*, from J.D. Hooker, *Rhododendrons of Sikkim-Himalaya* (1849), drawn by W.H. Fitch from a sketch by Hooker. Reproduced by kind permission of the Royal Botanic Gardens, Kew.

thereby identified with Hooker's patrons, friends, and accomplices, some of the most spectacular sights in the Himalayan landscape were populated with his personal associations.[142]

Hooker left his mark on Sikkim in other ways, too. Not content merely to describe the landscape in words, he drew up a detailed topographical map of Sikkim, of sufficient accuracy to be of military use to the British for decades to come as the autonomy of the state was steadily undermined.[143] Hooker reckoned that his last long journey through Sikkim, though blighted by his "captivity" and the loss of some of his most treasured plant collections, had "answered my purposes beyond my most sanguine expectations." It had allowed him to "survey the whole country, and to execute a map of it," and Campbell "had gained that knowledge of its resources which the British government should all along have possessed, as the protector of the Rajah and his territories."[144] Territorial acquisition was not the only measure of imperial advance. Even a relatively remote region like Sikkim might be appropriated by science, annexed by aesthetics as much as ensnared through economics. Sikkim, reduced in size, struggled on as a semi-independent state (until incorporated into the Indian Union in 1975), but Hooker's involvement in this far corner of the Himalaya showed how closely the quest for botanical and geographical knowledge might be entwined with the wider colonizing process.

Tropics into Text

In the published version of his journey in the *Himalayan Journals* Hooker gave only the briefest account of his voyage out to India via the Mediterranean, Egypt, the Red Sea, Ceylon, and Madras, beginning his narrative instead with his arrival in Calcutta. The reasons for this are not hard to find. Eager to publicize his son's "botanical mission" to India, William Hooker printed extracts from Joseph's private letters, covering the early part of his travels, in his *Journal of Botany*. He even, without consulting his son, had them printed up as a book, much as he prepared illustrations and descriptions of Joseph's newly discovered Darjeeling–Sikkim rhododendrons for publication.[145] However, when Hooker's travel *Notes on a Tour* appeared, a reviewer in the *Athenaeum* subjected them to a scathing review, suggesting that (to judge by his letters) Joseph had nothing new to contribute to botanical knowledge, nor yet much talent as a travel writer. "There must," the reviewer declared, "be something very extraordinary in the style of the writer—either the humour must be great or the pictorial power unrivalled—to command attention to such subjects. Dr Hooker has no pretensions of the kind..." Besides, he added dismissively, "ordinary Englishmen" now knew the route to India "nearly as well as that to the Isle of Wight," and apart from Hooker's description of Aden, the rest of his voyage to Calcutta was "about as interesting as a voyage to Gravesend would be."[146]

Hooker was understandably aggrieved by this review (which soon reached him in the Himalaya) and, for the time being at least, it discouraged him from believing that he should attempt to publish a narrative of his journey. The publication of his more strictly botanical work, and especially the preparation of the *Flora Indica* with Thomson, seemed a more urgent priority. It was some years after his return from India, and especially with encouragement from his wife, Frances, whom he married in 1851, and from Humboldt, that Hooker decided to take up the task of transforming his travel notes into a book.[147] Hooker perhaps felt that his personal experience of India and the Himalaya, the sensations and visual impressions it produced, and the sense of almost Humboldtian achievement he felt as a result of his travels, required more than the kind of technical and "philosophical" treatment given in his and Thomson's introductory essay to the *Flora Indica*. India's tropicality (or the partial want of it) called for narration and not just taxonomy. The *Journals* also met Hooker's longstanding desire to be part of the great tradition of travelers and travel writers. As he put it to one fellow botanist: "To write a book of the sort, after travels of the sort, has been the pole-star of my life from earliest childhood."[148] The publication, also in 1855, the same year as the *Flora*, of the richly illustrated volume on Himalayan plants dedicated to J.F. Cathcart, completed a trilogy in which the Indian flora and all that gave it meaning and context could be understood in three complementary ways—the visual, the taxonomic, and the narrative.

When Hooker published his *Himalayan Journals* in 1854, he argued that the previous publication of his journey to Calcutta obviated the need for again covering that portion of his travels; since the same argument could have been made of most of his journey, accounts of which had also previously appeared in print, perhaps he was still smarting from the *Athenaeum*'s attack. Combined with his failure to gain entry to Nepal in 1850 and his recourse instead to the Khasi hills and eastern Bengal, the effect was to make his narrative one concerned exclusively with his travels *within* India rather than encompassing those *to* India as well. This created a narrative which, in one of its several aspects, was about a quest for the tropics within India itself. Here was a fabled region that had been heard about and glimpsed (in Brazil, in Ceylon, even in what remained of the botanic garden at Calcutta) which proved disappointingly elusive in the dreary plains of Bengal and Bihar, but which began to reveal itself in the foothills of the Himalaya and in the lush "tropical" vegetation of Sikkim. But the quest did not end there. Hooker's narration took him beyond the tropical into the temperate and alpine reaches of the high Himalaya, through the ordeal of "captivity," and then, after leaving Darjeeling, back into the lowlands of Bengal, the Khasi hills, and finally Chittagong, all of which added new layers of scenic beauty and scientific complexity to his understanding of the tropics. Even more clearly than in the writings of previous naturalists in India and its margins, Hooker presented the tropics as a narrative of subcontinental proportions, to be experienced and understood by passing through, beyond, and back into them several times over.

To narrativize the Indian tropics in this way and still to be faithful to his scientific agenda was no easy task. Thomson had attempted something of the sort in his own account of his travels in the western Himalaya and Tibet in 1852, but, lacking in any compelling sense of vitality, or even literary pretensions, it had not been a success. One reviewer commended it as a "straightforward, unaffected narrative," adding that if it was "wholly devoid of exaggeration or egotism," it was also "loaded with botanical names and geographical details." Worse still, it was "deficient in the interest which a personal narrative and the power of animated description can alone convey."[149]

Nor were Hooker's *Himalayan Journals* entirely free from these pitfalls. Certainly, when it appeared in 1854 the work was favorably received by the scientific community in Britain. Darwin, to whom the work was dedicated, was particularly enthusiastic. It was, he wrote on completing the first volume, a book that would become "a standard," not so much because it contained "real solid matter," but because it gave "a picture of the whole country,—one can feel that one has seen it . . . & one *realises* all the great Physical features."[150] Edward Forbes, the naturalist whose poor opinion of Thomson's narrative has just been quoted, was also broadly appreciative of Hooker's *Journals*. Contrasting it with the work of other Himalayan travelers and naturalists, he observed:

> the mantle of Humboldt has not in general descended on them ... they appear to have been deficient in many of the qualities of the philosophic traveller, in habits of generalisation, and, not least of all, in the art of communicating with the world, in a perspicuous and interesting style, a knowledge of what they saw.[151]

Hooker, he felt, had "advanced a step beyond his predecessors"—in his attention to the interest of the "general reader," as well as his "scientific acquirements" and "his outfit for observing facts and collecting specimens." He wished, though, that Hooker had gone further in revising his journals. Had he more thoroughly recast his material, Forbes suggested, he might have produced a more interesting book.[152]

Sixty years later, Hooker's biographer, Leonard Huxley, also rated the *Journals* highly, claiming that they were "an instant success" and ensured for their author "the highest reputation as a scientific traveller."[153] He cited F.O. Bower's assessment that the *Journals* stood alongside Darwin's account of the *Beagle* voyage and Wallace's *Malay Archipelago*, the three together forming "a veritable trilogy of the Golden Age of travel in pursuit of science."[154] But such high praise was surely excessive. Hooker's *Journals* appeared in an abbreviated second edition in 1855 (with the technical appendices removed) but thereafter were only reprinted late in his own lifetime, in 1891 and again in 1905. Many readers found the work over-long, tedious in its botanical and topographical detail, and rather awkwardly divided between Hooker's personal adventures and his scientific observations. "A narrative of nearly eight hundred pages," complained the *Spectator*, "requires to be lightened by every artifice of composition."[155] Others, while praising some of Hooker's descriptive passages, were distracted by the conflict with the Raja of Sikkim, whose insulting behavior toward a British subject appeared to be the work's main message. Imperial rights and barbarous wrongs seemed more important than accounts of obscure epiphytes and yet more glacial moraines.

Hooker's *Journals* demonstrate, nonetheless, the extent to which an early Victorian scientific writer was prepared to go, and the range of devices he was prepared to employ, in order to render his tropical travels and natural history accessible to a wider audience. Apart from the maps and numerous engravings with which the text was adorned, the printed word (and the multiplicity of images and allusions it could conjure up) was consciously deployed to engage, entertain, and inform. In so doing, Hooker made the tropics a central theme of his work. Even if their success among the general public was limited, the *Himalayan Journals* were one of several contemporary sources that helped to consolidate the idea of the tropics as both a scientific concept and a popular imaginative trope, and one that was as applicable to India (albeit with certain qualifications) as to Tahiti, Brazil, Mauritius, or Ceylon. It was part of Hooker's achievement to bring India and more specifically the eastern Himalaya (a region, as one reviewer pointed out, "not strictly'" within the tropics and yet possessing vegetation "of a tropical character")[156] more securely within the imaginative domain of the tropics.

CONCLUSION

IN THE COURSE OF THE EARLY NINETEENTH CENTURY INDIA BECAME "tropicalized." For a region as topographically and climatically diverse as India, so deficient in many of the seemingly characteristic scenic tropes of the quasi-Edenic tropics, so clearly possessing a long history of civilizations, of powerful states and literate cultures, such a conceptualization was by no means easy or self-evident. That India had by mid-century largely succumbed to tropicality was due to many factors and not one alone. But, as this book has tried to demonstrate, the increasing tendency to represent India as wholly or partly tropical stemmed from the profound epistemological reorientation that occurred as colonial rule was consolidated and South Asia more fully integrated into wider systems of power and knowledge. Part of that process involved the explicit downgrading of indigenous knowledge and agency, and even of the scholarly Orientalism that had formed part of the West's earlier acquisitive, and inquisitive, drive. Instead, India was interpreted in relation to perceptions and values that were largely external to itself and alien to its history and culture. India could not stand alone, nor speak for itself. In an age of globalizing empires and universalizing systems of knowledge, it needed to be represented as part of something else. And, in no small measure, that "something else" was nature. Just as, under an increasingly intense and exacting imperial gaze, other lands became Oriental or Arctic,[1] so India became (in many important respects) tropical.

To a degree, as the opening chapters of this book have tried to suggest, the tropicalization of India was a process that occurred first at the level of perception and imagination. In this regard, it has been argued, the anticipation of India's tropicality—through travel literature, through novels and poetry, through pictorial art—played a vital, preconditioning role. So, too, did the Romantic sentiments and sensibilities of those European travelers who sought to annex India—not least India's landscapes—to their own emotional and cultural world, or who by their intimate correspondence helped created an empire of affect in which India was more widely understood and identified with through the personal experiences of relatives, friends, and compatriots. But it has been one of the ambitions of this book to go beyond impressions and imagination, to argue that even before the mid-century climacteric of the Indian Rebellion and the transfer of authority from Company to Crown, the emerging understanding of India as tropical had acquired significant purchase in more practical and technical ways.

In particular, botany has been used here to show how the idea of the tropics influenced the manner in which India's plant "treasure" was presented to Western science (and the careers in science that grew out of the appropriation and transfer of such esteemed "riches"), how a tropical–temperate divide informed plant taxonomy and the biogeography of Indian flora, and how economic botany, allied to "improvement," began to reshape Indian agriculture and the wider environment. In thus utilizing the paradigms of tropicality, botanical science kept pace with similar developments in tropical medicine and helped to anticipate and advance the disciplinary spread of tropicality into other fields of imperial science. If tropicality found one of its early routes into India through a Romantic evocation of the tropics, it found part of its subsequent elaboration and fulfillment through such technical and eminently practical fields as tropical agriculture. The tropicalization of India was more than a mere effect of the imagination.

That said, though, there remained a prevailing tension in India's tropicality. For those travelers whose first fond sighting of the tropics was in the Caribbean or Brazil, or whose impressions of the tropics came first from Humboldt or Darwin, or even from the pages of *Paul and Virginia*, India could be a bitter disappointment. Much of the subcontinent lay within tropical latitudes but appeared untropically gaunt and bare. It was situated close to the luxuriant and self-evidently tropical lands of Ceylon and Southeast Asia, and yet it was plagued by famine and its "unclothed" plains lay "sterile" and "barren" before the eye. To be sure, the tropics were seldom, except in wildest fantasy, seen as merely Edenic: to even the most casual traveler it was obvious that they teemed with all manner of biting, stinging, and bloodsucking insects, were bedeviled by snakes and scorpions, cursed by sudden and deadly diseases, and were home to raging tempests and crashing surfs of a violence unequalled in Europe.

Across most of the tropical world these natural menaces and melodramas were compensated for by the wealth of natural abundance, of landscapes and vistas in which the senses could revel with pleasure and delight. But India, seemingly, had too few of these compensations. It had aplenty the disease of the tropics, its parasites and pests, but too little of India looked like Malabar or the quintessentially tropical botanic garden Nathaniel Wallich had presided over in Calcutta. Some travelers, like Victor Jacquemont, never satisfied their lust for the tropics in India; others (notably Joseph Hooker), having at first been bitterly disappointed, were eventually able to bring to the idea of India's scenic and scientific tropicality a new complexity and vibrancy and, further, to entrench this authoritative idea in the botanical science of the region.[2]

By the latter part of the nineteenth century some parts of South Asia seemed, by virtue of their climate, vegetation, scenery, and even their diseases, to fit almost paradigmatically into the normative tropics,[3] while others, characterized by semi-arid savannas or high alpine pastures, were far more difficult to locate within that overarching framework. And yet, after a flurry of mid-century speculation, to which Hodgson and Hooker were conspicuous contributors, the idea that the valleys and foothills of the Himalaya might be suited for European colonization—India's White Highlands—and thereby more closely integrated into an empire of settlement, began to wane, thus steering India still further toward tropical alterity.[4] But well before that time the fact that so much of India failed to look like the imagined tropics helped, conversely, to feed the determination to transform India, to create through an alliance of colonial capitalism and prospective Romanticism, a vision of an India so "improved" as to come close to ideals of tropical abundance and productivity. In falling short of the idealized tropics, India added to the more complex understanding of what the tropics actually were—diverse and not homogeneous, characterized by dry savannas and scrubby "jungles" as well as by luxuriant plant-life and dense rainforest, places of poverty, hardship, and death as well as fecundity, pleasure, and plenty.

The complex and multi-stranded nature of the process of perceptual and scientific change overtaking India needs, however, to be constantly borne in mind. It was not just the internal diversity of India (itself so broadly conceived in the early nineteenth century as at times to embrace Nepal, Sikkim, Burma, and beyond) that called for a series of different, and to a degree contending, topographical tropes. Individuals, too, over time and in various contexts, might articulate significantly different understandings of the Indian landscape and its attendant sciences. For instance, when the Irish-born soldier and botanist Edward Madden first traveled extensively in India in the late 1820s and early 1830s, much of his personal concern was with recognizing the "biblical" features in the landscape and in recording those plants that he had first encountered textually in the Bible but now saw for the first time. By the late 1830s and 1840s, as his acquaintance with the Indian countryside and Indian botany grew, and as he traveled widely in Rajasthan and the hill country of Kumaon, so his travel narratives, exhibited a more "Orientalist" character, relating plants and places to Hindu myth and legend. Some of this work appropriately found its way to European readers in India (and eventually further afield) through the pages of the *Journal of the Asiatic Society of Bengal*. Finally, after he had retired to Edinburgh in the early 1850s and become a significant figure in scientific circles there, his articles on Indian botany assumed a more technical, less subjective character and, with the Bible and Orientalism now largely eschewed, made extensive use of the tripartite division of vegetation between tropical, temperate, and alpine zones.[5] The subject of Madden's traveling gaze remained much the same throughout—the Indian landscape and its plant-life—but, over a twenty-year period, at different stages in his career and for different audiences, he presented that material in significantly different ways.

By mid-century, both science and India were rapidly changing. The death of Humboldt and the publication of Darwin's *Origin of Species*— both in 1859—helped signal science's radical shift. Striving for new levels of authority and objectivity, the practitioners of science were growing increasingly wary of the Romantic strain, which had previously been so conspicuous in their personal approach to, and literary representation of, nature.[6] Even Hooker's *Himalayan Journals*, published in 1854, still intermittently exhibited a Romantic spirit, but contained considerably fewer references to *Rasselas*, Walter Scott, and Salvator Rosa, or to personal friends and private recollections, than had his original travel notes and writings. The indulgent Orientalist sensuality of *Lalla Rookh* had given way to Turner's vast and luminous canvases, with their hints of the dawning of a new imperial and industrial age. And where an earlier writer like Bishop Heber had charmed (or infuriated) his readers with his loose lyricism and uncritical analogies, Hooker strove to discipline his more impulsive associations and to bend them to the more exacting task of topographical depiction and botanical analysis. Science never ceased to travel, but it felt less compulsion to do so—the landscape (and the nature it held) was assuming less importance as a site of operations and as a resource than the laboratory. The natural sciences felt less need to wrap their observations and speculations in a finely spun narrative cocoon. Scientific travel did not cease to have a role (and one can certainly find examples of it in late nineteenth-century India), but, in a disciplinary field like botany, the scientific gaze was becoming less immediately dependent upon travel.

India, too, was changing, not least under the compulsions of technological innovation. Hooker traveled to and from Darjeeling the hard way—by palanquin, by boat, by pony, or simply by walking. Most of his exploration of Sikkim was done on foot, and the relative inaccessibility of the region made it possible for him to see himself as a resolute explorer, defying fatigue, altitude sickness and obstruction, and to peer into Tibet as if into another, lost, world. He relished being a pioneer, going where few, if any, Europeans had previously trod, and so becoming a great "Indian traveller." It seemed essential as much to his science as to his personal reputation that he did so. And yet, within two decades of his Himalayan adventure, as the railroads snaked north from Calcutta, and Darjeeling became only a few days' journey from the Indian metropolis, so even Sikkim fell "within easy reach of the traveller" and tourists could gaze in relative comfort at the "sylvan wonders of Sikkim" that Hooker, through such personal labor, had first brought to their attention.[7] The Himalayan frontier did not shed its mystique, but a decade or two after Hooker and Hodgson had sat by the fireside at "Bryanstone," smoking their cheroots, arguing and speculating, there remained few outstanding geographical issues still clamoring to be resolved.

When Hooker left for India in 1847 photography, too, like the railroad, was still in its infancy. What he could not capture in words of Himalayan scenes and flora, had to be painstakingly reproduced through his many landscape sketches and plant drawings. By the time of the Indian Mutiny ten years later photography already had an established place in India, too, as pictures of the shattered Residency at Lucknow or the dangling figures of hanged sepoys powerfully demonstrated. The advent of photography did little for botany (unlike ethnography where it had a dramatic and enduring effect),[8] but it did render less necessary the lengthy scenic descriptions and pen and ink sketches with which Hooker sought to illustrate and embellish his *Himalayan Journals*. Within twenty years of his journey, European photographers were making accessible to a wide audience images of Himalayan scenery, many of the kind over which Hooker had labored so long. The coming of the railroad and the dawning of photography were but two of the technologies that made India more visible to the outside world, more an exhibit or a commodity, and so rendered the experience of travel less necessary, less revelatory.

Joseph Hooker has been used in this book to show the elaboration and culmination of several interlocking trends in early nineteenth-century India—the scenic evaluation and scientific understanding of India, the role of travel and travel writing, the emergence of botany as one of the principal routes to the appropriation and tropicalization of India. He (and to a degree his father's more distant engagement with India before him) illuminates the many paradoxes of the period. He shows how science was reaching out from its metropolitan bases to establish a firmer hold over science in the colonies, and yet how important local expertise (like Hodgson's and Campbell's) and the authority of having traveled, of having personally seen and experienced another place, remained. Increasingly assured in his place in metropolitan science, not least as Darwin's confidant, Hooker also helped institutionalize the idea of the tropics in modern scientific thought and professional practice. By the botanical and geographical detail of his writing, and by narrativizing, through travel and text the complex ecology that combined yet distinguished tropical and temperate plant-life in the eastern Himalaya, he helped to give added authority to the idea of tropical difference: both at a generalized level of perception and categorization and in the more localized distribution of characteristically tropical and temperate flora.

In this process, as in so much else, Hooker did not act alone. In its constituent elements, his botany had abundant local precedent—not least in the travels, taxonomy, and texts of Wallich, Royle, Wight, and his own collaborator Thomson. The practical interdependence of colonial and metropolitan naturalists was as evident as was the persistent feeling that the pursuit of science in India was variously disadvantaged—or backward—compared to that in the metropole. And yet, reliant though he was in many ways upon colonial knowledge (and, more remotely, indigenous agency and knowledge), Hooker deployed his wider experience, his "philosophical" stance and urge to systematize, to carry local observation and accumulated knowledge to a new theoretical level in science and to help consolidate the burgeoning idea of "the tropical world" in the popular imagination of Europe.[9] Such a development was by no means confined to botany, influential and instrumental though that science undoubtedly was. Other areas of scientific activity—earlier perhaps in the case of medicine or agriculture, later in the case of veterinary science or soil science, or in the "race science" of ethnography—were moving in a similar direction and using the idea of the tropics to enlarge their professional domains and scientific credibility. Indeed, it was not uncommon by the end of the nineteenth and early years of the twentieth century for authoritative accounts of one "tropical" specialty to invoke and reinforce another. A botanist's treatise on "tropical agriculture" might thus not only draw upon the apparently shared experience of India, Ceylon, Java, and Malaya, but also allude (as if unproblematically) to the shared hazards of "tropical disease," the deficiencies of "tropical soils," and the characteristic "indolence" of all "tropical races."[10]

The invocation of what has here been called tropicality—the ideas, associations, and practices that congealed around the central idea of tropical difference—should not be understood as representing some kind of absolute difference, an alterity beyond all comparison and comprehension. Even chalk and cheese have their commonality. Observers like Hooker well knew that the tropics and the temperate zone were not separated by a single, unbridgeable divide: there were inevitably areas of interpenetration, a blurring at the margins, enclaves of otherness within one or other generalized domain. And yet, despite knowing this, there remained something that, even under close botanical scrutiny, distinguished one from the other, which called for other kinds of technical expertise and knowledge, or even summoned up a different kind of emotional response and scenic sensibility. Although in many respects the world was becoming more accessible to European control, even though the universalizing ambitions of science were increasingly asserted and realized, a variety of specialisms, built around geographical, climatic, biological, and ethnographic difference, was apparently becoming more (and not less) necessary. In an age unprecedented alike in science and in empire, tropicality was scaling new heights.

NOTES

INTRODUCTION

1. Carter, *Road*.
2. Thomas, *Colonialism's Culture*, 2.
3. Taussig, *Shamanism*, 334–5.
4. Writers sometimes referred, as in Europe, to the "environs" of a town or village. The term "ecology" was similarly not used in scientific literature in India before the 1900s.
5. For example, Arnold, *Colonizing*; Grove, Damodaran, and Sangwan, *Nature*; Harrison, *Climates*.
6. Cohn's other modalities were historiography, surveying, enumeration, museology, and surveillance, though clearly some of these, especially the last, overlap with observation and travel. Cohn, *Colonialism*, 5–11.
7. Crosby, *Ecological Imperialism*.
8. A classic statement of this was Thomson, "Natives;" but many Europeans believed India capable of environmental amelioration, including measures that would eliminate disease, curb drought, transform agriculture and facilitate white settlement. This book is not primarily concerned, however, with European acclimatization in the tropics. See Anderson, *Cultivation*; Harrison, *Climates*; Livingstone, "Climate's Moral Economy."
9. Cosgrove and Daniels, *Iconography*, 1; also Cosgrove, "Social Formation."
10. Notably Carter, *Road*; Griffiths and Robin, *Ecology*; Neumann, *Imposing Wilderness*. See also the "Introduction" to Beinart and McGregor, *Social History*, 4–6, 14–15, for the importance of landscape traditions in colonial Africa.
11. Green, *Spectacle*. The landscape as "the work of the mind" has also been tellingly discussed by Schama, *Landscape*, though, as will be evident from the early chapters of this book, in this case the "memory" evoked by Indian landscapes

was often of landscapes that lay elsewhere—in Britain or in "tropical" Brazil and the West Indies.

12. Drayton, *Nature's Government*, and Guha, *Rule*. While excellent in its coverage of the metropolitan forces behind nineteenth-century "improvement," and especially those that emanated from Kew Gardens, Drayton's study fails to recognize the extent to which such ideas and practices had acquired a dynamic force of their own within colonial territories like India by the early decades of the century and were not dependent upon repeated stimulus from Kew. Equally, as this study will try to show, economic botany was only one of the ways in which botany served the empire and its colonizing ambitions.

13. As in the case of French and German influences on "scientific forestry" in late nineteenth-century India: see Rajan, "Imperial Environmentalism."

14. Said, *Orientalism*.

15. Not all historians would agree: see Harrison, *Climates*, for a dissenting view. The main arguments for the present claim will be found here in chapters 4–6.

16. See Dunlap, *Nature*.

17. Bayly, *Empire*; Raj, "Colonial Encounters." For the "dialogic" idea, see Irschick, *Dialogue*.

18. E.g., Dirks, "Introduction."

19. Pratt, *Imperial Eyes*, 4, 6.

20. As this book is concerned with European travel, it does not seek to address the question of Indian travel and its relation to the "colonial gaze," about which a significant literature has begun to emerge: e.g., Grewal, *Home*, chapter 4.

21. E.g., Sangwan, "Strength."

1 / ITINERANT EMPIRE

1. Unless otherwise specified, "India" in this book refers to the whole of the subcontinent, except Ceylon, including the present states of India, Pakistan, and Bangladesh; as will be evident however the Himalayan regions, including Nepal, Sikkim, and Bhutan, as well as neighboring areas such as Burma, and Afghanistan also featured prominently and influentially in the India travel and scientific literature of the time.

2. Bevan, *Thirty Years*, vol. 1: v; cf. Malcolm, *Memoir*, vol. 2: 276, 282.

3. Roberts, *Scenes*, vol. 2: 32.

4. Ibid., vol. 1: 297.

5. Kaye, *Selections*, 80.

6. Bayly, *Imperial Meridian*; Peers, *Between Mars and Mammon*.

7. Hamilton, *East-India Gazetteer*, vol. 1: xii.

8. Forster, *Journey*, vol. 1: 191; Hove, *Tours*, 51.
9. Burnes, *Travels*, vol. 1: xiii. Richard Burton took the view that disguise (in his case as an Indian–Arab merchant) was the best means to gain uninhibited access to Indian society, but that was from choice, not necessity. "Early Days in Sind," in Burton, *Selected Papers*, 18–19.
10. The number of doctors (one of the main kinds of scientific travelers in this period) was particularly significant. In the mid-1830s, there were 745 European surgeons and assistant surgeons in India, nearly half in the Bengal Presidency: Crawford, *History*, vol. 1: 215.
11. For instance, Emma Roberts, born c.1794, was the posthumous daughter of Captain William Roberts, and first visited India in 1828 with her sister and brother-in-law, a captain in the Bengal Infantry. When her sister died in 1831, she returned to Britain, but went back again to India, dying there in 1840. Sengupta, *Cameos*, 69–79.
12. Griffith, *Journal*, i–v. For botanists generally, see Desmond, *European Discovery*.
13. In charge of the museum from 1841 to 1862, Blyth seems hardly to have left Calcutta during that entire time. As a result, as he informed Charles Darwin, he lacked the "great & needful advantages of travel and personal observation elsewhere." Blyth to Darwin, 4 Aug. 1855, Burkhardt and Smith, *Correspondence*, vol. 5: 392.
14. On Heber, see chapter 3 below.
15. See Lee-Warner, *Dalhousie*.
16. Forster, *Journey*, vol. 1: 3.
17. Mouat, *Rough Notes*, 76.
18. Lee-Warner, *Dalhousie*, vol. 1: 347. For a similar sentiment, see the letters of Fanny and Emily Eden, 3 April 1836 and 31 Aug. 1836, in Eden, *Letters*, vol. 1:132, 231.
19. *Athenaeum*, 13 Dec. 1851, 1304.
20. Murray, *Account*, vol. 3: 338.
21. *Athenaeum*, 13 Dec. 1851, 1304.
22. Ibid., 12 June 1852, 649–50.
23. The first Cook's tour to India was in 1873: Brendon, *Cook*, 143–8.
24. Joseph Hooker (hereafter JH) to William Hooker (WH), 1 Feb. 1849, IL, RBG.
25. [Kaye], "English," 3.
26. See Deloche, *Transport*.
27. [Kaye], "English," 28; cf. Hoffmeister, *Travels*, 198.
28. Mackintosh, *Memoirs*, vol. 1: 378–9; Smith, *Lawrence*, vol. 1: 38.
29. Hooker, "Extracts" (1849), 7.
30. Roberts, *Scenes*, vol. 1: 214.

31. Bowrey, *Geographical Account*.
32. Singh, *Colonial Narratives*, chapter 1.
33. E.g., see Foster, *Embassy*. An exception might also be made for Edward Terry, whose descriptions of India between 1616 and 1619 mark him out as a discerning observer: Foster, *Early Travels*, 295–306.
34. See Charlton, *New Images*, and Thacker, *Wildness*, for changing European sensibilities to nature. For the dramatic changes in writing and publishing from the mid-eighteenth century onwards, see Butler, "Romanticism."
35. Hodges, *Travels*, 23, 28, 37. For the picturesque and "idyllic" strain in Hodges (despite the recent famine of 1770), see Teltscher, *India Inscribed*, 127–8.
36. Archer, *Early Views*; Godrej and Rohatgi, *Scenic Splendours*; Tillotson, *Artifical Empire*.
37. Notably in *The Oriental Annual, Or Scenes in India* (London, 1834–40), which initially served as a vehicle for William Daniell's "unrivalled" depictions of India. Several of the illustrations used in this book are taken from R. Montgomery Martin's *Indian Empire Illustrated*. Although dating from c. 1861 this volume reproduced, with scant acknowledgment, many of Roberts's scenic descriptions and illustrations from the earlier works of Elliott and White, sometimes captioned or partly redrawn to relate them to the events of 1857–8.
38. [Gibbes], *Hartly House*, 20–1, 24, 67, 92, 99, 113. For this novel, see Nussbaum, *Torrid Zones*.
39. [Gibbes], *Hartly House*, 46. For the importance of Thomson and other poets in influencing British sensibilities to nature, see Butler, "Romanticism," 41–2.
40. Cf. Pratt, *Imperial Eyes*, 59–60. Roberts's work is particularly expressive of this. Apart from her *Scenes*, see her descriptions in Elliott, *Views*, White, *Views*, and Martin, *Indian Empire*.
41. Hooker, "Extracts" (1849), 3; *Himalayan Journals*, vol. 2: 290, 354.
42. Roberts, *Scenes*, vol. 1: 3; vol. 2: 135.
43. Barrow, *Making History*; Dirks, "Guiltless Spoilations;" Tillotson, *Artificial Empire*.
44. Quoted in Barrell, *Infection*, 150.
45. Bellew, *Memoirs*, vol. 1: 7.
46. Graham, *Journal*, iii.
47. For a general account of the development of travel writing, see Korte, *English Travel Writing*.
48. Mackintosh noted that while Britons in India gossiped endlessly about "home," "Indian topics" were "very uninteresting in England": Mackintosh, *Memoirs*, vol. 1: 216. Fifty years later, Dalhousie remarked that "the Indian Empire bores the Commons." Baird, *Dalhousie*, 202.
49. Howison, *Foreign Scenes*, vol. 1: 202–3.

50. *Athenaeum*, 18 Feb. 1854, 209.
51. Ibid., 20 Nov. 1852, 1268.
52. Edney, *Mapping*; Kejariwal, *Asiatic Society*; Marshall, *British Discovery*.
53. In addition to Edney, *Mapping*, see Headrick, *Tools*.
54. Mellor, "Romanticism," 148.
55. Bearce, *British Attitudes*; Drew, *India*; Leask, *Romantic Writers*. For India's role in stimulating European Romanticism, see Halbfass, *India*; Schwab, *Oriental Renaissance*.
56. Stokes, *Utilitarians*, 10–15; cf. Bayly, *Imperial Meridian*, 154–9.
57. Bewell, *Romanticism*; Fulford and Kitson, *Romanticism*; Lee, *Slavery*; Makdisi, *Romantic Imperialism*. For Romanticism generally, see McCalman, *Oxford Companion*.
58. See Foucault, "Governmentality," and for some consideration of its colonial contexts, see Scott, "Colonial Governmentality."
59. Foucault, *Birth*; *Discipline*; *Order*.
60. E.g., Sloan, "Gaze;" Green, *Spectacle*.
61. Pratt, *Imperial Eyes*, 7, 201–4; cf. Spurr, *Rhetoric*, chapter 1.
62. Cf. Neumann, *Imposing Wilderness*, chapter 1.
63. Carter, *Road*, 69.
64. Ibid., 9, 67.
65. Tod, *Annals*, vol. 1: 4.
66. Humbley, *Journal*, 8.
67. Heyne, *Tracts*; Roberts in White, *Views*, vii, 85, 95; Murray, *Account*, vol. 3: 14.
68. "March between Mhow and Saugor," 805.
69. Arnold, "Race."
70. For examples, see Sleeman, *Rambles*; Spry, *Modern India*.
71. This narrative strand in early colonial science has been effectively discussed in relation to the "journey-like" maps of the period: Barrow, *Making History*, 62–4.
72. Bevan, *Thirty Years*, vol. 1: 157; Mackintosh, *Memoirs*, vol. 2: 161; Malcolm, *Memoir*, vol. 1: vi; Orme, *History*, 300.
73. Cleghorn, "Report," 79.
74. Turner, *Account*.
75. Cohn, *Anthropologist*, 632–82; cf. Mitchell, *Colonising Egypt*. For India and the Great Exhibition, see Royle, *Culture*. The first major Indian exhibition was in Madras in 1855.
76. One of the best-known works of nineteenth-century travel writing about India, Eden's *Up the Country*, was published in 1866 but recounted her experiences thirty years earlier.
77. See Arnold, *Science*.

78. Hamilton, *East-India Gazetteer*, vol. 1: 533.
79. "Introduction," to Arnold, *Warm Climates*, 6; Stepan, *Picturing*.
80. Said, *Orientalism*. For India's subsequent "tropicality," see Arnold, "India's Place." On "imaginative geographies," see Cosgrave, *Social Formation*; Flint, *Imaginative Landscape*; and the "Introduction" to Lowenthal and Bowden, *Geographies*. Cf. Aravamudan, *Tropicopolitans*, which is principally concerned with the representation of "tropical people" as colonized subjects within European literature and thereby fails to problematize the idea of "the tropics" and to reflect on how such concepts were worked out in the discursive practices of "the tropical world" itself.
81. Cohn, *Colonialism*.
82. The only detailed biography remains Huxley, *Life*; but see Desmond, *Hooker*.
83. Brockway, *Science*; Drayton, *Nature's Government*.
84. It is, however, beyond the scope of this book to trace the development of Hooker's ideas beyond his Indian years. For his wider place in bio-geographical thinking, see Browne, *Secular Ark*.
85. In 1909, two years before his death and already in his nineties, Hooker published a magisterial survey of Indian botany: Hooker, "Botany."

2 / IN A LAND OF DEATH

1. See Curtin, *Death*.
2. [Gibbes], *Hartly House*, 1.
3. Darwin, *Voyage*, 322.
4. Martin, *Tropical Climates*, 58.
5. Between 1815 and 1855, an estimated 100,000 British soldiers of the Company and Royal armies died in India (exclusive of campaign casualties); at a cost of £100 a head to the state, this amounted to a loss of £10 million: J.R. Martin in "Report of the Commissioners Appointed to Inquire into the Organization of the Indian Army," *Parliamentary Papers*, 1859, 167.
6. Martin, *Tropical Climates*, 51, 402.
7. [Lawrence], "English Women," 124.
8. [MacMullen] *Camp*, 137–42.
9. Ewart, *Digest*, 2, 27–31.
10. Ibid., 139–40, 152.
11. Between 1790 and 1836, of the 4,525 civil servants recruited for Bengal, 90 died in the first five years of service, with a further 72 in the second quinquennium, and 41 in the third. Prinsep, "Corrected Estimate," 346.
12. Quoted in Pennant, *View*, vol. 2: 325.

13. Tennant, *Indian Recreations*, vol. 1: 78.
14. Howison, *Foreign Scenes*, vol. 2: 20–1.
15. Eden to the Countess of Buckinghamshire, 9 Aug. 1836, in Eden, *Letters*, vol. 1: 210.
16. For the impact of cholera and other epidemics, see Arnold, *Colonizing the Body*.
17. Tod, *Annals*, vol. 2: 630–1. By mid-century the class differential had become more evident. Ewart (*Digest*, 153), noted that each year 17.4 soldiers per 1,000 were attacked by cholera, of whom 7 died. Among officers only 7.3 per 1,000 were attacked and 1.2 died.
18. Gleig, *Munro*, vol. 2: 312–15.
19. Annesley, *Sketches*, vol. 1: 21–2.
20. Hickey, *Memoirs*, vol. 3: 203, 315.
21. Edwardes and Merivale, *Lawrence*, vol. 1: 141–2.
22. Ibid., 142.
23. Dalhousie to Sir George Couper, 8 Aug. 1851, in Baird, *Dalhousie*, 175. Dalhousie was also concerned about the "grievous" sickness and mortality among European soldiers in the Punjab and the heavy military and financial costs that resulted. His interest in improving transportation in India partly stemmed from this concern: ibid., 150–1, 177.
24. Dalhousie to Couper, 10 July 1849, ibid., 83.
25. Ibid., vii.
26. Dalhousie to Couper, 19 June 1853, ibid., 257.
27. Harrison, *Climates*, chapter 3.
28. In addition to Martin, *Medical Topography*, see Rankine, *Notes*, and Taylor, *Sketch*.
29. Cf. Riley, *Eighteenth-Century Campaign*.
30. Hooker, *Himalayan Journals*, vol. 2: 254, 263, 272.
31. Buchanan, *Account*, 65.
32. Tod, *Annals*, vol. 2: 264, 266, 617–18.
33. See Pratt, *Imperial Eyes*, 155–71, for a more explicitly gendered reading of Graham as a travel writer.
34. Graham, *Journal*, 141.
35. Eden, *Letters*, vol. 1: 119. Eden was (mis)quoting Pope's "Elegy to the Memory of an Unfortunate Lady" (1717): "By foreign hands thy dying eyes were closed." The passage also occurs in Mackintosh, *Memoirs*, vol. 2: 119.
36. Campbell, *Romantic Ethic*, 140.
37. Russell, *Journal*, 137.
38. Roberts, *Scenes*, vol. 2: 34.
39. Ibid., vol. 1: 108.
40. Ibid., vol. 2: 37–8.

41. Ibid., 34–5.
42. For dying abroad, especially in the tropics, as a "bad death," see Jalland, *Death*, 68–9.
43. Roberts, *Scenes*, vol. 2: 47–8.
44. Ibid., vol. 2: 48, 51.
45. Johnson, *Oriental Voyager*, 280; Annesley, *Sketches*, vol. 1: 101.
46. M'Cosh, *Assam*, 108.
47. Burton, *Goa*, 130; cf. Skinner, *Excursions* vol. 1: 207.
48. *Oriental Annual* 1835, 217–19.
49. Heber, *Narrative*, vol. 1: 351–5.
50. For one such account, culminating in "horror" and "disgust," see "Mr Pearson's Report," in *Transaction of the Missionary Society for the Year 1817*, vol. 4 (London: London Missionary Society, 1818), 398.
51. Tennant, *Indian Recreations*, vol. 1: 108; cf. Roberts in White, *Views*, vol. 1: 101–2; Heber to Mrs Douglas, 10 Jan. 1824, Heber, *Narrative*, vol. 3: 262.
52. Martin, *Medical Topography*, 52.
53. Cf. Barrow, *Making History*, 43–50.
54. Hodges, *Travels*, 87–94; Roberts, *Scenes*, vol. 2: 39–40; Skinner, *Excursions*, vol. 2: 302.
55. Tod, *Annals*, vol. 2: 702.
56. M'Cosh, *Assam*, 98–9.
57. Mackintosh to his wife, 23 Feb. 1810, Mackintosh, *Memoirs*, vol. 2: 4.
58. For sensibility as a middle-class virtue, see Campbell, *Romantic Ethic*, 139–42.
59. Edwardes and Merivale, *Lawrence*, vol. 2: 20–35.
60. Institutionalizing and restricting the mobility of poor whites was a persistent feature of nineteenth-century British India: Arnold, "European Orphans."
61. [Lawrence], "English Women," 107–8.
62. Heber, *Narrative*, vol. 1: 413.
63. Ibid.
64. Singh, *Colonial Narratives*, chapter 2.
65. [Kaye] "English in India," 292.
66. The converse of this was the view that India was governed by a clique of Company men, trained at Haileybury and its army college, Addiscombe, who formed a much intermarried dynasty and shared the same "class doctrine and sentiment": *Athenaeum*, 27 Mar. 1852, 344.
67. Edgeworth to her stepmother, 7 Jan. 1822, Colvin, *Edgeworth*, 313.
68. For the gendered connotations of "sensibility," see G.J. Barker-Benfield, "Sensibility," in McCalman, *Oxford Companion*, 102–14.
69. Hunter, *Hodgson*, 67–81.
70. Munro to his sister, 22 July 1805, Gleig, *Munro*, vol. 1: 403.

71. Ibid., xi–xii; cf. Stein, *Munro*.
72. Munro to his brother, 24 Oct. 1792, Gleig, *Munro*, vol. 1: 154–5. James Munro briefly served in India before being invalided home with dysentery.
73. Munro to Erskine, 1 Mar. 1790, ibid., 98.
74. Munro to Erskine, 30 June 1799, ibid., 243.
75. Cf. Tod's account of his gardens in Rajasthan: *Annals*, vol. 2: 700, and Madden in Rajasthan (30 Oct. 1836): "These gardens are undoubtedly what the Persians called *Paradises*." "Itineraries," MP, RBG.
76. Munro to his wife, 30 May 1821, Gleig, *Munro*, vol. 2: 211.
77. Munro to his wife, 7 July 1826, ibid., 301.
78. Ibid., 297.
79. Edgeworth to her stepmother, 20 Jan. 1831, Colvin, *Edgeworth*, 473.
80. WH to JH, 16 July 1841, AL, RBG.
81. Hooker, *Himalayan Journals*, vol. 2: 185. See also Hooker, "Extracts" (1850), 12.
82. Heber, *Narrative*, vol. 1: 7; Lawrence and Woodiwiss, *Journals*, 58.
83. Jameson, *Report*, 5.
84. Shteir, *Cultivating Women*, mentions only a few of the many women with botanical interests who visited India in this period. Others were Anna Maria, the wife of William Jones (Jones, *Letters*, vol. 2: 695, 892, 900, 902), and Lady Dalhousie, mother of the future governor-general: *Curtis's Botanical Magazine*, 27–8.
85. JH to Bentham, 27 Nov. 1842, Huxley, *Life*, vol. 1: 167.
86. Hooker and Hooker, "Botany;" Huxley, *Life*, vol. 1: 37.
87. Lyell to his father, 11 Jan. 1849, Lyell, *Life*, vol. 2: 153. Lyell later wrote to Hooker himself in similar terms, deploring Williams's death as a "most unfortunate event," which made him "the more desirous to see you safe back again." Lyell had not known Williams personally but believed "much knowledge must have died with him." Lyell to JH, 23 July 1849, PL, RBG.
88. JH to his mother, 1 Feb. 1849, IL, RBG.
89. JH to WH, 1 Feb. 1849, IL, RBG.
90. Hunter, *Hodgson*, 31–2.
91. Ibid., 70, 82; Bacon, *First Impressions*, vol. 2: 195–8.
92. *Hooker's Journal of Botany* 1 (1849), 155.
93. Hooker and Thompson, *Flora Indica*, 60–4.
94. Desmond, *Dictionary*, 299–300; Gardner, "Notes," 402.
95. Griffith, *Journal*.
96. JH to WH, 20 Jan. 1848, IL, RBG.
97. Hooker, *Illustrations*, i–iv.
98. Ibid., plate 21. Another species, a rhododendron, was named, with "melancholy satisfaction," after the late Lord Auckland (see plate 12). For an

earlier example of South Asian plants being named after the botanist's colleagues, patrons, and deceased friends, see Wallich, *Plantae Asiaticae*.

99. "The woods and jungles are full of peacocks, another symbol of Hindooism": Hamilton, *East-India Gazetteer*, vol. 1: 17.

100. Roberts, *Scenes*, vol. 2: 3–8.

101. Jones to Earl Spencer, 18 Aug. 1787, Jones, *Letters*, vol. 2: 752.

102. Madden, "Miscellaneous Notes, 1830–49," MP, RBG.

103. Madden, "Itineraries," MP, RBG. For a similar attitude to the Middle East, see Melman, *Women's Orients*, 168–9.

104. Edwardes and Merivale, *Lawrence*, vol. 1: 151.

105. Strictly speaking, Heber was not an evangelical, but he was influenced by them: for his background and religious outlook, see the "Introduction" to Laird, *Heber*, 17–20.

106. Heber, *Narrative*, vol. 1: 103.

107. Edwardes and Merivale, *Lawrence*, vol. 1: 165.

108. Ibid., vol. 1: 182–96, 214–24; vol. 2: 246–7. For Victorian attitudes to the death of children, see Jallard, *Death*, chapter 6.

109. Ward, *View*, vol. 1: xxxvi.

110. Buchanan, *Christian Researches*, 22, 29.

111. Ibid., 19, 23–4, 28.

112. Archer, *Tours*, vol. 2: 146–7; Wakefield, *Traveller*, 144–7; Ward, *View*, vol. 1: xliii–xliv.

113. Roberts in White, *Views*, 106–7.

114. Roberts, *Scenes*, vol. 2: 222–3. Apart from *Frankenstein*, Roberts and Lawrence had clearly read their Gothic novels, finding evocations of the "Radcliffe school" and the *Mysteries of Udolpho* in India's moonlit scenes, castles, and dungeons: Roberts, *Scenes*, vol. 1: 217; Lawrence and Woodiwiss, *Journals*, 128.

115. Seshadri, *Anglo-Indian Poet*, 59–60.

116. Leyden, like many of his contemporaries in the Company service, has been seen as more representative of the Scottish Enlightenment than of evangelism: see Rendall, "Scottish Orientalism."

117. Heber, *Narrative*, vol. 1: 2–7; vol. 3: 223. Cf. Ward, *View*, vol. 1: xli. For later European images of the Sundarbans, see Greenough, "Hunter's Drowned Land."

118. Duff, *India*, 204–5.

119. Ibid., 205.

120. Ibid.

121. Ibid., 208–9.

122. Bevan, *Thirty Years*, vol. 1: 5–10; [MacMullen], *Camp*, 69–70.

123. Edwardes and Merivale, *Lawrence*, vol. 1: 159; Lawrence and Woodiwiss, *Journals*, 109.

3 / ROMANTICISM AND IMPROVEMENT

1. Warfare might, however, be seen as a source of Romanticism rather than its antithesis, even during the inglorious Afghan War: [Kaye], "English," 4–7.
2. Bearce, *British Attitudes*, chapter 4; Stokes, *English Utilitarians*, 9–18.
3. Especially Bewell, *Romanticism*; Fulford and Kitson, *Romanticism*; Lee, *Slavery*; Makdisi, *Romantic Imperialism*.
4. Butler, *Romantics*, 184. On the problems of interpreting Romanticism, see Lovejoy, "Discriminations," and Porter and Teich, *Romanticism*.
5. Pratt, *Imperial Eyes*, 137–8.
6. For the view that travel was central to early nineteenth-century Romantic writing, see Cardinal, "Romantic Writing."
7. Notably, Cunningham and Jardine, *Romanticism*; Knight, *Science*; Paradis and Postlewait, *Victorian Science*.
8. Howison, *Foreign Scenes*, vol. 1: 36.
9. *Athenaeum*, 4 Nov. 1843, 976.
10. Tickell, "Memoir," 708.
11. Heber, *Narrative*, vol. 3: 246.
12. Ibid., vol. 2: 290.
13. Ibid., 291. For the "picturesque" as applied to ruins, see Hussey, *Picturesque*, 117.
14. Shelley's poem was widely known to travelers: e.g., Skinner, *Excursions*, vol. 2: 108.
15. Tennant, *Indian Recreations*, vol. 2: 127.
16. Archer, *Tours*, vol. 2: 26–7.
17. Mackintosh, *Memoirs*, vol. 2: 77.
18. Ibid., 78.
19. Roberts in Elliott, *Views*, vol. 1: 59.
20. Ibid., 59–60.
21. Ibid., 35.
22. Ibid., 13.
23. Lloyd, *Narrative*, vol. 1: 18, 51.
24. Ibid., 267.
25. E.g., Leckie, *Journal*, 64.
26. For the origin of the term, see Zimmermann, *Jungle*, vii–viii, 10–18. In Charles Wilkins's "Glossary" of 1812 (Firminger, *Fifth Report*, vol. 3: 22) "jungle" is derived from the Sanskrit *jangala* and Hindustani *jangal* and further glossed as: "A wood or thicket, a country overrun with wood or long grass, in a rude and uncultivated state."
27. Heyne, *Tracts*, 33, 238.
28. E.g., Edgeworth, "Botanico-Agricultural Account."

29. Hamilton, *East-India Gazetteer*, vol. 2: 725. Cf. Herbert, "Particulars," 95–6.
30. [Deane], *Tour*, 73–4; Hamilton, *East-India Gazetteer*, vol. 1: 18, 30, 39.
31. Welsh, *Reminiscences*, vol. 1: 92–122.
32. Sen, *Santals*, 52; Turner, *Account*, 21. On the "anomalous" nature of these jungle tracts, see Sivaramakrishnan, "British Imperium."
33. Peers, "Habitual Nobility," 558.
34. Inden, *Imagining India*, 86–7. It was in this extended sense that Carlyle spoke of paganism as a "bewildering, intricate jungle of delusions, confusion, falsehoods and absurdities": Carlyle, *Heroes*, 4.
35. Eden, *Up the Country*, 70.
36. Roberts, *Scenes*, vol. 2: 28; Madden, 2 Feb. 1830, "Itineraries," MP, RBG.
37. Tennant, *Indian Recreations*, vol. 2: 27; Perrin, *Voyage*, vol. 1: 26–9; Lawrence and Woodiwiss, *Journals*, 64.
38. Cleghorn, "Report," 80. Dhak (*Butea frondosa*), jujube (*Ziziphus jujuba*), and acacia (*Acacia arabica*) were among the trees most commonly associated with India's dry jungles.
39. [Seton-Karr], "Plains," 9.
40. Lloyd, *Narrative*, vol. 1: 128.
41. Malcolm, *Memoir*, vol. 1: 13; vol. 2: 234–45.
42. Browne, *India Tracts*, 9–10; Hunter, *Annals*, 64–6.
43. Malcolm, *Memoir*, vol. 2: 232.
44. Tickell, "Memoir," 703.
45. See Vicziany, "Imperialism."
46. The northern route, typically from Calcutta along the Ganges valley to the cities and mountains of North India, was followed by several artists including William Hodges and the Daniells; see Archer, *Early Views*, chapter 2, and for some of its scenic and ethnographic tropes, Cohn, *Colonialism*, 6–7.
47. Buchanan, *Journey*, vol. 1: 2–17, 32, 35.
48. Thomson, "Sketch," 197; Hooker, *Himalayan Journals*, vol. 2: 283.
49. Buchanan, *Journey*, vol. 1: 6.
50. [Buchanan], "Notices," 173–7.
51. Buchanan's instructions specifically enjoined him to report on the state of agriculture and its "improvement": Buchanan, *Journey*, vol. 1: viii–ix.
52. Ibid., 30. The lack of hedges was often remarked upon as a reason for the backwardness of "Indian husbandry" and its want of "improvement" compared with Britain. Identifying suitable hedging plants thus became a botanical preoccupation: Cleghorn, "Hedge Plants."
53. [Sherer], *Sketches*, 158.
54. Buchanan, *Journey*, vol. 1: 126. Critics, however, pointed out that by traveling so rapidly (covering eight or nine miles a day) and with little knowledge

of local languages and practices, Buchanan was easily misled as to the resources and industriousness of the peasant population: [Hamilton] "Review."
55. Briggs, *Age*, 1–3; Drayton, *Nature's Government*.
56. Guha, *Rule*.
57. Browne, *India Tracts*.
58. Quoted in Guha, *Rule*, 17. For "improvement" as a continuing state concern, see Rosselli, *Bentinck*.
59. Buchanan, *Journey*, vol. 1: 82.
60. Ibid., 82–3.
61. Ibid., vol. 2: 42, 96, 127, 165. That Tipu was known as the "Tiger of Mysore" may have encouraged an association between human and animal tyranny, but there is little evidence of it in contemporary writers for whom the negative connotations of tigers needed little embellishment.
62. Ibid., vol. 2: 122; cf. *Oriental Annual* 1834, 38, 64. For evolving attitudes to Indian wildlife, see Greenough, "*Naturae Ferae*," Rangarajan, "Raj."
63. Womack, *Improvement*, 3. This argument runs counter to the familiar view that Romanticism represented an escape from tamed landscapes to wild ones and from science to emotion and communing with untouched nature: e.g., Worster, *Nature's Economy*, 81–92.
64. For Scott, see below. Unlike his first-hand *Tour in Scotland* (1769), Pennant's *View of Hindoostan* (1798) was compiled from the work of others, including Hodges, Rennell, and Thomas Daniell.
65. Buchanan, *Journey*, vol. 1:170; vol. 2: 122.
66. Gleig, *Munro*, vol. 2: 303, 308; Heyne, *Tracts*, 236; *Oriental Annual* 1834, 60–1.
67. Buchanan, *Journey*, vol. 2: 167.
68. Ibid., 347.
69. Ibid., 390.
70. Grove, "Indigenous Knowledge."
71. Buchanan, however, visited Malabar at a poor season for botanizing and, given his official responsibilities, had little time for plants: Prain, "Sketch," xiv.
72. For a recent assessment, see Peabody, "Tod's *Rajast'han*."
73. Tod, *Annals*, vol. 1: chapter 1.
74. Ibid., vol. 2: v.
75. Porter and Teich, 5. For instance, Tod's contemporaries John Malcolm and Mountstuart Elphinstone also wrote histories of India and adjoining regions.
76. Notably Forbes, *Oriental Memoirs*.
77. Chandler, *Dream*.
78. Tod, *Annals*, vol. 1: 622. Tod's quotation is from Byron's "Childe Harold's Pilgrimage," (1818), Canto IV, verse 129.
79. Roberts in Elliott, *Views*, vol. 1: 10; cf. Archer, *Tours*, vol. 2: 69.

80. Tod, *Annals*, vol. 1: 562–3. References to *Rasselas* and the "happy valley" the prince inhibited are legion (though sometimes the phrase was ironically inverted to "unhappy valley"): e.g., M'Cosh, Assam, 17; Skinner, *Excursions*, vol. 2: 135. Africa, at least the Africa represented in *Rasselas* and the *Travels* of James Bruce and Mungo Park, was a surprisingly common motif in early nineteenth-century travel writing in India.
81. Tod, *Annals*, vol. 1: 563.
82. Ibid., 564–8, 665.
83. Ibid., 572–3.
84. Ibid., vol. 2: 550.
85. Ibid, vol. 1: 574.
86. Ibid., 577.
87. Ibid., 578.
88. Edward Madden's account of his journeys in Rajasthan in 1836 exhibits a similarly rich range of tropes and images: "Itineraries," MP, RBG.
89. Tod, *Annals*, vol. 1: 582.
90. Ibid., 583; cf. ibid., vol. 2: 571. On Rosa, see Hussey, *Picturesque*, 8.
91. Tod, *Annals*, vol. 1: 584.
92. Ibid., 584–5.
93. Ibid., vol. 2: 575–6.
94. Bellew, *Memoirs*, vol. 1: 3. Technically, a European was a "griffin" only during the first year's residence in India.
95. Jacquemont, *Voyage dans l'Inde*, vol. 1: 479–80.
96. [Long], "Grand Trunk Road," 170. "[O]f all unquestioned authorities, no one has held so supreme or so lasting a sway as Bishop Heber. To him India has been made over, as one might suppose, in perpetual possession": [Keane], "Accepted Travellers," 280.
97. Roberts, *Scenes*, vol. 2: 290.
98. Heber, *Life*, vol. 1: 377–80, 500–1, 514; vol. 2: 94–117.
99. Ibid., vol. 2: 142.
100. Ibid., 95; Laird, *Heber*, 20–5.
101. [Keane], "Accepted Travellers," 298.
102. Heber, *Narrative*, vol. 1: xvi, xlvii; vol. 3: 224–5.
103. The content of these works has been extensively discussed in connection with Romantic literature (e.g., Leask, *British Romantic Writers*; Majeed, *Ungoverned Imaginings*), but their immense popularity deserves to be stressed. First published in 1817, Moore's "Oriental Romance" passed through twenty editions by 1842: apart from numerous translations, it was also adapted for the theatre and opera house. Southey's *Curse of Kehama* enjoyed less immediate success but entered its fourth edition within eight years of its first publication and was widely reprinted thereafter. Butler ("Romanticism," 38) points out that *Kehama*'s theme,

the cruelty of Hinduism, "supported Southey's serious journalistic campaign to persuade the British public of the need to impose a strong Christian government on India."

104. Southey, *Curse,* chapters 1, 11, 14.
105. E.g., Murray, *Account,* vol. 3: 42, 157.
106. One of Scott's early admirers was James Macintosh: *Memoirs,* vol. 1: 254, 262; vol. 2: 81.
107. Scott, *Heart,* 393, 452.
108. Heber, *Narrative,* vol. 1: 272, 342; vol. 2: 52, 240; vol. 3: 22. Cf. Archer, *Tours,* vol. 1: 276; vol. 2: 31.
109. E.g., Heber, *Narrative,* vol. 1: 28, 114, 237; vol. 2: 52, 153, 410.
110. Ibid., vol. 3: 316, 397.
111. Ibid., 321–2.
112. Ibid., vol. 1: 245–6.
113. For the "logic of association," see Carter, *Road,* 44–5, 60.
114. Martin, *Medical Topography,* 75.
115. JH to Elizabeth Rigby, 29 July 1848, PL, RBG.
116. Darwin to JH, 10 Mar. 1854; JH to Darwin (c. 25 Mar. 1854) in Burkhardt and Smith, *Correspondence,* vol. 5: 182, 185. That Hooker was aware of the dangers of "recollections" and "associations" that might impair more objective observation can be seen in Hooker and Thomson, *Flora Indica,* 25–6.
117. As Hooker remarked ("Observations," 382), "A stranger in India is overwhelmed with local details." The point was made about geography but had wider connotations.
118. Nicolson, *Mountain Gloom.*
119. Roberts in Elliott, *Views,* vol. 1: 114; Howison, *Foreign Scenes,* vol. 1: 161–2. As the travels of Thomas Munro and James Tod discussed elsewhere suggest, not all Europeans felt so confined; but even Tod found the *"fraicheur"* of the mountains of Rajasthan so "exhilirating" after the heat of the neighboring plains as to "[make] us quite frantic." Tod, *Annals,* vol. 1: 573.
120. Skinner, *Excursions,* vol. 1: 217.
121. Herbert, "Particulars,"116. Cf. Hooker, "Extracts" (1850), 88.
122. Cf. Schama, *Landscape.*
123. The greatest exception being Turner's 1783 embassy to Bhutan and Tibet. From the 1820s, the travels of William Moorcroft and George Trebeck provided a further influential source and model, this time of the western Himalaya: see Moorcroft and Trebeck, *Travels,* Bayly, *Empire,* chapter 3.
124. Fraser, *Journal,* 56, 59. A Calcutta-based merchant, Fraser was also a prolific amateur artist: see Godrej and Rohatgi, *Scenic Splendours,* 38–40.
125. Fraser, *Journal,* 107–8.
126. Lloyd, *Narrative,* vol. 1:145, 153. Consciously or not, such early

nineteenth-century writers were echoing Bernier a hundred and fifty years earlier, who found himself in Kashmir "transferred from the Indies to Europe." Bernier, *Travels*, 405.

127. Fraser, *Journal*, 110.
128. Ibid., 131, 133. Cf. Archer, *Tours*, vol. 1: 207–8.
129. Fraser, *Journal*, 168–9.
130. Royle, *Illustrations*, vol. 1: 15; Hooker, *Himalayan Journals*, vol. 1: 109, 112–13.
131. Fraser, *Journal*, 139.
132. Ibid., 140.
133. Batten, *Official Reports*, 209–12; Thomson, "Sketch," 198.
134. Edwardes and Merivale, *Lawrence*, vol. 2: 13–15.
135. Herbert, "Particulars," 92.
136. Archer, *Tours*, vol. 1: 244–5.
137. Ibid., 314.
138. Skinner, *Excursions*, vol. 1: 261; vol. 2: 41–52.
139. Heber, *Narrative*, vol. 2: 150–3, 193. Heber's reference to the Himalaya as the "Indian Caucasus" perhaps echoed Shelley's *Prometheus Unbound*, but the usage was considerably older: cf. Bernier, *Travels*, 395; Rennell, *Memoir*, 302.
140. Hooker, *Himalayan Journals*, vol. 1: 123, 264.
141. Parish, "Journal," 401, 405; Roberts in Elliott, *Views*, vol. 1: viii.
142. Cunningham, "Notes," 172.
143. Ibid., 174.
144. Hooker, *Himalayan Journals*, vol. 2: 130–1.
145. Skinner, *Excursions*, vol. 2: 157.
146. Edwardes and Merivale, *Lawrence*, vol. 2: 14; Gerard, "Observations," 249, 267.
147. Shore, "Report," 18.
148. Herbert, "Report," viii, xxv.
149. Minute, 31 Dec. 1824, Gleig, *Munro*, vol. 2: 170–1.
150. E.g., Tennant, *Indian Recreations*.
151. Carey's Preface to Roxburgh, *Flora Indica*, vol. 1.
152. This missionary outlook, and the equation of Christianity with cultivation and civilization, was not unique to India: see Comaroff and Comaroff, *Revelation*, vol. 2: 121–6, for the South African case.
153. Carey, "Prospectus," 213.
154. Ibid., 214.
155. Royle, "Essay," 372. Hooker visited Napleton's garden in 1848 and considered it a model establishment: *Himalayan Journals*, vol. 1: 93.
156. Wallich, "Brief Notice," 137–9, though as Royle, *Essay*, 196–7, pointed out, much of the work of the botanic garden was itself directed toward "improvement."

157. Leycester, "Introductory Discourse," 3.
158. When, for instance, Captain W.H. Sleeman was not tracking down Thugs, he was inducing the peasants of Central India to adopt "Tahitian" sugarcane: [Temple], "Agri-Horticultural Society," 345.
159. *Journal of the Agricultural and Horticultural Society* 5 (1846): 41–2, 82–6, 83–4, 180–3.
160. Howison, *Foreign Scenes*, vol. 2: 102.
161. Cf. Grove, *Green Imperialism*; Mann, *British Rule*.
162. Edgeworth, "Botanico-Agricultural Account;" Jameson, "Physical Aspects."
163. Cunningham, *History*, 3.
164. Browne, *Indian Infanticide*, 77.
165. Humbley, *Journal*, 209–10.
166. [Smith], "Canals," 165.

4 / FROM THE ORIENT TO THE TROPICS

1. Suleri, *Rhetoric*, 12.
2. For the Portuguese role in establishing pan-tropical links, see Russell-Wood, *World*, chapter 5, and for the converse argument about the creation of temperate "neo-Europes," see Crosby, *Ecological Imperialism*.
3. The dreamlike quality and perceived primitivism of the Pacific's tropical islands is captured in Hermann Melville's semi-autobiographical novels *Typee* (1846) and *Omoo* (1847). See Charlton, *New Images*, chapter 6, and Frost, "New Geographical Perspectives," for the Pacific voyages and their literary impact.
4. E.g., de Léry, *History*; Oviedo, *Natural History*; cf. Dunn, *Sugar*, chapter 9.
5. A key work in linking slavery with the "torrid zone" was John Stedman's *Expedition to Surinam* (1796): see Bewell, *Romanticism*, 88–97; Pratt, *Imperial Eyes*, 92–102. For the inimical climate of the tropics, see Kupperman, "Fear."
6. An invaluable source remains Smith, "European Vision."
7. Humboldt, *Personal Narrative*. For the wider picture, see Mackay, *Wake*; Miller and Reill, *Visions*.
8. Glacken, *Traces*, 544.
9. Grove, *Green Imperialism*.
10. E.g., Bernardin de Saint-Pierre, *Voyage*; Marsden, *History*.
11. Bernardin de Saint-Pierre, *Paul and Virginia*. Humboldt and Hooker were among its many admirers.
12. Bellew, *Memoirs*, vol. 1: 33.
13. Anderson, "Climates," 140–1.
14. For this shift, see Pratt, *Imperial Eyes*, 22–3; Stepan, *Tropical Nature*, chapters 1–2.
15. Cannon, *Science*, 73–110; Nicolson, "Humboldt."

16. Humboldt, *Personal Narrative*; Humboldt, *Cosmos*, vol. 1: 3–14; vol. 2: 87.

17. *Athenaeum*, 8 Feb. 1851, p. 164, reviewing Richard Schomburgk's natural history of Guiana; cf. Haeckel, *Visit*. For Humboldt's compelling vision of the tropics, see Pratt, *Imperial Eyes*, 111–25, and for his artistic legacy, Manthorne, *Tropical Renaissance*.

18. Wallace's *Tropical Nature* gives one of the most evocative accounts of the tropics by a nineteenth-century naturalist.

19. Mackay, *In the Wake*, 172–81; Carter, *Banks*, 272.

20. Jones, *Letters*, vol. 2: 816, 901. Earlier writers noted India's tropical location but seldom made further comment: e.g., Edward Terry in Foster, *Early Travels*, 298.

21. Trautmann, *Aryans*, chapter 2.

22. Forbes, *Oriental Memoirs*, vol. 1: 12, 23, 60, 103.

23. Cook, "Rennell," 5.

24. Markham, *Rennell*, v, 85–9. Cf. Barrow, *Making History*; Bravo, "Precision."

25. Barrow, *Making History*, chapter 2.

26. Rennell, *Memoir*, iv–v.

27. Ibid., xxix.

28. Bernier, *Travels*, 393–402.

29. Rennell, *Memoir*, 58.

30. Ibid., 242.

31. Ibid., 60–1.

32. Orientalism provided an important link between pre-colonial and British topographical ideas and representations. Rennell, like Tod, shows how this continuity could be achieved. Richard Eaton (*Essays*, 250–1) has also pointed out how Robert Orme's late eighteenth-century account of the debilitating climate of Bengal drew directly on earlier Mughal sources. Orme was an influential writer (though even he mixed European and Oriental influences), but, just as new ideas of landscape and scenery were encroaching on India from Europe, so by the early nineteenth century his work was supplanted by the new medical topographies which relied far less on indigenous sources for their understanding of the relationship between climate, landscape, and disease, and were more heavily influenced by West Indian precedents or by recent European medical literature.

33. "An Account of the Ganges and Burrampooter Rivers," in Rennell, *Memoir*, 346. On the inundations caused by "great tropical rivers," including the Hugli, see Piddington, "Fertilising Principle."

34. Edney, *Mapping*.

35. E.g., Hamilton, *East-India Gazetteer*, vol. 1: 23–8, 366–7.

36. Pennant, *View*, vol. 2: 182, 222.

37. Moore, *Lalla Rookh*, "Notes."

38. Said, *Orientalism*, 49–72. There have been many critiques of Said's work. For one of the most incisive, see Behdad, *Belated Travelers*, 10–13.
39. Said, *Orientalism*, chapter 1; Cohn, "Command," 276–329; Kejariwal, *Asiatic Society*; Kopf, *British Orientalism*.
40. *Oriental Annual*, 1834–40.
41. [Lawrence and Lawrence], "Romance," 377–8.
42. Ibid.
43. Skinner, *Excursions*, vol. 1: 43–4. Cf. Graham, *Journal*, 333; Roberts, *Scenes*, vol. 1: 204; vol. 2: 295–6, 304.
44. For a distinction between "scholarly" and "popular" Orientalism, see Mukherjee, *Jones*, 3.
45. But for a more Hinduized version of an "Oriental" landscape, see Tod's *Annals* for Rajasthan and Madden, "Turree," for Kumaon.
46. On this mission, see Olaf Caroe's "Introduction" to Elphinstone, *Account*, v–xxvi.
47. Ibid., 2–3.
48. Ibid., 5.
49. Ibid., 15.
50. Ibid., 23.
51. Ibid., 46.
52. Ibid., 53–4. Plantains refers here to the round-leaved, low-growing plants of the genus *Plantago*, with their rat-tailed seed spikes, commonly found (uninvited) in English lawns, and not the genus *Musa*, the banana or plantain tree.
53. Ibid., 73.
54. Tod, *Annals*, vol. 2: 173, 190, 264–7, 292, 298–9.
55. Moore, *Lalla Rookh*, 91, 324.
56. Burnes, *Travels*, vol. 1: 6–7, 15, 46–50, 59.
57. Burton, *Sindh*, 2, 43, 166.
58. Ibid., 1.
59. Stocks, "Botany," "Balsam Trees." Stocks also wrote botanical entries for George Stack's *Dictionary of Sindhi and English* (Bombay, 1855).
60. Stocks to WH, 16 Mar. [1848], DC 54, RBG.
61. Burton, *Sindh*, 1.
62. Stocks's aim to publish a natural history of Sind died with him: see William Hooker's obituary in *Hooker's Journal of Botany* 6 (1854): 308–10. The term "Oriental," rarely used in Indian botany, was sometimes applied to the flora of the Middle East, from the Levant to Afghanistan: Hooker and Thomson, *Flora Indica*, 57; Hooker, "Botany," 158, 209–10.
63. Champion, "L'image;" Deleury, *Les Indes*; Lowe, *Critical Terrains*.
64. Marshall, *Jacquemont*, 3.

65. Ibid., 6, 13.
66. Brown, *Jacquemont*; Phillips, Introduction to Jacquemont, *Letters*, xiii–xx.
67. Théodoridès, "Humboldt," 43–4.
68. Jacquemont to Chaper, 6 Aug. 1828, in Marshall, *Jacquemont*, 239.
69. For his impressions of this journey, see Jacquemont, *Voyage*, vol. 1.
70. Jacquemont to Humboldt, 31 July 1828, in Jacquemont, *Voyages en Amérique*, 62.
71. Hooker and Thomson, *Flora Indica*, 63.
72. Ibid., 52, 64.
73. Jacquemont, *Voyage*, vol. 3: 30; Zimmermann, *Jungle*, 14. Jacquemont was not alone in seeing the Indian landscape in these proto-ecological terms: see Edgeworth, "Botanico-Agricultural Account."
74. Jacquemont, *Voyages en Amérique*, 61–5.
75. Hickey, *Memoirs*, vol. 2: 37, 49, 50, 53–4.
76. Graham, *Journal of a Voyage*, 147. For Graham in Brazil, see Pratt, *Imperial Eyes*, chapter 7. The unfavorable contrast between "tropical" India, overcrowded and caste-ridden, and Brazil, as a domain of relatively untouched nature, has persisted: see Lévi-Strauss, *Tristes Tropiques*, especially 181: "In America, what I saw in the first place was the physical universe, whereas in India I saw only human beings."
77. Jacquemont to his father, 24 Dec. 1829, *Letters*, 68.
78. Howison, *Foreign Scenes*, vol. 2: 41. For the association of the tropics with sexual desire, see Nussbaum, *Torrid Zones*.
79. Jacquemont, *Voyage*, vol. 1:179–82.
80. Jacquemont to his father, 22 June 1830, *Letters*, 109. There is a certain irony in this longing for "tropical" Brazil, since in the eighteenth century the Portuguese had tried to "Orientalize" Brazil: Freyre, *Mansions*, chapter 9.
81. Jacquemont to his father, 24 Dec. 1829, *Letters*, 59.
82. Ibid.
83. Jacquemont, *Voyage*, vol. 2: 14.
84. Jacquemont to his father, 10 Jan. 1831, *Letters*, 156.
85. Jacquemont, *Voyage*, vol. 1: 182. The theatricality of the tropics is well conveyed in James Tennent's glowing account of arriving at Galle on the coast of Ceylon at dawn in November 1845: "If, as is frequently the case, the ship approaches the land at daybreak, the view recalls, but in an intensified degree, the emotions excited in childhood by the slow rising of the curtain in a darkened theatre to disclose some magical triumph of the painter's fancy, in all the luxury of colouring and all the glory of light." Tennent, *Ceylon*, vol. 2: 99.
86. E.g., Heyne, *Tracts*, 232, Roberts, *Scenes*, vol. 1: 177. Cf. Carter, *Road*, 43.
87. Jacquemont, *Voyage*, vol. 1: 307–8.
88. Ibid., 308–11. India did not have black slaves like the West Indies and

Brazil, but it is a further pointer to the role of travel literature in informing impressions of India and colonial ethnography that many Europeans likened India's tribal populations to "Negroes": e.g., Hooker, *Himalayan Journals*, vol. 1: 19; [Sherer], *Sketches*, 154, 257–8. See Arnold, "Race," for the racial typologies of early nineteenth-century India.

89. Gourou, *Tropical World*; cf. Arnold, "'Illusory Riches.'"
90. Orme, *History*, vol. 2: 4.
91. Eden, *Up the Country*, 65–7.
92. Arnold, "Hunger;" Pennant, *View*, vol. 2: 233–4; Tod, *Annals*, vol. 2: 298.
93. Grove, *Green Imperialism*, 332–41.
94. Jacquemont, *Voyage*, vol. 1: 446. Many travelers were struck by the cultural as well as topographic change from deltaic Bengal to the more arid north and northwest. For some "the Orient" began with the first camels sighted in the vicinity of Patna or Benares: Heber, *Narrative*, vol. 1: 371; vol. 3: 318; Hooker, *Himalayan Journals*, vol. 1: 79; Roberts in Elliott, *Views*, vol. 1: 43.
95. Jacquemont to his father, 10 Mar. 1830, *Letters*, 74.
96. Jacquemont to his father 10 Jan. 1831, ibid., 151.
97. Jacquemont to Victor de Tracy, 28 May 1831, ibid., 221–2.
98. Jacquemont to his father, 12 Mar. 1831, ibid., 170; Jacquemont to Chaper, 16 Dec. 1831, in Marshall, *Jacquemont*, 254.
99. *Himalayan Journals*, vol. 1: 6, 72, 102. Unlike Jacquemont, Hooker had briefly visited Egypt *en route* to India and so seen something of the Middle East for himself.
100. Zastoupil and Moir, *Great Education Debate*.
101. Ferguson, *Essay*, 110.
102. Pennant, *Indian Zoology*, 45.
103. Robert Kyd, "Some Remarks on the Soil and Vegetation of the Western Side of the River Hooghly" (1791), 92, 96, 103, Kyd Papers; Piddington, "Researches."
104. "Both *surf* and *suffe*... were originally used especially in reference to the coast of India, which suggests an Indic origin for the words": *The Barnhart Dictionary of Etymology* (1988), 1095. But cf. Walter W. Skeat, *An Etymological Dictionary of the English Language* (1882), 613; Ernest Weekley, *An Etymological Dictionary of Modern English* (1921), col. 1449, for likely English origins.
105. Beaglehole, *Journals*, 137, 155, 304; Hawkesworth, *Account*, vol. 1: 4, 92, 99. But "surf" was also to be found in the very un-tropical waters of the Strait of Magellan (Hawkesworth, *Account*, 83, 87), and in his 1818 novel *The Heart of Mid-Lothian* (422), Scott located "surf" on the chilly banks of the Clyde.
106. *Oxford English Dictionary* (1989), 285–6.
107. Hickey, *Memoirs*, vol. 1: 163–6; cf. Fay, *Original Letters*, 163.
108. Marsden, *History*, 34–7.

109. Moseley, *Treatise*. For a comparable French work, see Desportes, *Histoire*.
110. Dancer, *Medical Assistant*, iii.
111. Hunter, *Observations*, 6–7; Moseley, *Treatise*, 22–36.
112. Johnson, *Influence*; cf. Moseley, *Treatise*, 2–3, 17, 71. For Johnson, see Harrison, "Tropical Medicine."
113. Martin, *Medical Topography*, 155–8; cf. Moseley, *Treatise*, 44–8.
114. Wallace, *Voyage*, 159–60.
115. Reece, *Medical Companion*, xi, xvi.
116. Wade, *Paper*, 41.
117. Ibid., 50.
118. Annesley, *Researches*, vol. 1: vii, 7, 52, 64–5.
119. Twining, *Clinical Illustrations* (1832), 561.
120. Twining, *Clinical Illustrations* (1835), vol. 1: 45–6.
121. E.g., MacGregor, *Practical Observations*.
122. Fosberg, "Tropical Floristic Botany," 90.
123. Ibid., 91.
124. Hooker and Thomson, *Flora Indica*, 45–6, 54–6.
125. Humboldt, *Aspects*, 223–4.
126. Royle, *Fibrous Plants*, 69, 91, 103.
127. The *Shorter Oxford English Dictionary* (1944) dates "tropical fruits" to c. 1700. See Robertson, *Discovery of Tahiti*, 121, for this usage, and, for India (particularly in contrast to "European" fruits), Hamilton, *East-India Gazetteer*, vol. 1: 45, 81–5.
128. Jacquemont, *Voyage*, vol. 1: 181; Marsden, *History*, 97; Moore, *Lalla Rookh*, 324.
129. E.g., *Baburnama*, 343–7.
130. Foster, *Early Travels*, 297.
131. Johnson, *Oriental Voyager*, 81.
132. Hooker, *Himalayan Journals*, vol. 1: 61, 159–61.
133. Heber, *Narrative*, vol. 2: 227.
134. Hickey, *Memoirs*, vol. 4: 230.
135. Dalhousie to Couper, 7 Aug. 1852, in Baird, *Dalhousie*, 215.
136. Pennant, *Indian Zoology*.
137. Hooker and Thomson, *Flora Indica*, 84–6, 115–16.
138. Crawfurd, *History*, vol. 1: 11; vol. 3: 68, 213.
139. E.g., Hamilton, *East-India Gazetteer*, vol. 1: 533, quoting Crawfurd.
140. Hoffmeister, *Travels*, 97–9.
141. Ibid., 102.
142. Hooker, "Extracts" (1848), 315–16.
143. *Athenaeum* 10 July 1847, 726, reviewing Hoffmeister.
144. Hoffmeister, *Travels*, 196, 199. Tennent, another Humboldtian, who also

first visited Ceylon in 1845, contrasted its unfolding "scene of loveliness and grandeur" with "the melancholy delta of the Ganges and the torrid coast of Coromandel." Tennent, *Ceylon*, vol. 1: 3.

5 / NETWORKS AND KNOWLEDGES

1. For a recent reappraisal, see the Introduction to Roy MacLeod, *Nature*.
2. Desmond, *European Discovery*, chapters 4–6; Grove, *Green Imperialism*, chapter 7.
3. Hooker, *Journal*, v.
4. Allan, *Hookers*; Drayton, *Nature's Government*, 143–6.
5. Charles Lyell to his father, 20 July 1817, in Lyell, *Life*, vol. 1: 41–2.
6. Mary Turner to JH, 26 Mar. 1841, Elizabeth Palgrave to JH, 13 July 1842, AL, RBG.
7. W.J. Palgrave to WH, 12 Apr. 1848, DC 54, RBG.
8. Browne, *Darwin*, 11–13.
9. The nature and range of William Hooker's scientific correspondence is further discussed in Secord, "Corresponding Interest."
10. For Hooker's move to Kew, see Drayton, *Nature's Government*, 153–69.
11. Lady Dalhousie to WH, 4 Feb. 1833, 4 Mar. 1833, 18 July 1833, DC 53, RBG; *Curtis's Botanical Magazine*, 27–8.
12. Hooker and Thomson, *Flora Indica*, 70.
13. Dalhousie to WH, 16 Aug. 1847, 26 Aug. 1847, DC 54, RBG; Hooker, *Himalayan Journals*, vol. 1: x.
14. Desmond, *European Discovery*, 103, 141.
15. Eden, *Letters*, vol. 1: 114–15, 170; vol. 2: 52.
16. Jacquemont to Victor de Tracy, 1 Sept. 1829, in *Letters*, 14.
17. Grove, *Green Imperialism*, 407–13.
18. Although "no quarter of the globe" was "so rich in plants" as India, the plains were generally poor in species (Hooker, *Flora*, v); Hooker and Thomson, *Flora Indica*, 93–4.
19. On the "magnificent" and "stately" magnolias, see Wallich, *Tentamen*, 1–4.
20. [Burkill], "Jack's Letters,"161. However, thirty years later in eastern India, Joseph Hooker witnessed the wholesale plunder of orchids for the European market: Hooker, *Himalayan Journals*, vol. 2: 321–2; Huxley, *Life*, vol. 1: 337. Wallich's nephew Charles Cantor was among the Calcutta agents involved in the collection and sale of Indian orchids: see "A List of Terrestrial and Epiphytical Orchideae found in Assam and the Neighbouring Hills," enclosed with Wallich to Bentham, 20 Aug. 1850, BC, RBG.

21. WH in *Hooker's Journal of Botany* 6 (1854), 185.
22. Ibid.; Hooker and Thomson, *Flora Indica*, 59.
23. Wallich to WH, 2 Sept. 1818, 13 Oct. 1818, 8 Oct. 1819, DC 52, RBG.
24. Royle to WH, 1 Dec. 1829, DC 52, RBG.
25. Carey to WH, 10 Dec. 1829, 16 June 1830, DC 52, RBG.
26. Hooker and Thomson, *Flora Indica*, 58–9; Thomson, "Notes," 408.
27. Wallich to WH, 21 June 1832, DC 53, RBG; de Candolle and Radcliffe-Smith, "Wallich."
28. Wallich to WH, 15 Oct. 1832, DC 53, RBG.
29. "A List of the Orchideae found in Assam and the Neighbouring Hills," *Hooker's Journal of Botany* 2 (1850), 286; Hooker and Thomson, *Flora Indica*, 23.
30. WH to Lindley, 20 Feb. 1838, LC, RBG.
31. Burkill, *chapters*, 27.
32. Falconer to WH, 20 May 1837, DC 53, RBG.
33. In 1855 Thomson complained that the Calcutta garden lacked an adequate herbarium and that the library was "entirely deficient in modern botanical works." Since it did not even possess a set of the Wallachian herbarium for its own reference, he hoped to retrieve one from the Linnean Society in London. Thomson, "Report on the Hon'ble Company's Botanic Garden," Calcutta Botanic Garden Papers, RBG. Not all the Siwalik fossils, however, went to London: some remain on display at the Indian Museum, Calcutta. Others were exhibited at Saharanpur in the 1830s and 1840s: see Madden, "Itineraries," 3 Feb. 1837, MP, RBG, for an enthusiastic account.
34. Falconer to WH, 3 July 1848, DC 54, RBG.
35. Hooker, *Himalayan Journals*, vol. 1: ix.
36. A.C. Mcrae to WH, 7 Apr. 1849, DC 54, RBG.
37. JH to Darwin, 13 Oct. 1848, Burkhardt and Smith, *Correspondence*, vol. 4: 172.
38. JH to WH, 1 Feb. 1849, IL; Falconer to WH, 7 Mar. [1850], DC 54; MJ, RBG, 530–53.
39. Falconer to WH, 3 July 1848, DC 54, RBG.
40. But see WH to N.A. Dalzell, 17 Nov. 1848, DC 54, RBG.
41. On one occasion, Stocks referred to the appearance of a plant as resembling "nothing so much as the anus of horse contracting after defecation." Stocks to WH, 15 Dec. 1852, DC 55, RBG. When Hooker published Stocks's letter in his *Journal of Botany*, he tactfully omitted the remark, which Stocks had himself called "unsavoury."
42. Stocks to WH, 15 Apr. 1848, DC 54, RBG. On Stocks, see also Noltie, *Dapuri Drawings*, 62–3. As conservator of forests for Sind, Stocks was one of the few among William Hooker's correspondents to touch upon issues of deforestation and desiccation in his letters: see Stocks to WH, 20 Feb. 1849, DC 54, RBG.

43. Wight to WH, 7 Apr. 1835, DC 52; Dalzell to WH, 27 Feb.1849, DC 54, RBG.
44. J.S. Law to WH, 13 Mar.1847, DC 54, RBG.
45. Jenkins to WH, 24 Sept. 1846, DC 54, RBG.
46. WH to Munro, 28 Feb.1848, MC, RBG.
47. Hooker and Thomson, *Flora Indica*, 69–71.
48. Colley, *Captives*, 347–63.
49. JH to Hodgson, 19 Sept. 1849, HP, RAS.
50. Falconer to WH, 30 June [1847], DC 54, RBG.
51. Thomson, *Western Himalaya*.
52. Hooker claimed that he had been "pledged" to Thomson "as a travelling companion for 25 years... the whole of our scientific studies, reading & traveling, collecting &c were pursued with the one end of travelling together as men." JH to Hodgson, 19 Sept. 1849, HP, RAS.
53. Thomson to his father, 2 Jan. 1850, IL, RBG.
54. Huxley, *Life*, vol. 1: 357.
55. Falconer to WH, 18 Mar. 1854, PL, RBG.
56. Thomson, "Notes," 405.
57. Roxburgh, *Plants*, vol. 1: i; Wallich, *Plantae*, vol. 1: i; Wight and Arnott, *Prodromus*, v.
58. Roxburgh, *Plants*.
59. Royle, *Illustrations*; *Manual*.
60. Desmond, *European Discovery*, chapter 16.
61. Royle to WH, 16 Sept. 1832, DC 53, RBG.
62. Royle, *Essay* (1840); *Manual* (1847); *Culture* (1851); *Fibrous Plants* (1855).
63. Royle, *Illustrations*, vol. 1: vii; 1840, iv, 45, 192–3.
64. Royle, "List."
65. Royle, *Illustrations*, vol. 1: xxx, 4.
66. Ibid., xxxiii.
67. Royle, *Essay*, 245–7.
68. Dittelbach, "Global Physics."
69. See Royle's correspondence in DC 54, RBG.
70. JH to Dalzell, 17 Nov. 1848, DC 54, RBG. Hooker and Thomson also used Royle's herbarium: *Flora Indica*, 64.
71. JH to WH, 12 Sept. 1848; JH to WH, 11 Apr. 1849, IL, RBG.
72. Hooker and Thomson, *Flora Indica*, 51–2.
73. Royle, "Account," 48; *Illustrations*, vol. 1: 2.
74. Lack of precise information about plant locations was the bane of early colonial botany: Thomson, "Notes," 409–10.
75. Hooker and Thomson, *Flora Indica*, 107–8.
76. Stocks to WH, 1 Sept. 1850, DC 54, RBG.

77. Wight, "Letters," 156. On Wight and his associates, see Noltie, *Indian Botanical Drawings*, 22–4.
78. See the Wight-Hooker correspondence in DC 53–4, RBG.
79. Stocks to WH, 6 July 1850, DC 54, RBG.
80. Wight, "Letters," 160–1.
81. Ibid., 168–81.
82. Wight to Arnott, 27 Sept. 1836, Wight, "Letters," 196. Wight's work was reviewed in Royle, *Essay*.
83. E.g., Wight, *Illustrations*, vol. 2: 161, 189.
84. [Batten], "Works," 164.
85. Wight, "Letters," 179.
86. Hodgson to J.E. Gray, 1 Jan. 1845, HP, NHM.
87. Morrell and Thackray, *Gentlemen*, 502–3.
88. Hooker and Thomson's remark (*Flora Indica*, 12) that "It cannot be too strongly impressed upon all students of botany, that it is only after much preliminary study, and with the aids of a complete library, and an herbarium containing authentic specimens of a very large proportion of known species, that descriptive botany can be effectively carried out," must have seemed a very daunting prescription.
89. Wight and Arnott, *Prodromus*, xxx.
90. Hooker and Thomson, *Flora Indica*, 44, 48–9.
91. Ibid., 50.
92. Wight to WH, 12 Apr. 1851, DC 54, RBG.
93. Cleghorn, "Obituary," 363–88.
94. "Dr Wight's Return to England," *Hooker's Journal of Botany* 5 (1853): 247–8.
95. See Hunter, *Hodgson*, and Waterhouse, *Origins*, for Hodgson's career as a naturalist.
96. Hodgson to Johnston, 20 June 1835, HP, NHM.
97. Ibid.
98. Griffith to Munro, 20 May 1844, MC, RBG.
99. Wallich, *Plantae*, vol. 3: v.
100. Hooker and Thomson, *Flora Indica*, 61.
101. However, during his stay in Calcutta in 1843–5, Griffith was active in the Agricultural and Horticultural Society and served as a vice-president.
102. Griffith to WH, 6 Aug. 1840, DC 54, RBG.
103. Griffith to WH, 3 Feb. 1843, DC 54, RBG.
104. "William Griffith's Instructions regarding his Botanical Collections," DC 54, RBG.
105. M'Clelland to WH, 6 July 1846, DC 54, RBG; "Address of the President," 23 June 1847, *Report of the Seventeenth Meeting of the British Association*, xli.

106. *London Journal of Botany* 7 (1848): 446.
107. JH to WH, 20 Jan. 1848, IL, RBG.
108. JH to WH, 11 July 1850, IL, RBG; cf. Hooker and Thomson, *Flora Indica*, 60, 62.
109. Hooker, *Himalayan Journals*, vol. 2: 244.
110. Ibid.
111. Hooker, "Extracts" (1849), 4–5.
112. JH to WH, 20 Jan. 1848, IL, RBG.
113. Cf. Bellon, "Hooker's Ideals."
114. *Hooker's Journal of Botany* 4 (1852): 93.
115. For this dispute and the background to it, see also Sangwan "Strength," 227–8.
116. J. M'Clelland, "Memorandum Regarding the Differences between Dr Wallich and the late W. Griffith," June 1848, RBG Library.
117. In the "Wallich Catalogue" in the RBG Library, Wallich (Dec. 1829) indicated that his plants were arranged according to the Natural System by Royle.
118. Griffith to Munro, 9 Nov. 1844, MC, RBG.
119. Griffith's scorn was not directed at Wallich alone. He was also scathing about de Candolle: Griffith to Munro, 20 May 1844, MC, RBG.
120. Wallich to WH, 8 Mar. 1853, DC 55, RBG.
121. E.g., Grove, *Green Imperialism* and "Indigenous Knowledge;" Raj, "Colonial Encounters."
122. Dirks, "Foreword," xii.
123. Jones, *Works*, vol. 5: 1–162.
124. Heyne, *Tracts*, 127–9. On indigenous landscape categories, see Zimmermann, *Jungle*.
125. Heyne, *Tracts*, 238.
126. Ibid., 165.
127. Tod, *Annals*, vol. 2: 269.
128. Ibid., 271, 300.
129. For an example of this trend, see the reports on Kumaon in Batten, *Official Reports*.
130. Buchanan, *Account*, 100.
131. Royle, *Illustrations*, vol. 1: 46–8. Cf. Hooker and Thomson, *Flora Indica*, 3–4.
132. Jones, *Works*, vol. 5: 62.
133. Buchanan, *Journey*, vol. 1: 181–2.
134. Prain, "Sketch," xxxii.
135. Wallich, *Tentamen*, 7; cf. Wight and Arnott, *Prodromus*, xxiii–iv.
136. Hooker and Thomson, *Flora Indica*, 36.
137. Ibid., 11, 38–9.

138. *Himalayan Journals*, vol. 1: 155, 158; vol. 2: 268; Huxley, *Life*, vol. 1: 260.
139. JH to Hodgson, 5 Nov. 1848, IJ, RBG.
140. Hooker and Thomson, *Flora Indica*, 44.
141. I do not, therefore, entirely accept the view that in India "colonial knowledge was derived to a considerable extent from indigenous knowledge, albeit torn out of context and distorted by fear and prejudice": Bayly, *Empire*, 7. Rather, colonial knowledge either sought to mediate between indigenous and metropolitan knowledge, or was seen from a metropolitan perspective as the empirical frontier of knowledge-gathering (and the first line of knowledge-processing), often marred by its association with, or inability to distance itself sufficiently from, indigenous knowledge.
142. Wallich, *Plantae*, vol. 1: 2–3.
143. Royle, "Account."
144. Stocks, "Botany."
145. Roxburgh, *Plants*, vol. 1: 3–7, 11, 57.
146. Agrawal, "Dismantling."
147. Stocks, "Notes," 551–2.
148. Royle, *Illustrations*, vol. 1: 2.
149. Heyne, *Tracts*, 248.
150. Thomson, "Notes," 407; Wallich, *Tentamen*, 5–6; Wallich, *Plantae*, vol. 2: 31; vol. 3: 5.
151. Wight, "Letters," 159–60, 179–80; Hooker, *Himalayan Journals*, vol. 1: 115; vol. 2: 321–2. Hooker sometimes employed as many as fourteen collectors at a time.
152. Cathcart in Darjeeling employed a "corps" of Lepcha collectors who were sent to scour the forests and bring back any plant they could find in flower: Hooker, *Illustrations*, iii. Thomson's brother Gideon in Madras did his collecting almost entirely through Indians deputed to collect for him, one of whom was paid the substantial sum of Rs 20 to 25 a month (£2–£2 10s): Hooker, "Extracts" (1848), 320; Hooker and Thomson, *Flora Indica*, 73. Hooker paid his Lepcha collectors a more modest 8 to 20 shillings a month: *Himalayan Journals*, vol. 1: 115. Some of his collectors appear in Fig. 1.
153. Hooker and Thomson, *Flora Indica*, 3; Thomson, "Notes," 405–6.
154. Madden, "Turree," 416.
155. Noltie, *Indian Botanical Drawings*, 13–17, 28–30.
156. Graham, *Journal*, 146.
157. Royle, *Illustrations*, vol. 1: 3.
158. Hooker, *Illustrations*, iii; JH to WH, 27 Apr. 1850, in the RBG copy of *Illustrations*.
159. Cited in Cleghorn, "Obituary," 26.
160. Wallich, *Plantae*, vol. 1: x.
161. Desmond, "Roxburgh's Plants," 27–9; Hooker, *Illustrations*, i.

6 / BOTANY AND THE BOUNDS OF EMPIRE

1. For Hooker's ability to stand outside his own scientific community and subject it to critical scrutiny, see Beer, *Open Fields*, 197–200.
2. For the critical importance to itinerant naturalists like Alfred Russel Wallace and Joseph Hooker of local "networks of colonial culture," see Camerini, "Remains," and "Wallace."
3. JH to WH, 7 Apr. 1848, IL, RBG.
4. Browne, *Secular Ark*, 81.
5. Huxley, *Life*, vol. 1: 37.
6. Hooker and Thomson, *Flora Indica*, 68.
7. For these deaths, see Huxley, *Life*, vol. 1: 20–2, and the correspondence in AL, RBG.
8. JH to WH, 7 Apr. 1848, IL, RBG.
9. [Forbes], "Himalayan Journals," 55.
10. Huxley, *Life*, vol. 1: 216.
11. "J.D. Hooker Testimonials," RBG; Huxley, *Life*, vol. 1: chapter 1.
12. Desmond, *Hooker*, 93–4. The apparent resemblance between ancient fossils and living plant and animal forms was one of the sub-themes of Hooker's Indian travels (*Himalayan Journals*, vol. 1: 1–2, 7–8, 54), and further illustrates the way in which the tropics were often seen to reflect a much earlier period of the earth's history.
13. Huxley, *Life*, vol. 1: 200.
14. JH to Frances Henslow, 26 Oct. 1848, IL, RBG.
15. Darwin to JH, 7 Apr. 1847, in Burkhardt and Smith, *Correspondence*, vol. 4: 30; JH to Dawson Turner, 26 Apr. 1847, in Huxley, *Life*, vol. 1: 222; JH to Professor Wheatstone, 15 Feb. 1848, IL, RBG.
16. E.g., JH to Darwin, 3 Feb. 1849, in Burkhardt and Smith, *Correspondence*, vol. 4: 194–202.
17. Cited in Huxley, *Life*, vol. 1: 216.
18. Ibid., 53, 92–4.
19. Ibid., 167, 217.
20. J.S. Law to JH, 1 Feb. 1847, DC 54, RBG.
21. Stocks to WH, 15 Apr. 1848, 25 Oct. 1848, DC 54, RBG.
22. Munro to WH, 21 Mar. 1848, DC 54, RBG.
23. Huxley, *Life*, vol. 1: 180, 185.
24. Humboldt, *Cosmos*, vol. 2: 373–404.
25. Humboldt to JH, 30 Sept. 1847, in "Hooker's Botanical Mission," 604–6.
26. JH to Hodgson, 12 Aug. 1849, HP, RAS.
27. Huxley, *Life*, vol. 2: 127, 223.
28. Ibid., vol. 1: 3; Porter, "Road."
29. E.g., Hooker, *Himalayan Journals*, vol. 2: 48, 131, 171, 185, 263, 401.

30. Huxley, *Life*, vol. 1: 303, suggests that Hooker climbed higher than Humboldt and so eclipsed the latter's achievement.
31. Hooker, *Himalayan Journals*, vol. 1: 5.
32. Ibid., 2–3; *Curtis's Botanical Magazine*, 87–8.
33. Hooker, *Himalayan Journals*, vol. 2: 265.
34. Wallich to Munro, 11 Feb. 1848, MC, RBG.
35. JH to Frances Henslow, 5 Jan. 1848, IL, RBG.
36. JH to WH, 8 Jan. 1848, IL, RBG.
37. JH to WH, 17 Nov. 1847, 23 June 1849, IL, RBG.
38. Hooker, "Extracts" (1848), 314–16.
39. Hooker, *Himalayan Journals*, vol. 1: 1.
40. Ibid., 12, 18, 32, 34, 54, 63.
41. Hooker, *Himalayan Journals*, vol. 1: 7, 49; Hooker and Thomson, *Flora Indica*, 73.
42. Hooker, *Himalayan Journals*, vol. 1: 24.
43. Ibid., 43. Hooker's later interest in forest conservation has been much remarked upon, but it does not appear to have been one of his primary concerns in India in 1848–50: cf. Huxley, *Life*, vol. 2: 7; Grove, *Green Imperialism*, 426–31. He visited Darjeeling and Sikkim before "the reckless clearances took place which [later] resulted in the modification of the climate": "Hooker's Recollections," 251.
44. Hooker and Thomson, *Flora Indica*, 94–5; Thomson, "Sketch," 197. Nor was Hooker opposed to burning the grass jungles of the Tarai, believing them to be "a most serious obstacle to civilization & all advancement of the human race." 8 Mar. 1849, IJ, RBG.
45. Hooker, *Himalayan Journals*, vol. 1:100–8.
46. Ibid., 104, 107. For consideration of a comparable passage from Humboldt, see Pratt, *Imperial Eyes*, 123.
47. Hooker, *Himalayan Journals*, vol. 1: 109.
48. 10 Dec. 1848, IJ, RBG.
49. [Forbes], "Himalayan Journals," 62.
50. Hooker, *Himalayan Journals*, vol. 1:157.
51. Ibid., 194, 196.
52. Ibid, vol. 2: 18–19.
53. Ibid., 181.
54. Ibid., vol. 1: 125.
55. Ibid., 125–6.
56. Hooker, *Rhododendrons*, plate 27.
57. Hooker, *Himalayan Journals*, vol. 2: 33, 37, 98, 105, 157.
58. Ibid., 336.
59. See Hooker's explanation why *R. dalhousiae* often grew epiphytically even though, unlike orchids, it had no specific mechanism for doing so: "Climate," 72.

60. Hooker and Thomson, *Flora Indica*, 20–3, 101–2. Hooker addressed the question of variation more fully in his Tasmanian flora (*Botany of the Antarctic Voyage*), published shortly after Darwin's *Origin of Species*.
61. Huxley, *Life*, vol. 1: 449–50; vol. 2: 28.
62. Hooker, "Climate," 69–71.
63. This visual image was captured not only in Hooker's prose but also in the plates of his Himalayan flora (Hooker, *Illustrations*), which, in contrast to the individual specimens normally shown in botanical prints, depicted plants in their "native localities." See Figs 2 and 15 for examples.
64. "In determining what may be called the tropic of vegetation, regard must be had not only to the latitude and isothermal lines, but to the abundance of the vegetation and its character." Hooker, *Flora Tasmaniae*, vol. 1: xxxviii.
65. HJ to WH, 23 Sept. 1849, IL, RBG.
66. Cf. Paradis, "Darwin," 85–6.
67. For the contrast with the Hooker's parents, see Huxley, *Life*, vol. 1: 16–20.
68. Quoted in ibid., 241.
69. Hooker, "Extracts" (1849), 170: the final phrase was omitted in *Himalayan Journals*, vol. 1: 74.
70. Ibid., vol. 1: 11; Huxley, *Life*, vol. 1: 257; JH to Hodgson, 29 Oct. 1848, IJ, RBG.
71. Hooker, "Extracts" (1850), 114.
72. Hooker, *Himalayan Journals*, vol. 1: 315–16, 324–5.
73. Ibid., 147.
74. Paradis, "Darwin," 86.
75. Hooker, *Himalayan Journals*, vol. 1: 266.
76. The impression Turner's paintings made on Hooker is discussed in JH to Elizabeth Rigby, 29 July 1848, PL, RBG.
77. Hooker, *Himalayan Journals*, vol. 1: 123.
78. Huxley, *Life*, vol. 1: 274.
79. Hunter, *Hodgson*, 242–9.
80. E.g., Hodgson, "Route," based on the report of two Nepalese emissaries. For Hodgson's published works, see Hunter, *Hodgson*, and Waterhouse, *Origins*.
81. Hodgson to Sir Alexander Johnston, 20 June 1835, HP, NHM.
82. Hodgson, "New Species," 186.
83. Hunter, *Hodgson*, 333, 368–75.
84. Huxley, *Life*, vol. 1: 262.
85. JH to WH, 3 Oct. 1849, IL, RBG.
86. Hooker, *Himalayan Journals*, vol. 1: xiv.
87. JH to "my dear Uncle," 17 Mar. 1849, IL, RBG.
88. Entries for Mar. 1849, IJ, RBG.
89. JH to WH, 23 Sept. 1849, IL, RBG. "I have not the most ordinary capacity

for languages, & feel this to be a terrible drawback to any undertaking wherein I must seek as much by mouth as by my legs and eyes": JH to Hodgson, 23 Sept. 1849, HP, RAS.

90. JH to WH, 1 Feb. 1849, IL, RBG.

91. JH to Darwin, 13 Oct. 1848, Burkhardt and Smith, *Correspondence*, vol. 4: 171.

92. Darwin to JH, 6 Oct. 1848, ibid., 169.

93. JH to Darwin, 24 June 1849, Burkhardt and Smith, *Correspondence*, vol. 4: 241.

94. Hodgson to Johnston, 20 June 1835, HP, NHM.

95. JH to WH, 24 Aug. 1849, IL, RBG.

96. JH to Hodgson, 28 Oct. 1848, IJ, RBG.

97. Ibid., 28 Feb. 1849, RBG.

98. JH to Hodgson, 27 Sept. 1849, HP, RAS.

99. Hodgson to WH, 8 Dec. 1848 and 20 June 1849, IL, RBG.

100. Hodgson to WH, 8 Dec. 1848, IL, RBG; "Hooker's Recollections."

101. Herbert, "Report;" Markham, *Memoir*.

102. Madden, "Turaee;" Thomson, *Western Himalaya*; Strachey, "Physical Geography."

103. For Hodgson's ethnographic and linguistic studies, see his *Essays*, Part 2, and Waterhouse, *Origins*.

104. JH to Darwin, 13 Oct. 1848, in Burkhardt and Smith, *Correspondence*, vol. 4: 173.

105. Hooker, *Himalayan Journals*, vol. 2: 386–401.

106. "On the Physical Geography of the Himayala" (1849), in Hodgson, *Essays*, Part 2, 1–28.

107. But cf. Hodgson, "Migration," 123, for the seasons in the Kathmandu valley as "essentially tropical." Other naturalists, better acquainted with medicine and botany, adopted the terms more readily, even with respect to bird migration: see Jameson, "Geographical Distribution," 326–7.

108. Pemble, *Invasion*.

109. See the correspondence and newspaper clippings in HP, RAS.

110. "On the Colonization of the Himalaya by Europeans" (1856), in Hodgson, *Essays*, Part 2, 83–9, and Hooker's evidence, 14 Feb. 1859, to the committee on colonization and settlement in India, *Parliamentary Papers* (1859), VII, 1–9.

111. Hooker, *Himalayan Journals*, vol. 1: 109, 112–20.

112. Hooker, "Extracts" (1850), 90–1.

113. JH to WH, 20 Oct. 1848, in Huxley, *Life*, vol. 1: 270.

114. JH to Hodgson, 12 Nov. 1848, IJ, RBG.

115. Huxley, *Life*, vol. 1: 264–7.

116. Herbert, "Particulars," 91, 94; Raja of Sikkim to Campbell, 7 Oct. 1848, IJ, RBG.

117. Lee-Warner, *Dalhousie*, vol. 2: 146.
118. Hooker, "Extracts" (1850), 90.
119. Raja of Sikkim to Campbell, 7 Oct. 1848, IJ, RBG.
120. Hooker, *Himalayan Journals*, vol. 1: 117.
121. JH to his mother, 10 June 1848, in Huxley, *Life*, vol. 1: 252.
122. Smith, *Lawrence*, vol. 1: 159.
123. Ibid., 276.
124. Dalhousie to JH, 1 Sept. 1848, 13 Feb. 1849, PL, RBG.
125. Huxley, *Life*, vol. 1: 254.
126. Hodgson to Johnston, 20 June 1835, HP, NHM.
127. Campbell published 27 articles in the Asiatic Society *Journal* alone: *Centenary Review*, 122–3.
128. Minutes of the Agricultural and Horticultural Society of India, 9 March 1848, AHSI, Calcutta; *Himalayan Journals*, vol. 1: 100.
129. JH to Hodgson, 27 Sept. 1849, HP, ZSL.
130. JH to Hodgson, 7 Aug. 1849, HP, RAS.
131. Huxley, *Life*, vol. 1: 272.
132. JH to Hodgson, 4 Sept. 1849, HP, RAS.
133. Entry for 5 Oct. 1849, IJ, RBG.
134. Diary entry, 11 Nov. 1849, IJ, RBG. Cf. *Himalayan Journals*, vol. 2, chapters 25–6; Huxley, *Life*, vol. 1, chapters 15–16.
135. H.M. Elliott to Sir James Colvile, n.d., IJ, RBG.
136. Dalhousie to JH, 12 Dec. 1849, PL, RBG.
137. Diary entry for 16 Nov. 1849, IJ, RBG; JH to Hodgson, 18 Dec, 1849, HP, RAS; JH to his mother, 31 Jan. 1850, in Huxley, *Life*, vol. 1: 320–1.
138. JH to Frances Henslow, 3 Dec. 1849, IL, RBG.
139. JH to Hodgson, 12 Nov. 1849, 5 Dec. 1849, 14 Dec. 1849, HP, RAS.
140. Hodgson to WH, 1 Dec. 1849, IL, RBG.
141. JH to WH, 2 Jan. 1850, IL, RBG.
142. Hooker, *Himalayan Journals*, vol. 2: 7.
143. Huxley, *Life*, vol. 1: 275, 327.
144. Hooker, *Himalayan Journals*, vol. 2: 238.
145. Hooker, *Notes on a Tour*.
146. *Athenaeum*, 21 Oct. 1848, 1049–50.
147. Huxley, *Life*, vol. 1: 255, 339–41; Humboldt to JH, 16 July 1851, PL, RBG.
148. Huxley, *Life*, vol. 1: 363.
149. [Forbes], "Himalayan Journals," 80.
150. Darwin to JH, 1 Mar. 1854, in Burkhardt and Smith, *Correspondence*, vol. 5: 179.
151. [Forbes], "Himalayan Journals," 58–9.
152. Ibid., 59.
153. Huxley, *Life*, vol. 1: 363.

154. Quoted in ibid., 412.
155. *Spectator*, 4 Mar. 1854, 253.
156. *Quarterly Review*, no. 167 (1865): 183.

CONCLUSION

1. For the significance of this geopolitical trope (which was also reflected in the designation of highland zones in India and elsewhere "alpine" or "arctic," see Loomis, "Arctic Sublime."
2. See especially Hooker's 1909 essay, "Botany," where the tripartite division of India between tropical, temperate, and alpine zones remains fundamental and the botanical geography of South Asia still begins (167) with the eastern Himalaya and the "tropical zone of Sikkim."
3. Again the southwest provided one of the most convincing examples of India's tropicality: see Logan, *Malabar*, vol. 1: 29–31, with its approving reference to Wallace's *Tropical Nature*.
4. As late, however, as the 1870s Hodgson and Hooker were cited in support of the idea that there might one day arise "cheerful English homesteads" set "amidst the orchards and sheep-walks of the north." Newall, *Highlands*, 15.
5. Madden, "Itineraries" and "Notes on Plants," MP, RBG; "Turaee;" "Occurrence of Palms;" "Elucidation."
6. Cunningham and Jardine, *Romanticism*; Knight, *Science*.
7. Hartwig, *Tropical World*, 89.
8. Pinney, *Camera Indica*. For early examples of Himalayan photography, see Falconer, *India*, plates 74–6.
9. E.g., Hartwig, *Tropical World*, where Hooker is cited alongside such other authorities as Humboldt, Darwin, Forbes (on India), Tennent (on Ceylon), and Livingstone (on Africa), and where climate, plants, and animals are all seen as elements of an overarching "tropical nature."
10. Willis, *Agriculture*, vi, 4, 12. Willis was director of the botanic garden at Peradeniya in Ceylon when he wrote this book. The idea of "tropical races" was still relatively rare in the 1850s but had become widespread by the end of the century: Alatas, *Myth*.

BIBLIOGRAPHY

ARCHIVES

Agri-Horticultural Society, Calcutta
   Minutes of the Agricultural and Horticultural Society of India
Natural History Museum, London [NHM]
   Hodgson Papers [HP]
Oriental and India Office Collections, British Library, London
   Kyd Papers Mss Eur 95/1
Royal Asiatic Society, London [RAS]
   Hodgson Papers [HP]
Royal Botanic Gardens, Kew [RBG]
   Bentham Correspondence [BC]
   Calcutta Botanic Garden Papers
   Director's Correspondence [DC]
   Falconer Papers [FP]
   Joseph Hooker: Antarctic Letters, 1839–43 [AL]
   Joseph Hooker: Indian Letters, 1847–51 [IL]
   Joseph Hooker: Indian Journals [IJ]
   Joseph Hooker: Manuscript Journal [MJ]
   Joseph Hooker: Private Letters [PL]
   Lindley Correspondence [LC]
   Madden Papers [MP]
   Munro Correspondence [MC]
Zoological Society of London [ZSL]
   Hodgson Papers [HP]

OFFICIAL REPORTS AND PUBLICATIONS

Great Britain
Report of the Commissioners Appointed to Inquire into the Organization of the Indian Army. *Parliamentary Papers*, 1859, v (Cmd 2515).
Report on Colonization and Settlement (India). *Parliamentary Papers*, 1859, VII.

SERIALS

Asiatic Researches
Athenaeum
Calcutta Journal of Natural History
Calcutta Review
Gleanings in Science
Hooker's Journal of Botany
Journal of the Agricultural and Horticultural Society of India
Journal of the Asiatic Society of Bengal
London Journal of Botany
Oriental Annual

PRINTED BOOKS AND ARTICLES

Agrawal, Arun. "Dismantling the Divide between Indigenous and Scientific Knowledge." *Development and Change* 26 (1995): 413–39.
Ahluwalia, H.P.S. *Eternal Himalaya*. New Delhi: Interprint, 1982.
Alatas, Syed Hussein. *The Myth of the Lazy Native: A Study of the Image of the Malays, Filipinos and Javanese from the 16th to the 20th Century and its Function in the Ideology of Colonial Capitalism*. London: Frank Cass, 1977.
Allan, Mea. *The Hookers of Kew, 1785–1911*. London: Michael Joseph, 1967.
Anderson, Warwick. "Climates of Opinion: Acclimatization in Nineteenth-Century France and England." *Victorian Studies* 35 (1992): 135–58.
———. *The Cultivation of Whiteness: Science, Health and Racial Destiny in Australia*. New York: Basic Books, 2003.
Annesley, James. *Researches into the Causes, Nature, and Treatment of the Most Prevalent Diseases of India*. 2 vols. London: Longman, Rees, Orme, Brown and Green, 1828.
———. *Sketches of the Most Prevalent Diseases of India*. 2 vols. London: Thomas and George Underwood, 1825.
Aravamudan, Srinivas. *Tropicopolitans: Colonialism and Agency, 1688–1804*. Durham: Duke University Press, 1999.
Archer, E.C. *Tours in Upper India and in Parts of the Himalaya Mountains*. 2 vols. London: Richard Bentley, 1833.

Archer, Mildred. *Early Views of India: The Picturesque Journeys of Thomas and William Daniell, 1786–1794.* London: Thames and Hudson, 1980.
Arnold, David. *Colonizing the Body: State Medicine and Epidemic Disease in Nineteenth-Century India.* Berkeley: University of California Press, 1993.
———. "European Orphans and Vagrants in India in the Nineteenth Century." *Journal of Imperial and Commonwealth History* 7 (1979): 104–27.
———. "Hodgson, Hooker and the Himalayan Frontier, 1848–50." In *The Origins of Himalayan Studies: Brian Houghton Hodgson in Nepal and Darjeeling, 1820–1858*, edited by David M. Waterhouse, 189–205. London: RoutledgeCurzon, 2004.
———. "Hunger in the Garden of Plenty: The Bengal Famine of 1770." In *Dreadful Visitations: Confronting Natural Catastrophe in the Age of Enlightenment*, edited by Alessa Johns, 81–111. New York: Routledge, 1999.
———. "'Illusory Riches': Representations of the Tropical World, 1840–1950." *Singapore Journal of Tropical Geography* 21 (2000): 6–18.
———. "India's Place in the Tropical World, 1770–1930." *Journal of Imperial and Commonwealth History* 26 (1998): 1–21.
———. "Race, Place and Bodily Difference in Early Nineteenth-Century India." *Historical Research* 77 (2004): 254–73.
———. *Science, Technology and Medicine in Colonial India.* Cambridge: Cambridge University Press, 2000.
———, ed. *Warm Climates and Western Medicine: The Emergence of Tropical Medicine, 1500–1900.* Amsterdam: Rodopi, 1996.
The Baburnama: Memoirs of Babur, Prince and Emperor, edited by Wheeler M. Thackston. New York: Oxford University Press, 1996.
Bacon, Thomas. *First Impressions and Studies from Nature in Hindostan.* 2nd ed. 2 vols. London: W.H. Allen, 1837.
Baird, J.G.A., ed. *Private Letters of the Marquess of Dalhousie.* Edinburgh: William Blackwood and Sons, 1910.
Barrell, John. *The Infection of Thomas De Quincey: A Psychopathology of Imperialism.* New Haven: Yale University Press, 1991.
Barrow, Ian J. *Making History, Drawing Territory: British Mapping in India, c.1756–1905.* New Delhi: Oxford University Press, 2003.
Batten, J.H. *Official Reports on the Province of Kumaon.* Agra: Secundra Orphan Press, 1851.
———. "Works on the Himalaya." *Calcutta Review* 4 (1845): 162–77.
Bayley, H.V. (comp.). *Dorjé-ling.* Calcutta: G.H. Huttmann, 1838.
Bayly, C.A. *Empire and Information: Intelligence Gathering and Social Communication in India, 1780–1870.* Cambridge: Cambridge University Press, 1996.
———. *Imperial Meridian: The British Empire and the World, 1780–1830.* London: Longman, 1989.

Bearce, George D. *British Attitudes Towards India, 1784–1858.* Oxford: Oxford University Press, 1961.
Beer, Gillian. *Open Fields: Science in Cultural Encounter.* Oxford: Clarendon Press, 1996.
Behdad, Ali. *Belated Travelers: Orientalism in the Age of Colonial Dissolution.* Cork: Cork University Press, 1994.
Beinart, William and JoAnn McGregor, eds. *Social History and African Environments.* Oxford: James Currey, 2003.
Bellew, F.J. *Memoirs of a Griffin.* 2 vols. London: W.H. Allen, 1843.
Bellon, Richard. "Joseph Hooker's Ideals for a Professional Man of Science." *Journal of the History of Biology* 34 (2001): 51–82.
Bernardin de St Pierre, Jacques-Henri. *Paul and Virginia.* London: Peter Owen, 1982.
———. *A Voyage to the Isle of France.* London: Vernor and Hood, 1800.
Bernier, François. *Travels in the Mogul Empire.* Westminster: Archibald Constable, 1891.
Bevan, H. *Thirty Years in India.* 2 vols. London: Pelham Richardson, 1839.
Bewell, Alan. *Romanticism and Colonial Disease.* Baltimore: Johns Hopkins University Press, 1999.
Biswas, Kalipada. *The Original Correspondence of Sir Joseph Banks relating to the Foundation of the Royal Botanic Garden, Calcutta.* Calcutta: Royal Asiatic Society of Bengal, 1950.
Bowrey, Thomas. *A Geographical Account of Countries Round the Bay of Bengal, 1669 to 1679.* Cambridge: Hakluyt Society, 1905.
Bravo, Michael T. "Precision and Curiosity in Scientific Travel: James Rennell and the Orientalist Geography of the New Imperial Age." In *Voyages and Visions: Towards a Cultural History of Travel*, edited by Jas Elner and Joan-Pau Rubies, 162–83. London: Reaktion Books, 1999.
Brendon, Piers. *Thomas Cook: 150 Years of Popular Tourism.* London: Secker and Warburg, 1991.
Briggs, Asa. *The Age of Improvement, 1783–1867.* London: Longman, 1959.
Brockway, Lucile H. *Science and Colonial Expansion: The Role of the British Botanic Gardens.* New York: Academic Press, 1979.
Brown, Alexander W., et al. *Jacquemont.* Paris: Muséum National d'Histoire Naturelle, 1959.
Browne, J. *India Tracts.* London: East India Company, 1788.
Browne, Janet. *Charles Darwin: The Power of Place.* London: Jonathan Cape, 2002.
———. *The Secular Ark: Studies in the History of Biogeography.* New Haven: Yale University Press, 1983.
Browne, John Cave. *Indian Infanticide.* London: W.H. Allen, 1857.

Buchanan, Claudius. *Christian Researches in Asia.* 5th ed. London: T. Cadell and W. Davies, 1812.
Buchanan, Francis. *An Account of the Kingdom of Nepal.* Edinburgh: Archibald Constable, 1819
———. *A Journey from Madras through the Countries of Mysore, Canara, and Malabar,* 3 vols. London: T. Cadell & W. Davies, 1807.
———. [as Francis Hamilton]. "Some Notices Concerning the Various Plants of India." *Transactions of the Royal Society of Edinburgh* 10 (1826): 171–86.
Burkhardt, Frederick and Sydney Smith, eds. *The Correspondence of Charles Darwin,* vol. 4. Cambridge: Cambridge University Press, 1988.
———. *The Correspondence of Charles Darwin,* vol. 5. Cambridge: Cambridge University Press, 1989.
Burkill, I.H. *Chapters on the History of Botany in India.* Delhi: Government of India, 1965.
———. "William Jack's Letters to Nathaniel Wallich, 1819–21." *Journal of the Straits Branch of the Royal Asiatic Society* 73 (1916): 147–268.
Burnes, Alexander. *Travels into Bokhara.* 3 vols. London: John Murray, 1834.
Burton, Richard F. *Goa, and the Blue Mountains.* London: Richard Bentley, 1851.
———. *Sindh, and the Races that Inhabit the Valley of the Indus.* London: W.H. Allen, 1851.
———. *Selected Papers on Anthropology, Travel and Exploration,* edited by N.M. Penzer. London: A.M. Philpot, 1924.
Butler, Marilyn. "Romanticism in England." In *Romanticism in National Context,* edited by Roy Porter and Mikulas Teich, 37–67. Cambridge: Cambridge University Press.
———. *Romantics, Rebels and Reactionaries: English Literature and Its Background, 1760–1830.* Oxford: Oxford University Press, 1981.
Camerini, Jane R. "Remains of the Day: Early Victorians in the Field." In *Victorian Science in Context,* edited by Bernard Lightman, 354–77. Chicago: University of Chicago Press, 1997.
———. "Wallace in the Field." In *Science in the Field* (*Osiris* 11), 1996, edited by Henrika Kuklick and Robert E. Kohler, 44–65.
Campbell, Colin. *The Romantic Ethic and the Spirit of Modern Consumerism.* Oxford: Blackwell, 1987.
Cannon, Susan Faye. *Science in Culture: The Early Victorian Period.* New York: Dawson, 1978.
Carey, William. "Prospectus of an Agricultural and Horticultural Society in India." *Transactions of the Agricultural and Horticultural Society of India* 1 (1838): 211–21.
Carlyle, Thomas. *On Heroes, Hero-Worship, and the Heroic in History.* Boston: Ginn, 1901.

Cardinal, Roger. "Romantic Travel." In *Rewriting the Self: Histories from the Renaissance to the Present*, edited by Roy Porter, 135–55. London: Routledge, 1997.
Carter, Harold B. *Sir Joseph Banks, 1743–1820*. London: British Museum, 1988.
Carter, Paul. *The Road to Botany Bay: An Essay in Spatial History*. London: Faber and Faber, 1987.
Centenary Review of the Asiatic Society of Bengal from 1784 to 1883. Calcutta: Thacker, Spink, 1885.
Champion, Catherine. "L'image de l'Inde dans la fiction populaire française aux XIXe et XXe siècles." In *Rêver l'Asie: Exotisme et littérature coloniale aux Indes, en Indochine et en Insulinde*, edited by Denys Lombard, 43–68. Paris: Editions de l'école des hautes études en sciences sociales, 1993.
Chandler, Alice. *A Dream of Order: The Medieval Ideal in Nineteenth-Century English Literature*. London: Routledge and Kegan Paul, 1971.
Charlton, D. G. *New Images of the Natural in France: A Study in European Cultural History, 1750–1800*. Cambridge: Cambridge University Press, 1984.
Cleghorn, Hugh. "On the Hedge Plants of India." *Transactions of the Botanical Society of Edinburgh* 4 (1853): 83–100.
———. "Obituary Notice of Dr Robert Wight." Reprinted from *Transactions of the Botanical Society of Edinburgh*. Edinburgh: Neill, 1873.
———, et al. "Report of the Committee Appointed by the British Association to Consider the Probable Effects... of the Destruction of Tropical Forests." *Report of the Twenty-First Meeting of the British Association for the Advancement of Science, 1851*. London: John Murray, 1852.
Cohn, Bernard S. *An Anthropologist Among the Historians and Other Essays*. Delhi: Oxford University Press, 1990.
———. *Colonialism and Its Forms of Knowledge: The British in India*. Princeton: Princeton University Press, 1996.
———. "The Command of Language and the Language of Command." In *Subaltern Studies IV*, edited by Ranajit Guha, 276–329. Delhi: Oxford University Press, 1985.
Colley, Linda. *Captives: Britain, Empire and the World, 1600–1850*. London: Jonathan Cape, 2002.
Colvin, Christina, ed. *Maria Edgeworth: Letters from England, 1813–1844*. Oxford: Oxford University Press, 1971.
Comaroff, John L. and Jean Comaroff. *Of Revelation and Revolution. Volume Two: The Dialectics of Modernity on a South African Frontier*. Chicago: University of Chicago Press, 1997.
Cook, Andrew S. "Major James Rennell and *A Bengal Atlas* (1780 and 1781)." *India Office Library and Records Report, 1976*. London: India Office, 1978.
Cosgrove, Denis E. *Social Formation and Symbolic Landscape*. London: Croom Helm, 1984.

——— and Stephen Daniels, eds. *The Iconography of Landscape*. Cambridge: Cambridge University Press, 1988.
Crawford, D.G. *A History of the Indian Medical Service, 1600–1913*. 2 vols. London: W. Thacker, 1914.
Crawfurd, John. *History of the Indian Archipelago*. 3 vols. Edinburgh: Constable, 1820.
Crosby, Alfred W. *Ecological Imperialism: The Biological Expansion of Europe, 900–1900*. Cambridge: Cambridge University Press, 1986.
Cunningham, Andrew and Nicholas Jardine, eds. *Romanticism and the Sciences*. Cambridge: Cambridge University Press, 1990.
Cunningham, Joseph Davey. *A History of the Sikhs*. London: John Murray, 1849.
———. "Notes on Moorcroft's Travels in Ladakh." *Journal of the Asiatic Society of Bengal* 13 (1844): 172–222.
Curtin, Philip D. *Death by Migration: Europe's Encounter with the Tropical World in the Nineteenth Century*. Cambridge: Cambridge University Press, 1989.
Curtis's Botanical Magazine Dedications, 1827–1927. London: Curtis's, n.d.
Dancer, Thomas. *The Medical Assistant or Jamaica Practice of Physic*. Kingston: Alexander Aikman, 1801.
Darwin, Charles. *The Voyage of the Beagle*. Harmondsworth: Penguin, 1989.
D[eane], A. *A Tour through the Upper Provinces of Hindostan*. London: C. and J. Rivington, 1823.
de Candolle, Roger and Alan Radcliffe-Smith. "Nathaniel Wallich and the Herbarium of the Honourable East India Company." *Botanical Journal of the Linnean Society* 83 (1981): 325–48.
de Léry, Jean. *A History of a Voyage to the Land Called Brazil*. Berkeley: University of California Press, 1990.
Deloche, Jean. *Transport and Communications in India Prior to Steam Locomotion*. 2 vols. Delhi: Oxford University Press, 1993.
Deleury, Guy (comp.). *Les Indes Florissantes: Anthologie des Voyageurs Français (1750–1820)*. Paris: Robert Laffont, 1991.
Desmond, Ray. *Dictionary of British and Irish Botanists and Horticulturalists*. London: Taylor and Francis, 1977.
———. *The European Discovery of the Indian Flora*. Oxford: Oxford University Press, 1992.
———. *Sir Joseph Hooker: Traveller and Plant Collector*. Woodbridge: Antique Collectors' Club, 1999.
———. "William Roxburgh's Plants of the Coast of Coromandel, 1795–1820." *Hortulus Aliquando* 2 (1977): 23–41.
Desportes, Pouppé. *Histoire des Maladies de S. Domingue*. Paris: Lejay, 1770.
Dirks, Nicholas B. Foreword to *Colonialism and Its Forms of Knowledge: The British in India* by Bernard S. Cohn, ix–xvii. Princeton: Princeton University Press, 1996.

———. "Guiltless Spoliations: Picturesque Beauty, Colonial Knowledge, and Colin Mackenzie's Survey of India." In *Perceptions of South Asia's Visual Past*, edited by Catherine B. Asher and Thomas R. Metcalf, 210–32. New Delhi: Oxford University Press, 1994.

Dittlebach, Michael. "Global Physics and Aesthetic Empire: Humboldt's Physical Portrait of the Tropics." In *Visions of Empire: Voyages, Botany, and Representations of Nature*, edited by David Philip Miller and Peter Hanns Reill, 258–92. Cambridge: Cambridge University Press, 1996.

Drayton, Richard. *Nature's Government: Science, Imperial Britain, and the Improvement of the World*. New Haven: Yale University Press, 2000.

Drew, John. *India and the Romantic Imagination*. Delhi: Oxford University Press, 1987.

Duff, Alexander. *India, and India Missions*. Edinburgh: John Johnstone, 1839.

Dunlap, Thomas R. *Nature and the English Diaspora: Environment and History in the United States, Canada, Australia, and New Zealand*. Cambridge: Cambridge University Press, 1999.

Dunn, Richard S. *Sugar and Slaves: The Rise of the Planter Class in the English West Indies, 1624–1713*. Chapel Hill: University of North Carolina Press, 1972.

Eaton, Richard M. *Essays on Islam and Indian History*. New Delhi: Oxford University Press, 2000.

Eden, Emily. *Letters from India*. 2 vols. London: Richard Bentley, 1872.

———. *Up the Country: Letters Written to Her Sister from the Upper Provinces of India*. London: Virago Press, 1983.

Edgeworth, M.P. "Botanico-Agricultural Account of the Protected Sikh States." *Journal of the Asiatic Society of Bengal* 7 (1838): 751–66.

Edney, Matthew H. *Mapping an Empire: The Geographical Construction of British India, 1765–1843*. Chicago: Chicago University Press, 1997.

Edwardes, Herbert Benjamin, and Herman Merivale. *Life of Sir Henry Lawrence*. 2nd ed. 2 vols. London: Smith, Elder, 1872.

Elliott, Robert. *Views in India, China, and on the Shores of the Red Sea*. 2 vols. London: H. Fisher and R. Fisher, 1835.

Elphinstone, Mountstuart. *An Account of the Kingdom of Cabul*. 3rd ed. 2 vols. Karachi: Oxford University Press, 1972.

Elsner, Jas and Joan-Pau Rubies, eds. *Voyages and Visions: Towards a Cultural History of Travel*. London: Reaktion Books, 1999.

Ewart, Joseph. *A Digest of the Vital Statistics of the European and Native Armies in India*. London: Smith, Elder, 1859.

Falconer, John. *India: Pioneering Photographs, 1850–1900*. London: British Library, 2001.

Fay, Eliza. *Original Letters from India (1779–1815)*. London: Hogarth Press, 1925.

Ferguson, Adam. *An Essay on the History of Civil Society*. Edinburgh: Edinburgh University Press, 1966.

Firminger, W. K., ed. *Fifth Report from the Select Committee of the House of Commons on the Affairs of the East India Company, 1812.* Calcutta: R. Cambray, 1918.
Flint, Valerie J. *The Imaginative Landscape of Christopher Columbus.* Princeton: Princeton University Press, 1992.
[Forbes, Edward]. "Himalayan Journals." *Edinburgh Review* 103 (1856), 55–81.
Forbes, James. *Oriental Memoirs.* 2nd ed. 2 vols. London: Richard Bentley, 1834.
Forster, George. *A Journey from Bengal to England through the Northern Part of India.* 2 vols. London: R. Faulder, 1798.
Fosberg, F. R. "Tropical Floristic Botany." In *Tropical Botany*, edited by Kai Larsen and Lauritz B. Holm-Nielsen, 89–105. London: Academic Press, 1979.
Foster, William, ed. *Early Travels in India, 1583–1619.* Reprinted New Delhi: S. Chand, 1968.
———, ed. *The Embassy of Sir Thomas Roe to India, 1615–19.* 2nd ed. London: Oxford University Press, 1926.
Foucault, Michel. *The Birth of the Clinic: An Archaeology of Medical Perception.* London: Tavistock Publication, 1973.
———. *Discipline and Punish: The Birth of the Prison.* Harmondsworth: Penguin Books, 1979.
———. "Governmentality." In *The Foucault Effect: Studies in Governmentality*, edited by Graham Burchell, Colin Gordon, and Peter Miller, 87–104. Chicago: University of Chicago Press, 1991.
———. *The Order of Things: An Archaeology of the Human Sciences.* London: Tavistock Publications, 1970.
Fraser, James Baillie. *Journal of a Tour through Part of the Snowy Range of the Himala Mountains.* London: Rodwell and Martin, 1820.
Freyre, Gilberto. *The Mansions and the Shanties: The Making of Modern Brazil.* New York: Alfred A. Knopf, 1963.
Frost, Alan. "New Geographical Perspectives and the Emergence of the Romantic Imagination." In *Captain James Cook and His Times*, edited by Robin Fisher and Hugh Johnston, 5–19. London: Croom Helm, 1979.
Fulford, Tim and Peter J. Kitson, eds. *Romanticism and Colonialism: Writing and Empire, 1780–1830.* Cambridge: Cambridge University Press, 1998.
Gardner, George. "Notes on a Botanical Visit to Madras, Coimbatore, and the Neelgherry Mountains." *London Journal of Botany* 4 (1845): 393–409.
Gerard, J.G. "Observations on the Spiti Valley and Circumadjacent Country within the Himalaya." *Asiatic Researches* 18 (1833): 238–78.
[Gibbes, Phoebe]. *Hartly House.* Calcutta: Thacker, Spink, 1908.
Glacken, Clarence J. *Traces on the Rhodian Shore: Nature and Culture in Western Thought from Ancient Times to the End of the Eighteenth Century.* Berkeley: University of California Press, 1967.
Gleig, G.R. *The Life of Major-General Sir Thomas Munro.* 2 vols. London: Henry Colburn and Richard Bentley, 1831.

Godrej, Pheroza and Pauline Rohatgi. *Scenic Splendours: India through the Printed Image*. London: British Library, 1989.
Gourou, Pierre. *The Tropical World: Its Social and Economic Conditions and Its Future Status*. London: Longman, 1953.
Graham, Maria. *Journal of a Residence in India*. Edinburgh: Archibald Constable, 1812.
———. *Journal of a Voyage to Brazil*. New York: Frederick A. Praeger, 1969.
Green, Nicholas. *The Spectacle of Nature: Landscape and Bourgeois Culture in Nineteenth-Century France*. Manchester: Manchester University Press, 1990.
Greenough, Paul. "Hunter's Drowned Land: An Environmental Fantasy of the Victorian Sunderbans." In *Nature and the Orient: The Environmental History of South and Southeast Asia*, edited by Richard H. Grove, Vinita Damodaran, and Satpal Sangwan, 237–72. Delhi: Oxford University Press, 1998.
———. "*Naturae Ferae*: Wild Animals in South Asia and the Standard Environmental Narrative." In *Agrarian Studies: Synthetic Work at the Cutting Edge*, edited by James C. Scott and Nina Bhatt, 141–85. New Haven: Yale University Press, 2001.
Grewal, Inderpal. *Home and Harem: Nation, Gender, Empire, and Cultures of Travel*. London: Leicester University Press, 1996.
Griffith, William. *Journal of Travels in Assam, Burma, Bootan, Affghanistan and the Neighbouring Countries*. Calcutta: Bishop's College Press, 1847.
Griffiths, Tom and Libby Robin, eds. *Ecology and Empire: Environmental History of Settler Societies*. Edinburgh: Keele University Press, 1997.
Grove, Richard. *Green Imperialism: Colonial Expansion, Tropical Island Edens and the Origins of Environmentalism, 1600–1860*. Cambridge: Cambridge University Press, 1995.
———. "Indigenous Knowledge and the Significance of South-West India for Portuguese and Dutch Constructions of Tropical Nature." *Modern Asian Studies* 30 (1996): 121–43.
———, Vinita Damodaran, and Satpal Sangwan, eds. *Nature and the Orient: The Environmental History of South and Southeast Asia*. Delhi: Oxford University Press, 1998.
Guha, Ranajit. *A Rule of Property for Bengal: An Essay on the Idea of Permanent Settlement*. Paris: Mouton, 1963.
Haeckel, Ernst. *A Visit to Ceylon*. London: Kegan Paul, Trench, 1883.
Halbfass, Wilhelm. *India and Europe: An Essay in Understanding*. Albany, NY: State University of New York Press, 1988.
[Hamilton, Alexander]. Review of Francis Buchanan, *A Journey from Madras*, *Edinburgh Journal* 13 (1808), 82–100.
Hamilton, Walter. *The East-India Gazetteer*. 2nd ed. 2 vols. London: W.H. Allen, 1828.
Harrison, Mark. *Climates and Constitutions: Health, Race, Environment and British Imperialism in India, 1600–1850*. New Delhi: Oxford University Press, 1999.

———. "Tropical Medicine in Nineteenth-Century India." *British Journal for the History of Science* 25 (1992): 299–318.
Hartwig, G. *The Tropical World*. London: Longman, Green, Longman, Roberts and Green, 1863.
Hawkesworth, John, ed. *An Account of the Voyages ... for Making Discoveries in the Southern Hemisphere*. 3 vols. London: W. Strehan and T. Cadell, 1773.
Headrick, Daniel R. *The Tools of Empire: Technology and European Imperialism in the Nineteenth Century*. New York: Oxford University Press, 1981.
Heber, Amelia. *The Life of Reginald Heber*. 2 vols. London: John Murray, 1830.
Heber, Reginald. *Narrative of a Journey through the Upper Provinces of India*. 3rd ed. 3 vols. London: John Murray, 1828.
Herbert, J.D. "Particulars of a Visit to the Siccim Hills." *Gleanings in Science*, 15 (1830): 89–96; 16 (1830): 114–24.
———. "Report of the Mineralogical Survey of the Himmalaya Mountains." *Journal of the Asiatic Society of Bengal* 11 (1842): i-clxiii.
Heyne, Benjamin. *Tracts, Historical and Statistical, on India*. London: Robert Baldwin, 1814.
Hickey, William. *Memoirs of William Hickey*, edited by Alfred Spencer. 4 vols. London: Hunt and Blackett, 1913–25.
Hodges, William. *Travels in India during the Years 1780, 1781, 1782, and 1783*. London: the author, 1793.
Hodgson, B.H. *Essays on the Languages, Literature, and Religion of Nepal and Tibet*. London: Trubner, 1874.
———. "On the Migration of the Natatores and Grallatores." *Asiatic Researches* 18 (1833): 122–28.
———. "On a New Species of Buceros." *Asiatic Researches* 18 (1833): 178–86.
———. "Route of Two Nepalese Embassies to Pekin." *Journal of the Asiatic Society of Bengal* 25 (1856): 473–97.
Hoffmeister, W. *Travels in Ceylon and Continental India*. Edinburgh: William P. Kennedy, 1848.
Hooker, Joseph Dalton. "Botany." In *Imperial Gazetteer of India*, vol. 1. London: Oxford University Press, 1909.
———. "On the Climate and Vegetation of the Temperate and Cold Regions of East Nepal and the Sikkim Himalaya Mountains." *Journal of the Horticultural Society of London* 7 (1852): 69–131.
———. "Extracts from the Private Letters of Dr J.D. Hooker." *London Journal of Botany* 7 (1848): 297–321. Continued in: *Hooker's Journal of Botany* 1 (1849): 1–14, 81–9, 113–20, 129–36, 161–75, 361–70, and ibid., 2 (1850): 11–23, 52–9, 88–91, 112–18.
———. *Flora Antarctica: The Botany of the Antarctic Voyage: Part 1*. London: Reeve Brothers, 1847.
———. *The Flora of British India*, vol. 1. London: L. Reeve, 1875.

———. *Flora Tasmaniae: The Botany of the Antarctic Voyage: Part III*. London: Lovell Reeve, 1860.
———. *Himalayan Journals*. 2 vols. London: John Murray, 1854.
———. "Dr Hooker's Botanical Mission to India." *London Journal of Botany* 6 (1847): 604–8.
———. "Sir Joseph Hooker's Recollections of Hodgson's Darjiling Days." In William Wilson Hunter, *Life of Brian Houghton Hodgson*, 248–55. London: John Murray, 1896.
———. *Illustrations of Himalayan Plants*. London: Lovell Reeve, 1855.
———. "Notes, Chiefly Botanical, made during an Excursion from Darjiling to Tonglo." *Journal of the Asiatic Society of Bengal* 29 (1849): 419–46.
———. *Notes on a Tour in the Plains of India, the Himala, and Borneo*. London: Reeve, Benham and Reeve, 1848.
———. "Observations made when following the Grand Trunk Road." *Journal of the Asiatic Society of Bengal* 17 (1848): 355–411.
———. *The Rhododendrons of Sikkim-Himalaya*. London: Reeve, Benham, Reeve, 1849.
——— and Thomas Thomson. *Flora Indica*. Vol. 1. London: W. Pamplin, 1855.
——— and William Hooker. "Botany of the Niger Expedition." *London Journal of Botany* 6 (1847), 125–39.
Hooker, William Jackson. *Journal of a Tour in Iceland*. London: Vernor, Hood and Sharpe, 1811.
Hove, A.P. *Tours for Scientific and Economical Research Made in Guzerat, Kattiawar, and the Conkuns, in 1787–88*. Bombay: Government of Bombay, 1855.
Howison, John. *Foreign Scenes and Travelling Recreations*. 2 vols. Edinburgh: Oliver and Boyd, 1825.
Humbley, W.W.W. *Journal of a Cavalry Officer*. London: Longman, Brown, Green, and Longman, 1854.
Humboldt, Alexander von. *Aspects of Nature*. London: H.G. Bohn, 1849.
———. *Cosmos: Sketch of a Physical Description of the Universe*. 5 vols. London: George Bell and Sons, 1901
———. *Personal Narrative of a Journey to the Equinoctial Regions of the New Continent*. London: Penguin, 1995.
Hunter, John. *Observations on the Disease of the Army in Jamaica*. London: G. Nicol, 1788.
Hunter, William Wilson. *Annals of Rural Bengal*. 5th ed. London: Smith, Elder, 1872.
———. *Life of Brian Houghton Hodgson*. London: John Murray, 1896.
Hussey, Christopher. *The Picturesque: Studies in a Point of View*. London: Frank Cass, 1983.
Huxley, Leonard. *Life and Letters of Joseph Dalton Hooker*. 2 vols. London: John Murray, 1918.

Inden, Ronald. *Imagining India*. Oxford: Blackwell, 1990.
Irschick, Eugene F. *Dialogue and History: Constructing South India, 1795–1895*. Berkeley: University of California Press, 1994.
Jacquemont, Victor. *Letters from India, 1829–1832: Being a Selection from the Correspondence of Victor Jacquemont*. London: Macmillan, 1936.
———. *Voyages en Amérique et aux Indes: Lettres Ecrit de 1826 à 1832*. Paris: Les Belles Lectures, 1952.
———. *Voyage dans l'Inde, 1828 à 1832*. 3 vols. Paris: l'Institut de France, 1841.
Jalland, Pat. *Death in the Victorian Family*. Oxford: Oxford University Press, 1996.
Jameson, William. "On the Geographical Distribution of the Vulturidae, Falconidae, and Strigidae." *Journal of the Asiatic Society of Bengal* 8 (1839): 321–7.
———. "On the Physical Aspects of the Punjab." *Journal of the Horticultural Society of London* 8 (1853): 273–313.
———. *Report upon the Botanical Gardens of the Government, North-Western Provinces*. Roorkee: Thomason College Press, 1855.
Johnson, James. *The Oriental Voyager*. London: James Asperne, 1807.
———. *The Influence of Tropical Climates, More Especially the Climate of India, on European Constitutions*. London: J.J. Stockdale, 1813.
Jones, William. *The Letters of Sir William Jones*, edited by Garland Cannon. 2 vols. Oxford: Clarendon Press, 1970.
———. *The Works of Sir William Jones, vol. V*, edited by Lord Teignmouth. Delhi: Agam Prakashan, 1979.
[Kaye, J.W.]. "The English in India." *Calcutta Review* 1 (1844): 1–41.
———. "The English in India: Our Social Morality." *Calcutta Review* 1 (1844): 290–6.
Kaye, J.W., ed. *Selections from the Papers of Lord Metcalfe*. London: Smith, Elder, 1855.
[Keane, H.G.]. "Accepted Travellers." *Calcutta Review* 27 (1856): 277–313.
Kejariwal, O.P. *The Asiatic Society of Bengal and the Discovery of India's Past*. Delhi: Oxford University Press, 1988.
Knight, David M. *Science in the Romantic Era*. Aldershot: Ashgate, 1998.
Kopf, David. *British Orientalism and the Bengal Renaissance: The Dynamics of Indian Modernization, 1773–1835*. Berkeley: University of California Press, 1969.
Korte, Barbara. *English Travel Writing: From Pilgrimages to Postcolonial Explorations*. Basingstoke: Palgrave, 2000.
Kupperman, Karen Ordahl. "Fear of Hot Climates in the Anglo-American Colonial Experience." *William and Mary Quarterly* 41 (1984): 213–40.
Laird, M.A., ed. *Bishop Heber in Northern India: Selections from Heber's Journal*. Cambridge: Cambridge University Press, 1971.
[Lawrence, Henry and Honoria Lawrence]. "Romance and Reality of Indian Life." *Calcutta Review* 2 (1844): 377–443.

[Lawrence, Honoria]. "English Women in Hindustan." *Calcutta Review* 4 (1845): 96–127.
Lawrence, John and Audrey Woodiwiss, eds. *The Journals of Honoria Lawrence: India Observed, 1837–1854*. London: Hodder and Stoughton, 1980.
Leask, Nigel. *British Romantic Writers and the East: Anxieties of Empire*. Cambridge: Cambridge University Press, 1992.
Leckie, David Robinson. *Journal of a Route to Nagpore*. London: John Stockdale, 1800.
Lee, Debbie. *Slavery and the Romantic Imagination*. Philadelphia: University of Philadelphia Press, 2002.
Lee-Warner, William. *The Life of the Marquis of Dalhousie*. 2 vols. London: Macmillan, 1904.
Lévi-Strauss, Claude. *Tristes Tropiques*. Harmondsworth: Penguin, 1976.
Leycester, W. "Introductory Discourse." *Transactions of the Agricultural and Horticultural Society of India* 1 (1838): 1–9.
Livingstone, David N. "Climate's Moral Economy: Science, Race and Place in Post-Darwinian British and American Geography." In *Geography and Empire*, edited by Anne Godlewska and Neil Smith, 132–54. Oxford: Blackwell, 1994.
Lloyd, William. *Narrative of a Journey from Caunpoor to the Boorendo Pass in the Himalayan Mountains*. 2 vols. London: J. Madden, 1840.
Logan, William. *Malabar*. 2 vols. Madras: Government Press, 1887.
[Long, J.]. "The Grand Trunk Road: Its Localities." *Calcutta Review* 21 (1853): 170–224.
Loomis, Chauncey C. "The Arctic Sublime." In *Nature and the Victorian Imagination*, edited by U.C. Knoepflmacher and G.B. Tennyson, 95–112. Berkeley: University of California Press, 1977.
Lovejoy, Arthur O. "On the Discrimination of Romanticisms." In his *Essays in the History of Ideas*. Baltimore: Johns Hopkins Press, 1948.
Lowe, Lisa. *Critical Terrains: French and British Orientalisms*. Ithaca: Cornell University Press, 1991.
Lowenthal, David and Martyn J. Bowden, eds. *Geographies of the Mind: Essays in Historical Geosophy in Honor of John Kirtland Wright*. New York: Oxford University Press, 1976.
Lyell, Mrs, ed. *Life, Letters and Journals of Sir Charles Lyell*. 2 vols. London: John Murray, 1881.
McCalman, Iain, ed. *An Oxford Companion to the Romantic Age: British Culture, 1776–1832*. Oxford: Oxford University Press, 1999.
M'Cosh, John. *Topography of Assam*. Calcutta: G.H. Huttmann, 1837.
MacGregor, W.L. *Practical Observations on the Principal Diseases Affecting the Health of the European and Native Soldiers in the North-Western Provinces of India*. Calcutta: W. Thacker, 1843.

Mackay, David. *In the Wake of Cook: Exploration, Science and Empire, 1780–1801*. London: Croom Helm, 1985.

MacLeod, Roy, ed. *Nature and Empire: Science and the Colonial Enterprise* (*Osiris* 15), 2000.

Madden, Edward. "The Turaee and Outer Mountains of Kumaoon." *Journal of the Asiatic Society of Bengal* 17 (1848): 349–450; 18 (1849): 603–44.

———. "On the Occurrence of Palms and Bambus, with Pines and Other Forms Considered Northern, at Considerable Elevations in the Himalayas." *Transactions of the Botanical Society of Edinburgh* 4 (1853): 185–96.

———. "Elucidation of Some Plants Mentioned in Francis Hamilton's Account of the Kingdom of Nepal." *Transactions of the Botanical Society of Edinburgh* 5 (1858): 116–40.

Marshall, J.F. *Victor Jacquemont: Letters to Achille Chaper*. Philadelphia: The American Philosophical Society, 1960.

Marshall, P.J. *The British Discovery of Hinduism in the Eighteenth Century*. Cambridge: Cambridge University Press, 1970.

Martin, James Ranald. *The Influence of Tropical Climates on European Constitutions*. London: John Churchill, 1856.

———. *Notes on the Medical Topography of Calcutta*. Calcutta: G.H. Huttmann, 1837.

Martin, R. Montgomery. *The Indian Empire Illustrated* (vol. III of *The Indian Empire*). London: London Printing and Publishing Co., n.d. (1861).

Mellor, Anne K. "Romanticism, Gender and the Anxieties of Empire." *European Romantic Review* 8 (1997): 148–54.

Melman, Billie. *Women's Orients: English Women and the Middle East, 1718–1918*. Basingstoke: Macmillan, 1992.

Miller, David Philip and Peter Hanns Reill, eds. *Visions of Empire: Voyages, Botany and Representations of Nature*. Cambridge: Cambridge University Press, 1996.

Mitchell, Timothy. *Colonising Egypt*. Cambridge: Cambridge University Press, 1988.

Moorcroft, William and George Trebeck. *Travels in the Himalayan Provinces of Hindustan and the Panjab*. 2 vols. London: John Murray, 1841.

Moore, Thomas. *Lalla Rookh*. 9th ed. London: Longman, Hurst, Rees, Orme and Brown, 1818.

Morrell, Jack and Arnold Thackray. *Gentlemen of Science: Early Years of the British Association for the Advancement of Science*. Oxford: Clarendon Press, 1981.

Moseley, Benjamin. 1789. *A Treatise on Tropical Diseases, on Military Operations and on the Climate of the West-Indies*. 2nd ed. London: T. Cadell, 1789.

Mouat, Frederic J. *Rough Notes on a Trip to Reunion, the Mauritius and Ceylon*. Calcutta: Thacker, Spink, 1852.

Mukherjee, S.N. *Sir William Jones: A Study in Eighteenth-Century British Attitudes to India*. 2nd ed. London: Sangam Books, 1987.

Murray, Hugh, et al. *Historical and Descriptive Account of British India*. 3rd ed. 3 vols. Edinburgh: Oliver and Boyd, 1840.
Neumann, Roderick P. *Imposing Wilderness: Struggles over Livelihood and Nature Preservation in Africa*. Berkeley: University of California Press, 1998.
Newall, D.J.F. *The Highlands of India*. London: Harrison, 1882.
Nicolson, Malcolm. "Alexander von Humboldt, Humboldtian Science and the Origins of the Study of Vegetation." *History of Science* 25 (1987): 167–94.
Nicolson, Marjorie Hope. *Mountain Gloom and Mountain Glory: The Development of the Aesthetics of the Infinite*. Ithaca: Cornell University Press, 1959.
Noltie, H.J. *The Dapuri Drawings: Alexander Gibson and the Bombay Botanic Gardens*. n. p.: Antique Collectors' Club, 2002.
———. *Indian Botanical Drawings, 1793–1868*. Edinburgh: Royal Botanic Garden Edinburgh, 1999.
Nussbaum, Felicity A. *Torrid Zones: Maternity, Sexuality, and Empire in Eighteenth-Century English Narratives*. Baltimore: Johns Hopkins University Press, 1995.
Orme, Robert. *A History of the Military Transactions of the British Nation in Indostan from the Year MDCCXLV*. 2nd ed. 2 vols. London: F. Wingrave, 1803.
Oviedo, Gonzalo Fernandez. *Natural History of the West Indies*. Chapel Hill: University of North Carolina Press, 1959.
Paradis, James. "Darwin and Landscape." In *Victorian Science and Victorian Values: Literary Perspectives*, edited by James Paradis and Thomas Postlewait, 85–110. New Brunswick: Rutgers University Press, 1985.
Parish, W.H. "A Journal of a Trip through the Kohistan of the Jullunder." *Journal of the Asiatic Society of Bengal* 18 (1849): 360–409.
Parks, Fanny. *Wanderings of a Pilgrim in Search of the Picturesque*. 2 vols. Reprinted Karachi: Oxford University Press, 1975.
Peabody, Norbert. "Tod's *Rajast'han* and the Boundaries of Imperial Rule in Nineteenth-Century India." *Modern Asian Studies* 30 (1996): 185–220.
Peers, Douglas. M. *Between Mars and Mammon: Colonial Armies and the Garrison State in Early Nineteenth-Century India*. London: I.B. Tauris, 1995.
———. "'The Habitual Nobility of Bearing': British Officers and the Social Construction of the Bengal Army in the Early Nineteenth Century." *Modern Asian Studies* 25 (1991): 545–69.
Pemble, John. *The Invasion of Nepal: John Company at War*. Oxford: Clarendon Press, 1971.
Pennant, Thomas. *Indian Zoology*. 2nd ed. London: Robert Faulder, 1790.
———. *The View of Hindoostan*. 4 vols. London: Henry Hughs, 1798.
Perrin, M. *Voyage dans l'Indostan*. 2 vols. Paris: Imprimerie de le Normant, 1807.
Piddington, Henry. "On the Fertilising Principle of the Inundations of the Hughli." *Asiatic Researches* 18 (1833): 224–6.
———. "Researches on the Gale and Hurricane in the Bay of Bengal on the 3rd,

4th, and 5th of June, 1839." *Journal of the Asiatic Society of Bengal* 8 (1839): 559–89.
Pinney, Christopher. *Camera Indica: The Social Life of Indian Photographs.* London: Reaktion Books, 1997.
Porter, Duncan M. "On the Road to the *Origin* with Darwin, Hooker, and Gray." *Journal of the History of Biology* 26 (1993): 1–38.
Porter, Roy and Mikulas Teich, eds. *Romanticism in National Context.* Cambridge: Cambridge University Press, 1988.
Prain, D. "A Sketch of the Life of Francis Hamilton (once Buchanan)." *Annals of the Royal Botanic Garden, Calcutta* 10 (1905): i–lxxv.
Pratt, Mary Louise. *Imperial Eyes: Travel Writing and Transculturation.* London: Routledge, 1992.
Prinsep, H.T. "Corrected Estimate of the Risk to Civil Servants of the Bengal Presidency." *Journal of the Asiatic Society of Bengal* 6 (1837): 341–6.
Raj, Kapil. "Colonial Encounters and Forging of New Knowledge and National Identities: Great Britain and India, 1760–1850." In *Nature and Empire: Science and the Colonial Enterprise (Osiris* 15), edited by Roy MacLeod, 119–34.
Rajan, Balachandra. *Under Western Eyes: India from Milton to Macaulay.* Durham: Duke University Press, 1999.
Rajan, Ravi. "Imperial Environmentalism or Environmental Imperialism? European Forestry, Colonial Foresters and the Agendas of Forest Management in British India, 1800–1900." In *Nature and the Orient: The Environmental History of South and Southeast Asia,* edited by Richard H. Grove, Vinita Damodaran, and Satpal Sangwan, 324–71. Delhi: Oxford University Press, 1998.
Rangarajan, Mahesh. "The Raj and the Natural World: The War against 'Dangerous Beasts' in Colonial India." In *Wildlife in Asia: Cultural Perspectives,* edited by John Knight, 207–32. London: RoutledgeCurzon, 2004.
Rankine, Robert. *Notes on the Medical Topography of the District of Sarun.* Calcutta: G.H. Huttmann, 1839.
Reece, Richard. *The Medical Companion for Visitors to the East and West Indies.* London: Longman, Hurst, Rees, Orme and Brown, 1817.
Rendall, Jane. "Scottish Orientalism: From Robertson to James Mill." *Historical Journal* 25 (1982): 43–69.
Rennell, James. *Memoir of a Map of Hindoostan.* 2nd ed. London: n. p., 1792.
Report of the Seventeenth Meeting of the British Association for the Advancement of Science, June 1847. London: John Murray, 1848.
Riley, James C. *The Eighteenth-Century Campaign to Avoid Disease.* Basingstoke: Macmillan, 1987.
Roberts, Emma. *Scenes and Characteristics of Hindostan.* 3 vols. London: W.H. Allen, 1835.

Robertson, George. *The Discovery of Tahiti: A Journal of the Second Voyage of H. M. S. "Dolphin" Round the World, 1766–1768*. London: Hakluyt Society, 1948.
Rosselli, John. *Lord William Bentinck: The Making of a Liberal Imperialist, 1774–1839*. London: Sussex University Press, 1974.
Roxburgh, William. *Flora Indica*. 2 vols. Serampore: Serampore Mission Press, 1820, 1824.
———. *Plants of the Coast of Coromandel*. 3 vols. London: George Nicol, 1795, 1798, 1819.
Royle, J. Forbes. "Account of the Honorable Company's Botanic Garden at Saharanpur." *Journal of the Asiatic Society of Bengal* 1 (1832): 41–58.
———. *On the Culture and Commerce of Cotton in India*. London: Smith, Elder, 1851.
———. *Essay on the Productive Resources of India*. London: W.H. Allen, 1840.
———. *The Fibrous Plants of India*. London: Smith, Elder, 1855.
———. *Illustrations of the Botany and Other Branches of the Natural History of the Himalayan Mountains*. 2 vols. London: W.H. Allen, 1839.
———. "List of the Articles of Materia Medica Obtained in the Bazaars of the Western and Northern Provinces of India." *Journal of the Asiatic Society of Bengal* 1 (1832): 458–71.
———. *A Manual of Materia Medica and Therapeutics*. London: John Churchill, 1847.
Russell, Joshua. *Journal of a Tour in Ceylon and India*. London: Houlston and Stoneman, 1852.
Russell-Wood, A.J.R. *A World on the Move: The Portuguese in Africa, Asia and America, 1415–1808*. Manchester: Carcanet, 1992.
Said, Edward W. *Orientalism*. London: Routledge and Kegan Paul, 1978.
Sangwan, Satpal. "The Strength of a Scientific Culture: Interpreting Disorder in Colonial Science." *Indian Economic and Social History Review* 34 (1997): 217–50.
Savage, Victor R. *Western Impressions of Nature and Landscape in Southeast Asia*. Singapore: Singapore University Press, 1984.
Schwab, Raymond. *The Oriental Renaissance: Europe's Rediscovery of India and the East, 1680–1800*. New York: Columbia University Press, 1984.
Scott, David. "Colonial Governmentality." *Social Texts* 43 (1995): 191–220.
Scott, Walter. *The Heart of Mid-Lothian*. London: Penguin, 1994.
Secord, Anne. "Corresponding Interests: Artisans and Gentlemen in Nineteenth-Century Natural History." *British Journal for the History of Science* 27 (1994): 383–408.
Sen, Suchibrata. *The Santals of Jungle Mahals: An Agrarian History, 1793–1861*. Calcutta: Ratna Prakashan, 1984.
Sengputa, Anjali. *Cameos of Twelve European Women in India (1757–1857)*. Calcutta: Rddhi-India, 1984.

Seshadri, P. *An Anglo-Indian Poet: John Leyden*. Madras: Higginbotham, 1912.
[Seton-Karr, W.S.]. "The Plains of the Lower Ganges." *Calcutta Review* 9 (1848): 1–28.
Schama, Simon. *Landscape and Memory*. London: HarperCollins, 1995.
Shelley, Mary. *The Last Man*. Oxford: Oxford University Press, 1994.
[Sherer, M.]. *Sketches of India*. 4th ed. London: Longman, Rees, Orme, Brown and Green, 1826.
Shore, F.J. *Report on the Dehra Doon, 1827–28*. Calcutta: Samuel Smith, 1836.
Shteir, Ann B. *Cultivating Women, Cultivating Science: Flora's Daughters and Botany in England, 1760 to 1860*. Baltimore: Johns Hopkins University Press, 1996.
Singh, Jyotsna G. *Colonial Narratives/Cultural Dialogues: "Discoveries" of India in the Language of Colonialism*. London: Routledge, 1996.
Sivaramakrishnan, K. "British Imperium and Forested Zones of Anomaly in Bengal, 1767–1833." *Indian Economic and Social History Review* 33 (1996): 243–82.
Skinner, Thomas. *Excursions in India*. 2nd ed. 2 vols. London: Richard Bentley, 1833.
Sleeman, W.H. *Rambles and Recollections of an Indian Official*. Reprinted Karachi: Oxford University Press, 1973.
Sloan, Phillip. "The Gaze of Natural History." In *Inventing Human Science: Eighteenth-Century Domains*, edited by Christopher Fox, Roy Porter, and Robert Wokler, 112–51. Berkeley: University of California Press, 1995.
[Smith, R. Baird]. "Canals of Irrigation in the N. W. Provinces." *Calcutta Review* 12 (1849): 79–183.
Smith, Bernard. *European Vision and the South Pacific*. 2nd ed. New Haven: Yale University Press, 1985.
Smith, R. Bosworth. *Life of Lord Lawrence*. 2 vols. London: Smith, Elder, 1883.
Southey, Robert. *Poems of Robert Southey*, edited by Maurice H. Fitzgerald. London: Oxford University Press, 1909.
Spurr, David. *The Rhetoric of Empire: Colonial Discourse in Journalism, Travel Writing, and Imperial Administration*. Durham: Duke University Press, 1993.
Spry, Henry H. *Modern India*. 2 vols. London: Whittaker, 1837.
Stein, Burton. *Thomas Munro: The Origins of the Colonial State and His Vision of Empire*. Delhi: Oxford University Press, 1989.
Stocks, J.E. "Botany (Chiefly Economic) of Scinde." *London Journal of Botany* 7 (1848): 539–50.
———. "On two Balsam Trees of Scinde." *Hooker's Journal of Botany* 1 (1849): 257–63.
———. "Notes Written during a Short Botanical Excursion to Shah Bilawul." *London Journal of Botany* 7 (1848): 550–6.
Stokes, Eric. *The English Utilitarians and India*. Oxford: Clarendon Press, 1959.
Stepan, Nancy Leys. *Picturing Tropical Nature*. London: Reaktion Books, 2001.
Strachey, R. "On the Physical Geography of the Provinces of Kumaon and Garhwal

in the Himalaya Mountains." *Journal of the Royal Geographical Society of London* 21 (1851): 57–85.

Suleri, Sara. *The Rhetoric of English India*. Chicago: Chicago University Press, 1992.

Taussig, Michael. *Shamanism, Colonialism, and the Wild Man: A Study in Terror and Healing*. Chicago: University of Chicago Press, 1986.

Taylor, James. *A Sketch of the Topography and Statistics of Dacca*. Calcutta: G.H. Huttmann, 1840.

Teltscher, Kate. *India Inscribed: European and British Writing in India, 1600–1800*. Delhi: Oxford University Press, 1995.

[Temple, Richard]. "The Agri-Horticultural Society of India." *Calcutta Review* 22 (1854): 341–59.

Tennant, William. *Indian Recreations*. 2nd ed. 2 vols. London: Longman, Hurst, Rees and Orme, 1804.

Tennent, James Emerson. *Ceylon: An Account of the Island: Physical, Historical, and Topographical*. 3rd ed. 2 vols. London: Longman, Green, Longman and Roberts, 1859.

Thacker, Christopher. *The Wildness Pleases: The Origins of Romanticism*. London: Croom Helm, 1983.

Théodoridès, Jean. "Humboldt and England." *British Journal for the History of Science* 3 (1966): 39–55.

Thomas, Nicholas. *Colonialism's Culture: Anthropology, Travel and Government*. Cambridge: Polity Press, 1994.

Thomson, Arthur. "Could the Natives of a Temperate Climate Colonize and Increase in a Tropical Country and Vice Versa?" *Transactions of the Medical and Physical Society of Bombay* 6 (1843), 112–38.

Thomson, Thomas. "Notes on the Herbarium of the Calcutta Botanic Garden." *Journal of the Asiatic Society of Bengal* 25 (1856): 405–18.

———. "Sketch of the Climate and Vegetation of the Himalaya." *Proceedings of the Philosophical Society of Glasgow* 3 (1851): 193–204.

———. *Western Himalaya and Tibet*. London: Reeve, 1852.

Tickell, [S.R.]. "Memoir on the Hodésum." *Journal of the Asiatic Society of Bengal* 9 (1840): 694–709, 783–808.

Tillotson, Giles. *The Artificial Empire: The Indian Landscapes of William Hodges*. Richmond: Curzon Press, 2000.

Tod, James. *Annals and Antiquities of Rajasthan*. 2nd ed. 2 vols. Calcutta: Higginbotham, 1873.

Trautmann, Thomas R. *Aryans and British India*. Berkeley: University of California Press, 1997.

Turner, Samuel. *An Account of an Embassy to the Court of the Teshoo Lama in Tibet*. London: G.W. Nicol, 1800.

Twining, William. *Clinical Illustrations of the More Important Diseases of Bengal*. Calcutta: W. Thacker, 1832; 2nd ed. 2 vols. 1835.

Vicziany, Marika. "Imperialism, Botany and Statistics in Early Nineteenth-Century India: The Surveys of Francis Buchanan (1762–1829)." *Modern Asian Studies* 20 (1986): 625–60.
Wade, John Peter. *A Paper on the Prevention and Treatment of the Disorders of Seamen and Soldiers in Bengal*. London: J. Murray, 1793.
Wakefield, Priscilla. *The Traveller in Asia*. London: Darton, Harvey and Darton, 1817.
Wallace, Alfred Russel. *Tropical Nature and Other Essays*. London: Macmillan, 1878.
Wallace, James. *A Voyage to India*. London: T. and G. Underwood, 1824.
Wallich, Nathaniel. "A Brief Notice concerning the Agricultural and Horticultural Society of India." *Hooker's Journal of Botany* 1 (1853): 137–9.
———. *Plantae Asiaticae Rariores*. 3 vols. London: Trettel, Wurtz and Richter, 1830, 1831, 1832.
———. *Tentamen Florae Napalensis Illustratae*. Serampore: Asiatic Lithograph Press, 1826.
Ward, William. *A View of the History, Literature, and Mythology of the Hindoos*. 2nd ed. 3 vols. London: Kingsbury, Parbury and Allen, 1822.
Waterhouse, David M., ed. *The Origins of Himalayan Studies: Brian Houghton Hodgson in Nepal and Darjeeling, 1820–1858*. London: RoutledgeCurzon, 2004.
Welsh, James. *Military Reminiscences*. 2 vols. London: Smith, Elder, 1830.
White, George Francis. *Views in India, Chiefly Among the Himalaya Mountains* (1838). Reprinted in Ahluwalia, *Eternal Himalaya*, 1982.
Wight, Robert. *Illustrations of Indian Botany*. 2 vols. Madras: American Mission Press, 1850.
———. "Recent Botanical Letters of Dr Robert Wight." *Journal of Botany* 3 (1841), 156–201.
——— and G.A. Walker Arnott. *Prodromus Florae Peninsulae Indiae Orientalis*. Vol. 1. London: Parbury, Allen, 1834.
Willis, J.C. *Agriculture in the Tropics: An Elementary Treatise*. Cambridge: Cambridge University Press, 1909.
Womack, Peter. *Improvement and Romance: Constructing the Myth of the Highlands*. Basingstoke: Macmillan, 1989.
Worster, Donald. *Nature's Economy: A History of Ecological Ideas*. Cambridge: Cambridge University Press, 1985.
Zastoupil, Lynn and Martin Moir, eds. *The Great Education Debate: Documents Relating to the Orientalist-Anglicist Controversy, 1781–1843*. Richmond: Curzon Press, 1999.
Zimmermann, Francis. *The Jungle and the Aroma of Meats: An Ecological Theme in Hindu Medicine*. Berkeley: University of California Press, 1987.

INDEX

Abu'l Fazl, 116, 117
Aden, 221
Afghanistan, 13, 121–2, 124, 127, 134, 144, 145, 160, 214, 217; botany of, 16, 167, 172
Africa, 7, 27, 29, 42, 52, 63, 74, 89, 112, 114, 164, 186, 210
Agra, 127, 134
agriculture, 4, 6, 83–5, 86, 90, 106–8, 133, 163, 168, 226
Agricultural and Horticultural Society of India, 106–8, 166, 192
Akbar, 80, 136
Alexander of Macedonia, 116, 122, 124, 125, 136
Alps, 7, 103
Amazon, 117
America, tropical, 7, 130–2, 139, 141, 143, 145
Amherst, Lord and Lady, 152
Amherstia nobilis, 152, 181
Anderson, Warwick, 113
Andes, 63, 164, 189, 209
Anglo-Gurkha War, 99, 154, 211, 213
Anglo-Sikh Wars, 13, 108–9

Annesley, James, 141
Anson, George, 112
Antarctic 7, 38, 39, 63, 160, 187, 188, 191, 199, 209
Arabia, 7, 36, 52, 122, 123, 125
Arabian Nights, 96, 120, 121, 125, 134
Archer, E. C., 102
Arctic, 151, 149, 225
Arnott, G. A. Walker, 166, 168, 169
Arrian, 116, 117, 124
Asiatic Society of Bengal, 16, 17, 27, 107, 118, 119, 145, 169, 192; *Journal* of, 31, 169, 228
Assam, 16, 24, 27, 54, 157, 159, 164, 172, 175, 182
associations, 6, 7, 10, 23, 25, 36, 62, 93, 96–7, 98, 200, 202, 220
Athenaeum, 220, 221
Auckland, Lord, 45, 152, 172, 191–2, 205, 218
Aurangzeb, 120, 136
Australia, 7, 18, 30, 43–4, 113, 164, 212
Awadh, 13, 135, 152, 214
Aylmer, Rose, 144

Bahawalpur, 122
Baluchistan, 63, 125, 158, 181
Banks, Joseph, 114, 149, 151, 162, 184
Barbados, 130
Barrackpore, 50, 152
Benares, 18, 19, 127, 135, 202
Bengal, 12, 34, 57, 69, 149; European residents in, 44–5; European travel in, 17, 64, 127, 134, 22; landscapes and perceptions of, 21, 82, 84, 85, 87, 97, 116, 131, 133, 141, 146, 164, 193
Bengal Army, 63, 76, 162
Bengal Medical Service, 18, 39, 43, 64, 150, 160, 163, 186, 215
Bentham, George, 63, 155, 164, 189
Bentinck, Lord, 53, 107, 127
Berhampore, 51, 79
Bernier, François, 11, 21, 116, 118, 125, 127
Bhagalpur, 107, 186
Bhotias, 180, 212, 214
Bhutan, 16, 34, 119, 172, 174, 211, 212, 217
Bible, 36, 68, 118, 177, 228
Bihar, 12, 107, 193
Bikaner, 122
Bligh, William, 143
Blyth, Edward, 17
Bombay, 12, 15, 17, 34, 63, 76, 127, 159, 189
Bombay Army, 52, 150
Bombay Medical Service, 63, 158
Bonpland, Aimé, 113
Borneo, 64
botanic gardens: *see under* Calcutta, Kew, Saharanpur
botanical illustrations, 170, 183–4, 221
botany, 5, 6, 8, 9, 29, 37, 142, 147–8, 150; associated with mortality, 62–7; development of in India, 39, 67, 125, 133, 145, 151–2, 154–5, 158–70, 172, 174–6, 178–84, 186, 189–90; economic, 38, 162–6, 168, 172, 181, 226; Linnaean, 59, 169, 174, 176, 177, 179, 182; medical, 162, 178–80; Natural System of, 169, 174, 183; Oriental, 125, 137; religion and, 68, 106, 203, travel and, 16–17, 33, 125, 127; tropical, 40, 63, 87, 113, 142–3, 154, 156, 162, 164, 168, 174–5, 176, 188, 193–6
Bougainville, Louis Antoine de, 112
Bower, F. O., 223
Brahmaputra, 15, 24, 117
Brazil, 7, 98, 113, 130, 131, 132, 136, 143, 164, 222, 224, 226; botany in, 65, 190
British Association for the Advancement of Science, 82, 169, 174
British Museum, 206
Browne, James, 85
Browne, Janet, 150
Buchanan, Claudius, 69–70, 71
Buchanan, Francis, 49, 93, 114, 152, 178, 179, 182; travels in South India, 83–8, 90, 106
Buddhism, monuments, 78, 203; relationship to landscape and nature, 67, 121, 180, 203; Western scholarship on, 40, 205, 207
Bukhara, 124, 160
Burma, 13, 16, 27, 47, 214, 228; as tropics, 36, 145, 144, 146; botany in, 152, 154, 155, 157, 172
Burnes, Alexander, 124, 125
Burton, Richard, 29, 52–3, 124–5
Byron, Lord, 89, 95, 96

Calcutta, 12, 19, 20, 24, 53, 65, 76, 83, 95, 97, 99, 127, 146, 154, 156, 193, 229; botanic garden, 106, 107, 133, 146, 149, 152, 157, 160–3, 168, 174–

6, 181, 183, 193, 222, 227; Europeans in, 22, 44–5, 144, 192; as a scientific centre, 17, 34, 48, 106, 119, 140, 141, 145, 155, 157, 169, 172, 184; as seat of government, 17, 192, 213, 214, 216–18; *Calcutta Journal of Natural History*, 169
Campbell, Archibald, 213–17, 218, 220, 230
canals, 76, 78, 85, 93, 106, 108–9, 133, 135
Candolle, Alphonse de, 155
Cape of Good Hope, 18, 38, 127, 166
Carey, William, 106–7, 155
Caribbean, 36, 226; *see also* West Indies
Carnatic, 84, 86, 88, 90, 106
Carter, Paul, 3, 30
Cathcart, J. F., 65, 67, 183, 184, 218, 221
Central America, 36, 113
Central Asia, 36, 190
Central India, 13, 31, 82–3
Ceylon, botany and, 65, 145, 149, 150, 159; European travel and, 15, 17, 18, 193, 220; tropical perceptions of, 36, 97, 112, 136, 146, 222, 224, 227, 231
Chardin, John, 118
Chimborazo, 164, 191, 210
China, 164, 203, 210, 212, 213
Chittagong, 48, 84, 87, 98, 114, 160, 164, 222
cholera, 43, 44, 45–6, 47, 51, 61, 69, 92, 139
Christianity, 68–70, 72–3, 75, 81, 94, 95, 103, 106, 108
Church of Scotland Mission, 72
Cleghorn, Hugh, 33, 82
Cleveland, Augustus, 54
Clive, Robert, 18
Cohn, Bernard, 4
Coimbatore, 168

Coleridge, Samuel Taylor, 28, 95
colonial knowledge, 4, 5, 8, 10, 33, 37, 180–1, 185
colonial science, 9, 34, 40, 147–8, 161, 164–5, 168–70, 176–7, 185–6, 209, 230–1. *See also* botany, development of in India
Colvile, James, 192
Cook, James, 22, 30, 97, 186
Cosgrove, Denis, 5
Court of Directors, 13, 155, 161, 162, 164
Crawfurd, John, 145
Crosby, Alfred W., 5
Cunningham, J. D., 103–4
Curse of Kehama, 95, 120, 135. *See also* Southey
Cuvier, Georges, 126

Dalhousie, Lord, 9th Earl, 47
Dalhousie, Lord, 10th Earl, 13, 17, 18, 46–7, 55, 57, 144; relations with J. D. Hooker, 40, 127, 151, 192–3, 205, 212–15, 217, 218
Dalhousie, Lady, wife of 9th Earl, 151, 156
Dalhousie, Lady, wife of 10th Earl, 47, 192, 218
Damodar, 131, 193
Daniell, Thomas, 22, 118, 119
Daniell, William, 22
Daniels, Stephen, 5
Darjeeling, 19, 40, 48, 64, 65, 103, 157, 160, 171, 184, 190, 192, 195–6, 199, 202, 203, 205–6, 208, 212–18, 222, 229.
Darwin, Charles, 38, 43, 94, 98, 114, 132, 137, 150, 155, 157, 185, 188, 189, 191, 199–200, 201, 208, 210, 222, 226, 228; and *The Voyage of the "Beagle"*, 40–1, 203, 208, 223

Davis, Samuel, 119
Defoe, Daniel, 96, 112
Dehra Dun, 105, 106
Delhi, 20, 77, 78, 118, 121–3, 127, 131, 134, 135
De Quincey, Thomas, 25, 39
deserts, 27, 89, 122–3, 125, 178
Dow, Alexander, 118
Duff, Alexander, 72–3, 106
dysentery, 43, 63, 127,139, 144

East India Company, 9, 12–13, 15, 16, 17, 25–6, 39, 40, 57, 126, 226; botany and, 57, 63, 149, 152, 156–61, 164, 167–70; as a patron of science, 65, 161–2, 164, 186, 189, 201, 207; policies of, 28, 68, 69, 74, 106, 133, 161–2, 166, 213, 214; surgeons, 47, 71, 83, 142–4, 163, 166–7, 174. See also Court of Directors
Eden, Emily, 45, 50, 81, 133
Edgeworth, Maria, 57–8, 61, 183
Edgeworth, Thomas Pakenham, 57
Edinburgh, 26, 162, 166, 169, 228
Edinburgh University, 156, 188
Egypt, 18, 151, 220
Ellenborough, Lord, 205, 214
Elphinstone, Mountstuart, 118, 121–4, 125, 127
ethnography, 31, 200, 206, 207, 210, 211, 215, 231
European colonization and settlement in India, 7, 18, 105, 106, 212, 215, 227
Europeans, mortality in India, 42–7, 50–4, 55, 76; soldiers and their families, 43–4, 48, 52, 56–7, 62, 212
evangelicals, 69, 71, 73, 74, 202
Everest, George, 116
Everest, Mount, 210
Ewart, Joseph, 43

Fa Hsien, 11
Falconer, Hugh, 156–9, 161, 168, 175, 183, 189, 218
Falkland Islands, 38, 187
famine, 74, 108–9, 227; in Bengal 1770, 57, 82, 96, 133
Ferguson, Adam, 98, 136
Firishta, 116, 118
Fitch, W. H., 184
Flora of British India (Hooker), 39, 154
Flora Indica (Hooker and Thomson), 38, 39, 145, 160, 161, 179, 199, 221
Forbes, Edward, 222–3
Forbes, James, 114–15
Forster, Georg, 112
Forster, George, 15, 18
Forster, Johan Reinhold, 112
Foucault, Michel, 28–9, 32
Francis, Philip, 85
Fraser, James Baillie, 99–100, 102
Fraser, William, 134, 135

Gama, Vasco da, 12
Ganges, 19, 53, 67, 102, 117, 145
gardens, 60, 65, 123, 192. See also horticulture
Gardner, Edward, 154
Gardner, George, 65
gaze, 6, 21, 28–9, 33, 34; traveling gaze, 5, 29–34, 41, 98, 148, 228–9
geology, 15, 24, 64, 129, 188, 189, 206, 209–11
Gibbon, Edward, 118
Glasgow, 40, 58, 59, 155, 156, 159, 160, 166, 186, 188
Glasgow University, 151
Gourou, Pierre, 133
governmentality, 28, 34
Govindoo, 184
Graham, Maria, 50, 118, 130, 183
Graham, Robert, 166

Great Exhibition, 34, 165
Griffith, William, 16–17, 63, 65, 67, 144, 157, 159, 167, 172, 174–6
Grove, Richard, 112
Gurkhas, 13, 213

Hafiz, 118
Haileybury, 57
Haiti (Santo Domingo), 126, 127, 130, 131, 144
Hakluyt's *Voyages*, 138
Halhed, H. B., 119
Hardwar, 70–1
Hartly House, 22
Hastings, Warren, 17, 18, 57
Heber, Amelia, 94, 97
Heber, Reginald: early career of, 94–5; *Narrative* of, 93–4, 98, 120; travels and observations of, 17, 53, 56–8, 69, 72, 73, 77, 78, 96–8, 103, 106, 121, 135, 144, 229
Henslow, Frances, later wife of J. D. Hooker, 188, 221
Henslow, John Stevens, 188
Herbert, J. D., 105–6
Heyne, Benjamin, 80, 177–8, 182
Hickey, William, 46, 130, 139, 144
Himalaya, 13, 24, 35, 49, 64, 105, 119, 145, 164, 189, 190, 212, 221; European travel and, 15, 17, 27, 32, 80, 98–100, 102–4, 121, 127, 131, 148, 156, 160, 165, 185, 193–6, 198–9, 203–4, 222–4, 230; flora of, 62, 67, 100, 151, 152, 154, 157, 160, 163, 165, 180, 184, 189, 198–200, 214, 230; geography of, 206, 209–11, 215, 229
Himalayan Journals (Hooker), 38, 40–1, 98, 118, 180, 185–6, 189, 191, 203, 207, 209, 210, 218, 220, 221–4, 228, 230
Hindu Kush, 123, 124

Hindu medicine, 163
Hinduism, 26; associations with landscape and nature, 67, 86, 102, 190, 228; critiques and negative images of, 68–73, 81, 202, 203
Hindus, 21, 48, 88, 115, 121; death rites of, 52–3, 67, 73; pilgrimages of, 69–71, 102
Hodges, William, 22, 118
Hodgson, Brian Houghton, 40, 58, 64, 103, 160, 171, 191–2, 203, 212, 227, 230; career of, 205–6; relations with J. D. Hooker, 206–11, 213, 215–18, 229
Hoffmeister, W., 146
Hooker, Joseph Dalton: as a botanist, 38–9, 65, 67, 100, 129, 157, 165, 170, 174–6, 179, 180, 182–4, 188, 195–6, 198–201, 207–8, 209, 218–20, 230–31; captivity of, 216–18, 220, 222; contacts of, 39, 127, 150–1, 157, 159–61, 164, 192; in Darjeeling, 19, 64, 184, 202–3, 205, 207–11, 212, 215; early life and career of, 37–40, 186–8; family of, 64, 149–50; in the Himalaya, 185, 186, 189, 194–5; perceptions of landscape and scenery, 24, 48, 62, 121, 202–4; in Sikkim, 15, 27, 104, 174, 180, 191, 196, 198; in Tibet, 27, 196; as a traveler, 20, 27, 32, 63–5, 83, 87, 98, 103, 104, 118, 148, 186, 207–8, 215–16, 220, 229; as a travel writer, 94, 135, 220–4; tropics and, 24, 38, 41, 130, 144, 146, 188–9, 227, 231. *See also under* Dalhousie, Hodgson; *Himalayan Journals*, and other works.
Hooker, Lady Maria, 149, 150, 209
Hooker, Mary Hariette, 62
Hooker, William, brother of J. D. Hooker, 187

Hooker, William Jackson, 18, 39, 40, 62, 149–51, 184, 209, 218, 220; herbarium of, 151, 187; at Kew Gardens, 148, 151, 158, 159, 161, 166, 175, 188; networks and correspondence of, 40, 63, 125, 148, 150–2, 154, 155–64, 166–7, 169, 170, 172, 174, 176, 185, 190–2
horticulture, 60, 62
Hove, Anton, 15
Howison, John, 45
Hugli, 71, 72–3, 95, 138
Humboldt, Alexander von, 39, 112, 113–14, 127, 130, 132, 137, 141, 164, 188, 208; influence on other naturalists, 38, 114, 129–30, 143, 145, 185, 186, 189, 190–1, 193, 200–2, 209, 221, 226; *Personal Narrative* of, 40–1, 114, 140, 191
Humboldt, Wilhelm von, 190
Huxley, Leonard, 187, 205, 223

Ibn Battuta, 11
Iceland, 149
Illustrations of Himalayan Plants (Hooker), 38, 65–6, 184, 221
improvement, 4, 6, 7, 8, 29, 33, 48, 82–5, 100, 124,133, 163, 166, 178, 192, 213, 215, 226, 227; associated with Romanticism, 86, 90, 92–3, 104, 105–9, 227
India, French interests in, 125–6; as a "land of death," 3, 42–9, 50–4, 61, 69–73, 92, 94; Government of, 214, 217, 218; landscapes of, 4, 6, 7, 21–5, 27, 32–3, 38, 54, 59–60, 67–8, 76–109, 110, 122–5, 132–3, 135–6, 147, 186, 194–6, 222, 225–9; location of, 36, 37, 144–7; tropicalization of, 5, 7–8, 35–6, 41, 114–15, 136–46, 154–6, 162–4, 211, 222, 225–8, 230

India House, 65, 164
India Office, 212
indigenous knowledge, 8, 37, 38, 40, 49, 148, 162, 163, 176–82, 185, 225
Indus, 15, 19, 27, 123, 124, 141
Islam, 134

Jack, William, 63, 144, 145, 154
Jacquemont, Victor: early life and career of, 126; and Orientalism, 134, 135; as a travel writer and naturalist, 94, 129, 130–4, 152, 157, 179; travels in India, 39, 63, 83, 87, 127, 165; and the tropics, 24, 127, 130–1, 133–4, 135, 137, 144, 227
Jagannath, 69, 70, 96, 117
Jalland, Pat, 52
Jang Bahadur, 211
Jamaica, 130, 140, 187
Jameson, William, 161
Java, 71, 112, 145, 231
Jenkins, F., 159
Johnson, James, 140, 141
Johnson, Samuel, 89
Johnston, Alexander, 127, 171
Jones, Anna Maria, 158
Jones, William, 27, 68, 72, 114, 118, 119, 158, 177, 179, 180
jungle, 72, 80–2, 106, 117, 131, 137, 177, 228
Jungle Mahals, 81, 85

Kabul, 124
Kali, 71
Kangchenjunga, 196, 205, 209–10, 213
Kanpur, 162
Karachi, 181
Kashmir, 21, 116, 118, 127, 134, 156, 160, 181
Kathmandu, 58, 64, 102, 154, 171, 182, 205, 206, 215

INDEX

Kaveri, 86
Kew Gardens, 19, 39, 40, 62, 125, 148, 151, 152, 157, 159, 161, 170, 174, 175, 188, 189
Khasi hills, 98, 152, 160, 174, 221, 222
Kindersley, Mrs, 44
King's College London, 164
Kipling, Rudyard, 34, 79
König, Johan, 149, 183
Koran, 118
Kumaon, 64, 99, 103, 105, 108, 127, 156, 157, 205, 211, 228
Kyd, Robert, 133, 149

La Condamine, Charles Marie de, 117
Ladakh, 127
Lahore, 124, 134
Lalla Rookh, 28, 95, 97, 118, 119, 120, 121, 124, 134, 135, 144, 229
Lambton, William, 116
Law, J. S., 189
Lawrence, Henry, 56, 58, 102, 120–1
Lawrence, Honoria, 46, 50, 56, 58, 68, 69, 73, 102, 120–1, 205
Lawrence, John, 20
Lepchas, 180, 182, 202, 212, 215, 217
Leyden, John, 71–2, 144
Lindley, John, 151, 155, 158, 164, 172, 188, 191
Linnean Society, 155
Lloyd, William, 80, 82, 100
London, publishing in, 26; scientific circles in, 155–7, 169
Lucknow, 230
Lyell, Charles, 64, 155, 188

Macaulay, T. B., 135
M'Clelland, John, 65, 174, 175
M'Cosh, John, 54
Mackintosh, James, 20, 50, 58, 78

Madden, Edward, 68, 81, 183, 210, 218, 228
Madeira, 138, 189
Madras, 12, 20, 34, 63, 76, 83, 130, 139, 141; Government of, 167; Presidency, 17, 60–1, 149, 167, 168
Madras Medical Service, 33, 166
magnolias, 154, 155, 198
Malabar, 87, 114, 127, 135, 167, 190, 227
Malacca, 16, 144, 172, 174
malaria, 43, 44, 48, 49, 63, 125, 139, 156
Malaya, 155, 210, 231
Malcolm, John, 82, 122
mangoes, 20, 81–2, 87, 90, 118, 143
Maratha Wars, 15, 17, 82
Marathas, 13, 89, 93, 96
Marsden, William, 139, 144
Martin, James Ranald, 43, 47–8, 98, 140
Marwar, 49, 89, 90, 91, 123, 178
Mauritius, 112, 224
medical topography, 47–9, 54, 62, 140, 178
medievalism, 88–9, 134
Megasthenes, 11
Metcalfe, Charles, 13
Mewar, 89, 90, 93
Middle East, 36, 119, 121, 123
Milton, John, 96, 118
missionaries, 68, 70, 72, 106
Moore, Thomas, 28, 95, 96, 118. *See also Lalla Rookh*
Moseley, Benjamin, 139, 140, 141
Mughals, 77, 90, 108, 116, 118, 119, 120, 121, 133, 134, 135
Mukherji, Kali Kumar, 157
Munro, Erskine, 58, 59, 60
Munro, James, 59
Munro, Jane, 60–1
Munro, Thomas, 46, 50, 58; life and observations of, 59–61, 95, 105

Munro, William, 172, 190, 192
Murdan Ali, 183
Mutiny and Rebellion, 1857, 13, 18, 34, 41, 43, 212, 226, 230
Mysore, 13, 20, 59, 83, 86, 88, 90

Nagpur, 13
natural history, *see* botany, geology, zoology
Nepal, 13, 63, 103, 156, 171, 178, 182, 196, 203, 205–6, 211–12, 215, 217, 218, 221, 228; flora and natural history of, 152, 154, 155, 179, 206
New Guinea, 145
New Zealand, 18, 38, 187, 212
Niger expedition, 63
Nilgiris, 53, 152, 159
North America, 22, 76
Northern Circars, 12, 34
Notes on a Tour (Hooker), 220

Opium War, 212
orchids, 156, 159, 201
Orient, 36–7, 60, 119–24, 134–7, 144
Oriental Annual, 119, 121
Orientalism, 7–8, 22, 28, 31, 35, 36, 37, 72, 74, 77, 78, 88, 95, 96, 110–11, 119–21, 126, 135, 136, 163, 177, 180, 181, 207, 225, 228, 229
Orme, Robert, 133
ornithology, 64, 206

Pacific, 36, 112, 114, 139, 186
Palgrave, W. J., 150
Palni hills, 152, 167
Parasnath, 193, 202
Park, Mungo, 186
Paul and Virginia, 112, 193, 226
Peel, Lawrence, 192, 218
Penang, 17, 145, 154
Pennant, Thomas, 86, 118, 137, 145

Peradeniya, 65
Permanent Settlement, 85, 105
Persia, 36, 121, 122, 125, 134, 144
Persian, 31, 134, 135
Peshawar, 121, 123
photography, 229–30
picturesque, 22, 23, 25, 76, 81, 89, 93, 103, 130, 134, 193
plant anatomy, 172, 174
plant collectors, 9, 152, 154, 165, 167, 182–3
plant geography, 38, 113, 129, 164, 165–6, 168, 198–201, 209, 210, 226
plant taxonomy, 129, 142, 158, 168, 179–80, 221
Prasad, Vishnu, 183
Pratt, Mary Louise, 8, 29
Prinsep, Henry, 44
Punjab, 13, 122, 124, 127, 129, 134, 156, 214
Puri, 69–70, 71, 117

Raffles, Stamford, 63
railroads, 17, 27, 34, 76, 135, 229, 230
Rajasthan, 45–6, 49, 106, 122, 178; travels in, 54, 88–93, 123, 127, 133, 228
Rajmahal, 54, 77, 97, 117
Rajputs, 88, 89, 92, 97
Ranjit Singh, 124, 126, 127, 134, 135
Rasselas, 89, 229
Reece, Richard, 140
Rennell, James, 115–17, 118, 122
Réunion, 127, 131
rhododendrons, 100, 154, 164, 180, 192, 196, 198–9, 215, 220, 221
Rhododendrons of Sikkim-Himalaya (Hooker), 38
Rio de Janeiro, 127, 189
Roberts, Emma, 12, 20, 21, 24, 50, 51–2, 71, 78–9, 81, 89, 94, 135

Romanticism, 6, 17, 25, 27–8, 32, 59–60, 74–5, 86, 126, 178, 201–2; in India, 74–6, 88, 89–100, 102–6, 110, 120–21, 226, 228–9; and science, 32, 34, 75, 110, 186, 202, 204; and the tropics, 112, 130, 226
Rosa, Salvator, 92, 96, 229
Ross, James, 38, 187, 189
Roxburgh, William, 106, 149, 152, 154, 161, 162, 170, 174, 179, 181, 183, 184
Royal Asiatic Society, 127
Royal Society, 149, 156, 176
Royle, J. Forbes, 100, 129, 143, 155, 156, 161–6, 168, 172, 176, 179, 181–3, 190, 231

Sagar island, 71–2, 95
Sagauli, Treaty of, 211, 213
Saharanpur botanic garden, 108, 155, 156, 157, 161, 163–5, 168, 181, 183
Said, Edward, 7–8, 74, 111, 119, 121, 136
Saint-Pierre, Henri Bernardin de, 112. *See also Paul and Virginia*
Sanskrit, 31, 80, 119, 177, 179, 207
sati, 53, 69, 96
Scotland, 83, 86, 96, 100
Scots in East India Company service, 63, 83–4, 86, 99, 156, 215
Scott, Walter, 71, 86, 95, 96, 229
Serampore, 68, 69, 152, 155
Shakespeare, William, 96, 118
Shelley, Mary, 71, 104
Shore, F. J., 105
Sikhs, 17, 89, 96
Sikkim, 15, 27, 40, 174, 180, 196, 198, 199, 205, 207, 211–18, 220, 228, 229; Diwan of, 214, 216, 217; landscapes of, 98, 196, 198; Raja of, 206, 212, 213–14, 215–17, 223

Simla, 17, 46, 151
Sind, 13, 17, 43, 124–5, 144, 158, 159, 172; botany in, 63, 181, 190
Singapore, 17, 63, 144, 145
Siwalik fossils, 156–7, 209
Skinner, Thomas, 121
Smith, R. Baird, 109
South America, 84, 157, 162, 164, 194
Southeast Asia, 36, 113, 137, 142, 144–5, 151, 154, 227
Southey, Robert, 28, 95, 96
steamships, 19, 24, 27, 78
Stocks, John Ellerton, 63, 125, 158–9, 166, 172, 181–2, 190
Sumatra, 16, 36, 63, 112, 136, 145, 146
Sundarbans, 24, 71–2, 193
surf, 138–9
Survey of India, 16, 116, 209
Syria, 125

Tahiti, 97, 224
tamarinds, 81, 82, 90
Tarai, 49, 81, 194, 207, 209, 211
Tasmania, 38, 187
Tavernier, John Baptiste, 118
Teesta, 194, 196, 217
Tennant, William, 45, 77, 106
Terry, Edward, 144
Thomson, James, 22
Thomson, Thomas, 38, 39, 129, 159–61, 168, 170, 174, 183, 186, 210, 217, 218, 222, 231
Tibet, 27, 34, 36, 121, 127, 160, 186, 196, 203, 205, 211, 212, 213, 216, 217, 222, 229
Tickell, S. R., 76
tigers, 67, 71, 72, 82–3, 86
Tipu Sultan, 13, 83, 85
Tod, James, 45–6, 49, 54, 88–93, 96, 97, 106, 123, 133, 178
Tranquebar Mission, 149

travel, European, 15–21, 22, 83, 98, 116, 119, 206; scientific, 16, 28, 30–3, 38–9, 40–1, 86–7, 92, 126, 152, 165, 169, 185–6, 188, 191, 201, 205, 216, 221–3

travel writing, 9, 11–12, 20–8, 31–2, 34, 220–4. *See also* Buchanan, Elphinstone, Heber, Hooker, Jacquemont, Roberts, Tod

tropical diseases and medicine, 43, 48, 111, 136, 139–41, 172, 226, 231

tropicality, 10, 35–7, 38, 110–15, 117, 138, 163, 186, 199–201, 224, 225–8, 231–2

tropics, European mortality in, 42, 63, 65; ideas and expectations of, 5, 24, 35–7, 38, 87, 111, 126, 130–2, 136, 146, 168, 189–90, 193, 222, 223; poor, 37, 132–3, 227; sensuality of, 24, 36, 130–1, 132, 137, 143–4, 146

Turner, Dawson, 149–50, 189

Turner, Gurney, 39, 64, 65, 150, 186

Turner, J. M. W., 204, 229

Turner, Samuel, 34, 119, 121, 186

Twining, William, 141

University College London, 151, 158, 172, 191

van Rheede, Hendrick, 87, 127

Victoria, Queen, 215

Vogel, J. R. T., 63, 65

Wade, J. P., 141

Wallace, Alfred Russel, 38, 114, 137, 185, 223

Wallace, James, 140

Wallich, Nathaniel, 129, 145, 152, 154–8, 161, 170, 172, 175–6, 179, 181, 182, 184, 227, 231

Wallichian herbarium, 129, 155, 189

Ward, William, 69

Wellesley, Lord, 13, 83

West Indies, 7, 43, 55, 94, 112, 114, 130, 139–40, 157, 164, 187

Wilkins, Charles, 119

Williams, D. H., 64, 65, 193

Wight, Robert, 159, 166–70, 172, 174, 176, 179, 182, 201, 231

Wordsworth, William, 96, 102

Womack, Peter, 86

women, as botanists, 62, 158; as travelers and travel writers, 16, 20, 49–52, 71, 78–80

Yamuna, 79–80, 102, 108

zoology, 28, 64, 129, 137, 171, 206–11

LIBRARY OF CONGRESS CATALOGING-IN-PUBLICATION DATA

Arnold, David, 1946–
The tropics and the traveling gaze : India, landscape,
and science, 1800–1856 / David Arnold.
p. cm. — (Culture, place, and nature)
Includes bibliographical references and index.
ISBN 0-295-98581-X (hardback : alk. paper)
1. Human ecology—India—History—19th century.
2. India—Colonization—History—19th century.
3. Europeans—Travel—India—History—19th century.
4. Travelers' writings, European—History and criticism.
5. India—Description and travel.
I. Title. II. Series.
GF661.A76 2006
304.2'0954'09034—dc22
2005023751

www.ingramcontent.com/pod-product-compliance
Lightning Source LLC
Chambersburg PA
CBHW030608230426
43661CB00053B/1899